10th Brief Edition

Principles of SPEECH COMMUNICATION

Bruce E. Gronbeck
The University of Iowa

Douglas Ehninger

Alan H. Monroe

with Kathleen German
Miami University–Oxford, Ohio

HarperCollins*Publishers*

An Instructor's Guide with Test Bank to accompany *Principles of Speech Communication,* Tenth Brief Edition, is available. It may be obtained through a Scott, Foresman representative or by writing to Speech Communication Editor, College Division, Scott, Foresman and Company, 1900 East Lake Avenue, Glenview, Illinois, 60025.

Photo and literary credits
appear on pages 396–97,
which constitutes a
legal extension of
the copyright page.

Library of Congress Cataloging-in-Publication Data

Gronbeck, Bruce E.
  Principles of speech communication.

  Ehninger's name appears first on the earlier edition.
  Includes bibliographies and index.
  1. Public speaking.   I. Ehninger, Douglas.
II. Monroe, Alan Houston.   III. Title.
PN4121.E36   1988   808.5'1   87-12728
ISBN 0-673-18708-X
ISBN 0-673-48722-9

5 6 - KPH - 92 91

Publication of *Principles of Speech Communication,* Tenth Brief Edition, celebrates more than fifty years of service to students and instructors of public speaking. It also celebrates a time of unparalleled popularity for the field of communication—both on campus and in the realm of public activity.

On campus, communication departments of all types are generally overflowing with students. In many colleges, such departments have more majors than most of the other liberal arts units. Their graduates have less trouble than many in finding jobs, because, according to Department of Labor statistics, between a quarter and a third of *all* entry level positions in the country call for oral communication skills. Communication majors move into a kaleidoscopic array of careers in the broadcasting and video industries, politics, advertising and public relations, public service organizations, religion, film making, sales and promotion, travel industries, teaching, and countless other careers.

Communication is no less an important topic of conversation outside the ivied halls of old schools and the cement walls of modern colleges. Leaders of our government have "credibility gaps"; they find "a failure to communicate" when talking with other world leaders; some become known as "Great Communicators." Political rhetoric regularly is labeled "sharp" or "dull" and even "eloquent." The electronic church is controversial in part because of the communication practices of its evangelists, and the established churches seek new ways to revitalize speaker-audience relationships. Bumperstickers and billboards scream at us daily to "COMMUNICATE!"

Indeed, our entire culture—our folkways and stocks of shared knowledge—can be conceived of as one great big conversation. The idea of "conversation," of the exchange of thoughts and sentiments, captures perfectly the way Americans think of their culture. We think of ourselves as talking through problems over a cup of coffee, in public hearings, or over call-in phone lines. The idea of conversation in a time of full electrification— when each of us seems wired to everyone else thanks to phones, computers, and fiber optics—is comforting. The idea that you and I still can talk each other into and out of mindsets and activities is comforting, for it means that you and I and he and she and we and they still count.

This is an exciting time to be teaching or taking a course in speech communication. Whatever else it may be, this is the Age of Communication. This is a time when students need to acquire and hone their oral communication skills in order to grow and prosper. That's what this book is about. Students will grow and prosper as oral communicators if they (1) understand the conceptual bases of communication processes,

(2) acquire a vocabulary for expertly talking about and analyzing the communicative messages of others, and (3) put their learning into practice, giving speeches for others to respond to and to help them improve. Communication skills grounded in understanding, tied to a vocabulary that allows one to think and talk about them precisely, and engrained by guided practice are lifelong skills. The good habits established today are valuable resources for tomorrow.

Principles of Speech Communcation has a long and successful track record in communication studies. It has a continuing commitment to a particularly useful and time-tested method of teaching public speaking skills. Organizationally, this book allows students to gain an overview of the process of public speaking, then to learn the basic principles of speech preparation, and finally to put those principles into practice as they prepare and deliver speeches tailored to a variety of occasions and audiences. The "Monroe formula" for teaching public speaking has become the most widely used organizational pattern for public speaking textbooks, and it still works; it allows students to internalize particular principles before combining them in "complete" speeches.

Other continuing strengths include features that have been part of the book's success from edition to edition: Monroe's Motivated Sequence; the treatment of forms of supporting materials; the factors of attention; emphasis on speeches to inform, persuade, and actuate; types of imagery; and various kinds of introductions, organizational patterns, and conclusions. Such features provide a solid teaching foundation for both seasoned instructors of public speaking and newcomers to the field.

Principles of Speech Communication, Tenth Brief Edition, also reflects some of the excitement that characterizes communication studies today. Like its predecessors, this edition incorporates the latest thinking of scholars in rhetorical and communication theory and research. At the same time, it is blazing new trails in speech communication pedagogy:

- This is the first college-level public speaking book to be printed entirely in full color; this use of color, we hope, will enhance not only the appearance of the book, but the clarity and usefulness of the visual illustrations.

- The new "In Pursuit of Excellence" sections provide mini-breaks in the text giving students brief encounters with special ideas and problems.

- Specially set-off typographically are classroom examples involving problems frequently faced by student speakers; they allow readers to profit from someone else's successes—and failures.

- As always, a key feature of *Principles of Speech Communication* is the large number of sample speeches and outlines; they, too, permit students to see how others encounter and (usually) overcome rhetorical problems.

● As helps to the instructor, there is a number of extra teaching aids—a thoroughgoing Instructor's Guide with test items, a videotape of sample student speeches, a set of 35mm color transparencies on visual aids, and a computerized test bank.

Overall, *Principles of Speech Communication,* Tenth Brief Edition, is only the lead scout for students beginning studies in communicaiton. My hope is to provide a good start on both a short trip through the college communication curriculum and a long journey through a lifetime of communicative encounters.

ACKNOWLEDGMENTS

A book such as this one, of course, is not the product of one professor and his predecessors. Because *Principles of Speech Communication* has been in the hands of so many instructors and students over half a century, it has been evaluated and re-evaluated by several generations of users and experts. The Tenth Brief Edition has been built on expert opinion acquired through a nationwide users' questionnaire graciously returned to us by the following speech instructors: Anne Barron, Xavier University of New Orleans; Wanda Bellman, Black Hills State College; Melvin H. Berry, Nicholls State University; Edwin F. Buck, Purdue University—North Central; Darlene Christian, Platt College; Deborah Craig Claar, Penn Valley Community College; James M. Cunningham, Embry-Riddle Aeronautical University; Ronald Danko, Hartnell Community College; Ann B. Dofin, Florida Junior College (Kent Campus) at Jacksonville; Millard F. Eiland, Prairie View A&M University; J. Owen Eister, Cuesta College; Jonathan R. Eller, United States Air Force Academy; Wilma Frank, Rockland Community College; James W. Gibson, University of Missouri—Columbia; Bob Hatfield, University of Louisville; Marilyn Hoffs, Glendale Community College; John R. Landress, Copiah Lincoln Junior College; Lloyd McBride, Seton Hall University; B. P. McCabe, Southern Connecticut State University; Charles R. Newman, Parkland College; Dorothy O. Norton, University of Tennessee; Richard E. Porter, California State University, Long Beach; Jack B. Schriber, University of Southern Indiana; Doug Trank, University of Iowa; Allen Williams, Grambling State University; James Wolf, Miami-Dade Community College—South; and J. R. Zrubek, Texas State Technical Institute.

I also gratefully acknowledge the advice and suggestions provided by the manuscript reviewers: Edwin F. Buck, Purdue University—North Central; B. P. McCabe, Southern Connecticut State University; Nancy

Richards, Brigham Young University; and June Wells, Indian River Community College.

As author, I owe a great debt to Professor Kathleen German of Miami University of Ohio. She took in hand three pivotal chapters and reworked them in fresh and innovative ways; her strong sense of public accountability, student needs, and classroom pedagogy as director of the basic course at Miami University shows through in every paragraph she wrote. As well, her *Instructor's Guide to Using Principles of Speech Communication* and her package of color transparencies provide fine additions to our services for teachers.

I owe an additional round of thank-you's to three other people. I have been a father for over eighteen years; my three children are old enough now to assist me with library work. Christopher, Jakob, and Ingrid Gronbeck hit the stacks and the magazine racks last summer to take part in the search for resource material. I have doted on their virtues often, but with no greater admiration than I do at their dedication to the task of helping me prepare this book.

Finally, I owe perhaps my greatest debts of all to Scott, Foresman and Company, whose extensive resources have been mobilized for this textbook; its talented editors, designers, and production people have devoted untold hours to this project, and it has made a major investment in communication studies through the pedagogical package it has built for *Principles of Speech Communication*. The Editor-in-Chief of the College Division, Dick Welna, has been closely involved with this book over many editions. The shape of the Tenth Brief Edition has been contoured by Barbara Muller, the Acquisitions Editor and a long-time friend. Developmental Editor Louise Howe took my prose in hand and guided it toward our goals with firmness yet accommodation. And the word-by-word manuscript preparation came from Project Editor Deb DeBord, who provided the final hue and polish. From these individuals who constructed the book, I look to those in marketing and promotion: Carl Tyson, Meredith Hellestrae, and the army of dedicated sales representatives who carry this book out into colleges and universities—to you.

A publishing company the size of Scott, Foresman and Comany commands the talent and resources necessary to move this book through its second half-century. Without these company commitments to sustained excellence, to innovation from within tradition, the words of three generations of authors—of Alan Monroe (1903–75), Douglas Ehninger (1913–79), and me—would leave but faint traces on the landscape of time. I thank them for the opportunities they have provided.

B. E. G.

CONTENTS

> IN PURSUIT OF EXCELLENCE   *53*
> *Ethics and Public Speaking*

> SAMPLE SPEECH   *65*
> *Have You Checked Lately? by Deanna Sellnow*

● SAMPLE SPEECH MATERIALS FOR STUDY AND ANALYSIS

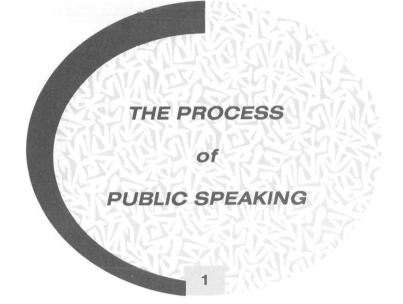

THE PROCESS
of
PUBLIC SPEAKING

1

What we call *public address, public speaking,* or *speech communication* is both a public act and a personal activity. Public speaking is simultaneously a set of individual mental and motor activities that allow "a speech" to flow out of your mouth (the "speaking") and an act whereby you attempt to influence your peers (the "public" aspect). The prefix *com-* (from the Latin *cum,* meaning "with") and *munus* (referring to a service performed for society) are combined in our word *communication*—which means sharing experience publicly for the common good. Communicating publicly, therefore, is part of most adults' lives. People are frequently called on to present oral messages of some length and complexity to groups of listeners.

PUBLIC SPEAKING SKILLS: PUBLIC SERVICE AND PERSONAL SURVIVAL

Given the historical roots of the idea of "communication," it is not surprising that public speaking *skills* are important to each of us. Public speaking skills are required by everyone in a society so that they can (1) contribute to the common good and (2) survive, and even get ahead, within that society.

Public Service: The Roles of Speechmaking

There are many reasons why society needs your speaking skills. "No Man is an *Iland,* intire of it selfe"; wrote John Donne; "every man [and woman] is a peece of the *Continent,* a part of the *maine;* . . . "[1] Although written over three hundred fifty years ago, these words capture an essential view of human life: The world has few places for hermits; everyone is a part of everyone else through language, custom, work relations, and family ties. One of the primary ways you become and stay a part of everyone else is through public talk—from informal chit-chat to more formal speeches. Through speaking publicly, you share ideas with others (informative speaking), construct warm relationships with them through humor (entertaining speaking), and influence their attitudes and actions (persuasive speaking).

To be sure, many media of communication are available these days—print, electronic, and film mass media; billboards; even skywriting and signal flags. However, face-to-face, speaker-to-audience public speaking has several advantages over other media:

1. It is the most humane and human mode of exchange in that people are actually present, confronting each other.
2. *Feedback,* the chance to ask for clarification or explanation, is directly available; further, feedback allows speakers to adjust their messages in midstream—even in midsentence—when they see frowns or signs of audience befuddlement.
3. Only in oral communication are ideas—information, beliefs, attitudes, and values—presented to others by a living, breathing human being, by someone with faults, virtues, vices, wisdom, silliness, and all of the other characteristics we share.

Ultimately, then, "public service" through speechmaking is a social responsibility. If you are not willing to do your part to maintain and improve society, who will? You cannot surrender all of the decision making and information sharing to others, because if you do, you are reduced to a state of complete dependence. The flow of words—and good ideas—from speakers is the lifeblood of a democratic society.

Personal Survival: The Roles of Speech Training

Despite the importance of speechmaking to society, people do not speak in public only for altruistic or humanitarian reasons. Public speaking skills are also necessary for personal survival. Unless you have the speaking talents

Why study speech communication? Because every public speaking situation is an opportunity to improve your relationships and further career goals. You can learn the skills necessary to survive, even thrive, in your community and on the job.

necessary to engage in committee discussions, employment interviews, conferences with clients, and meetings with supervisors, you may be in trouble on the job.[2] Your speechmaking skills also affect your ability to change people's minds at neighborhood or corridor meetings; at city or student councils; at political conventions and public hearings; and in the innumerable associations, clubs, and pressure groups that lobby the government. The power of public talk is as important in government as it is in the world of work.

You will survive as a fully developed, thinking, and forceful human being to the degree that you have learned and practiced speechmaking and other oral communication skills. Ultimately, you speak not only to serve others but also to achieve your own goals on the job and in the public forum. And, you might even have fun doing it; human beings talk with others both to survive and to play a little.

Before you plunge into the activities that will improve your speaking skills, however, it is helpful to visualize the whole process, to think about the various elements that make up communication in general and public speaking in particular. The rest of this chapter will be an examination of those elements and of the competencies they demand of you.

BASIC ELEMENTS IN THE SPEECHMAKING PROCESS

There are many types of speeches. Some, such as presidential inaugural addresses, are highly formalized; others, such as a few remarks from your seat in a marketing class, may be very informal. Some speeches are read to an audience; watch the next press conference on television. Others are given in an impromptu, off-the-cuff manner, as when you plead for three extra points on the essay test. After-dinner speeches tend to be humorous, while funeral sermons are dignified and serious.

Despite such differences in formality, presentation, and tone, however, all speeches share some features. Let us examine those features one at a time and then see how they interact dynamically—with each element affecting all the others—to produce a process called a *speech transaction*. The idea of "transaction" carries with it the notion of exchange, of a kind of interpersonal bartering. Public speaking is a complex, two-way—not a simple, one-way—activity. More will be said about transactions after we look at each element.

The Speaker

From the speaker's viewpoint, there are four key elements in every speech transaction: (1) communicative purpose; (2) knowledge of subject and communication skills; (3) attitudes toward self, listeners, and subject; and (4) degree of credibility.

Speaker's Purpose

Every speaker has a purpose. We all know some random talkers, of course, but generally you speak to achieve a goal. That goal can be as simple as the wish to appear sociable or as complex as the desire to alter someone's ideas without appearing to be rude. You may wish to entertain, call attention to a problem, refute an assertion, ward off a threat, or establish or maintain your status or power.

John visited his speech instructor the day before he was to speak. 'What's your purpose, John?' she asked. 'I want to talk about bike lanes downtown.' 'No, no, John,' she said, 'I don't want to know your topic. Tell me your purpose: What do you want to achieve in this speech?' 'I just want to get through it without fainting, ma'am,' came the response. John fully understood his private purpose. He did not yet under-

stand that audiences *also* want you to have them *in mind*
when you talk.

Speaker's Knowledge

*In every speaking situation, the speaker's knowledge of the subject and
mastery of communication skills affect the character of the message and the
effectiveness with which it is transmitted.* Sometimes you listen to somebody
just because you *like* to listen to them—you like the zaniness of talk from
someone like David Letterman or Bill Cosby. Usually, though, audiences
demand to hear something worth thinking about or doing. If you have only
surface knowledge of a topic, listeners feel cheated. You had better say
something important.

Also, to succeed, you will need to acquire and refine a series of
fundamental speaking skills. In this book we will often talk about *communication skills,* a phrase that encompasses a wide variety of abilities—setting
communicative goals, finding and assembling relevant information, organizing messages in coherent and powerful ways, illustrating them visually
when useful, and delivering them with clarity and punch. You already
possess many of the requisite skills; after all, you have been talking most of
your life. Through practice, instruction, reading, and observation of other
speakers, you will gain the rest.

Speaker's Attitudes

*In every speaking situation, the speaker's attitudes toward self, listeners, and
subject significantly affect what is said and how it is said.* All of us have
mental pictures of ourselves as persons—self-concepts or images of the kind
of individuals we are and of how others perceive us.[3]

Your *self-image* influences how you will behave in particular situations.
If you have little confidence in your abilities or are unsure of your
information, you tend to speak hesitantly. Your voice becomes weak, your
body stiffens, and you watch the floor rather than your listeners. If you are
overly self-confident, you tend to move in the other direction—becoming
overbearing, disregarding listeners' needs for facts and proofs, and riding
roughshod over the feelings of others. Ideally, you should have enough self-
confidence to believe in yourself and, yet, enough sensitivity to the audience's
intelligence, needs, and integrity to treat them like human beings.

Part of that treatment of others comes from your perception of your
status, or relationship to them—as their parent or child, instructor or
student, supervisor or employee. These role positions, in turn, affect your
power relationships with and modes of address to audiences. If you perceive
someone as intellectually inferior, you tend to use simple vocabulary, clear
structure, and concrete ideas; if someone seems politically inferior, you

might talk condescendingly, self-indulgently, and assured of your own status. Or, if you view your listeners as superior, you will likely talk in a deferential or highly qualified manner. Hence, you must think seriously about speaker-audience role relationships and adjust your speaking style to your attitudes toward your listeners.

Finally, your speaking behavior is influenced by *how you feel about the subject* you are discussing. Do you really believe what you are saying? Is the subject interesting to you, or did you pick it just to have something to say? Is your subject relevant to anyone else? Your personal answers to these questions are reflected in the ways in which you use your voice and body, in the intensity of your language, even in your selection of ideas. People can tell whether you are engaged with your subject. A disquieting thought, perhaps, but true, is that as a speaker you verbally and nonverbally convey how you feel about yourself, your listeners, and your subject matter.

Speaker's Credibility

In every speaking situation, the speaker's success in winning agreement, inspiring confidence, or promoting ideas is significantly affected by the listeners' estimate of his or her credibility. The term *credibility*—and its relatives, *image* or *ethos* (Greek for "character")—refer to the degree to which an audience finds you trustworthy, competent, sincere, attractive, and dynamic. Research has repeatedly demonstrated that a speaker who can raise an audience's estimate of these qualities will significantly heighten the impact of the speech. The following generalizations about credibility and communication have been verified by research:

1. References to yourself and your own experience—provided they are not boasting or excessive—tend to increase your perceived trustworthiness and competence; references to others (authorities) tend to increase your perceived trustworthiness and dynamism.
2. Using highly credible authorities increases your perceived fairness.
3. If you can demonstrate that you and your audience share common beliefs, attitudes, and values, your credibility will increase.
4. Well-organized speeches are more credible than poorly organized ones.
5. The more sincere you appear to be, the better your chances of changing your listeners' attitudes.[4]

As these generalizations suggest, your ability to project yourself as a competent, trustworthy, sincere, attractive, fair, and dynamic speaker may well determine the fate of your message. The message and the messenger are usually inseparable in people's minds.

SHYNESS AND PUBLIC COMMUNICATION

"What other dungeon is so dark as one's own heart! What jailer so inexorable as one's self!"

—Nathaniel Hawthorne

Do you think of yourself as shy? If so, does it bother you at all? Does it affect your willingness and ability to talk in public? What can be done about it? While not everyone suffers from heavy-duty "speech fright" of the type that paralyzes only a very small percentage of public speakers, many more people think of themselves as shy, and they let shyness affect their public speaking behaviors to one degree or another.

A leading psychologist, Stanford's Philip G. Zimbardo, defines it formally as "an apprehensiveness about certain social situations due to excessive preoccupation with being critically evaluated, resulting in a variety of behavioral, physical, cognitive, and emotional reactions" (Zimbardo, Glossary, page xv). "Shyness" thus comes in many varieties. It is a matter of bashfulness at one extreme, social paralysis at the other, with the middle ground being a state in which you lack self-confidence and are easily embarrassed. Shy people manifest their shyness in many ways, as the following table indicates. In all, about 40 percent of American college students describe themselves as "currently shy," another 40 percent indicate that they used to be shy by nature (disposition), and about 15 percent see themselves as "situationally shy"—in certain social situations they find unpleasant. To get at the roots of shyness, which can vary markedly from individual to individual, Zimbardo developed *The Stanford Shyness Survey*, a diagnostic tool that describes shyness in personal terms rather than on the basis of "expert" categories.

Using such instruments as the Shyness Survey, therapists can tailor treatment programs to individual needs: (1) They can help individuals build new social skills, teaching them *how* to act in situations that are new or strange. (2) They can suggest exercises to boost self-esteem if it appears that a person consistently thinks of him- or herself in negative terms. (3) If a shy person's physiological reactions (see the table) are dominant, anxiety management is taught —breathing exercises, relaxation techniques, muscle-flexing, and so on. (4) Occasionally group and individual sessions devoted to "cognitive reorganization" are undertaken; here, individuals learn the bases of their shyness, come to understand that it need not destroy social relations, and attribute different sorts of significance to it than they had before. (5) Group sessions can also be used as practice arenas, just as your speech classroom is, where shy people can be guided through their interactions with others step by step. All of these techniques probably are more effective than those offered in many quick-fix self-help books.

Shyness is probably at the base of what we usually call "speech fright" or "communication apprehension." If you are shy, one of the goals you ought to set for yourself in this classroom is the control and redirection of those feelings. Talk with your instructor, and perhaps other professionals on campus, if you want help.

TO READ: For statements from shy people as well as for the statistics cited here, see Philip Zimbardo, Paul Pilkonis, and Robert Norwood, "The Silent Prison of Shyness," Office of Naval Research Technical Report Z-17 (Stanford, CA: Stanford University, November 1974). A more condensed summary of their ideas can be found in Philip G. Zimbardo, *Psychology and Life,* 11th ed. (Glenview, IL: Scott, Foresman and Company, 1985), 447–50. The table included here is from this book, and is reprinted with the permission of Philip Zimbardo.

Inventory of Shyness Reactions

Physiological Reactions	% Shy Students
Increased pulse	54%
Blushing	53%
Perspiration	49%
Butterflies in stomach	48%
Heart pounding	48%

Thoughts and Feelings	% Shy Students
Self-consciousness	85%
Concern about impression management	67%
Concern for social evaluation	63%
Negative self-evaluation	59%
Unpleasantness of situation	56%

Overt Behaviors	% Shy Students
Silence	80%
No eye contact	51%
Avoidance of others	44%
Avoidance of action	42%
Low speaking voice	40%

(Adapted from Zimbardo, Pilkonis, and Norwood, 1974)

The Message

In all speech communication transactions, the message the speaker transmits is made up of the same three variables: content, structure, and style.

Content

Obviously, the messages we transmit to our listeners have content, that is, are about something we want them to be aware of. What is less obvious, however, are the many different sorts of content that go into a message. There are, of course, "ideas"—assertions about the state of the world, facts and figures, analogies and examples, and generalizations as well as more specific statements. But the content of a speech also includes your feelings about those ideas, interpretations of ideas you wish your audience to accept, courses of action you want the listeners to pursue, and beliefs you are attempting to challenge. Many different kinds of "meanings" make up the content of a speech.

Structure

Any message we transmit is necessarily structured or organized in some way, simply because we say some things first; others second; and still others third, fourth, and so on. Even if you seem to ramble, listeners will look for a coherent pattern in your message. It is important, then, to provide a pattern in order to guide the audience's search for coherence. That structure may be as simple as numbering points ("First, I will discuss . . . , next I will . . . and finally, I will. . . .") or as complex as a full outline with points and subpoints.

Style

The third variable in every spoken message is style. Just as you must select and arrange the ideas you wish to convey to audiences, so must you select words, arrange them in sentences, and decide how to reveal your self-image to that group of listeners. Selecting and arranging words, as well as revealing ourselves to be a certain sort of person, are matters of style. Given the innumerable words from which to choose, the great varieties of sentence structures, and even the many kinds of self-images available to the speaker, many styles are possible. Styles can be "personal" or "impersonal," "literal," or "ironic," "plain" or "elevated," even "philosophical" or "poetic"; such labels refer to particular combinations of vocabulary, syntax (sentence arrangement), and images of the speaker. What we call style, therefore, really has nothing to do with "prettiness" or "stylishness"; rather, it includes those aspects of language use that convey impressions of speakers, details of the world, and emotional overtones.[5]

The Listeners

In all forms of speech, the listeners—like the speaker—have goals or purposes in mind. Moreover, the way a message is received and responded to varies according to the listeners' (1) purpose; (2) knowledge of and interest in the subject; (3) level of listening skills; and (4) attitude toward self, speaker, and ideas presented.

Listeners' Purpose

Listeners always have one or more purposes they want to fulfill. Listeners, no less than speakers, enter into the speech transaction in search of rewards. They may wish to be entertained, informed, advised, or guided. These purposes form their expectations—expectations, as we shall see, that control to whom, how, and why they listen. Speakers who violate those expectations—turning an informative talk, say, into a political harangue—risk ineffectiveness or failure.

Listeners' Knowledge of Subject

In speech transactions, the listeners' knowledge of and interest in the subject significantly affect how they receive and respond to the message. Speakers often are told to address listeners "where they are." "Where they are" is determined by two factors: their knowledge of the topic and their personal interest in it. A knowledgeable audience is bored by an elementary speech, whereas one with little knowledge is confused by a technical description. Disinterested listeners may even go so far as to walk out on a speaker who has not made the topic relevant to their interests. Audience analysis, therefore, is a matter of (1) gauging listeners' prior knowledge so as to achieve an appropriate level of sophistication in the speech and (2) finding ways to make the message relevant to listeners' beliefs, desires, and motivational drives.

Listeners' Command of Listening Skills

Audience members vary in their abilities to process oral messages. Some people were raised in homes where complex oral exchanges occurred, and others were not; some people have acquired, by whatever means, the ability to follow long chains of reasoning, while some struggle to "see the point" in such messages; most younger children cannot yet concentrate on difficult speeches, while most college students have been taught to do so. All of this means that as a speaker you must attempt to gauge an audience's listening skills. Because so many audiences are heterogeneous, you often must visually survey the listeners, looking for signs of understanding or puzzlement, acceptance or rejection. Those signs, or cues, are termed *feedback*—

reactions "fed back" to speakers during or after their talks. Reading feedback is often your only way of assessing a listener's skill of comprehension.

Listeners' Attitudes

In every speech encounter, the listeners' attitudes toward themselves, the speaker, and the subject significantly affect how they interpret and respond to the message. Just as your communicative behavior is influenced by your attitude toward self, subject, and listener, so do these same factors affect your listeners' responses. Listeners with low self-esteem tend to be swayed more easily than those whose self-image is stronger. Listeners whose opinions seem to be confirmed by the views of the speaker are also susceptible to great influence. Moreover, as a rule, people seek out speakers whose positions they already agree with, and they retain longer and more vividly ideas of which they strongly approve.[6] In other words, listeners' attitudes— which comprise another extremely important area for audience analysis— can be used (or, conversely, must be overcome) by speakers who wish to maximize their communicative effectiveness.

The Channels

All speech communication is affected by the channels through which the message is transmitted. The transaction between speakers and listeners occurs through several channels. The *verbal channel* carries the words, the culture's agreed-upon symbols for ideas. The *visual channel* transmits the gestures, facial expressions, bodily movements, and posture of the speaker; these tend to clarify, reinforce, or add emotional reactions to the words. At times the visual channel may be supplemented with a *pictorial channel*—so-called "visual aids," such as diagrams, charts, graphs, pictures, objects, and the like. The *aural channel*—also termed the *paralinguistic medium*—carries the tones of voice, variations in pitch and loudness, and other vocal modulations produced by the speaker's stream of sounds. Like the visual channel, the aural channel heightens some meanings and adds others. Because these four channels are seen and heard by listeners simultaneously, the "message" is really a combination of several messages flowing through all of these pathways. You must learn to control or shape the messages flowing through all four channels.

The Communicative Situation

All speech communication is affected by the physical setting and social context in which it occurs.

Physical Setting

The physical setting of the speech influences listeners' expectancies as well as their readiness to respond. People waiting in the quiet solemnity of a cathedral for the service to begin have quite different expectations than do theatergoers gathered to witness the opening of a new Broadway play. Listeners at an open-air political rally anticipate a different sort of message from those gathered in a college classroom to hear a lecture on political theory.

The furniture and decor of the physical space also make a difference. Comfortable chairs and soft-hued drapes tend to put discussion groups at ease and to promote a more productive exchange. The executive who talks to an employee from behind a large desk set in the middle of an impressively furnished office gains a natural advantage not only because of a superior position but also because of the physical setting.

Social Context

Even more important than physical setting in determining how a message will be received is the social context in which it is presented. A *social context* is a particular combination of people, purposes, and places interacting communicatively. *People* are distinguished from each other by such factors as age, occupation, power, degree of intimacy, and knowledge. These factors in part determine how one "properly" communicates with others. You are expected to speak deferentially to your elders, your boss, an influential political leader, a stranger whose reactions you cannot immediately predict, and a sage. The degree to which people are seen as superior to, equal with, or inferior to each other in status helps determine each one's communicative style. Certain *purposes,* or goals, are more or less appropriately communicated in different contexts as well. Thus, a memorial service is not a time for attacking a political opponent—a "meet the candidates" night is. In some contexts it is considered unreasonable to threaten someone before you have tried to find reasonable compromises. Some *places* are more conducive to certain kinds of communicative exchanges than others. Public officials are often more easily influenced in their offices than in public forums, where they tend to be more defensive; sensitive parents scold their children in private, never in front of their friends.

Another way of saying all this is to observe that societies are governed by customs, traditions, or what we call *communication rules.* A communication rule is a guide to communicative behavior; it specifies what can be said to whom and in what circumstances. While communication rules are guides to communicating, they can, of course, be broken. Occasionally, rule breaking is inconsequential; sometimes it determines success or failure; always, it involves a certain amount of risk.[7]

In summary, the social context in which we speak determines an audience's judgment of *appropriateness* and *competency*. We learn to communicate appropriately and competently by learning and, usually, following the communication rules that govern our society. You have spent your lifetime learning those rules; throughout this book we will cite many of the more explicit ones that govern public speaking.

A MODEL OF THE SPEECHMAKING PROCESS

All speeches entail a complex pattern of interaction among the five primary elements: speaker, message, listeners, channels, and situation. The model of the speechmaking process contained in this chapter is termed a *transactional model* because:

- Both speakers and listeners have mutual rights and responsibilities.
- Both speakers and listeners generally are aware of each other's needs and purposes, and so, consciously adapt their messages—speeches and feedback—to the others' presumed conditions and situations.
- Both speakers and listeners are bonded together in a common culture through *communication rules,* which influence the ways in which they behave in each other's presence.

Thus, I prepare a speech to "give" you, and you in turn give me your attention and reactions (feedback). From among all of the things I *could*

The Speech Communication Transaction

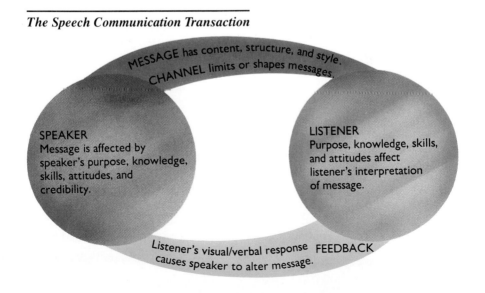

MESSAGE has content, structure, and style.
CHANNEL limits or shapes messages.

SPEAKER
Message is affected by speaker's purpose, knowledge, skills, attitudes, and credibility.

LISTENER
Purpose, knowledge, skills, and attitudes affect listener's interpretation of message.

Listener's visual/verbal response FEEDBACK causes speaker to alter message.

say about a subject, I *actually* select only a few, tailoring (adapting) them to your interests, wants, and desires as well as to limitations of time and space. And, as I assert my right to speak to other members of this culture, so you also assert your right to listen or not, your right to react as you see fit. Hence, the *transactional* aspects of the public speaking process integrate the various elements so as to make them interdependent. That interdependence is achieved through innumerable communication rules.

Indeed, because speeches almost always represent transactions whose appropriateness is determined by cultural rules or expectations, throughout this book you will find explicit pieces of advice—do's and don'ts—that you ought to follow. It is not really "wrong," for example, to skip a summary at the end of your speech, but most audiences expect that summary. If you omit it, they might even question your *communicative competence,* that is, your ability to construct a speech in accordance with their expectations. These sorts of expectations do not have to be followed slavishly, for conditions and even speaker talents vary from situation to situation; but, you will want to follow the rules of communication most of the time, because you want listeners to evaluate your ideas, not your communication skills.

THE SKILLS AND COMPETENCIES NEEDED FOR SUCCESSFUL SPEECHMAKING

Because public speaking is an interactive process through which people transact various kinds of business, you must acquire certain skills (psychomotor abilities) and competencies (mental abilities to identify, assess, and plan responses to communication problems). Five basic qualities merit your attention: (1) integrity, (2) knowledge, (3) sensitivity to listener needs and to speaking situations, (4) oral skills, and (5) self-confidence and control.

Integrity

Your reputation for reliability, truthfulness, and concern for others is perhaps your single most powerful means of exerting rhetorical influence over others. Integrity is important, especially in a day of electronic advertising and mass mailings—when every pressure group, cause, and special interest can worm its way into the public mind, often with conflicting analyses and recommendations for action. Listeners who have no personal experience with a particular subject will seek information and advice from speakers they trust. You must earn their trust if you want to succeed.[8]

Knowledge

Expertise is also essential. No one wants to listen to an empty-headed prattler; speakers should know what they are talking about. So, even though you know a lot about a topic through personal experience, take time to do some extra reading, talk with other local experts, and ask classmates what aspects of the topic *they* (not you) are interested in.

'Nothing galls me more than someone who doesn't take the time to check out the local situation,' noted Mary Beth. 'Take that guy talking yesterday about substituting soccer for football in the schools. Here he was in Iowa City, a town of 55,000 with 1500 kids playing in soccer leagues, and two male and one female high-school teams. Why, the 1984 Junior Olympics, including an international soccer tournament, were held here. The guy hadn't bothered to find out about any of this. He just ran at the mouth about his own experiences. Boy, did he miss an opportunity!' Yes, and he missed a chance to gain an ally in his audience. Mary Beth left disgusted.

Rhetorical Sensitivity

Sometimes we talk publicly simply to be talking—for purely *expressive* reasons. Usually, however, we speak for *instrumental* reasons—to pass on ideas or to influence the way others think or act. The most successful speakers are "other-directed," concerned with meeting their listeners' needs and solving their problems through public talk. These speakers are rhetorically sensitive to others.

Rhetorical sensitivity refers to speakers' attitudes toward the process of speech composition.[9] More particularly, rhetorical sensitivity is the degree to which speakers (a) recognize that all people are different and complex and, hence, must be considered individually, (b) avoid rigid communication practices by adapting their messages and themselves to particular audiences, (c) consciously seek and react to audience feedback, (d) understand the limitations of talk (sometimes even remaining silent rather than trying to express the unexpressible), and (e) work at finding the right set of arguments and linguistic expressions to make particular ideas clear and attractive to particular audiences.

Being rhetorically sensitive does not mean saying only what you think the audience wants to hear. Rather, it is a matter of careful self-assessment, audience analysis, and decision making. What are your purposes? To what degree will they be understandable and acceptable to others? To what degree can you adapt your purposes to audience preferences while still maintaining your own integrity and self-respect? These questions are faced by rhetorically sensitive speakers, and they demand that you be sensitive to *listener needs, the demands of speaking situations, and the requirements of self-respect.* Rhetorical sensitivity, then, is not so much a skill as a competency—a way of thinking and acting in the world of communication.

Oral Skills

Fluency, poise, control of voice, and coordinated movements of your body mark you as a skilled speaker. These skills do not come naturally—they are homegrown through practice. Such practice is not a matter of acquiring and rehearsing a bag of tricks. Rather, your practice both inside and outside your classroom should aim at making you an animated, natural, and conversational speaker. Indeed, many successful public speakers—discounting the high ceremonial situations of politics and religion—seem to be merely *conversing* with their audiences. That should be your goal: to practice being natural, to practice conversing with others in public.

Self-Confidence and Self-Control

The competent speaker has self-confidence and self-control. Gaining these qualities usually entails overcoming a series of fears.[10] Audiences are more likely to accept ideas from self-confident than from self-doubting persons. In Chapter 3 we will talk a good deal more about self-assurance and control.

First, however, we will continue our general orientation to speechmaking by looking at it from the other end—from the view of listeners.

CHAPTER SUMMARY

Public speaking is both a public act and a personal activity—a matter of both *public service* and *personal survival.* It is comprised of a set of *skills* (psychomotor activities) and *competencies* (mental abilities to identify, assess, and make plans to solve communication problems). It is useful to think of speechmaking as a *communication transaction,* a two-way exchange between speaker and audience. A complete speech transaction is composed of five elements and several subelements: the *speaker* (purpose, knowledge, attitudes, credibility), the *message* (content, structure, style), the *listeners* (purpose, knowledge of the subject, command of listening skills, attitudes), the *channels,* and the *communicative situation* (physical setting, social context). Overall, a successful speaker, in following this culture's *communication rules,* must exhibit five basic skills and competencies to do well: *integrity, knowledge, rhetorical sensitivity, oral skills,* and *self-confidence and self-control.* These ideas will be expanded considerably through the rest of this book.

Oral Activities

1. Interview the leader of a local group that schedules public lectures, the director of the campus speakers' bureau, or another person in a position to discuss speech skills highly prized in "professional" speakers. Bring a list of those skills to class and be prepared to compare your notes with others'.
2. Talk with another classmate in preparation for introducing him or her to the rest of the class. Concentrate on obtaining, selecting, and ordering your information for public presentation.
3. Prepare an inventory of your personal speech needs and speaking abilities. (Your instructor may make this the first assignment in a personal communication journal that you will maintain throughout the term.) In your inventory, offer thoughtful responses to the following items:

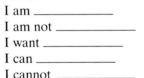

   I am _____
   I am not _____
   I want _____
   I can _____
   I cannot _____

Reference Notes

1. From "Meditation XXVII" by John Donne, reprinted in *The Complete Poetry and Selected Prose of John Donne & The Complete Poetry of William Blake,* intro. Robert Silliman Hillyer, The Modern Library (New York: Random House, Inc., 1946), 332.
2. Carol H. Pazandak, "Followup Survey of 1973 Graduates, College of Liberal Arts," Minneapolis: University of Minnesota, 1977 (multilith); Jack Landgrebe and Howard Baumgartel, "Results of the Graduation Requirement Questionnaire for College of Liberal Arts and Science Alumni," Lawrence: College of Liberal Arts and Science, University of Kansas (typescript); "Instruction in

Communication at Colorado State University," Fort Collins: College of Engineering, Colorado State University, July 1979 (multilith); Edward Foster et al., "A Market Study for the College of Business Administration, University of Minnesota, Twin Cities," Minneapolis: University of Minnesota, November 1978 (multilith). These and other studies of communication and employment are reported in Samuel L. Becker and Leah R. V. Ekdom, "That Forgotten Basic Skill: Oral Communication," *Association for Communication Administration Bulletin, #33* (August 1980).

3. For a discussion of interrelationships between self-concept and communication, see Gordon I. Zimmerman, James L. Owen, and David R. Seibert, *Speech Communication: A Contemporary Introduction,* 2nd ed. (St. Paul: West Publishing Co., 1977), esp. pp. 32–43; and Gail E. Myers and Michele Tolela Myers, *The Dynamics of Human Communication: A Laboratory Approach,* 3rd ed. (New York: McGraw-Hill Book Co., 1980), Chapter 3, "Self-Concept: Who Am I?", 47–72.

4. These and other generalizations relative to source credibility are most usefully summarized in Stephen W. Littlejohn, "A Bibliography of Studies Related to Variables of Source Credibility," *Bibliographic Annual in Speech Communication: 1971,* Ned. A. Shearer, ed., (New York: Speech Communication Assoc., 1972), 1–40; cf. Ronald L. Applebaum et al., *Fundamental Concepts in Human Communication* (San Francisco: Canfield Press, 1973), 123–46.

5. For a useful discussion of communication stylistic choices, see Gary Cronkhite, *Public Speaking and Critical Listening* (Menlo Park: The Benjamin-Cummings Publishing Co., Inc., 1978), esp. pp. 255–72.

6. See the personality analysis of receivers in Michael Burgoon, *Approaching Speech Communication* (New York: Holt, Rinehart & Winston, Inc., 1974), 64–69.

7. Much research on physical setting and social context is summarized in Mark L. Knapp, *Essentials of Nonverbal Communication* (New York: Holt, Rinehart & Winston, 1980), Chapter 4, "The Effects of Territory and Personal Space," 75–96. The determinative aspects of social expectations in human communication generally are discussed in such books as John J. Gumperz and Dell Hymes, eds., *Directions in Sociolinguistics: The Ethnography of Communication* (New York: Holt, Rinehart & Winston, 1972) and Peter Collett, ed., *Social Rules and Social Behavior* (Totowa, NJ: Rowman and Littlefield, 1977). More specifically, the current state of our knowledge about "rules" and their importance in communication is documented in Susan B. Shimanoff, *Communication Rules: Theory and Research,* Sage Library of Social Research, 97 (Beverly Hills: Sage Publishing, 1980).

8. A fuller discussion of the role that personal integrity plays in successful public communication may be found in Otis M. Walter, *Speaking to Inform and Persuade* (New York: The Macmillan Co., 1966), Chapter 8, "The *Ethos* of the Speaker."

9. See Roderick P. Hart and Don M. Burks, "Rhetorical Sensitivity and Social Interaction," *Speech [Communication] Monographs* 39 (1972): 75–91; and Roderick P. Hart, Robert F. Carlson, and William F. Eadie, "Attitudes Toward Communication and the Assessment of Rhetorical Sensitivity," *Communication Monographs,* 47 (1980): 1–22.

10. "What Are Americans Afraid Of?" *The Bruskin Report,* 13, #53; "Surveys Reveal Students' Concern Over Jobs, Public-Speaking Anxiety," *Pitt News* (May 1978): 4.

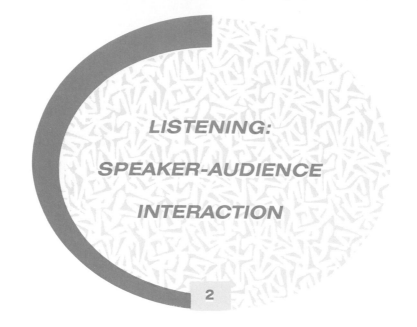

LISTENING:

SPEAKER-AUDIENCE

INTERACTION

2

Listening is an activity so common to human experience that you probably think little or nothing of it. When was the last time you listened to someone? Probably just a few moments ago. Listening accounts for over 40 percent of all your communicative time; more time is spent listening than writing, reading, or speaking.[1] Listening is extremely important in our culture because through it we learn the rules and expectations of others, their feelings and moods, and information we require to lead comfortable lives. Children do almost all of their learning aurally. Even adults—through conversations, group meetings, and public talks—acquire an amazing amount of data, ideas, and good sense by listening to others.

Listening is the central conduit in the speechmaking process. Speakers reach out to their audiences through that conduit, and, in turn, listeners in face-to-face situations can send messages back to speakers. In particular, listeners can provide three kinds of feedback: (1) *direct feedback* in the form of verbal or written comments; (2) *indirect feedback,* as in nods, laughs, frowns, and other signs that a person is or is not understanding and accepting a message; and (3) *delayed feedback,* such as when politicians find out how well they communicated in October by counting the votes in November.

Overall, public speaking is not a one-way process. Because listeners can provide three kinds of feedback, oral communication is a dynamic process that integrates speakers and listeners into what is called a speech transaction. Both speakers and listeners modify each other's thoughts and actions—one by making a speech and the other by reacting to it. Hence, this chapter is subtitled "speaker-audience interaction" because of the mutual influence, the interaction process that occurs during speechmaking.

Before we begin, please note the vocabulary we will be using through this book. A *hearer*, as will be obvious in the next section, is a person physiologically capable of receiving oral signals. A *listener* is someone who not only receives the signals but mentally processes them. An *audience* is a collection of listeners and hearers, that is, a group capable of hearing a message and, speakers hope, containing some active listeners. Finally, an *auditor* is a single member of an audience; it is a word used interchangeably with "listener."

In this chapter, we will discuss listening behavior in general. That will allow us to characterize more precisely both listeners' and speakers' responsibilities in the speech transaction. Finally, to help you refine your listening skills, we will conclude this chapter with some advice on classroom listening.

LISTENING BEHAVIOR

Hearing and Listening

To listen to a message, you first must hear it. Hearing is a *physiological process* whereby sound waves traveling through the air make impact on the eardrum. Hearing is affected by both the laws of physics and the neurophysiology of the body. One's hearing can be impaired in many ways: by distracting noises in the environment, by sound too loud or too soft for the aural mechanism, or by illness or other physiological impediments. Generally, then, hearing is a process out of the speaker's control, except when it comes to the matters of speaking volume and, occasionally, distracting sounds. Listening, on the other hand, is primarily a *psychological process* whereby people attach meanings to aural signals.[2] Once sound reaches the brain, listening begins. After sound waves are translated to nerve impulses by the middle ear and auditory nerve, they are sent to the brain for interpretation. Those interpretation processes—registering impul-

The Types of Feedback

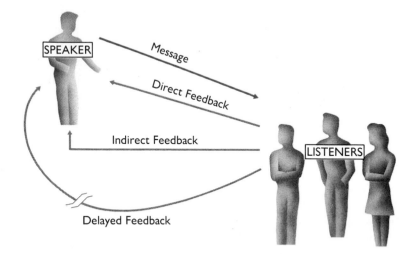

ses, assigning them to meaningful contexts, and evaluating them—comprise the heart of listening.

All of this becomes complicated by the fact that people who can hear a message do not always listen to it. The physiological mechanisms for transmitting and receiving sounds may be working perfectly, yet, for any number of reasons, the receiver may choose not to listen. Getting an audience to listen, therefore, is one of the public speaker's primary goals.

Characteristics of Listeners

We have noted that listening is a joint responsibility. Both speaker and listeners must make sure that intended messages are taken in, comprehended, interpreted, and evaluated fully. Yet problems can arise. Few of us are good listeners. Although researchers vary in their assessments of the average listening comprehension rate, they agree that we do not utilize our listening potential.[3] Some studies indicate that we may be listening at only a 25 percent comprehension rate, understanding only one fourth of all of the information received aurally. There are several reasons why people are poor listeners. As a speaker, you must adjust your message to avoid these problems.

One reason we are poor listeners is that our complex minds can comprehend many more words per minute than speakers can produce. As listeners, we can mentally handle more than four hundred spoken words a minute, yet the average speaker produces between one hundred twenty-five and one hundred seventy-five words a minute. Stated in a different way, the listener needs only fifteen seconds of every minute to comprehend what the speaker says. The time lag thus created in the listener's mind presents special problems. In the excess time, the listener begins to think of other things; technically, extraneous thoughts begin to enter the listener's *internal perceptual field.* Recall a situation in which you began listening to a speaker but soon found yourself thinking about lunch or an upcoming test or appointment. This tendency for listeners to "drop in, drop out" poses many problems for the speaker trying to convey an understandable message, especially if the subject matter is complex.

Second, as listeners, we often bring our past—our feelings, values, and attitudes—into the communication setting. Sometimes the speaker will present a thought or word that triggers memories of a past experience. At that point we start to think about the experience and soon forget the message being presented.

Our attitudes, values, and beliefs can cause us to give personalized interpretations and meanings to spoken messages. When we do not agree with the message, we spend mental time "debating" the ideas of the speaker instead of listening for the full development of those ideas. Much faulty listening can be attributed to the fact that as listeners we do not give the speaker the benefit of a full presentation before drawing conclusions about the "rightness" or "wrongness" of the ideas. At times, our feelings color our reception so much that we attribute ideas to the speaker that were not actually presented. This happens especially when we disagree with the speaker.

A third problem is passive listeners. Listening is an active process. It takes energy, and many of us are lazy listeners. Being passive is much easier than concentrating on the speaker's message, but, unfortunately, it leads to ineffective listening. Think back for a moment to the last time you enjoyed a good movie. When you left the theater you may have felt tired even though you did nothing but watch and listen. Because you empathized with the actors, you were "living" the flow of events with the characters. This empathic response takes energy, the same type of energy you use when you are actively listening. It is easier to pretend to listen or to fake attention than it is to focus on the spoken message.

A fourth problem is that the physical setting can work against listening. Seats are hard; the room is too cold or too hot; the person next to you is coughing; the heater is making a distracting sound. Just as your other thoughts can invade your internal perceptual field, so also can distractions outside your body invade your *external perceptual field,* drawing your

The Perceptual Fields of the Listener

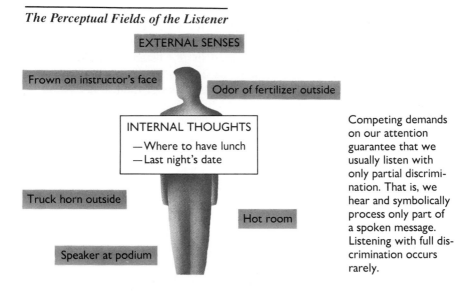

EXTERNAL SENSES

Frown on instructor's face

Odor of fertilizer outside

INTERNAL THOUGHTS
— Where to have lunch
— Last night's date

Truck horn outside

Hot room

Speaker at podium

Competing demands on our attention guarantee that we usually listen with only partial discrimination. That is, we hear and symbolically process only part of a spoken message. Listening with full discrimination occurs rarely.

attention away from the speech. Physical well-being and comfort often take priority with the listener.[4]

Fifth, the listener's own needs also may compete with the speaker's ideas. Perhaps you did not sleep well, have a cold, or are hungry. All of these personal factors compete for your energy and focus. Again, your physical needs as an individual win out over your intellectual needs as a listener.

Sixth, because it takes mental and physical energy to deal with words or concepts that we do not know, it is easier to turn off the listening process when the speaker uses unfamiliar language. As listeners, we assume that we are unable to understand what the speaker is talking about if the vocabulary is different or the ideas are new. Unfamiliarity requires energy that listeners may not be willing to expend.

And finally, preset ideas about the topic, the speaker, or the occasion also may interfere with adequate listening comprehension. If you have heard that Professor Smith is a boring lecturer, you will enter the class with that preset notion. Chances are that you will find that Professor Smith's lectures are boring, not because they are but because you allowed the reputation to interfere with the reality of the communication event. Many speakers are not given a fair hearing because the audience accepts conclusions about them or their topics beforehand.

What, then, can you as speaker expect from an audience? You know they probably will have other things on their minds, things of more concern to them than the information you want to share. They may not be physically or mentally prepared to listen. Their preconceived biases about you, the topic, or the words and ideas you present may interfere with acceptance of your message. Lastly, you know that you, as speaker, will have to make some adjustments and adaptations for your listeners just because they are listeners. We will talk about those speaker responsibilities later in this chapter.

Purposes of Listening

One last set of considerations complicates the speaker-audience relationship in respect to listening. Just as speakers' motivations for talking vary from situation to situation, so, too, do listeners' purposes. Those motivations determine *how* individuals in the audience listen to a speaker. Wolvin and Coakley identify five types of listening: listening for appreciation, discrimination, therapeutic value, comprehension, and critical analysis.[5]

Appreciative listening actually encompasses several different purposes. Some listeners simply come to hear and enjoy a "famous" speaker; some enjoy the "arts" of good public speaking, such as pleasing vocal modulation, clever uses of language, impressive phraseology, the powerful use of argumentative materials, and the like; and some members of audiences just like to attend such occasions as inaugurals or dedications of new city artworks. Appreciative listening, therefore, is undertaken by people principally concerned with something other than the primary message.

In *discriminative listening,* auditors are attempting to draw inferences about unstated matters—about what speakers "really" think, believe, or feel. You often draw conclusions about how angry your parents are with you based not on what they actually say, but on how they say it. Often, too, a president's attitude toward, say, some foreign policy controversy is determined as much by what he did not say as by what he did say: Was his commitment to an invasion absolute or not? How strong was his anti-Communist language? Did he dwell on the gory details of atrocities or pass them over? Were there signs of sincerity and deep commitments or only *pro forma* remarks he would be expected to offer? In other words, an important dimension of listening—especially of listeners' judgments regarding emotional impact, speaker credibility, and the urgency of some problem—has to do with relatively sophisticated inferences auditors draw from (rather than find in) speeches.

Therapeutic listening actually is more typical of interpersonal than of public communication. In therapeutic listening, the auditor acts as a sounding board for the speaker as that person attempts to talk through a problem, work out a difficult situation, or express deep emotional stress or confusion. Such therapy can also occur in public speaking situations, such as when a sports star apologizes for unprofessional behavior, a religious convert talks about a soul-saving experience, or a classmate reviews a personal problem and thanks friends for help in solving it. Equally important, therapeutic listening is used in times of joy, as when someone wants to tell others about a new love, a new baby, a promotion at work, or an award at school. In therapeutic listening, special social bonding occurs between speaker and listener; the speaker-audience relationship itself becomes recognized and even celebrated.

Listening for comprehension is probably the most common auditory activity. It occurs when the listener wants to gain additional information or insights being provided by the speaker. When you listen to radio or TV news programs to find out what is happening, to classroom lectures describing the four principal causes of World War II, or to an orientation official previewing your school's new registration process, you are listening to understand—to comprehend information, ideas, and processes.

The most sophisticated kind of listening is *critical listening*. It demands that auditors become fully engaged with the message not simply to understand it, but to interpret it, judge its strengths and weaknesses, and assign it some worth. You practice this sort of listening when you evaluate commercials, political campaign speeches, advice from career counselors, or arguments offered by people for or against some plan of action on the job. When listening critically, auditors decide to accept or reject and to act or delay action on the message.

Such variety in the purposes for listening has serious implications for both listeners and speakers. When you are in an audience, you must decide what your purpose is so that you listen accordingly. Appreciative listeners are highly selective people, watching for metaphors, listening to speaking tones, and searching out memorable phrasings; at the other extreme, critical listeners work hard to catch every piece of relevant information, judge the soundness of competing arguments, and rationally decide whether to accept some proposal. Therapeutic listeners must decide when to positively reinforce speakers through applause or other signs of approval; those listening for comprehension must learn to sort out the important from the unimportant ideas. Discriminative listeners must search for clues to unspoken ideas or feelings especially important to themselves. As your skill in listening increases, and as you work to think explicitly about your own purposes *before* attending to a speech, you will find your experiences with public speeches becoming more pleasurable and complete.

Speakers likewise must consider these purposes for listening before talking. In part, speakers can determine the kinds of listening that occur. For example, you can increase the amount of appreciative listening that occurs by the way you phrase ideas and the number of humorous anecdotes you offer—by the general tone or atmosphere you set. Sometimes you can force more critical listening by emphasizing the rationality of your arguments for or against a proposal. You can even produce some level of therapeutic listening by adopting a confessional tone.

In part, however, speakers *cannot* control listeners' motivations. Many will listen for their own purposes no matter what you do. Some speakers, for example, have reputations that, in effect, limit the messages they can get across to some audience members. For example, Al Capp, who drew *Li'l Abner* for years, was known to be a humorist, and when he tried to talk seriously about America's political problems in the 1960s, he generally disappointed student audiences; they wanted him to make them laugh, and they *would* laugh, no matter what he said. Similarly, William F. Buckley, Jr., is known for his intellectual sneer and well-turned phrases; his audiences wait for both, and were he not to provide them, people would leave his speeches wondering what was wrong with him. Ultimately, then, understanding the range of purposes listeners have helps speakers set goals and expectations.

LISTENERS' RESPONSIBILITIES

Having generally reviewed hearing-listening, characteristics of listeners, and the purposes of listening, we can move directly to the heart of public speaking—the responsibilities of both listeners and speakers to make speech communication a rewarding experience. We will begin from the audience side, suggesting ways of improving listening skills through the analysis of self, speaker, and message.

Analysis of Self

To become a better listener in public settings, you first must identify your listening patterns and preferences, think about them in terms of their productivity, and then decide which to continue and which to alter. Think about times when you feel you are a good listener, when listening is easy for you and when you remember most of the content of the message. What types of settings are these? How do you keep your attention focused on the message and the speaker? Think also about those times when it is difficult for you to listen for comprehension and critical analysis. Why is it difficult to listen? Are you uninterested in the subject? Are you bored or tired? Taking stock of your listening habits will help you recognize your strong and weak listening abilities.

Think also about your listening preferences. Are there people to whom you prefer to listen? Are some classes especially exciting for you even though they are required lecture courses? What features of these people and classes cause you to think and listen with an eager ear? By quickly scanning your habits, patterns, and preferences for listening, you can begin to identify and reinforce positive aspects of your listening behavior.

In addition to reviewing your listening behavior, you can begin to correct poor habits by preparing to listen. Just before the speaker begins, ask yourself this series of questions:

1. *What is my purpose in listening?* Do I expect to gain information and understanding or to make a critical decision based on the speaker's presentation? Think about your listening behavior when a teacher announces "This material will be on the next test." You probably pay particular attention to that material, making sure that you understand it. By recognizing why you are listening, you can better analyze the message.

2. *Am I impartial about the topic being presented?* If you are not willing to let the speaker fully develop ideas before you draw conclusions, you may be wasting the speaker's time and yours. That does not mean that you cannot disagree; every listener has the duty to question and evaluate the materials presented. However, you should suspend judgment until all of the ideas have been developed.

3. *How much do I know about the topic?* If you still have a great deal to learn, you can better direct your attention to listening. If you know a great deal about the topic, be prepared to compare the speaker's information to your knowledge. This may provide additional motivation for listening.

4. *What do I expect from this speech?* Be realistic. If a classmate is giving a speech about the stock market, you will be disappointed if you expect to learn the secret to small investments and quick return. If you expect only to increase your understanding of the way the stock market works, your expectations may be more easily satisfied.

5. *What do I know about the speaking situation?* If you can anticipate the length of and the occasion for the speech, you can better focus your attention. In your class, you will be listening to a variety of speeches. You will know through the description of the assignment how long these speeches will be. Mentally prepare yourself to focus your attention on the speech for the expected period of time.

6. *What can I expect from the listening environment?* Become aware of the physical environment. Note the temperature and sounds of the room. If you can deal with these and other possible distractions beforehand, you will be less likely to allow your attention to steal away after the speaker begins.

7. *What "trigger" words or ideas cause me to stray from the listening situation?* As you listen, do not let past experiences distract you from the current communication event. Take note of particular words that seem to pull you away from the speaker's message. After the listening situation is over, try to think why those words caused your attention to be redirected.

Analysis of the Speaker

Speaking does not occur in a vacuum. Both speaker and listener bring past experiences to the communication environment. In doing so, the listener attends not only to the message the speaker transmits but also considers the speaker's credibility. The following questions may help you decide how to view the speaker and what impact that view will have on your reactions:

1. *What do I know about this speaker?* Rightly or wrongly, the reputation of the speaker will influence how you listen to the message. If your previous experience with the speaker has been favorable, you will be more likely to be receptive to the message. If you have had a disagreement with the person or if you do not respect that person, you may allow such prior knowledge to color the way you understand the message. If you fail to listen carefully, you may never consider worthwhile ideas that deserve your attention.

2. *How believable is the speaker?* We tend to answer this question based on previous experiences with the speaker or on information about the speaker. If you know that the speaker has misled another audience, you will probably assume that you are being subjected to the same treatment. You may adjust your listening to search out unfounded conclusions, assuming they are untrue. In doing so, you may be listening for detail and not for the main ideas.

3. *Has the speaker prepared for the occasion by conducting adequate research and by considering relationships among ideas?* As listeners, we are more likely to accept messages that we perceive as carefully planned and researched. Yet just because a source has been cited by the speaker does not mean that careful research and planning have been conducted. You need to listen to the total presentation of ideas, noting the relationships between the message and the supporting materials. Your opinion about the speaker's believability is based partially on his or her knowledge of the subject. Suppose you decide to buy a new car. You enter a showroom eager to find out about fuel efficiency and car durability. When you mention these concerns, the salesperson begins a prepared speech about the new models, citing commendations from a driving magazine. Your interest will probably slacken because the person skirted the topics you were concerned about.

4. *What is the speaker's attitude toward this presentation?* As listeners, we use our ears and eyes to grasp meaning. We assess whether a message is worthy of our time in part by the attitudes the speaker projects. A speaker who appears flippant and uncaring creates an obstacle to productive listening. As listeners, we must be careful that the speaker's mannerisms do not divert our attention from the message.

Analysis of the Message

The message is the speaker's product. It gives information about the topic and expresses views. Therefore, the message should be the principal focus of the listener's energy. The receiver can better focus energy on the message by structuring listening behavior to answer three questions:

1. *What are the main ideas of the speech?* Try to discover the speaker's purpose for speaking and the ideas that contribute toward that purpose. Usually these can be found by determining the thesis of the speech and the statements that help the speaker explain the thesis. The main ideas serve as a skeleton on which the speaker builds the speech. The next time you listen to a commercial, listen for the main idea. What types of information does the advertiser give to encourage you to accept the product? Listen the same way to a speech. By focusing on the main idea, you can better recall the message.

2. *How are the main ideas arranged?* By searching for the speaker's pattern of organization, the listener can see more easily the relationships among the main ideas. If you know that the speaker is using a chronological or spatial pattern of development, it is easier to identify the main ideas and keep them ordered as the speech progresses.

3. *What sorts of supporting materials are used to develop the main ideas?* Consider the timeliness, the quality of the source, and the content of the supporting materials. Supporting materials are used to clarify, amplify, and strengthen the main ideas of the speech. Analyze these materials to help you evaluate the ideas presented. Check to make sure that the supporting materials, as well as the main ideas, make sense to you. If there is a discrepancy between your knowledge and the ideas presented by the speaker, find out why it exists. This should help you clarify the differences and reach a conclusion about the validity of the total message.

To focus your attention on the main ideas of the speech, on the pattern of development, and on the use of supporting materials, you should constantly *review, relate,* and *anticipate. Review* what the speaker has said. Take a few seconds to summarize the content of the message, to think about the way the materials have been developed. Mentally add to the summary review each time the speaker initiates a new topic for consideration. *Relate* the message to what you already know. Consider how important the message is to you and how you might use the information in the future. *Anticipate* what the speaker might say next. Given the development of the materials to that point, what is the speaker likely to say next? Use the anticipation stage as a way of continuing to focus on the content of the message. It is not important if you are right or wrong—the important element is that you have directed your attention to the message. By reviewing, relating, and anticipating, you can use up the extra time generated by the speech-thought lag and keep your attention focused on the message.

Listening is a complex process. Listeners may seek only to comprehend a message, or they may discriminate to discover "unspoken truths." At the same time, listeners bring their own ideas and attitudes to a speaking situation and may find fault with the structure of the speech or question the speaker's credibility. Thus, messages are shaped by the interactive elements that make up the listening process.

SPEAKER'S RESPONSIBILITIES

Even though it is the listener who finally judges the transmitted message, there are several steps that you as the speaker can take to help the listener. These efforts are concentrated in three areas: preparing the speech, capturing and holding attention, and presenting the speech.

Preparing the Speech

When preparing the speech, keep in mind that it is often difficult for the listener to follow the structure of your presentation and to keep track of what has been said. Try to use an organizational pattern that is suited to your purpose and is easy to follow. You may want to share the means of development with your audience in an initial summary or forecast early in the speech. This will help the listener follow your development.

Careful planning and preparation will help guarantee that your message is clearly presented and is easy to follow. Researching the topic area to select the most appropriate forms of support will help you develop your ideas fully. The supporting materials make it easier for the listener to remember the main ideas of your speech. Poor planning makes the audience lose respect for the speaker; if your topic is worth speaking about, it is worth preparing well.

When preparing your speech, anticipate points where your listeners will need special guidance. Forecasts and internal summaries will help the listeners focus on your ideas. Think about concepts that may be especially difficult for the listeners to understand. Try to present those concepts several times using different wording each time so that the listeners can better identify with the materials and ideas. Paraphrasing is a useful tool.

During your planning, keep your listeners in mind. If the audience is expecting a five-minute speech, tailor your presentation to that expectation. If you know the environment is going to be uncomfortable for the audience, try to adapt your speech topic and length to accommodate the physical situation.

*'The speech that stands out most clearly in my memory,'
Rich noted in reviewing this chapter, 'was on an August
Sunday morning when I was a kid. We were getting ready to
go to church camp after the service. The temperature was
already in the 90s by 10:30 in the morning. The church had
no air conditioning. And, of all things, this morning the
minister—probably worrying too much about our hormones—*

gave an extra-long sermon on keeping our bodies chaste. The longer he spoke, the more turned-off we became. Even my parents were wilted within ten minutes. They wound up complaining about a sermon they themselves had been trying to give me all week!'

Preparation also includes practice. While practicing your speech, work out awkward phrasing, get used to the sound of your own voice, and convince yourself that you are ready to take on the audience. The better prepared you are, the better you will feel about yourself and your speaking tasks.

Capturing and Holding Attention: Nine Factors

Listeners' behaviors vary considerably, thanks to thoughts and sensations moving through their internal and external perceptual fields. Essentially, listeners need reasons for *wanting* to listen. Yet, even when you have their attention, it tends to ebb and flow for reasons we have already noted. So, you must constantly be on the lookout for lapses in attention. James Albert Winans, a twentieth-century pioneer in public speaking instruction, expressed this problem succinctly: "Attention determines response." If you cannot gain and hold attention, you are in deep trouble.

What is attention? For our purposes, it can be thought of as *focus* on one element in a given perceptual field, with the result that other elements in that field fade and, for all practical purposes, cease to exist.[6] Consider, for example, a rock concert: Near the end of his concert, Billy Joel breaks into the verses of "Innocent Man." The crowd goes wild, and you join in the cheering. You love that song. You all become quiet during the middle verses, but, by the end, you cannot help yourself—you are singing all of the choruses at the top of your lungs, near to crying for the sheer sweetness of it all. At the end, the place erupts. Billy Joel obliges by repeating the last verse and chorus. Again the place explodes for three or four minutes. As the screaming finally ebbs, only then do you look around. You have spilled your soft drink on your new jeans, the person sitting to your right is sobbing uncontrollably, and you have to use the bathroom. Now that is paying attention! It is this focusing on one message source or stimulus to the greater or lesser exclusion of others that is called *attention*.

However, you are not Billy Joel singing "Innocent Man"; how can you capture and hold attention? Of course, a *vigorous and varied delivery* will help. Likewise, your reputation and trustworthiness (positive *ethos*) can command respect—and attention. *Lively and picturesque language* gives audiences "word-pictures" and makes it easier for them to stay with you. *Fundamentally, however, you will capture and hold attention through the types of ideas you present.* Some types of ideas or images have greater attention value than others.

Ideas can be presented in a variety of ways that have high attention value. Often called *the factors of attention,* these include the following:

1. Activity or movement
2. Reality
3. Proximity
4. Familiarity
5. Novelty
6. Suspense
7. Conflict
8. Humor
9. The vital

Activity

Suppose you have two TV sets side by side. One shows a singer performing motionless behind a microphone; the other set carries an MTV music video with motorcycles, dry-ice clouds, and three performers with orange hair leaping and running around the stage. Which one will you look at? Ideas that "move" likewise tend to attract attention. Stories in which something happens or in which there are moments of uncertainty usually have attention value.

In addition, a speech as a whole should "move"—it should march or press forward. Nothing is so boring as a talk that seems to stand still, providing far too much detail on a minor point. Instructions and demonstrations, particularly, demand orderly, systematic progress. Keep moving ahead, and an audience will be more likely to stay with you.

Reality

The earliest words you learned were names for tangible objects—"Mama," "milk," and "cookie." While the ability to abstract—to generalize—is one of the marks of human intelligence, nonetheless there persists in all of us an interest in concrete reality, the here-and-now of sense data. When you speak, refer to specific events, persons, places, and happenings. A few paragraphs ago, we could have written: "Consider, for example, a rock concert. Near the end of a concert, the singer breaks into the verses of one

The Factors of Attention

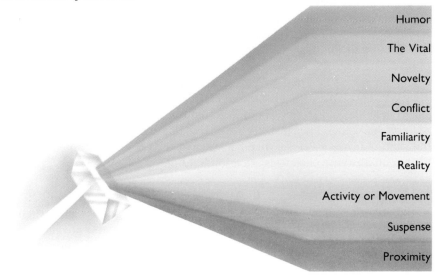

Humor

The Vital

Novelty

Conflict

Familiarity

Reality

Activity or Movement

Suspense

Proximity

of his well-known songs . . . . " As an example, such a depersonalized anecdote about "a singer" would not have as much human interest and memorability as one about a specific, named performer. Audiences can use specific details on which to hang ideas.

Proximity

A direct reference to a person in the audience, to a nearby object or place, to an incident that has just occurred, or to the immediate occasion usually helps you command attention. Talking about specific people in the audience—"Take John over there, and think what he'd look like with a shave, a three-piece suit, a Brooks Brothers shirt, a silk tie, and a black leather briefcase"—involves all of your listeners in your message; if people are sharing in a speech, they are likely to listen to it.

Or, consider the following introduction: "Do you realize how much fast food is consumed by our student body? Within four blocks of this classroom are nine restaurants, including a McDonalds, a Wendy's, a Godfather's Pizza joint, a Kentucky Fried Chicken franchise, and a Best Steak House. And, two of the others are local submarine houses. Even the student union runs a fast-food counter. A key question is, what are your lunch habits doing to your nutrition—to your body and your mind?" Such an introduction brings the speech topic home.

Familiarity

Especially in the face of new or strange ideas, references to the familiar are attention sustaining. A common device here is the *analogy:* If I explain that the London postal or zip codes are arranged like directions on a compass, with the initial letters indicating directions and the next set of numbers representing degrees or positions, then I will have used something familiar to explain something unfamiliar. And, I probably will have held your attention. The familiar is also *comfortable.* We like to sing songs we know and to hear the old stories about Washington, Lincoln, and Kennedy. We probably have such likes because we share "the familiar" with others, and that sharing brings us closer together. Hence, the comfortable anecdote—if it is not an absolute cliché—is attention holding.

Novelty

As the old adage has it, when a dog bites a man, it is an accident; when a man bites a dog, it is news. Novel happenings, dramatic advances, or unusual developments attract wide notice. Two special types of novelty are *size* and *contrast.* Insofar as size is concerned, especially large or especially small objects or amounts attract attention. For example, reference to a $10,000 automobile or to a $90,000 home would not stand out as unusual, but reference to a $30,000 automobile or to a $300,000 home would. In a speech on the high cost of national defense, a speaker caught the attention of his listeners with this sentence: "Considering that it costs more than $5000 to equip an average soldier for combat, it is disquieting to learn that in a year his equipment will be 60 percent obsolete."[7]

Although attention arousing in themselves, large and small figures become even more compelling when thrown into *contrast* with their opposites. Here is how Henry W. Grady, in an address at the University of Virginia, used novel or startling contrasts to focus attention on the gap between the rich and the poor:

> A home that cost three million dollars and a breakfast that cost five thousand are disquieting facts to the millions who live in a hut and dine on a crust. The fact that a man . . . has an income of twenty million dollars falls strangely on the ears of those who hear it as they sit empty-handed with children crying for bread.[8]

In utilizing the materials of novelty, be careful, of course, not to inject elements that are so different or unusual that they are entirely unfamiliar. As we have emphasized, your listeners must at least know what you are talking about, or their attention will soon waver. They must be able to relate what you say to things they know and—preferably—have a degree of experience with. Best results are achieved by the proper combination of the new and the old, of the novel and the familiar. Note, too, that novelty may gain attention but will not necessarily hold it.

Suspense

A large part of the interest in mystery stories arises from uncertainty about their outcome. When giving a speech, you can create uncertainty by pointing out results that have mysterious or unknown causes or by calling attention to forces that threaten uncertain effects. Introduce suspense into the stories you use to illustrate your ideas, especially in lectures or even in demonstrations. Mention valuable information you expect to divulge later in your talk but which requires an understanding of what you are now saying.

> *Lori and Richard both spoke on the same topic on the same day. Lori began her speech as follows: 'It all started innocently enough. First they told me I ought to know about the field generally before I did any advanced work in it. Then, the next semester they said I had to have a practical course before I could take a more theoretical one. Soon, they became more insidious and more subtle; the following semester I was told that while there wasn't room in the course I wanted to take, I could take a different one and learn pretty much the same thing. Soon I was done. And then I discovered I hadn't taken any of the courses I originally planned on taking. I was a victim of an over-structured major and just plain bad advice from a counselor.' Richard began his speech differently: 'I don't think this department ought to tell you what courses to take. I don't think the advisers are very good, either. I want to talk about this stuff today. . . . ' Lori's use of suspense earned many more positive audience comments than Richard's flat beginning.*

Conflict

The opposition of forces compels attention; just look at the ratings for prime time TV soap operas, which play off extremely strong interpersonal conflicts for their plots. Conflict, like suspense, suggests uncertainty; like activity or movement, it is dynamic. Hence, when then–President Jimmy Carter wanted to get the American public moving on energy conservation, he talked about energy saving as "the moral equivalent of war." The word "war"—suggesting conflict—gave him a dynamic metaphor. You can carry this further, too; take time to describe the *details* of the battles. For example, in an informative speech on big-city downtown renovations, you could easily describe the struggle between the downtown merchants, who want investments in parking lots and attractive visual projects, and the mall owners on the outskirts, who argue that such city-sponsored construction is wasting taxpayers' money and giving the downtown merchants an unfair competitive advantage. Talking merely about urban renewal and public dollars would not have nearly as much attention value as a description of the fight between downtown and outlying investment groups.

Humor

People usually pay attention when they are enjoying themselves. Humor relaxes both the speaker and listeners. It provides an attention getting change of pace, and it can establish a link between you and your audience— "the group that laughs together, stays together." When using humor to capture and hold attention, however, observe two guidelines:

1. *Be relevant.* Beware of wandering from the point, of telling a joke just for the sake of telling a joke. If it is not reinforcing an important point, forget it.

2. *Use good taste.* You probably do not want to tell a knee-slapper during a funeral and should refrain from telling off-color stories in a speech, which can offend audience members.

The Vital

Finally, people nearly always pay attention to matters that affect their health, reputation, property, or employment. When you hear "Students who take an internship while in college find jobs after school three times as fast as those who do not," you are likely to pay attention. When your future is on the line, so are you. Appealing to "the vital," therefore, is a matter of *personalizing* your topic and supporting materials, making them directly and unavoidably relevant, not just to groups, but to specific individuals in your audience.

The vital, humor, conflict, suspense, novelty, familiarity, proximity, reality, and activity or movement—these nine attention getters should be in your arsenal of rhetorical weapons. They give your speech sparkle, vivacity, and force; they help keep you and your words squarely in the middle of listeners' external and internal perceptual fields. They are designed to force an audience to keep coming back for more.

Presenting the Speech

The presentation of the speech can help the receiver be a better listener. See that your delivery style is appropriate for the audience, topic, and occasion. Be sure also that your nonverbal communication matches your verbalized thoughts and feelings so that you are not sending contradictory messages.

Interpreting audience feedback during the presentation will help you modify, adapt, or recast any ideas you see the audience is misunderstanding or doubting. If the listeners notice that you are making a sincere effort to communicate your thoughts, they will tend to be more receptive and try harder to be good listeners. Your use of feedback is one way the audience assesses your desire to communicate effectively. If nonverbal clues from the audience suggest that they are not understanding your message, quickly think back over what you have said and try to rephrase main points in simpler language. Include a brief internal summary of the points you have covered, and if the situation allows, ask for questions.

Finally, as a speaker, remember how it feels to be a listener. Consider your own positive and negative reactions to the ways other speakers present ideas. Avoid making some of the same errors that annoy you. Remember that good speakers are also good listeners. Review critiques of your speaking and try to correct any weaknesses before you speak again.

DEVELOPING LISTENING SKILLS IN THE CLASSROOM

Critical listening skills can be developed in several ways in the speech classroom and in other settings as well:

1. Practice critiquing the speeches of other students, taking part in post-speech discussions.

2. Listen critically to discussions, lectures, oral presentations, and student-teacher exchanges in your other classes, identifying effective and ineffective communicative techniques employed by a variety of people in several different contexts.

3. Make an effort to listen to speakers outside of class, in the community, carefully observing their successes and failures and analyzing why they meet with certain reactions.

4. Read the sample speeches in this book, taking them apart systematically in order to isolate the communicative cues that might have facilitated comprehension and acceptance.

Undoubtedly you will become a more informed listener after you have studied this book and carried out the classroom speaking assignments, but

Speech Evaluation Form

The Speaker
☐ poised?

☐ positive self-image?

☐ apparently sincere?

☐ apparently concerned about the topic?

☐ apparently concerned about the audience?

☐ apparently well prepared?

The Message
☐ suitable topic?

☐ clear general purpose?

☐ sharply focused specific purpose?

☐ well-phrased central idea or proposition?

☐ adequately supported (enough, varied, trustworthy sources)?

☐ supporting materials tailored to the audience?

☐ introduced adequately?

☐ concluded effectively?

☐ major subdivisions clear, balanced?

☐ use of notes and lectern unobtrusive?

Transmission
☐ voice varied for emphasis?

☐ voice conversational?

☐ delivery speed controlled?

☐ body alert and nondistracting?

☐ gestures used effectively?

☐ face expressive?

☐ language clear (unambiguous, concrete)?

☐ language forcible (vivid, intense)?

The Audience
☐ all listeners addressed?

☐ their presence recognized and complimented?

☐ their attitudes toward subject and speaker taken into account?

The Speech as a Whole
Audience's expectations met?

_____

_____

_____

_____

Short-range effects of the speech?

_____

_____

_____

_____

Long-range effects?

_____

_____

_____

_____

Possible improvements?

_____

_____

_____

_____

you can start now to become a more proficient listener. First, use the Speech Evaluation Form on page 40 as a checklist of listening concerns. Depending on the particular assignment, the nature of the audience, and the demands of the occasion, some of the checkpoints on the form will be more significant and applicable than others. For now, use the form as a general guide; later, concentrate on those aspects that are relevant to a specific speech assignment.

Second, participate regularly in post-speech evaluations, even of early classroom speaking assignments. Do not hesitate to provide direct feedback to your classmates, pointing out what was good, what worked and what did not seem to work so well, what was clear and what remained cloudy. Good, constructive classroom criticism is both positive and negative—but always supportive. Such oral commentary accomplishes two goals: it provides a beginning speaker with much-needed response, and it forces you, the listener, to verbalize your thoughts and recognize explicitly your standards and expectations. In this way, both you and the speaker gain; the speaker acquires a sense of the range of reactions being generated in an audience, and you gain a better sense of your own mind.

Listening, then, is a two-way process, a joint responsibility of speaker and listener. Only when both parties are sensitive to its points of breakdown and to techniques that can enhance it will oral communication be a successful transaction. Much of what we will have to say in later chapters will rest directly on this process.

CHAPTER SUMMARY

Public speaking is a two-way transaction; hence, listening is an important part of this process. *Hearing* is physiological, while *listening* is a psychological process in which people attach meanings to aural signals. People can be poor listeners for several reasons: (1) they may be distracted by other stimuli in their *internal* or *external perceptual fields;* (2) *past associations* may interfere with the present message; (3) some listeners may be *passive* rather than active; (4) the *physical setting* may make listening difficult; (5) a person's physical *needs* may compete with the speaker's ideas; (6) *unfamiliar language* may cause some listeners to tune out; and (7) *preset ideas* about the topic, speaker, or occasion may interfere with adequate listening comprehension. To become a better listener, you should become familiar with the different *purposes of listening*—appreciative listening, discriminative listening, therapeutic listening, listening for comprehension, and critical listening. Equally important, both listeners and speakers must be aware of their responsibilities to make the oral communication process work well. Listeners have responsibilities to analyze *themselves* (purposes, impartiality, knowledge, expectations, and familiarity with situations), *the speaker* (knowledge, believability, preparation, and attitudes), and *the message* (main ideas, their arrangement, and supporting materials). Speakers have responsibilities to *prepare* the speech well; to *capture and hold attention* (by considering the factors of activity or movement, reality, proximity, familiarity, novelty, suspense, conflict, humor, and the vital); and to *present* the speech in ways appropriate to the audience, topic, and occasion. When listening in *classrooms,* refine your skills and help others become better speakers with your *feedback* (direct, indirect, and delayed).

Oral Activities

1. As a check on listening abilities, participate in a class discussion on a controversial topic. Conduct the discussion with the rule that before anyone can speak, he or she first must summarize to the satisfaction of the previous speaker what that person said. As a result of this exercise, what conclusions can you draw about: (a) people's ability to summarize accurately and satisfactorily and (b) the manner in which good listening and feedback reduce the amount and intensity of disagreement?
2. List some ideas that trigger your prejudices. Choose one of them as the subject for a two- to four-minute speech. In that speech, concentrate on discussing why you hold this feeling and how analyzing it will affect your listening skills the next time you encounter the idea.
3. Keep a "Listening Log." For two or three days, record your oral communication interactions, noting (a) who you were listening to, (b) what your listening purposes were, and (c) how effectively you listened. After completing the log, look it over, focusing on your listening patterns. What sorts of changes should you make in your listening habits so as to improve them?

Reference Notes

1. See studies reviewed by Andrew Wolvin and Carolyn Coakley, *Listening* (Dubuque, IA: William C. Brown Co., 1982), Chapter 1.
2. Thomas Lewis and Ralph Nichols, *Speaking and Listening* (Dubuque, IA: William C. Brown Co., 1965), 6.

3. For a discussion, see Carl Weaver, *Human Listening* (Indianapolis, IN: Bobbs-Merrill Publishers, 1972), Chapter 1; and Larry L. Barker, *Listening Behavior* (Englewood Cliffs, NJ: Prentice-Hall, Inc., 1971), Chapter 3.

4. This discussion of internal and external perceptual fields is adapted from Wayne C. Minnick, *The Art of Persuasion* (Boston: Houghton Mifflin Co., 1957), 38–41.

5. The materials on purposes are drawn from Wolvin and Coakley, Chapters 4–8.

6. Psychologist Philip G. Zimbardo has likened attention to "a spotlight that illuminates certain portions of our surroundings. When we focus our attention on something and thus become conscious of it, we can begin to process it cognitively—converting sensory information into perceptions and memories or developing ideas through analysis, judgment, reasoning, and imagination. When the spotlight of attention shifts to something else, conscious processing of the earlier material ceases and processing of the new content begins." In *Psychology and Life*, 11th ed. (Glenview, IL: Scott, Foresman and Company, 1985), 191.

7. Neal Luker, "Our Defense Policy," a speech presented in a course in advanced public speaking at the University of Iowa.

8. From an address by Henry W. Grady, presented to the Literary Societies of the University of Virginia, June 25, 1889.

PLANNING and PREPARING the SPEECH

3

The first two chapters have provided a foundation for understanding the *process* of oral communication. Next we will turn our attention to the *practice* of speech. We start with planning. Planning ahead saves you time and keeps you from wandering aimlessly through the library or waiting for inspiration at your desk. We will examine speech planning and preparation in terms of seven steps. Finally, we will address two other preliminary considerations on many speakers' minds—speech fright and gaining self-confidence.

There is no magic formula for getting ready to talk publicly; the task can be irksome and frustrating. But, if you generally follow a series of steps—either in the order presented here or in another that works for you—you will be ahead of the game and in firmer control than if you do not. Those steps—selecting and narrowing the subject; determining the purposes; analyzing the audience and the occasion; gathering the material; making an outline; practicing the speech aloud; and delivering the speech—will all be reviewed in this chapter, although in varying degrees of completeness, for some will have complete chapters devoted to them. After reading this chapter, however, you will know enough to give your first classroom speeches and to make basic improvements in your other public talks.

SELECTING AND NARROWING THE SUBJECT

On many occasions, the subject of your speech will be determined—at least in part—by the group to whom you are talking. If you are speaking at a public hearing on a proposed rezoning of your neighborhood, you need not select a topic, for it is already determined. But, there are many speaking occasions in which you have to exercise some choice. You must do so in a speech classroom, of course. Of, if you are asked to deliver a lay sermon in church, you have to decide, for example, whether to talk about religious duty, liberation theology, or missionary efforts. If you are to speak to a Spanish Club, should you discuss employment opportunities for Spanish majors, Latin American tour packages, or the subtleties of Basque cooking?

When you are faced with the task of choosing a subject, follow these basic guidelines:

Select a subject about which you already know something and can find out more. Knowledge you already have can guide your efforts to find a suitable subject, to distinguish between good and bad ideas, to assess areas in which your knowledge is thin, to know where to locate additional and updated materials, and to tailor your talk to the specific audience you face. Also, of course, you will be a more confident—and probably more successful—speaker if you talk from personal knowledge rather than from second-hand information.

Select a subject that is interesting to you. Some speakers seek a topic to impress an audience, whether or not they are personally interested in it. That way of thinking can lead to disaster. If you are not interested in what you are discussing, you will find preparation dull, and, more important, your presentation will probably reflect your lack of motivation and enthusiasm.

Select a subject that will interest your audience. Some speakers are tempted to force a topic on an audience because "it's good for them." That method is unproductive. Remember that whatever the topic, it is the *speaker's* responsibility to make it interesting to an audience. A topic may be of interest to listeners for one or more of the following reasons:

1. It concerns their health, happiness, or security. For instance, you might talk to a senior citizens group about changes in Medicare regulations.

2. It offers a solution to a recognized problem. For example, you might suggest new ways your sorority can raise needed money.

3. It is surrounded by controversy or conflict of opinion.

Select a topic appropriate to the occasion. A demonstration speech on break-dancing might go over very well as an informative speech in your classroom, but it probably would be out of place at a senior citizens' center arts and crafts demonstration.

Once you have selected an interesting topic, your next task is to narrow it. That is, you must sort through all of the things you could say in order to find one, two, or three points you can establish, clarify, and support in the time you have available. Narrowing involves three primary considerations:

Narrow your subject so that you can discuss it adequately in the time you have. In a ten-minute speech, you cannot adequately cover "The Rise and Fall of Baseball as the Premier American Sport." Instead, you might describe three or four changes baseball has made in response to television coverage. Fit the breadth of your topic to the time available.

Narrow your subject so that it is neither above nor below the comprehension level of your audience. If, for example, you want to talk about laser technology to an audience of beginning students, you might choose to

Gathering information for your speech is an easier, more enjoyable task when you have narrowed your subject, determined your purpose, and analyzed your audience and the occasion.

describe only its most basic principles; to a group of physics majors, however, you would probably explain its latest applications in technical terms.

Narrow your subject to meet the specific expectations of your audience. An audience that comes to a meeting expecting to hear a talk on gun safety will probably be upset if you lecture instead on the need for stricter gun-control laws. The announced purpose of the meeting, the demands of the particular context, and the audience's traditions all affect their expectations of the speech.

Suppose, for example, you are to give an informative talk on gardening to members of a 4-H club. Within that general subject are countless narrower topics, including:

- the growth of personal or hobby gardening over the last decade (facts and figures on clubs, seed sales, the home canning industry, and so on);
- methods for preserving homegrown vegetables (canning vs. freezing vs. drying vs. cold storage);
- soil enrichment (varieties of natural and artificial fertilizers, the strengths and weaknesses of each);
- factors to consider when selecting vegetables to plant (plot size, family eating habits, amount of time available for tending, cost of supermarket vegetables of each type);
- available strains of any given vegetable (selection of seeds based on geography, climate, soil characteristics, regional pests/bacteria, uses to which vegetables will be put, germination and heartiness);
- literature on gardening (library books, television programs, governmental pamphlets, magazines, seed catalogs, fertilizer company brochures);
- varieties of gardening tools (inexpensive hand tools, medium-cost hand tools, expensive power machinery); and
- year-round gardening (window-box gardening, "grow" lights, cold frames, hot frames, greenhouses).

Given this list of subtopics, your procedures for narrowing might run something like this:

1. *Subjects I know something about:*
   methods for preserving homegrown food
   soil enrichment
   literature on gardening
   varieties of gardening tools
   year-round gardening

2. *Subjects interesting to me:*
   all except soil enrichment

3. *Subjects interesting to audience* (a 4-H club):
   methods for preserving homegrown food
   literature on gardening
   year-round gardening

4. *Subjects appropriate to occasion* (demonstration speech):
   all three are appropriate

5. *Topics I can talk about in the available time* (note narrowing):
   one or *two* methods of preserving homegrown food
   two or *three* kinds of gardening literature
   one kind of year-round gardening

6. *Topics I can fit to the audience comprehension level:*
   Because 4-H club members are experienced gardeners,
   —do not discuss home food preservation, as most of them already
      know a lot about this subtopic
   —do not discuss gardening literature, as few kids want to spend more
      time reading about gardening; in the past they have found it easier
      to learn from other gardeners than from books
   —they have shown interest before in the topic of year-round gardening
      (when Henry gave a speech on "grow" lights, they followed him
      easily and enthusiastically)

7. *Topics that will meet their expectations for a 4-H demonstration project:*
   year-round gardening, specifically, how to build an inexpensive homemade greenhouse

To summarize, selecting and narrowing a topic involves: (1) identifying topics about which you are knowledgeable and interested; (2) thinking about your audience's interests and abilities; (3) considering the demands of the occasion; and (4) narrowing the topic to a particular subtopic you can cover adequately (a) in the time available and (b) in accordance with audience and situational expectations. All of this may seem to be a complicated chore; yet, if you attack it systematically, you can often move easily through the rest of your speech preparation.

DETERMINING THE PURPOSES

Once you know what you want to talk about, the next questions you face deal with a series of "whys" already implicit in much that has been said: Why do *you* wish to discuss this subject? Why might an *audience* want to listen to you? Why is what you wish to discuss appropriate to the *occasion*? You should approach these "whys" in three ways: first, think about *general purposes* (the reasons people generally speak in public); next, consider the *specific purposes* (the concrete goals you wish to achieve in a particular speech); and then, focus your thoughts on the *central idea* or *claim* (the statement of the guiding thought you wish to communicate). In addition, you will probably want to put into words the working title of your speech. Selecting a provisional title early in the preparation process helps you keep your primary emphasis in focus and lets you announce it to others ahead of the actual presentation.

General Purposes

In most public speaking situations, you address listeners in order to inform, to entertain, to persuade, or to move them to action:

General Purpose	*Audience Response Sought*
To inform	Clear understanding
To entertain	Enjoyment and comprehension
To persuade or actuate	Acceptance of ideas or recommended behaviors

Usually you talk to others publicly because you possess some knowledge of potential relevance and benefit to them, or because you hope to alter their fundamental beliefs about the world, their attitudes toward life, or the

The General Purposes of Speech

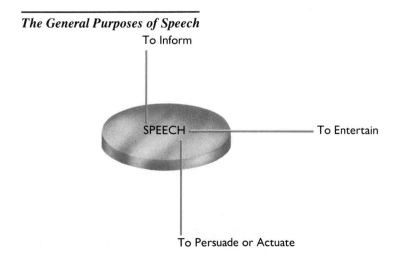

actions they have been or ought to be taking. Hence, to inform and to persuade or actuate are the major general purposes of the most speeches.

Sometimes, however, either because of the occasion or because of your personal talents, you may seek to entertain an audience as well as give them some ideas to think about. Those ideas are often similar to the subject matters of informative and persuasive talks; so, the speech to entertain, in many ways, is a species of the other two general kinds of speeches. Yet, because the techniques and general strategies you use in speeches to entertain differ substantially from those used in speeches to inform and to persuade or actuate, we will discuss the entertainment purpose separately. Most of this book will be devoted to informative and persuasive speaking. For now, we will briefly examine each of these three general purposes.

To Inform

When your overall object is to help listeners understand an idea, concept, or process or when you seek to widen their range of knowledge, the general purpose of your speech will be to inform. Such is the goal of scientists who report their research results to colleagues, of public figures who address community groups on subjects on which they are expert, of college lecturers and work supervisors.

To create understanding, you must change the level or quality of information possessed by your listeners. By providing examples, statistics, illustrations, and other materials offering data and ideas, you seek to expand or alter their stock of knowledge. Not only must an informative speech provide raw data, but its message and supporting materials must be structured and integrated in such a way that listeners perceive the whole. For example, an informative speech on how to build a stereo set must include the necessary instructions in an orderly sequence of steps. Understanding in this instance depends not only on learning *what* to do, but also on knowing *when* to do it and *why*. Some of your listeners may already be familiar with the information you are presenting but have not put the pieces together coherently. Your job as an informative speaker is to impart both knowledge and overall understanding.

In summary, when your purpose is to clarify a concept or process for your listeners, when you endeavor to explain terms or relationships, and when you strive in other ways to broaden your listeners' knowledge, your objective is to inform. With an informative speech, the response you seek is primarily conceptual or cognitive—an adjustment of an audience's *body of knowledge*. Several different types of speeches are considered to be informative: reports from committees or task forces, lectures, and demonstrations. All have information sharing as their primary thrust.

To Entertain

To entertain or amuse is often the purpose of an after-dinner speech, but talks of other kinds also may aim at producing enjoyment. A travel lecture, while presenting a good deal of information, can also entertain an audience with tales of adventure and misadventure. Club meetings, class reunions, and similar gatherings of friends and associates also provide settings for speeches to entertain. In these situations, speakers often depend primarily on humor in preparing their talks.

A speech to entertain, however, is *not* simply a comic monologue. Rather, the humor characteristic of speeches to entertain is highly purposive. Think of some of the great American humorists: Mark Twain used humor to describe life in the Midwest to Eastern audiences; Will Rogers' radio talks and commentaries on political realities during the Depression helped create a sense of American unity and common effort; Dick Cavett, in a speech reprinted elsewhere in this book, talks humorously with college students about the importance of preserving the English language.

In short, a speech to entertain is both humorous and serious. Evening entertainments, parodies, satires, and most other forms of public speaking humor are species of speeches to entertain. Because the skills they require are subtle and often difficult to master, we will discuss them late in this book, after you have acquired basic speechmaking competencies.

To Persuade or Actuate

A speaker whose purpose is to persuade or actuate seeks to influence listeners' minds or actions. While it may be argued that all speeches are persuasive to some degree,[1] there are many situations in which the speaker's primary purpose is outright persuasion. Promoters and public relations experts try to make you believe in the superiority of certain products, persons, or institutions; lawyers seek to persuade juries; social action group leaders exhort tenants to believe in landlord collusion; politicians debate campaign issues and strive to influence voters' thinking.

As a persuasive speaker, you usually seek to influence the beliefs and attitudes of your listeners. Sometimes, however, you will want to go a step further and try to move them to action. You may want them to contribute money, sign a petition, or participate in a demonstration. The distinguishing feature of an actuative speech is that instead of stopping with an appeal to their beliefs or attitudes, you ask your listeners to alter their behavior in a specified way.

Because the speech to persuade or actuate is usually designed to influence or alter listeners' beliefs and actions, you should fill it with well-ordered arguments supported by facts, figures, and examples. Additionally, you will have to go beyond "the facts," for persuasion is a psychological as well as a logical process. You will need to make strong motivational appeals to tap into the needs and desires of listeners. The person who seeks to change minds and move others to action, therefore, must be sensitive to both the rational and nonrational aspects of audience psychology—topics we will develop at some length shortly.

To inform, to entertain, and to persuade or actuate are the general purposes a speech may have. General purposes comprise the basic types of speeches and, as such, are important as overall orientations to your thinking about public talks. But just as subjects have to be narrowed, so do purposes.

Specific Purposes

A second important way to think about speech purposes is to consider them specifically—that is, to think about the challenges related to a particular topic explored in front of an actual audience on a real occasion by you, a human being. *Specific purposes are actual goals you want to achieve.* Although they are concrete, specific purposes can be extremely wide ranging. You may verbalize some of them; for example, you may tell an audience what you want them to understand or do as a consequence of your speech.

Some specific purposes are private, known only by you. For example, you probably hope to make a good impression on an audience, although you are not likely to say that aloud. Usually, a speech has short-term specific purposes and, occasionally, long-term specific purposes. If you are speaking to members of a local food cooperative on the virtues of baking their own

---

The Private and Public Purposes of Speech

PRIVATE
PURPOSE OF SPEECH
I hope I can make them understand how this system really works, because I'd like to lead the party myself.

PUBLIC
PURPOSE OF SPEECH
Today I would like to explain how the party caucus system works . . . .

ETHICS AND PUBLIC SPEAKING

"That man will go far; he believes all he says."

—Mirabeau speaking of Robespierre

Not only to believe all you say, but to believe as well in others and what they say, is the essence of ethics in public speaking situations. To do so is an act of supreme faith, and a compliment to those in whom you believe. Unscrupulous sales clerks, overzealous politicians, and friends who made promises but failed to keep them all have made most of us doubting Thomases. Speakers have great difficulty getting audience members to believe them.

The standards by which public speakers are judged come from four elements in the communication process:

1. *Self.* Each of us has, for better or worse, a personal ethic that allows us to do some things but not others. Where you draw the line determines how far you will go in using various kinds of emotional appeals and in letting yourself utter untruths.

2. *Situation.* Ethical standards also tend to vary, at least somewhat, from situation to situation. Parents tell "little white lies" about things children are too young to understand. In wartime, national leaders tend to downplay news of defeat and exaggerate victory. But we expect our close friends, our pastors, and our therapists to tell the truth. So, some ethical matters are situation bound. The question is, how far do and should those ethical standards vary across situations?

3. *Audience.* Some audiences are more gullible than others. What does this mean to you as a public speaker? Should you take advantage of less critical listeners, hoping to slide weak, unsupported items past them? If most of your audience is knowledgeable, should you pass over common information and value claims, even though others may not know that information or understand those values? Do you appeal to the majority? or to the lowest common denominator?

4. *Society.* Sometimes, too, you must think about societal norms in general. When someone says, "That's not the way we do things around here," he or she usually is signalling a social norm. Social expectations can be as important as the standards one finds in particular audiences.

What are we to make of all this? At least three overarching pieces of advice are dictated by these four centers for ethical standards in public speaking:

Respect the rights of others. Public speaking is, as we have been saying throughout this book, an act that intimately involves a series of others. They are parts of the transaction, and hence you must always take them into account—not trampling them and their abilities, treating them the way you want to be treated as part of an audience.

Test the ethical dimensions of your proposals. Can you support factually and valuatively your various claims? Are the motivational appeals you are using fair to your subject matter, your audience's predispositions, and your own sense of right? Does your proposal have ramifications that ought to be examined publicly before you can expect it to be accepted?

Subordinate techniques to ideas. Do not attempt to cover up bad logic or weak proposals with verbal diarrhea or slick delivery. Such habits as fast talking and smooth talking turn off more people than they capture. Competence is essential, of course, but if auditors decide you are using verbal and nonverbal techniques to cover up substantive shortcomings, you are dead ethically—and hence ineffective.

TO READ: For a general discussion of persuasion and ethics, see Herbert W. Simons, *Persuasion: Understanding, Practice, and Analysis,* 2nd ed. (New York: Random House, 1986), Chapter 5, "Persuasion and Image Management." To assess broader questions, see Henry W. Johnstone, Jr., "Communication: Technology and Ethics," in *Communication Philosophy and the Technological Age,* Michael J. Hyde, ed., (University, AL: University of Alabama Press, 1982), 38–53. And, to put questions of ethics in their legal frames, see Franklyn S. Haiman, *Speech and Law in a Free Society* (Chicago: University of Chicago Press, 1981).

bread, your short-term purpose might be to get people to go home that night and try out your recipe, while your long-term goal could be to have them change their food-buying and food-consuming habits.

Theoretically, you have any number of private and public, short-term and long-term specific purposes whenever you speak. Practically, however, you will want to reduce that mass of goals to a dominant one. We thus may define *the* specific purpose as the precise response that the speaker desires from the audience. Formulated into a clear, concise statement, the specific purpose identifies exactly what you want the audience to understand, enjoy, feel, believe, or do.

Suppose, for example, that you are asked to explain to the Campus Democrats how the party's caucus works, in preparation for their actual participation in the county caucuses during an election year. You might have several purposes: to demonstrate that caucusing allows for full grassroots participation in the electoral process, to review step-by-step the actual procedures for forming "candidate preference groups," to explain what happens when a candidate preference group is not viable according to party rules, and even to show that you are a knowledgeable person and hence a potential leader. The first of these specific purposes is a long-range goal, the next two are short-term goals designed to prepare listeners for actual participation in the county caucuses, and the fourth is a private purpose. All of these specific goals can be summarized, however, in a statement of *the* specific purpose: "to show members of the Campus Democrats how they can effectively participate in the county presidential caucuses in an election year."

Central Ideas or Claims

Once you have settled on the specific purpose, you are ready to translate that goal into concrete subject matter. You are ready to cast into words a central idea or claim (sometimes termed a *thesis statement*) that will form the controlling thought of your speech. A *central idea* is a statement that captures the essence of the information or concept you are attempting to communicate to an audience. A *claim* is a statement that phrases the belief, attitude, or action you wish an audience to adopt. Central ideas are characteristic of informative speeches (and some speeches to entertain), while claims form the core of persuasive, actuative, and some entertaining speeches.

The precise phrasing of central ideas and claims is very important because your wording captures the essence of your subject matter and purpose and guides audience expectations. Assume, for example, that you have decided to give an informative speech on building an inexpensive homemade greenhouse. You might decide to phrase your central idea for that speech in one of three ways:

Wording #1: "With only a minimum of carpentry skills, even a teenager can build a homemade greenhouse."

Wording #2: "With some creative searching around the home and neighborhood, anyone can build a homemade greenhouse for less than $150."

Wording #3: "Building an inexpensive homemade greenhouse will allow you to start garden plants early and grow some crops year-round."

Note that in the first version the stress is on audience members' abilities to complete the technical aspects of the task. Presumably, the speech would offer a step-by-step description of the construction process—preparing the bed, pouring cement for the foundation, erecting the superstructure, and covering that structure with transparent materials. The second version suggests quite a different speech, one focused on securing the materials. It might discuss places to find scrapped lumber, ways to get old storm windows to use as the greenhouse's glassed surface, areas in the neighborhood where one can get free sand for the cement. In contrast, the third version would discuss the actual construction of the greenhouse only superficially (perhaps with a handout on the construction process), concentrating instead on interior design—which shelves to reserve for seedlings; which shelves to prepare for year-round crops such as tomatoes, herbs, peppers, miniature fruit trees; and the like.

Phrasing a claim or thesis statement is an even more crucial preparatory act than phrasing a central idea, because the words you select can control several aspects of your relationship with your audience. Note the following examples:

Varying the audience's perception of the speaker's intensity:
1. "Do not eat cured pork because *it is unhealthy.*"
2. "Do not eat cured pork because *it is carcinogenic.*"
3. "Do not eat cured pork because *it will kill you.*"

As you move from version one to version three, you are phrasing your feelings in progressively more intense language; each successive version expresses your attitude more harshly.

Varying the reasons for taking some course of action:
1. "Make use of our school's Division of Career Planning because it can help you *plan your curriculum.*"
2. "Make use of our school's Division of Career Planning because it will help you *select your major.*"
3. "Make use of our school's Division of Career Planning because it will teach you how *to prepare résumés and to interview for jobs.*"
4. "Make use of our school's Division of Career Planning because it will put you *in touch with employers.*"

These four examples vary the rationales behind the actions you wish listeners to take. Presumably, one can take some course of action for any number of reasons; your claim should be phrased in a way that captures what you think will be the most compelling reasons for this *particular audience.*

Varying the evaluative criteria for judging something:
1. "The city's new landfill is an *eyesore.*" (esthetic judgment)
2. "The city's new landfill is a *health hazard.*" (personal-safety judgment)
3. "The city's new landfill is a *political payoff to the rich companies that supported the council members' campaigns.*" (political judgment)

Each of these claims condemns a civic project, but in a different way. The first version judges the landfill negatively on esthetic grounds, the second on safety grounds, and the third on political grounds. Were you to advocate the first version, you would need to demonstrate that (a) esthetic qualities are important criteria for judging landfills and (b) the landfill indeed will be visible to a significant number of community members. For the second version, you would need to argue successfully that health hazards are a matter of public concern, then that this particular landfill allows hazardous materials to be deposited. And, in defending the third version you would need to document (a) the campaign contributions and (b) the fact that major users or beneficiaries of the depository are the companies that gave the most money to the successful candidates. In each case, then, the selection of a particular evaluative criterion controls the main features of the speech.

Consider also these examples that put together, overall, what we have been saying about general purposes, specific purposes, and central ideas or claims:

Subject: cardiopulmonary resuscitation (CPR)
General purpose: to inform
Specific purposes:
- to explain the three life-saving steps of CPR
- to interest the auditors in signing up for a CPR course
- to impress on listeners their social responsibilities relevant to CPR
Central idea: "Cardiopulmonary resuscitation—CPR—is a three-step, life-saving technique for use in emergencies that anyone can learn."

Subject: accident insurance for students
General purpose: to actuate
Specific purposes:
- to get members of the student council to approve the group insurance policy offered by the ABC Insurance Company
- to provide inexpensive accident insurance for students currently without such protection
- to demonstrate that the ABC Insurance Company is the best one available for the money
- to overcome opposition from student council members and to remind the council of its obligations to its constituency
Claim: "The student council should approve the purchase of the group accident policy offered by the ABC Insurance Company."

Carefully explore your general and specific purposes before you begin to construct a public message. A sensitivity to general purposes will guide your thinking about speech materials and their structure. A realization of your specific purposes will allow you to understand your own hopes and fears, the range of effects you can expect to have on your audience, and the measures by which you can gauge the effects.

ANALYZING THE AUDIENCE AND THE OCCASION

Throughout this book, we have emphasized the notion that communication is a two-way process. If you accept that concept, then it is incumbent on you to act on it, that is, to take listeners consciously and systematically into account when preparing speeches. Often speakers forget to do that, becoming engrossed in their own interests and so impressed by ideas that seem important to them that they forget about listeners' interests and ideas.[2] It is a fairly safe assertion that more speeches fail for this reason than for any other.

The most important lesson you as a speaker can learn, therefore, is to see things from the standpoint of your listeners, to employ what researchers have called a *receiver orientation*.[3] You must regularly ask yourself, "How would I feel about this if I were in their place?" or "How can I adapt this material to their interests and habits, which are so different from mine?" To answer these questions requires a thorough analysis of audience members. You must find out which aspects of their *psychological and sociological background* will help you convince them to think or do as you want them to and which aspects will hinder you in those efforts.

Thus, audience analysis is a matter of finding out as much as you can about the people who compose the listening group—their age, gender, social-economic-political status, origins, backgrounds, prejudices, and fears. You also must try to find out how much they know about your subject, what they believe in and value, and what their attitudes are toward you and your subject. In your public speaking classroom, all this is easy enough to do— simply ask questions of your classmates. In other circumstances, you might have to become more creative and work harder. For that reason, the next chapter will be devoted to ways in which you can analyze your audience, *the* crucial step in speech preparation.

Almost equally important is the need to analyze the occasion on which you are speaking, for "audience" and "occasion" are usually inseparable for two reasons:

1. The occasion brings audience members together as part of a unique group and, hence, determines their *expectations*. The frame of mind you bring to a funeral is quite different from your thoughts on entering the campus auditorium to hear a comic monologue. Audience expectations of what will be discussed and how it will be presented differ markedly from one occasion to another.

2. In some occasions, the *communication rules*, as we discussed them earlier, are clear. If, for example, parliamentary procedure is being used at a business meeting, those rules will determine who can talk for how long and how often about what. The rules of parliamentary procedure are recorded in such books as *Robert's Rules of Order.* Other communication rules, however, are not recorded. No one tells the president-elect that the inaugural address must contain a greeting, a call for unity, a discussion of domestic policy, a discussion of foreign policy, and a final appeal to the deity. Yet all presidential inaugurals do contain those sections if only because presidents-elect read over the previous inaugural speeches before writing their own. Such traditions can be forged into unwritten communication rules, attached to particular occasions, and developed into constraints on speakers every bit as powerful as the written rules of parliamentary procedure.

How, then, can you analyze speech occasions as well as analyze your audience? The key variables you should think about include the nature of the occasion, the prevailing rules, and the physical conditions.

What Are the Nature and Purpose of the Occasion?

Is yours a voluntary or a captive audience? A voluntary audience attends a speechmaking event primarily because of interest in the speaker or subject. A captive audience is required to attend, perhaps at the explicit instruction of the boss or under threat of a failing grade in a course. In general, the more captive your audience, the less initial interest they will show, and the greater will be their resistance to accepting your information or point of view.

Are people interested in learning more about your subject—in taking some positive action concerning it—or have they perhaps come to heckle or embarrass you? Are your subject and purpose in line with the reason for the meeting, or are you merely seizing the occasion to present some ideas you think important? Are you one in a series of speakers whom the audience has heard over a period of weeks or months? If so, how does your speech subject relate to those previously presented? These are important questions to answer when you are analyzing the nature and purpose of the occasion. In other words, the nature and purpose of the occasion—as well as the interest level you can sense among those attending it—often dictate a series of general decisions you will make in your approach to the speech transaction.

What Are the Prevailing Rules or Customs?

Will there be a regular order of business or a fixed program into which your speech must fit? Is it the custom of the group to ask questions of the speaker after the address? Do the listeners expect a formal or informal speaking manner? Will you, as the speaker, be expected to extend complimentary remarks or to express respect for some tradition or concept? Knowing the answers to these questions will help you avoid feeling out of place and will prevent you from arousing antagonism with an inappropriate word or action.

What Are the Physical Conditions?

Will your speech be given out-of-doors or in an auditorium? Is the weather likely to be hot or cold? Will the audience be sitting or standing? If sitting, will the members be crowded together or scattered about? In how large a room will the speech be presented? Will an electronic public address system be used? Will facilities be provided for the audiovisual reinforcements you will use, or must you bring your own? Will you be seen and heard easily? Are there likely to be disturbances in the form of noise or interruptions from the outside? These and similar environmental factors affect the temper of the audience, their span of attention, and the style of speaking you will have to use as you make adjustments to the speech environment.

GATHERING THE SPEECH MATERIAL

Once you have carefully considered the subject and purpose of your speech and analyzed the audience and occasion, you will be ready to begin gathering material. Ordinarily you will start by drawing together what you already know about the subject and deciding roughly what ideas you

The Essential Steps in Planning, Preparing, and Presenting a Speech

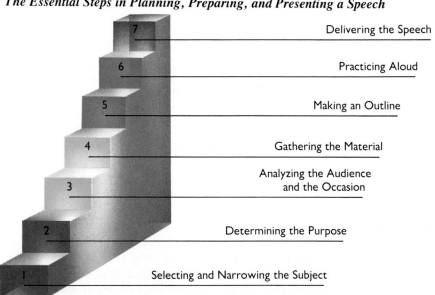

7 — Delivering the Speech

6 — Practicing Aloud

5 — Making an Outline

4 — Gathering the Material

3 — Analyzing the Audience and the Occasion

2 — Determining the Purpose

1 — Selecting and Narrowing the Subject

want to include. Nearly always, however, you will find that what you already know is not enough. You will need to gather additional information—facts, illustrations, stories, and examples—with which you can develop your speech. You can acquire some of this information through interviews and conversations with people who know something you do not know about the subject. You can gather other materials from newspapers, magazines, books, government documents, or radio and television programs. In particular, you should consult such sources as the "News of the Week in Review" section of *The New York Times, U.S. News and World Report, Wall Street Journal, Harper's,* and *The Observer* if you plan to deal with a current question of public interest. Many magazines of general interest are indexed in the *Readers' Guide to Periodical Literature;* numerous encyclopedias, yearbooks, government reports, almanacs, and other reference materials can be found in your college library. This important topic will be covered in detail in Chapter 5.

MAKING AN OUTLINE

Early in your preparation you may want to make a rough sketch of the points you wish to include in your speech. A complete outline, however, cannot be drawn up until you have gathered all of the necessary material. When this material is at hand, set down in final order the principal points you expect to present, together with the subordinate ideas that will be necessary to explain or prove these points.

In Chapter 6, you will find a number of specific patterns by which the ideas in a speech may be arranged. There, too, you will find the form that a complete outline should take. For the present, remember two simple but important rules: (1) arrange your ideas in a clear and systematic order and (2) preserve the unity of your speech by making sure that each point is directly related to your specific purpose.

PRACTICING ALOUD

With your outline completed, you are ready for the final step in preparation—practicing your speech for oral presentation. You probably will find that the best method is to talk through the outline aloud, following the planned sequence of ideas. Do this until you have learned this sequence thoroughly and can express each idea clearly and fluently. Then, putting the outline aside, think through the speech silently, point by point, to make certain that the ideas are fixed in your mind. Next, go through the speech aloud, but this time do not look at the outline at all. On your first oral trial, you may inadvertently omit some points and interchange others, but do not let this worry you. Practice until all of the ideas are expressed in their proper order and the words flow easily. The more surely you command your material, the more poised and confident you will be before the audience.

When you can go through the speech several times without forgetting any point or without hesitating unduly in putting your thoughts into words, your preparation is done. As you practice speaking from your outline, however, preserve a mental image of your listeners and project your speech as though you were actually talking to them. The good speaker talks *with* people, not *at* them.

DELIVERING THE SPEECH

For most beginners, actually delivering a speech is the hardest part of the process. Many feel anxious and nervous about standing before an audience. You may be saying to yourself, "I'm too nervous to stand up there"; "What will I do if I forget part of my speech?"; "My hands are trembling—how can I hold notes when I can't even keep my hands still?" Recognizing that these are common reactions is half the battle. Developing and communicating *confidence* is the other half.

Developing Confidence

The anxiety about speaking in public that you may feel just before getting up in front of an audience is part of of the general apprehension that many people have about any communication encounter. You do not wish to fail; at times, this fear of failure may overcome the desire to speak. If you have ever been reluctant to raise your hand in class and answer a question, you understand how apprehension can affect your behavior. We can distinguish two broad classes of this communication apprehension.[4] *State apprehension* refers to the anxiety you feel in particular settings or situations. You may find it easy to talk with friends but feel very uncomfortable when being interviewed for a job. You might not mind speaking within a small group in class, but presenting your ideas in a formal setting sends you into a near panic. The phenomenon known as "stage fright" is a common form of state apprehension. In its extreme form, stage fright is experienced physiologically as clammy hands; nervous knees; a dry mouth; and a trembling, cracking voice. Psychologically, stage fright is experienced as mental blocks— forgetting what you were going to say. The knowledge that you are going to be evaluated by others in a formal setting, whether in a classroom or in a town meeting, can cause some anxious moments.

While some aspects of nervousness are characteristic of the situation, others are a part of your own personality. This class of apprehension, called *trait apprehension,* refers to your level of anxiety as you face any communication situation. A high level of anxiety may lead people to withdraw from situations in which interpersonal or public communication with others is required. By attacking your "trait" fears as they manifest in speaking before others, you will be in a better position to reduce your overall level of anxiety. Although there is no foolproof program for developing self-confidence, there are some ways to achieve the confidence necessary to complete the speaking task.

1. *Realize that tension and nervousness are normal and even, in part, beneficial to speakers.* Fear is a normal part of living; learn how to control it and make it work for you. Remember that the tension you feel can provide you with energy and alertness. As adrenalin pours into your bloodstream, you experience a physical charge, increasing bodily movement, and psychological acuity. A baseball pitcher who is not "pumped up" before a big game may find that his fastball has no zip. A speaker who is not similarly charged will undoubtedly come across as dull and lifeless.

2. *Take comfort in the fact that tension is physiologically reduced by the act of speaking.* As you talk and discover that your audience accepts you and some of the things you are saying, your nervousness will tend to dissipate. Physiologically, your body is using up the excess adrenalin it generated; psychologically, your ego is getting positive reinforcement. Shortly after you have begun, you realize that your prior preparation is working in your favor and that you have the situation under control. Thus, the very act of talking aloud reduces fear.

3. *Talk about topics that interest you.* Speech anxiety arises in part because of self-centeredness; sometimes you are more concerned with your personal appearance and performance than with your topic. One means of reducing that anxiety is to select topics that are of deep interest to you, topics that will take your mind off of yourself. This makes the situation topic-centered rather than self-centered.

4. *Talk about subjects with which you are familiar.* Confidence born of knowledge increases your perceived credibility and helps control your nervousness. Have you ever wondered why you could talk at length with friends about your favorite hobby, sport, or political interests without feeling anxious, only to find yourself in a nervous state when standing in front of an audience to talk about something you just read in *Newsweek?* Knowing something about the subject may be part of the answer. Subject mastery is closely related to self-mastery.

5. *Analyze both the situation and the audience.* The more you know about the audience and about what is expected of you in a particular situation, the less there is to fear. In the speech classroom, students are usually less nervous during their second speech than during their first. They are more comfortable with the audience and are more aware of the demands of the situation. The same is true in other settings as well; careful analysis of the audience and their expectations goes a long way toward reducing a natural fear of the unknown.

6. *Speak in public as often as you can.* Sheer repetition of the public speaking experience will not eliminate your fears, but it will make them more controllable. As we have just seen, speaking a number of times in front of the same group can help reduce anxiety. Repeated experiences with different audiences and situations also will help increase your self-assurance and poise, which, in turn, will lessen your apprehension. As a student, force yourself to speak up in class discussions, join in discussions with friends and others, and contribute in meetings of organizations to which you belong. Find time to talk with people of all ages. Attend public meetings on occasion and make a few comments.

In summary, there are no shortcuts to developing self-confidence about speaking in public. For most of us, gaining self-confidence is partly a matter of psyching ourselves up, and partly a matter of experience. The sick feeling in the pit of your stomach probably will always be there, at least momentarily, but it need not paralyze you. As you gain experience with each of the essential steps—from selecting a subject to practicing the speech—your self-confidence as a speaker will grow. Certainly you will make mistakes of judgment, but each one is an opportunity to learn something about the complex process of communicating your ideas to others. One day your attention and energy will focus on your subject and your audience, and your fears will recede. You will find that you possess the skill required to control your anxiety and to succeed in presenting your ideas.

Communicating Confidence

If you are now ready to present your first speech, you may be asking, "How shall I deliver my message? Developing self-confidence is one thing, but how can I convey that self-confidence to an audience?" The following guidelines should help you communicate self-confidence.

1. *Be yourself.* Act as you would if you were having an animated conversation with a friend. Avoid an excessively rigid, oratorical, or aggressive posture. At the same time, do not become so comfortable in front of the group that you lean on the wall behind you or sprawl all over the lectern. When you speak, you want your listeners' minds to be focused on your ideas, not on the way you are presenting them.

2. *Look at your listeners.* Watch your listeners' faces for clues to their reactions. Without this essential information, you cannot gauge the ongoing effectiveness of your speech or make minor adjustments as you go along. People tend to mistrust anyone who does not look them in the eye. They also may get the impression that you do not care about them, that you are not interested in their reactions to your message.

3. *Communicate with your body as well as with your voice.* Realize that as a speaker you are being seen as well as heard. Bodily movements and changes in facial expression can help clarify and reinforce your ideas. Keep your hands at your sides so that when you feel an impulse to gesture, you can do so easily. If there is no lectern, do not be afraid to let your notes show. If you are working from an outline, use a hard backing to hold the papers firm (this will make your nervousness less visible). If you have notecards, hold them up so that you can see them clearly. Do not hide them so that referring to them becomes obvious, time consuming, and difficult. Avoid the impulse to curl papers or fold cards, only to uncrumple them to look at your notes. Let other movements of your body respond as your feelings and message dictate. Do not force your actions but do not hold them back when they seem natural and appropriate. In maintaining your self-confidence, remember that the tremor in your voice or your hand is not nearly as noticeable to your audience as it is to you. If you are being yourself, appropriate bodily responses will flow from the act of communicating.

. . . Sample Speech . . . .

The following speech by Deanna Sellnow, a student at North Dakota State University, focuses audience attention on the shortcomings in the methods of determining a person's credit rating. Notice the following features of her speech preparation:

1. *Deanna selected a topic—credit ratings—of importance to students about to enter the "real world" and just beginning to establish a credit rating.*
2. *She narrowed her concerns to two related subtopics (unprofessional information gathering and faulty formats), which she could handle adequately in the time she had.*
3. *Her persuasive purpose was clear.*
4. *The topic was appropriate to her audience and the occasion (a speech contest, where speeches are expected to be persuasive).*

5. The material came from varied and reliable sources.
6. The problem-solution format of her outline was clear.

The claim governing this speech is "The current system of reporting credit ratings does not adequately protect consumers."

HAVE YOU CHECKED LATELY?[5]
Deanna Sellnow

John Pontier, of Boise, Idaho, was turned down for insurance because a reporting agency informed the company that he and his wife were addicted to narcotics, and his Taco Bell franchise had been closed down by the health board when dog food had been found mixed in with the tacos. There was only one small problem. The information was made up. His wife was a practicing Mormon who didn't touch a drink, much less drugs, and the restaurant had never been cited for a health violation.   /1

An isolated case? A little dramatic, maybe, but I'm not so sure it was an isolated case. Few would argue with the contention of lenders that a financial background check is a price consumers must pay for the convenience of credit. But what are they really getting? The issue I would like to explore today is that of the accuracy of credit reporting. In exploring this topic, I think we need to try to identify some of the shortcomings involved in the current practices of credit reporting, identify why these shortcomings come about, and, finally, identify some measures we might take to improve the credit reporting system.   /2

Credit bureaus, private firms that exist by selling credit information, according to a July, 1982, issue of *U.S. News and World Report,* compile more than 25 million reports each year on consumers' dealings. Now stored in their computers are data on more than half the U.S. population, information that may be exchanged among lenders at the push of a button. Oil companies, insurance agencies, department stores, travel and entertainment card companies, as well as banks and finance companies, base their decisions for granting credit on credit reports. The possibility of having a credit request denied awaits each and every one of us; and, thus, it seems that a more crucial question becomes: why do negative credit reports come about? Some are legitimate—but how many? You begin to wonder when you listen to some of the people in the industry.   /3

According to a July, 1982, issue of *U.S. News and World Report,* a former credit bureau employee told the Senate Banking Committee that he had completely invented 25% of his reports, and that he was far from alone in doing so. One investigator even gave a clean bill of health to an applicant who turned out to be dead! Angele Khachadour, chief counsel to the State Insurance Commissioner of California, reported on one of the few studies done on credit reviews. The conclusion of this late 1960s study suggested that "nine out of every ten policy rejections were based on moral grounds, often bearing only tenuous connections to actuality." Despite the 1975 California legislative action to curtail this problem, Khachadour reports in a 1979 issue of *Saturday Review* that it is still common practice. So as you listen to the people in the industry, you really begin to wonder what's going on in the world of credit reporting. /4

Why do these shortcomings come about? We really can't blame the government for this one. The importance of this issue was recognized by Congress in 1974 when they passed the Equal Credit Opportunity Act prohibiting discriminating in the granting of credit on the basis of sex and marital status. In 1976, it was amended to include race, color, religion, national origin, and age as characteristics. And, in 1977, the Federal Trade Commission decided to devote a significant percentage of its resources to the handling of credit abuse problems. /5

Why, then, do these shortcomings come about? In part, because of the creativity and unprofessionalism of the investigators, and in part, because of the format the industry uses for credit reporting. I've already mentioned the investigator who testified to the fact that he had invented 25% of the information. That's certainly creative. How about the unprofessional behavior? Why does that occur? /6

Pressures of completing a quota of reports is one significant factor. Theodore P. VonBrand, presiding official of the Federal Trade Commission, stated, in his 16,000-page review of the system, that:

> "field representatives staggering beneath an impossible burden of reports—fifteen to twenty per day—often compensate by contacting unqualified sources, fake sources, hurry through interviews, and frequently fail to ask a full range of questions."

A limited time factor also contributes to his unprofessionalism. According to a 1979 issue of *Saturday Review*, the credit investigator is expected to speak to the applicant and two other people who know him, usually neighbors or business associates, when making a report. He is expected to ask each individual up to 30 questions in 20 minutes. A final major problem for these investigators is the unavailability of informants. According to James Traub, in a 1979 issue of *Saturday Review*, the investigators usually work during the day, so it is sometimes difficult to locate people. Also, asking for so much detailed and impressionistic information in such a short time span, the investigation leaves itself open to inaccuracy. Be it pressures, limited time, or unavailable informants, unprofessional behavior does occur. /7

And how about the other part of it—the format used in credit reporting—how does that account for shortcomings? /8

The first format in use today, and the most widely used, is the judgmental method. According to a 1982 issue of the *Journal of Marketing,* its framework consists of the three c's of credit: character, capacity, and capital. The investigator asks questions about the applicant's use of alcohol or narcotics—how much, how often, what kind, when, where—whom he is living with if not his wife, whether there is anything adverse about his reputation, life-style, and home environment, and if there are any reports of domestic troubles or dubious business practices. A major inadequacy of this approach is the source of the information. California's Angele Khachadour points out that neighbors simply don't know each other as well as they used to. /9

A second and more modern approach to credit reporting is the credit scoring system. This system proposes to eliminate such problems as credit officer error and irrelevant sources of information. According to Noel Capon, associate professor of Business at Columbia University, in the Spring, 1982, issue of the *Journal of Marketing,* the critical distinction between the credit scoring system and the judgmental method is that the credit scoring system is concerned solely with statistical predictability. Results from an interview with William Fair, chairman of Fair, Isaac, and Company, leading developer of credit scoring systems, indicate that any individual characteristic that can be scored, then, has potential for inclusion in the credit scoring system. Given the concern for creditworthiness, it is difficult to believe that some of the criteria revealed in the interview, such as hair color, zip code, and left- or right-handedness, are accepted components for prediction. According to a 1982 issue of *Credit Card Retailing,* this sole use of statistical prediction may also violate the constitutional guarantees of equal protection and due process clauses of the Fifth and Fourteenth Amendments. /10

While there is probably no way to guarantee that the investigators will do the job in the manner which they should, we can do something to insure that those seeking credit get a fair hearing. /11

We don't need government action this time. We need individual initiative. It is up to us, the consumers, to make use of the rights granted to us under the Equal Credit Opportunity Act and its amendments. If you haven't done so lately, check your credit records for errors and omissions. Tracking down the bureau that has your file—and believe me, if you have ever applied for credit you have a file—is relatively simple. The agencies are usually listed in the Yellow Pages, or you can contact them through your local Better Business Bureau. According to a March, 1979, issue of *Business Week,* most bureaus charge between three and eight dollars per interview. If you have any complaint, the bureau must either investigate it, or you have the right to submit a "Statement of Dispute" which becomes a permanent part of your file. Should the bureau refuse to resolve the dispute, you could also do as John Pontier did, and sue.   /12

It is best to check your file for accuracy before you even apply for credit. Even if you have had some credit in the past and/or if you are applying for the first time and find yourself turned down for a loan, mortgage, or some other type of credit, the lender must furnish the name and address of the bureau which supplied the information. And, in that case, you are entitled to a free copy of your file.   /13

Within the industry, we need to urge bureaus to rely less on third-party reports, or solely on statistics. The goal of unbiased credit judgments, which the credit scoring system employs, should be adapted to incorporate the relevant credit history which the judgmental method attempts to reveal. /14

When all is said and done, the major solution rests on our shoulders. We have the right to see our files and verify their validity. There is no reason for us to wait until, like John Pontier, of Boise, Idaho, we are denied the credit we deserve. We can, and should, check our files before we fall victim to inaccurate, irrelevant, and unmerited credit reports.   /15

• •

CHAPTER SUMMARY

Planning and preparing your speeches can involve seven steps: (1) *selecting and narrowing the subject,* making it appropriate to you, your audience, the occasion, and time limits; (2) *determining the general and specific purposes,* wording them in strategically sound ways; (3) *analyzing the audience and occasion* so as to discover aspects of both that should affect what you say and how you say it; (4) *gathering material* through library research, interviews, and the like; (5) *arranging and outlining the points* so as to package your ideas in clear and palatable ways; (6) *practicing your speech aloud,* drilling its main features into your body and brain; and (7) *delivering the speech* with enough self-confidence to overcome your own fears and convince the audience of your abilities.

This overview of the preparation and delivery processes is enough to get you started in early class assignments. From here on, this book will explore in more detail particular aspects of the topics we have introduced.

1. Listed below are two groups of three statements about a single topic. Read all three statements in each group and write what you believe to be the central idea of the group's message. Compare your phrasing of the central ideas with those of members of your class.
   a. Many prison facilities are inadequate.
   b. Low rates of pay result in frequent job turnovers in prisons.
   c. Prison employees need on-the-job training.

   a. There is a serious maldistribution of medical personnel and service.
   b. The present system of delivering medical service is excellent.
   c. Rural areas have a shortage of doctors.
2. Rewrite each of the following statements, making it into a clear and concise central idea for a speech:
   a. "Today I would like to try and get you to see the way in which the body can communicate a whole lot of information."
   b. "The topic for my speech has to do with the high amount of taxes people have to pay."
   c. "A college education might be a really important thing for some people, so my talk is on a college education."

Now rewrite the last two statements (b, c) as claims. Be ready to present your versions in a class discussion.

1. It can be argued that all speeches are persuasive because, presumably, *any* change in a person's stock of knowledge, beliefs, attitudes, or behavior is a kind of adjustment of the human mechanism that we can term the result of "persuasion," as long as symbols were used to produce the change. See, for example, Kenneth E. Andersen, *Persuasion: Theory and Practice,* 2nd ed. (Boston: Allyn and Bacon, Inc., 1978), Chapter 1, "The Nature of Persuasion." The opposing argument—that we ought to establish boundaries around the idea of "persuasion"—can be found in Herbert W. Simons, *Persuasion: Understanding, Practice, and Analysis,* 2nd ed. (New York: Random House, 1986), Chapter 2, "What Is Persuasion?" We will be following Simons here in technically separating informative and persuasive talk.
2. See Charles T. Brown and Charles Van Riper, *Speech and Man* (Englewood Cliffs, NJ: Prentice-Hall, Inc., 1966), 35–36.
3. In this connection, see especially David K. Berlo, *The Process of Communication* (New York: Holt, Rinehart & Winston, Inc., 1960), 52, 62.

4. James McCroskey, "Oral Communication Apprehension: A Summary of Current Theory and Research," *Human Communication Research* 4 (1977): 78 -96.

5. From "Have You Checked Lately?" by Deanna Sellnow. Reprinted from *Winning Orations,* 1983, by special arrangement with the Interstate Oratorical Association, Larry Schnoor, Executive Secretary, Mankato State University, Mankato, Minnesota.

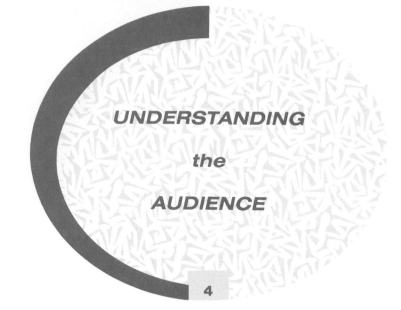

UNDERSTANDING

the

AUDIENCE

4

Public speaking is *audience-centered.* As earlier chapters have stressed, it is crucial that you interact with the people you are addressing. Selecting the topic, establishing your purpose, and narrowing the topic require consideration of your audience. Likewise, the remaining steps in speech preparation—selecting supporting materials, arranging the sequence of ideas, and developing introductions and conclusions—depend heavily on audience analysis. If you do not adapt to your listeners, you will probably not be a very effective speaker.

Because it is impractical to consider each listener as an individual, you must analyze listeners as members of a group—your audience. You should look for common denominators to help you target your messages to that group. Identifying the roles and physical characteristics of your listeners *(demographic analysis)* will help you locate the psychological components of your audience *(psychological profiling).* One theme will be stressed throughout this chapter: *The goal of audience analysis is to discover which facets of listeners' demographic and psychological characteristics are relevant to your speech purposes and ideas.* This information will help you discover ways to adapt your speech to your listeners.

ANALYZING THE AUDIENCE DEMOGRAPHICALLY

You can directly observe physical characteristics, so it is often easier to begin your audience analysis with these demographic factors. In any audience, you can identify traits that the members hold in common. When you begin your audience analysis, you will want to ask the following questions:

Age: Are my listeners primarily young, middle-aged, or older people? Does one age group seem to dominate a mixed audience? Is there a special relationship between age groups—parents and their children, for instance?

Gender: Is my audience predominantly male or female, or is the group equally made up of both genders?

Education: How much do my listeners already know about my subject? And, does their educational or experiential background allow them to learn about my subject easily and quickly?

Group Membership: Do these people belong to groups that represent special attitudes or identifiable values?

Cultural and Ethnic Background: Are members of my audience predominantly from particular cultural groups? Do my listeners share a special heritage?

The importance of demographic analysis for the speaker does not lie in simply finding answers to such questions. Rather, *the key here is to decide if any of these demographic factors will affect your listeners' ability or willingness to understand and accept what you want to say.* In other words, you must determine which factors are *relevant* to your audience and then shape your message accordingly.

For example, if you are addressing a group of senior citizens at a local seniors club, you obviously must consider *age* and *group affiliation.* You will probably adapt to your listeners by (1) speaking more loudly if their hearing is impaired, (2) choosing examples that are likely to be part of their experiential background, (3) considering their spare-time activities and interests, and (4) compensating for your lack of shared experiences through the use of local or common illustrations, examples, and other supporting material.

Demographic analysis can help you select and phrase your key ideas. It aids you in understanding your listeners by pinpointing the factors that may influence their ability to understand your message or accept what you say. Such variables as age or gender can determine how they experience events and what they think. So, demographic analysis can help you adapt your message more effectively to your listeners.

ANALYZING THE AUDIENCE PSYCHOLOGICALLY

It is also useful to divide audience members into psychological groups on the basis of fundamental beliefs, attitudes, and values. This is especially important if you intend to influence your listeners' thinking. You need to know what ideas they already accept before you can hope to alter their thoughts or actions. Sometimes, careful demographic analysis of your listeners can provide clues to how they think. For example, members of the National Rifle Association generally think constitutional rights are important; Daughters of the American Revolution are proud of their family heritage; and most Ph.D.'s believe education is fundamental to the development of human intellectual potential. Because beliefs, attitudes, and values are key concepts in discussing the psychology of listeners, we will define them carefully. Then, we will discuss some ways these concepts can be used by speakers who want to inform and persuade audiences.

Beliefs

Beliefs are ideas about what is true or false in the "real world." They arise from firsthand experience, evidence read or heard, authorities who have told us what is true, or even blind faith. So, you might believe that "Calculus is a difficult course" (firsthand experience), that "This university is dedicated to improving the quality of our lives through education" (university promotional literature), that "Learning is a lifelong activity" (something your parents or instructors have told you), or that "Getting an education increases your chances of landing a good job" (something you hope is true).

We hold beliefs for many reasons, and our beliefs can differ in important ways. Beliefs vary in the degree of *certitude* with which we hold them. We hold some beliefs to be externally verifiable—these we call *facts*—while others are personal *opinions*. Some beliefs are relatively open to change *(variable)*, while others are not *(fixed)*. And, both facts and opinions can be fixed or variable. Let us examine each of these subclasses.

Facts and Opinions

We all hold beliefs with varying degrees of certainty. *Facts* are those strong beliefs that you think are open to external verification. When you say "It's a fact that tomatoes are fruits," "Research has proven that infant blue

The Subclasses of Beliefs

	Beliefs of Fact	Beliefs of Opinion
Fixed Beliefs	● Americans who exercise live longer, healthier lives.	● Exercise is boring.
Variable Beliefs	● I might live longer and be healthier if I exercised.	● It might be fun to jog with Ed and Nancy.

whales gain an average of 10 pounds per day," or "It's a fact that whenever this country engages in a war, the economy booms," you are stating that you are very sure of those beliefs. Facts are usually held with certainty because you are convinced that you have hard evidence to back them up. In addition, you think that others can verify their accuracy. In sum, a fact is a belief that you hold firmly and think is supported with strong evidence.

However, opinions are another matter. When you identify an opinion, such as "It's my opinion that our current administration is neglecting the problems of the poor" or "In my opinion, he's right," you are signaling that your belief-statements are personal. You are letting your listeners know that your statements are being offered as your own views of a situation. You are telling them, at least indirectly, that your commitment to the statement is not especially strong and that you may not have sufficient external evidence to support the claim. Thus, an opinion is a personal belief held with less certitude and supported with less compelling external evidence than a fact.[1] Since both facts and opinions are matters of belief, however, the accuracy of their "truth" can be relative. Sometimes the difference between fact and opinion is blurred. In colonial America, for instance, many people knew "for a fact" that regular bathing caused illness, just as their ancestors knew that the earth was flat and located at the center of the universe. If an opinion is widely held, it may be taken as fact. It is important to recognize that opinions and facts are psychological concepts that can be believed both individually and collectively.

Fixed and Variable Beliefs

A second way of viewing beliefs is to determine their degree of *certainty*. Some beliefs are fixed, while others are open to change, or are variable. Fixed beliefs are those that have been reinforced throughout your life, making them central to your thinking. Obviously, many of your early childhood beliefs are fixed, such as "Bad behavior will be punished" and "If you work hard, you will succeed." Other beliefs become not only fixed but anchored as well; especially as you grow older, such beliefs harden in your mind and are highly resistant to change. For example, as people grow older, they tend to vote along political party lines election after election; they tend to purchase and drive the same kind of vehicles; they tend to believe that certain people and occupations are respectable and others are not; and they tend not to change religions or churches. Thus, the demographic variable of age may indicate fixed beliefs. Fixed beliefs become habituated and can even be called *stereotypes* because we often generalize our fixed beliefs to larger groups. For example, we might say, "All Republicans are honest," "People who do things like that should be arrested!" or "Never trust a German shepherd."

In contrast, variable beliefs are less well anchored in our minds and experiences. You might enter college thinking you are very well suited by temperament and talent to be a chemist; then, after an instructor has praised your abilities in a composition class, you might see yourself as predestined to be a writer; next, you take a marketing class and find out that you are very good at planning advertising campaigns and so on, as you experience one class after another until you somehow select a major and degree program. In this case, your beliefs about your talents and the best ways to use them change with your personal experiences. The testimony you have heard from various authority figures, instructors, and counselors has influenced these variable beliefs. And, since they are still not firmly fixed beliefs, they change as you encounter new experiences.

Before you speak, it is important to know which of your audience's beliefs are fixed (difficult to change) and which are variable (more easily altered). In addition, it is important to realize what information your listeners hold as fact and what is opinion. Assessing the nature of your audience's beliefs is important for three reasons:

1. You can reinforce or alter their beliefs using strategies similar to the ways in which people normally accept beliefs. For example, knowing that audiences often establish beliefs based on the statements of authorities will encourage you to use similar testimony as you seek to influence your listeners' views.

2. Such assessments should help you outline some of the appeals you can make within your speech. If audience analysis shows that your listeners consider empirical evidence to be factual, you can use scientific studies or statistical data in your speech. If, on the other hand, they believe in the divine inspiration of certain religious documents, you can cite quotations or examples from these sources. Such facts can be used to support your central idea or claim.

3. These assessments also allow you to set realistic expectations as you plan your talk. Not all audience beliefs are equally amenable to change through speeches. You should not try to accomplish impossible goals in a single speech. You will probably encounter psychological resistance when you try to destroy too many facts and fixed beliefs.

Later in this chapter we will discuss in more detail these questions of selecting belief-claims and setting speech goals.

'Ladies and gentlemen of the jury,' the defense lawyer said, 'my client's had to work for a living all of his life. He started out, like some of you did, at the bottom of the ladder. He's never asked for any special breaks and he's always treated those of you who know him as a neighbor fair and square. Why would he set fire to his own business—something he's worked so hard for? The night his building went up in smoke, so did half a lifetime of work—his dreams and those of his family. Arson is a serious crime and deserves our prosecution to the limits of the law. That's our duty as citizens of this country! But, let's not get carried away and accuse someone who's never even gotten a parking ticket! Let's go after the real criminals, not honest, law-abiding citizens like you and me.'

Attitudes

Now, let us move to the second aspect of psychological profiling—understanding audience attitudes. *Attitudes* may be defined as tendencies to respond positively or negatively to people, objects, or ideas. Attitudes express individual preferences or feelings, such as "Democracy is better than communism," "Discrimination is wrong," "The Statue of Liberty is a beautiful monument," and "I like my public speaking class."

Because attitudinal statements express our preferences, predispositions, reactions, and basic judgments, they often control our behavior. We
tend to do things we like and avoid things we dislike. As a speaker, you
should consider the dominant attitudes of your audience. Especially relevant
are the audience's attitudes toward you, your subject, and your speech
purpose. One dramatic example of the strength of attitudes occurred when
the Coca-Cola Company introduced "new Coke®"with disastrous results.
Even though extensive blind taste tests showed that people preferred the
new flavor, consumers reacted negatively to the "new Coke®" because of
their attitudes of loyalty to the classic formula. Their attitudes controlled
their purchasing behavior and the company was forced to "reintroduce"
Coca-Cola Classic®.

The Audience's Attitudes Toward the Speaker

The attitudes of an audience toward you as a speaker will be based in part
on your reputation. Your behavior during the speech will also influence the
audience's attitudes toward you as they assess and re-evaluate their previous
impressions. Two factors are especially important regarding your reputation:
(1) the amount of respect they hold for you and your subject and (2) the
listeners' feelings of friendliness toward you.

You might like rock music, but you probably do not copy the musicians'
life-styles. While you appreciate the music, you may not respect the
musicians' personal judgment. On the other hand, you may have great
respect for the foreign policy accomplishments of former President Richard
Nixon, but you may not like him as a person. Respect and friendliness are
two different attitudes. As a speaker you must consider both.

You can do several things to encourage positive audience attitudes
when you speak. You can enhance your listeners' respect for you and your
topic by (1) providing evidence of your intelligence and expertise during the
speech; (2) appearing to be fair, just, and sincere as you consider the topic;
and (3) providing clear, direct, well-documented arguments to support your
claim and central idea. You can strengthen your listeners' friendliness toward
you by (1) speaking energetically to suggest how important the topic is to
you and should be to them, (2) appearing alert but comfortable in your role
as a speaker, and (3) expressing your interest in them as listeners.

The Audience's Attitude Toward the Subject

Sometimes people are interested in a subject; sometimes they are apathetic
about it. In either case, the amount of interest they have can influence their
responses. Some researchers place *prior audience attitudes* among the most
crucial audience variables that determine speaking success.[2] If listeners feel
unfavorable toward the message, they may (1) distort the substance of the

message, (2) psychologically refuse to listen or even physically leave, (3) discredit you as a speaker, or (4) use similar defense mechanisms to avoid accurate perception of your intent as a speaker.

> *Andrew carefully prepared and delivered his persuasive speech to his public speaking class, warning them of the wickedness of drinking and the pitfalls of dating. At first he did not notice the smiles that suddenly froze on faces or the stony gazes of his audience. Even his instructor stared for a few minutes before he began to make notes on Andrew's critique sheet. Andrew went on to explain how they could find help in his religion. Mouths became hard lines and eyes turned toward desktops as he proceeded with the speech. Eventually Andrew noticed the changes in his listeners and thought to himself, 'They probably feel guilty—I'm really getting through to them—finally!' His classmates avoided him for weeks after the speech and his instructor commented on his critique form that he should get approval of the topic before he prepared his next speech. At the very least, some solid audience analysis would have prepared Andrew for his listeners' reactions.*

There are several ways in which you, as a speaker, can minimize these potentially negative attitude reactions. If your audience analysis indicates that listeners may be apathetic, you can stress ways in which the problem you are discussing directly affects them. It is important to neutralize their apathy by stressing the connections between your subject and their own lives. Use the available means for holding their attention to accomplish this. (See pages 38–39.) You may also arouse their curiosity about some novel aspect of the subject. When your listeners are apathetic, you must make a special effort to gain their interest.

Interest (or the lack of it) is only one aspect of an audience's attitude toward your subject. *Expectancy* is another. For example, as soon as we hear that a speech will be about the Gay Liberation movement, many of us begin to form favorable or unfavorable attitudes toward the speaker and the subject. As a general rule, the more the listeners know about your subject or the stronger their beliefs concerning it, the more likely they are to have well-defined expectations. These expectations may be troublesome, for frequently they operate as listening barriers or as filters that distort the meanings that the audience assigns to your message. The introduction of your speech presents a special opportunity to create or to correct these audience expectations. All the time you are talking, however, you should bear in mind the problem of listener expectation and adapt accordingly.

The Audience's Attitude Toward the Speech Purpose

It may surprise you that your audience holds attitudes toward your speech purpose even before you begin to speak. Your listeners represent many variations of attitude. For example, some may resent having to listen to you; others may be eager to learn new ideas; still others may be looking for an opportunity to argue with you about what you will say. Since audience predisposition is seldom uniform, it is best to determine which attitudes are predominant (through audience analysis) and to adapt your speech to those attitudes.

When the general purpose of your speech is *to inform,* your listeners' attitude toward your purpose will be governed largely by their attitude toward the subject; that is, they will be either interested or apathetic. When your general purpose is *to persuade,* however, the listeners' attitude toward the speech purpose will also be governed by their attitude toward the specific belief or action you urge; hence, their attitude will be one of the following:

1. favorable but not aroused;
2. apathetic to the situation;
3. interested in the situation but undecided what to do or think about it;
4. interested in the situation but hostile to the *proposed* attitude, belief, or action; or
5. hostile to any change from the present state of affairs.

Determining the predominant attitude of your audience toward your subject and purpose should guide you in selecting your arguments and developing the structure and content of your message. If your listeners are apathetic, begin your speech on a point of compelling interest or startling vividness. Show them how your subject affects them. If they are hostile to the proposal, you may wish to introduce it more cautiously, emphasize some basic principle with which you know they agree, and relate your proposal to it. If they are interested but undecided, provide plenty of proof in the form of factual illustrations, testimony, and statistics. If they are favorable but not aroused, try to motivate them by using appeals that directly touch their desires for pleasure, independence, power, creativity, ego satisfaction, and the like.

'I hate that commercial!' Barbara announced to the group of General Hospital regulars in the dorm lounge. 'After all, it's not her fault that his collar's dirty!'

'Maybe he never takes a bath,' Donna suggested, then laughed.

'Yeah, why do they always make her look so dumb?' someone else said.

After a minute of silence, as many of them nodded in agreement, Brian butted in—'The whole thing's kinda cute. She's just concerned about him. What's the big deal?'

Analysis of an audience made prior to a speech can never be fully correct. Even if it is close, audience attitudes may shift even while you are speaking.[3] This means that you must watch listeners' reactions closely to gauge their reactions to your message. The way listeners sit, their facial expressions, their audible reactions—laughter, applause, fidgeting, whispering—can all be clues to their attitude toward you, your subject, and your purpose. The conscientious communicator develops a keen awareness of these signs of audience feedback and adapts the message accordingly.[4]

Values

A third important component of audience psychology is values. Values are the basic components for organizing one's view of life. They are habitual ways of looking at the world or responding to problems. Values often are the foundation for beliefs and attitudes that cluster around them.

Attitudes, beliefs, and values are interdependent. That is, they tend to form consistent clusters that reinforce and repeat one another. Values are more basic than attitudes or beliefs because they represent broad categories that can motivate specific attitudes and beliefs. Thus, a person may hold a certain value, such as "Human life is sacred." That value can be expressed in multiple attitudes, perhaps including "Abortion is wrong" and "Mercy killing is immoral." Beliefs also may support this value, for example: "A fetus can survive as a human being," "Most Americans are opposed to abortion rights legislation," and "Religious authority ought to be respected on questions of morality."

Values, then, are an individual's habitualized reasons for holding particular attitudes and beliefs. But, even more broadly, we can talk about

Values and Related Beliefs/Attitudes

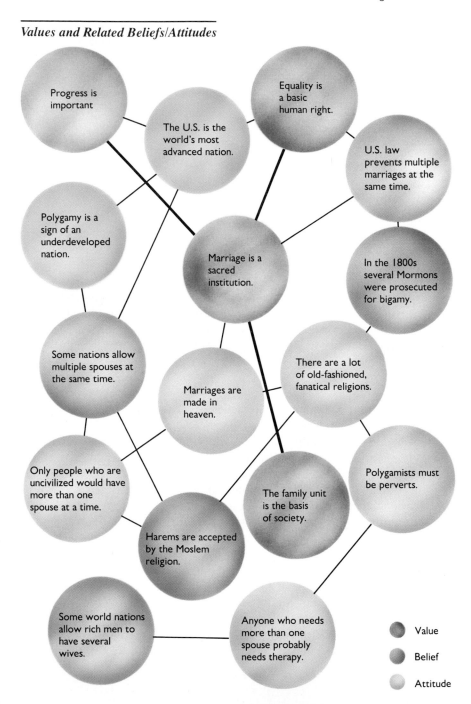

Progress is important

The U.S. is the world's most advanced nation.

Equality is a basic human right.

U.S. law prevents multiple marriages at the same time.

Polygamy is a sign of an underdeveloped nation.

Marriage is a sacred institution.

In the 1800s several Mormons were prosecuted for bigamy.

Some nations allow multiple spouses at the same time.

Marriages are made in heaven.

There are a lot of old-fashioned, fanatical religions.

Only people who are uncivilized would have more than one spouse at a time.

The family unit is the basis of society.

Polygamists must be perverts.

Harems are accepted by the Moslem religion.

Some world nations allow rich men to have several wives.

Anyone who needs more than one spouse probably needs therapy.

Value

Belief

Attitude

value orientations (sometimes called *ideologies*), which are the views of life taken by relatively large groups of people. Over the last three decades, for example, Americans have read about the Puritan Ethic, the Establishment, the Silent Majority, the Counterculture, Me-ism, Situational Ethics, Freaks, New Politics, the Old Guard, Libbers, Moonies, Rednecks, the Moral Majority, and Neo-Liberals.[5]

Discovering the values that your listeners habitually bring to bear on issues is a critical part of audience analysis. These values organize and often influence the beliefs and attitudes they express. For example, knowing that members of a student senate are strongly motivated by sociological issues (how the social life of the university will be affected) and pragmatic concerns (how much it will cost) will help you if you are trying to persuade them to allocate funds for bringing a rock group to campus. Unless you can discover *common ground*—shared values—among them, you may well be in communicative trouble. A search for common ground is a crucial step in audience analysis.

USING AUDIENCE ANALYSIS IN SPEECH PREPARATION

Identifying the demographic and psychological characteristics of your listeners is an important first step toward successful communication, but it is not enough. You are identifying such characteristics in order to discover what might affect the acceptance of you and your ideas. You are searching for *relevant* considerations. What you discover can help you better phrase your ideas, organize your speech, and determine your appeals. We will address such matters in Chapters 8, 9, and 10. For now, let us examine ways in which your audience findings help you prepare to speak.

Audience Targeting: Setting Realistic Purposes

Few of us have difficulty determining our overall or general speech purposes—to inform, to entertain, to persuade or actuate. Once this is done, you need to determine realistically what you can expect to accomplish with this audience in the time you have available. As you think about *targeting your audience,* four considerations should arise: your specific purpose, the areas of audience interest, the audience's capacity to act, and the degree of change you can expect.

Your Specific Purpose

Suppose you have a part-time job with your college's Career Planning and Placement Office; you know enough about its operations and have enough personal interest in it to want to speak about career planning and placement to different audiences. What you have discovered about different audiences should help you determine appropriate specific purposes for each. If you were to talk to a group of *incoming freshmen,* for example, you would know that they probably:

1. know little or nothing about the functions of a career planning and placement office (i.e., have few beliefs, none of which are fixed);
2. are predisposed to look favorably on career planning and placement (given job anxieties among college graduates);
3. are, at their particular stage of life and educational development, more concerned with such pragmatic issues as getting an adviser, registering, and learning about basic degree requirements than they are with such longer-range matters as post-degree placement (and may not value your information without motivation);
4. are likely, however, to see you as an authoritative speaker and, hence, are willing to listen to you.

Given these audience considerations, you probably should keep your speech fairly general: Feed them basic, not detailed, information about career planning and placement; remind them that the office can relieve many of their later anxieties as graduation nears; show them how thinking about possible careers will help them select majors and particular courses. You might phrase your specific purpose as follows: "To brief incoming freshmen on the range of services offered by the Career Planning and Placement Office." That orientation would include a basic description of each service and a general appeal to use the services to make some curricular decisions.

Were you, instead, to talk about this subject to a group of college seniors, you would address the audience differently. You would discover that they:

1. already know something about the Career Planning and Placement Office (since they probably have roommates and friends who have used or are preparing to use such services);
2. have strong positive feelings about career planning and placement (because they are hoping to use such services to find jobs when they graduate);
3. tend to value education pragmatically, that is, for how it has prepared them to "earn a decent living";
4. may view you as an unqualified speaker on this subject, especially if you are not a senior or are unemployed.

Given these factors, you should be much more specific in some areas. You would want to describe the special features of this office's operations rather than simply outline its general duties. Your listeners need to know "how" not "what," because they already know "what." You would reassure them that the office is successful in placing many students but suggest that they allow ample time for résumé development, job searching, and interviewing. Also, you should demonstrate your expertise by talking about career possibilities across a variety of fields (especially if you know what fields are represented in the group you are addressing). You might phrase your specific purpose like this: "To inform graduating seniors about Midstate University's philosophy of career planning and placement, about ways the office can help students find employment, and about specific types of information and assistance the office provides students." Audience analysis, therefore, will focus your specific purposes and determine which are most appropriate to your listeners.

In targeting your audience as a group, tailor your message to your specific purpose, the audience's interests and capacity to act, and the degree of change you can expect. For example, a class of first graders would probably prefer a general "Careers Day" introduction to firefighting, rather than a detailed discussion of the training required for the job.

Areas of Audience Interest

You can use both demographic and psychological analyses to help you decide what ideas will interest your listeners. This is critical in narrowing your topic choice and choosing specific ideas to develop. Suppose you know something about computer programming. An audience of industrial managers probably would be most interested in hearing how computers can make their companies more cost effective; a group of hospital administrators might want to learn how to enhance recordkeeping and patient services; the Internal Revenue Service would appreciate an application in tax fraud discovery; and, a mixed, "public" audience will be curious about how computers will transform their everyday lives in the twenty-first century.

Sometimes, however, you will want to *create a new set of interests in an audience.* For example, you might suppose that an audience of doctors will be interested in finding out about the latest drugs for pain therapy, given their medical-scientific values. Yet, you may want the audience to understand the psychological effects of such drugs and the related ethical questions of their use by unstable patients. You can create a new set of interests by *tying new interests to old ones.* For this speech, you might phrase your central idea as follows: "Knowing more about the psychological effects of the latest drugs available for pain therapy will make you a more humane as well as a more medically expert physician." Phrasing the central idea in this way explicitly ties the interests you are trying to create to ones the audience already has.

The Audience's Capacity to Act

As a speaker, *limit your request to an action that lies within your listeners' range of authority.* Do not ask them to accomplish the impossible. To demand of a group of striking workers that they place a tariff on imported goods is unrealistic. But if you ask them to picket the plant, you are more likely to get results.

You can often discover listeners' potential for action through an analysis of your audience. Demographic factors can be important here because they tell you about the channels of action available to your listeners. Voters can cast their ballots in elections, parents can teach their children, consumers can boycott products, and many others can contribute money. The psychological factors you discover through audience analysis can be used to stimulate listeners' motivation to act.

You determine ranges of authority through analysis of the audience, especially of demographic factors. In the case of a comparatively homogeneous audience (e.g., students), this is relatively easy to do. In the case of more heterogeneous groups, however, you may have to consider a broader range of capacities to act. So, in talking with a local school's PTA about instituting an after-school program of foreign language and culture instruction, you are addressing an audience comprised of school administrators (who can seek funding from the school board), teachers (who can volunteer instructional time), and parents (who can petition the school board, enroll their children, and volunteer to help with the program). Thus, you would have to include among your specific purposes goals for each of these subgroups of listeners.

Degrees of Change

Finally, as we suggested earlier, you must be realistic about the expected degree of change in your listeners' attitudes and beliefs. How much information can you present for consideration? If you have a time limit or if your average listener's attention span is short, you must limit the information you present. Such demographic factors as age and educational development will help you reach these answers. Also, deciding whether your information is new or already known will influence how much material you can cover in a single speech. How intensely can you motivate an audience to react to a topic? If your listeners are strongly opposed to downtown renovation, a single speech, no matter how eloquent, will probably not reverse their opinions. One attempt may only neutralize some of their objections—which is a more realistic goal for a single speech. How much action can you expect after your speech? If your prespeech analysis indicates that your listeners vehemently oppose nuclear power plants in your area, you can probably persuade many of them to work long hours at a variety of activities, such as picketing, lobbying, and telephone marathons. However, if they are only moderately committed to opposing nuclear facilities, you might ask for a small monetary donation and no actual time commitment.

In other words, audience analysis should help you determine how to phrase your specific purposes and central ideas for maximum effectiveness. Understanding your audience should also give you a more realistic expectation of what changes in behavior, attitudes, and commitments can occur in your listeners.

Audience Segmentation: Selecting Dominant Ideas and Appeals

So far, we have been dealing with audience analysis as it helps you target your audience as a group. Keep in mind, however, that no matter how people are crowded together, arranged in rows, or reached electronically, they are still individuals. As we noted when discussing psychological profiling, your beliefs, attitudes, and values, while influenced by your culture and society, are ultimately yours. They are the unique products of your experiences and your own thoughts.

Ideally, it would be most effective if you could approach each listener individually. Sometimes you can, but such communication is time consuming and inefficient when you are dealing with matters of broad public concern. Imagine for a minute the president of this country talking to each of us individually. It is impossible. However, through a televised public speech, he or she can talk to us in our own living rooms as though it were a personal conversation. It is necessary to find a compromise between thinking of audiences either as homogeneous masses or as solitary individuals. Advertisers use an approach called *audience segmentation.* Audience segmentation is a matter of dividing a mass audience as a series of subgroups, or "target populations," that hold common attitudes, beliefs, values, or demographic characteristics. A typical college student audience might be segmented by academic standing (freshmen through seniors), academic majors (art through zoology), classroom performance (A+ to F), and even extracurricular activities (ROTC, SADD, Young Democrats, Pi Kappa Delta).

Accurately Identifying Subgroups/Segments

It is important to carefully identify subgroups among your listeners. This will not only allow you to better phrase your appeals, but it will help you avoid irritating listeners unnecessarily. A speaker who began, "Because all you girls are interested in efficient cooking, today I want to talk about four ways a food processor will save you time in the kitchen," would probably alienate two subgroups in the audience: The females probably would be irritated with the stereotyped allusion to them as "girls," while the males who cook would be offended by having been left out. The appeal would be better phrased "Because everyone who cooks is interested in . . . . " Here, you are aiming the interest-appeal to the proper audience segment—the culinary masters. Similarly, unless you are sure there are no Roman Catholics in your audience, you probably will want to avoid blaming the Catholic religious hierarchy for the antiabortion movement in this country; because so many people in this country identify with businesses and industries, you probably would not want to blame "the business establishment" alone for inflation; and, you probably would be foolhardy to refer to "dumb jocks," "artsy-craftsy theater majors," and "computer fanatics" in a speech to your class on the goals of college education. This is *not* to say, of course, that you never directly confront beliefs, attitudes, and values of subgroups represented in your audience—that you always say what people "want" to hear. Obviously in some areas of this country, the church has been active in the Sanctuary Movement; some business practices have been responsible for

An audience is a collection of individuals who belong to various demographic and psychological subgroups. Audience analysis involves the careful identification of these subgroups.

part of the unemployment problem; and, government has contributed to environmental pollution. You can find ways to talk about those things, but be sure that you avoid stereotyped references to people and groups; that you avoid blanket condemnation of groups of people; and that, when possible, you work around controversial subjects. You should cite ample and unbiased evidence when you challenge a group's beliefs, attitudes, and sacred values.

Selecting Relevant Psychological Statements

Audience segmentation should also help you select statements of belief, attitudes, and values for inclusion in your speech. If you can accurately identify the relevant subgroups, you can include psychological appeals for each in your speech. This greatly increases the personal appeal and potential effectiveness of your message. Suppose you were to give a speech to a local Community Club about the importance of including women in its membership. Your initial segmenting of the audience tells you that the Club is composed of businessmen, medical professionals, educators, social service personnel, lawyers, and bankers. By thinking of the Club as segmented into such subgroups, you should be in a position to offer each subgroup some reasons to support your proposal. You might outline the appeals this way:

Claim: The membership of the Community Club should be extended to include women.

1. For doctors and hospital workers: a large percentage of the hospital staff is composed of women in all roles, including physicians, nurses, physical therapists, and administrators. Their expertise and commitment to helping others is the foundation of the Club's philosophy.

2. For social service workers: the social-team concept is important. It means working with everyone—including women.

3. For educators: the majority of our elementary and secondary school faculties are women. By limiting membership, we automatically exclude one of the most important resources for our young people—their classroom teachers.

4. And for those from community businesses: women control a large proportion of the financial resources of the community as investors, property owners, and heads of households. They could offer a significant contribution to the success of the Club.

This is just a sketch of several basic appeals; each would be expanded in an actual speech. From these examples, however, you can see how each is based on beliefs and attitudes you assume are important to segments of the audience. There is an implicit reference to medical ethics based on serving humankind, to the commitment of social services to help people from all strata of life, to educators' beliefs and attitudes that youth are a national resource, and to business commitments to financial responsibility and success. Thus, *audience analysis, in combination with audience segmentation, are valuable tools for selecting your main lines of appeal and argument.*

Choosing Among Valuative Appeals

And finally, as you might guess, audience segmentation will help you select a valuative vocabulary for your speeches. Even informative speeches, as we will discuss more fully later, need to contain appeals to audience interests. You can use a valuative vocabulary to motivate different segments of the audience to listen to and accept your information. So, for a class demonstration speech, you might say: "Today, I want to teach you three basic techniques of Oriental cooking—cutting meats and vegetables, using spices, and quick-cooking your food in a wok. If you learn these techniques, you'll expand your range of expertise in the kitchen *(personal value)*, you'll save money on your food and energy bills *(economic value)*, you'll prepare more than satisfying meals for your friends *(social value)*, and you'll prepare nutritious, healthful meals for everyone" *(pragmatic value)*. With that statement, you will have given your audience four different reasons for listening and will have a good chance of appealing to everyone in your speech. (If that is not enough, tell them the meals will be beautiful, too, and thereby add an *esthetic value*.)

Usually, however, valuative appeals are even more important to persuasive and actuative speeches. Because these speeches are attempts to alter people's beliefs, attitudes, and behaviors and because, as we noted, values are a body of beliefs and attitudes, valuative appeals are absolutely crucial for persuasive and actuative communications. For example:

Claim: The United States should adopt immediate, severe economic sanctions against nations, such as South Africa and Chile, that violate basic human rights.

1. *Politically,* getting tough with nations that consistently violate citizens' rights will increase international respect for the United States' commitment to support human rights. If successful, it may also gain a voice for previously disenfranchised peoples or groups.

2. *Pragmatically,* economic sanctions are effective and avoid violence. Nations violating human rights are more likely to respond to economic sanctions than to verbal threats.

3. *Psychologically,* we will increase the importance of preserving basic human rights throughout the world if we take them seriously enough to enforce them.

4. *Culturally,* treatment of groups or people as equals may enhance their opportunity to contribute to the development of their nation. Everyone will be richer because the nation is recognizing the heritage of all of its citizens.

5. *Sociologically,* we can promote a freer environment for the political/ social participation in nations if they abandon human rights violations.

6. *Economically,* individuals who have been denied access will have the opportunity to participate more fully in the resources of their nations.

While we have not used every conceivable value-term in this segmentation of appeals, the procedure should be clear: (1) Think through possible reasons people might accept your proposition in valuative terms. (2) Then, use a valuative vocabulary in phrasing your actual appeals for acceptance.

In conclusion, understanding your audience is certainly the most crucial step of speech preparation. The competent speaker makes many decisions about topic, specific purposes, phrasing for central ideas and propositions, dominant appeals, and phraseology based on demographical and psychological profiles of audience members. To help yourself with these tasks, you will want to (1) think through your personal experiences with identifiable groups in the audience, (2) talk with program chairpersons and others who can tell you "who" is in the audience and something about their interests, (3) ask speakers who have addressed this or similar audiences what to expect, and (4) even interview some people who will be there to find out more about their beliefs, attitudes, and values—their range of concerns.

These are not especially easy tasks, for most of us do not have available the resources of public opinion polls and extensive social-psychological target group profiles. You probably will be unable to precisely identify all possible facets of listeners' minds and habits. However, if you learn all you can about them and use that knowledge to help make some key prespeech decisions by discovering *relevant* considerations, you will significantly improve your chances for communicative success.

Sample Analysis *of an Audience* • • • • • • • •

In this chapter we have surveyed an array of choices you must make as you analyze your audience and occasion. If you work systematically, one step at a time, these choices will become clearer. Observe how one student analyzed her audience as she prepared a speech for increased understanding of acquired immune deficiency syndrome (AIDS).

AUDIENCE ANALYSIS: UNDERSTANDING AIDS

I. Basic Speaking Situation
  A. Title: "The Great American Plague: AIDS"
  B. Subject: What we should know about the coming crisis in American health—Acquired Immune Deficiency Syndrome
  C. General Purpose: To persuade
  D. Specific Purpose: To prove to members of a local political action caucus that AIDS poses a future national health threat
  E. Specific Audience: The political action caucus is a community group whose function is to promote political consciousness and action in the community. It consists of varied membership, including local housewives, business proprietors, the town mayor, the Chair of the state Republican Committee, and approximately a dozen interested listeners. A synopsis of the monthly meeting is broadcast over local radio stations and is included on the editorial page of the local newspaper (reaching a secondary audience).
  F. Proposition: "The caucus should be alerted to the pending crisis in national health."

II. Audience Analysis

  A. Demographic Analysis

     1. Age: Of the individuals attending the meeting, most are between thirty and sixty-five. The spectators are approximately twenty to thirty. Except for appeals to future events, age is probably not an important factor. The speaker is significantly younger than members of her audience (twenty-one). She will need to enhance her credibility as a speaker to compensate for her relative youth and inexperience.

     2. Gender: The caucus is a mixed group with slightly more women than men. Given the topic and proposition, there may be an initial attitude that AIDS is not a threat to either women or heterosexual males.

     3. Education: Approximately one third of the listeners have completed B.A. degrees in varied fields, including political science, pharmacy, nursing, home economics, and accounting. All but four of the remainder have finished high school; several have taken college courses. While several health professionals in the audience are familiar with disease history and control, most listeners are acquainted with the topic only through media coverage.

     4. Group Membership: All listeners are politically active, registered voters. Although they do not necessarily share party affiliation, they all agree that participation in the democratic process is vital.

     5. Cultural and Ethnic Background: Ethnic background is primarily European but should not be a factor on this topic. The community was shocked by the news of the recent AIDS death of a former resident. All members of the caucus were born and/or raised in this small Midwestern community with a mixed rural–small business economy.

  B. Psychological Analysis

     1. Beliefs

        a. Accepted Facts and Beliefs: Anyone who contracts AIDS will die of it. There is nothing that can currently be done to stop the disease. The incidence of AIDS is limited to homosexual populations primarily on the East and West Coasts. The resident who died had just moved to San Francisco, where it is thought that he may have contracted the disease.

        b. Fixed Beliefs: Homosexual behavior is morally wrong and should not be condoned. Only one or two members of the caucus would even consider hiring, renting to, or politically endorsing a person known to be homosexual. The medical profession has accounted for most breakthroughs in disease control and treatment.

        c. Variable Beliefs: Most probably believe that a degree of tolerance should be shown to members of unusual religious or political factions. Several would agree that the sexual revolution of the 1960s brought some advantages, such as greater openness, more individual responsibility, and better understanding of human sexuality.

2. Attitudes
   a. Audience Attitude Toward Speaker: The members of the caucus probably consider the speaker to be naive and idealistic on the topic. Her youthfulness severely undermines her credibility.
   b. Audience Attitude Toward Subject: The listeners are certainly hostile toward those they feel are guilty of spreading AIDS—the "promiscuous gay population." While they are curious about AIDS because of recent sensationalized media attention, they are probably not very concerned. They do not consider themselves likely targets of the disease.
   c. Audience Attitude Toward Purpose: Most are basically apathetic. While they are curious about the disease, they do not really care about it since they think it will not touch their lives. Several members are hostile, given their strong personal religious attitudes toward homosexuality.
3. Values
   a. Predominating Values: The political value of "majority rule" is strongly held by every listener. There is a positive commitment to democratic process and a pride in community political involvement at the state and national levels. They see themselves as "common people—the heart of America," fulfilling the American dream. Caucus members often point to community progress in civil rights issues, general educational reforms, and high voter turnout during elections.
   b. Relevant Value Orientation: Ideologically, while caucus members are voicing democratic principles, they are practicing those ideals in a limited sphere. They are promoting fair treatment for some minority issues, such as equal rights, but are unaware of or are denying others. It would be counterproductive to point out this hypocrisy to the group, since they take a great deal of pride in themselves and their local accomplishments.

III. Adaptive Strategies
  A. Audience Targeting
   1. Specificity of Purpose: To de-fuse one set of suspicions, to make it clear that this is not simply "a gay cause." While the speaker should recognize the importance of a good moral climate in this country, she also must stress the practical importance of treating disease regardless of moral issues. The speaker should emphasize that everyone's health may be affected if the disease is allowed to spread unchecked through ignorance or neglect.
   2. Areas of Audience Interests: Make sure to use the caucus members' fixed and anchored beliefs and values to advance the speaker's own goals. Stress their commitments to the welfare of the community and nation, their beliefs in the democratic process, and the rights of citizens in minority factions. Encourage their feelings of pride in previous civic

accomplishments and challenge them to face the coming AIDS crisis. In other words, show them that it is in their self-interest to confront and discuss unpopular issues for the well-being of the entire community.

3. Audience's Capacity to Act: The immediate goal is to increase their awareness of the AIDS crisis and encourage them to discuss it in future meetings. Point out that other Midwestern communities have debated the issues involved as they were faced with enrolling infected children in local schools. Stress predictions of future infection's affecting broader populations. Overcome audience apathy and hostility by encouraging members to discuss the disease in other groups such as the local PTA, religious organizations, community service groups, and the like.

4. Degrees of Change: Do not demand immediate commitments or political action. Push instead for an open forum for future debate on the issues.

B. Audience Segmentation

1. Accurate Identification of Subgroups: Emphasize the nature of the caucus' political rather than moral or personal involvement in community issues. Avoid stereotyping or judging religious or dogmatic individuals or groups. De-emphasize the sexual aspects of the issue. While these aspects might gratify the curious, they would strengthen the resistance of listeners who associate the disease only with those they consider to be undesirable members of the community.

2. Relevant Psychological Statements: Recognize the group's excellent efforts at political reform in local projects. Remember that listeners have taken the time to attend, and their commitments should be recognized. Stress the farsightedness of the group on difficult issues such as this one. Point out that, in a democracy, fair play requires that each side be given equal time and consideration before anyone reaches a final decision. Aim the bulk of the speech at gaining assent to open-minded discussions.

3. Relevant Valuative Appeals: Underscore the virtues of democratic process, freedom of expression, and the rights of all American citizens. Encourage pride in previous caucus accomplishments and channel motivation toward achieving new goals. Highlight, too, the fundamental importance of both medical and political progress in achieving success.

- -

With this prespeech audience analysis completed, the next steps in preparing the speech are clearer. The audience analysis points to the kinds of *supporting materials* needed. The speaker should:

1. Look up the history of AIDS in the United States.

2. Find out projected levels of AIDS infection in the future. This material should be available through the Center for Disease Control in Atlanta, Georgia.

3. Identify the populations that are currently infected by AIDS—men, women, children, homosexual, heterosexual.

4. Read local newspaper articles concerning the former community resident who died of AIDS.

5. If possible, interview community residents who knew the AIDS victim.

6. Search out examples of people who contracted the disease, including schoolchildren in Midwestern towns and medical personnel.

7. Develop a "typical" disease profile—what occurs in the body and how it copes with the disease.

8. Interview local medical authorities to discover the kinds of treatment currently used and the chances of AIDS occurring in local residents.

9. Read expert opinions and discussions of the disease, especially concerning the future rates of infection. Identify potential supporting material, such as authoritative statements, statistics, explanations, or illustrations.

10. Prepare a list of other Midwestern communities that have held community discussions or adopted measures regarding AIDS.

11. Anticipate and list potential questions and objections to the topic itself.

12. Check local and state medical codes and guidelines regarding infectious disease.

CHAPTER SUMMARY

Public speaking is *audience-centered.* The primary goal of audience analysis is to discover the facets of listeners' demographic and psychological backgrounds that are *relevant* to your speech purposes and ideas. Once you understand the makeup of your audience, you can adapt your speech purposes and ideas to best reach that audience. *Demographic analysis* concentrates on describing such audience characteristics as *age, gender, education, group membership,* and *cultural and ethnic backgrounds. Psychological analysis* seeks to identify the *beliefs, attitudes,* and *values* of audience members. Both demographic and psychological characteristics may affect your listeners' ability or willingness to accept and understand what you want to say. Audience analysis allows you to *set realistic speech purposes* and to *target* audience subgroups for more careful selection of ideas and appeals. Careful audience analysis is the first step in planning your speech.

Oral Activities

1. After your instructor has divided the class into four-person groups, meet with the other members of your group. Discuss the next round of speeches to be presented: the topics you intend to use, your general and specific purposes, development of your ideas or propositions, your speech outlines, and some useful kinds of supporting materials. Criticize each other's plans and preparation, offering suggestions for changes and more specific adaptations to your classroom audience. After discussing and evaluating the potential of your speech with a portion of your audience (your group), you should be able to develop and present a message more effectively adapted to the class as a whole.
2. Gather some magazine advertisements and bring them to class. Share your advertisements as a class or in groups. Speculate about the audiences for which they were intended. What attitudes are the advertisers trying to engage? Are they attempting to create beliefs? What tactics do they use? How effective do you think these tactics are?
3. As a group or individually, pretend you are the chief speech writer for each of the individuals listed below. Decide which audience subgroups you will need to address. What values, attitudes, and beliefs are they likely to hold? What can you say in your speech to engage their attention and support?
    a. The President of the United States addressing the nation on prime-time television concerning the latest international diplomacy development
    b. The president of your university student government welcoming freshmen to campus at the beginning of the academic year
    c. A defense lawyer conducting closing arguments in a jury trial for murder
    d. A ninth-grade teacher cautioning a class about the use of illegal drugs

Reference Notes

1. For more discussion, see Milton M. Rokeach, *Beliefs, Attitudes, and Values: A Theory of Organization and Change* (San Francisco: Jossey-Bass, 1968); and his *The Nature of Human Values* (New York: Collier-Macmillan, Free Press, 1973).
2. See Muzafer Sherif and Carl L. Hovland, *Social Judgment* (New Haven: Yale University Press, 1961).

3. Such changes during the course of a speech are often dramatic. See Robert D. Brooks and Thomas Scheidel, "Speech as Process: A Case Study," *Speech Monographs* 35 (1968): 1–7.

4. On adapting to feedback, see Paul D. Holtzman, *The Psychology of Speakers' Audiences* (Glenview, IL: Scott, Foresman, 1970), 33–36, 117.

5. See Robin M. Williams, "Changing Value Orientations and Beliefs on the American Scene," in *The Character of Americans: A Book of Readings,* rev. ed., Michael McGiffert, ed., (Homewood, IL: Dorsey Press, 1970), 212–30. Also remember that Gallup, Harris, and other polling organizations regularly issue reports on attitudes and values in America; check with the reference desk at your library.

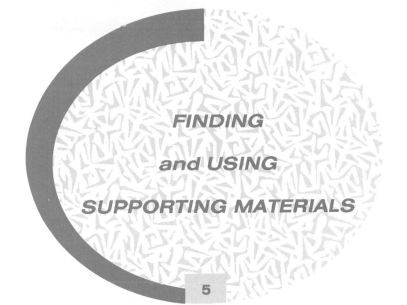

FINDING

and USING

SUPPORTING MATERIALS

5

Effective public speaking depends on more than the analysis of audience and occasion. Once you understand what you want to say and who your audience is, you must collect some substantive materials to fill out and support your ideas. If your purpose is to provide information on ways to seek employment, for example, you cannot simply assert the central idea "Summer employment opportunities are all around you." You must make it concrete; that central idea calls for examples of employment opportunities in your own community for students with various interests and talents. It also calls for precise information on how to obtain these jobs. Similarly, if you wish to argue "Nuclear power plants are unsafe and must be shut down," you should be ready to define "unsafe" precisely, to provide statistical and illustrative materials on the safety question, and to provide a plan for safely and practically shutting down existing facilities.

The forms of supporting materials identified in this chapter, therefore, are the medium of exchange between your ideas and the audience. Their functions are to amplify, clarify, or justify the beliefs, attitudes, and values you wish to convey to your listeners. These are the nutrients that bring your ideas to life and sustain them once they have been implanted in the minds of others. First we will define and illustrate the various types of supporting materials commonly used by speakers. Then we will suggest some possible ways of finding, recording, and using them.

FORMS OF SUPPORTING MATERIALS

The verbal supporting materials used to clarify, amplify, or justify your central ideas or claims can be divided into six categories: (1) explanation, (2) comparison and contrast, (3) illustration (hypothetical or factual), (4) specific instance, (5) statistics, and (6) testimony.

Explanation

An explanation is a description or expository passage that makes a term, concept, process, or proposal clear or acceptable. Explanations tell what, how, or why and are useful in showing the relationship between a whole and its parts. They also may give meaning to a difficult-to-envision concept.

For example, Vice-President and Director of the Health Care Policy and Program for Owens-Illinois, Inc., Richard J. Hanley, was attempting to help the Texas Medical Association understand what a "second opinion program" for insurance is and how it might affect doctors and patients. He needed a clear explanation, which follows:

> Let me describe how our second opinion program works. If a physician recommends that you have an elective surgical procedure that is on our mandatory second opinion list, you must call a toll-free number for assistance.
>
> The calls are handled by a staff of patient services coordinators, who are specially trained registered nurses. They can provide names of approved, board certified second-opinion physicians. Owens-Illinois currently has a panel of more than 2,000 physicians who have been approved to provide second opinions under our program. The list now includes more than a hundred here in Texas.
>
> The patient services coordinators also are available to answer questions to help clarify the decision facing the patient. Whether the second opinion confirms or disagrees with the first, the final decision is up to the patient.
>
> The list of mandatory second opinion procedures was developed with the advice of physicians and our insurance carriers. It is made up of procedures that are frequently recommended for conditions that may be amenable to other forms of treatment.
>
> These surgical procedures include: gallbladder, hernia, bunionectomy, knee, hysterectomy, prostate, cataract removal, nose surgery, varicose vein surgery, D&C, tonsils and adenoids, mastectomy, and back surgery.[1]

Computer technology has simplified the task of collecting supporting information literally by placing it at our fingertips.

In this explanation you can find many rhetorical factors at work: Mr. Hanley has (1) told *how* the procedure works, (2) mentioned *who* in Texas is a part of the program, (3) indicated *why* second opinions are required (in his reference to "other forms of treatment"), and (4) even listed *what* surgical procedures are covered. Especially for an audience of health care specialists, this explanation is particularly strong.

Although explanations are good ways to clarify an idea, they should not be too long or complicated. And, they should not have to carry the weight of your argument. For example, Mr. Hanley could be sure that, even after his explanation, some of the physicians needed more proof that second opinions would not undermine the authority of the first physician who offered an opinion and that second opinions would not significantly increase the cost of health care. Explanations clarify but seldom prove anything.

Comparison and Contrast

Comparisons point out similarities between something that is familiar to the audience and something that is not. Contrasts, on the other hand, clarify or support an idea by emphasizing differences.

Comparison

When used alone, comparisons are actually analogies connecting something already known or believed with an idea a speaker wishes to have understood or accepted. When, during the darkest days of the Civil War, critics attacked the administration's policies, Lincoln answered them by comparing the plight of the government with that of Blondin, a famous tightrope walker, attempting to cross the Niagara River:

> Gentlemen, I want you to suppose a case for a moment. Suppose that all the property you were worth was in gold, and you had put it in the hands of Blondin, the famous rope-walker, to carry across the Niagara Falls on a tightrope. Would you shake the rope while he was passing over it, or keep shouting to him, "Blondin, stoop a little more! Go a little faster!" No, I am sure you would not. You would hold your breath as well as your tongue, and keep your hands off until he was safely over. Now the government is in the same situation. It is carrying an immense weight across a stormy ocean. Untold treasures are in its hands. It is doing the best it can. Don't badger it! Just keep still, and it will get you safely over.

Contrast

Contrasts help clarify complex situations and processes by focusing on differences. A speaker explaining Australian football might want to contrast it with the rules governing football as it is played in the United States. To clarify Japanese Kabuki theater, a speaker may call on a theater system more familiar to the audience. Contrasts, further, can be used not only to clarify unfamiliar or complex problems, but also to strengthen arguments you wish to advance. Contrasts used as supporting material for propositions often employ examples, as in the case of a speech by George A. Biesel of Coe College. He was concerned about "orphan drugs," that is, drugs that can treat "small population diseases" but which are not manufactured by pharmaceutical companies because of low profitability. Contrasts helped him make his case:

> Why then aren't drug companies producing orphan drugs? The answer is simple—profit. Take for example this scenario. A doctor from the National Institute of Health has found a cure for a killer disease and is looking for a

company to market that cure. The offer is presented to a pharmaceutical company, which is told that only 25,000 people suffer from the disease. Immediately the door is closed, the request denied. The drug company is not interested in making a drug that will only be consumed by a limited number of people. To a pharmaceutical company, Valium, which can be consumed by 30 million people, is much more appealing than the haloperidol which would only be consumed by 10,000. The lack of profit creates more orphan drugs and leaves victims suffering.[2]

Comparison and Contrast Used in Combination

And finally, you can use comparisons and contrasts together so as to make statements about both of the contrasting ideas. For example, former U.S. Secretary of Health, Education, and Welfare Joseph A. Califano, Jr., traveled the country, addressing audiences composed of both smokers and nonsmokers. By combining comparisons and contrasts, he warned the smokers and psychologically reinforced the nonsmokers in this fashion:

> The tragic consequences of [smoking] are dramatically evident if we compare the later health consequences of smoking for two sixteen-year-olds: one who smokes a pack a day and one who does not. According to one estimate, the sixteen-year-old smoker has one chance in ten of developing a serious lung disease: lung cancer, emphysema, or chronic bronchitis, for example— providing he or she manages to avoid a crippling or killing heart attack. By contrast, the nonsmoker will have one chance in one hundred of contracting a serious lung disease, and will have only half the risk of the smoker of suffering a heart attack.[3]

Whatever the form of comparison or contrast used, at least one of the items should be familiar to the audience and distinct enough from the other that the difference is clear.

Illustration

A detailed narrative example of the idea or statement you wish to support is called an *illustration*. Sometimes an illustration describes or exemplifies a concept, condition, or circumstance; sometimes it shows or demonstrates the results of adopting a plan or proposal. Always, however, an illustration is an *extended example* presented in narrative form that has a striking or memorable quality.

There are two principal types of illustration: the *hypothetical* and the *factual*. The first tells a story that could have happened or probably will occur; the second tells what actually happened.

Hypothetical Illustration

A hypothetical illustration, although it is imaginary, must seem believable to the audience. Notice the details that Carl E. Bagge, President, National Coal Association, added to his story as he prepared to forecast the coal producers' fears and obstacles to growth by the year 2000:

> Exciting and important, [my] assignment also is challenging. All Mike [Schwartz, conference chair] has asked me to do is look 16 years into the future.
>
> To illustrate the challenge, I ask you to indulge me. Imagine a slight adjustment in time and purpose. Forget coal, but only for the time being, and 1984. Imagine we are at a nuclear technology conference in 1968—only 16 years ago.
>
> Imagine also that I am a nuclear power lobbyist instead of a coal digger. Since we have gone back 16 years, imagine I am 20 pounds lighter and my hair is darker just to round out the fantasy. My assignment now is to talk about trends and obstacles to nuclear power through the year 1985.
>
> First I would tell you that coal generation is all but dead, and I would prove it with projections and scholarly studies. I would dismiss it with the click of a slide projector switch. Coal is yesterday, I might have said.
>
> The only obstacle I would see to the advancement of nuclear generation would be the amount of electricity the United States could absorb. I might even crow some about how cheap this abundant power will be by 1985. I would brag that it will be so cheap we won't even bother to meter it.
>
> Moreover I would draw you a trend line for my product that, if plotted on a graph, would look like the ascending flight path of the space shuttle.
>
> And also everybody would have agreed with me.
>
> Yet today, on the eve of 1985, no new nuclear generating units are planned in the United States. Some that were not completed are being converted to coal. And the nuclear option is closed for the foreseeable future. It probably is closed well beyond the year 2000.[4]

Notice that Mr. Bagge has manipulated his illustration well in order to inject a little humor (about his weight and hair); to undercut one of his competitors (the nuclear lobby); and to make the point that the anticoal lobbyists have taken on coal before, will continue to attack coal, and yet (perhaps) will never get rid of it, thus protecting his own turf. But, of course, the fact that the speaker can manipulate such details may cause an audience to withhold acceptance of the story. When using a hypothetical illustration, be sure to let the audience know it is fictitious, and, as with explanations and comparisons, use it with other forms of support.

Factual Illustration

A factual illustration is a narrative that describes in detail a situation or incident that has actually occurred. Because details are brought into the story and because the incident actually happened, the factual illustration frequently has high persuasive value.

In a speech calling for the development of more creative industrial leaders, P. L. Smith, President and Chief Executive Officer of the General Foods Corporation, supported his call with the following factual illustration:

> An illustration of the fundamental importance of leadership is present at the Chrysler Co. Lee Iococca [sic] has turned this company around. Few of the environmental factors have changed significantly since Chrysler was on the brink of bankruptcy. They're still facing pretty much the same competition, the same taxes, the same unions, the same regulations.
>
> But what they have now is the vision and the commitment of one man—the leader at the top. And through the force of his personality, he has built a leadership team and influenced the behavior of employees, suppliers, investors, customers and even the government. This has turned around a $13-billion company with 80,000 jobs at stake.
>
> That's an incredible accomplishment! And it was done through leadership.[5]

Mr. Smith uses this extended illustration to visualize his central claim. He then goes on with a series of specific instances to supply additional proof for his claim.

Guidelines for Choosing Illustrations

Three considerations should be kept in mind when selecting illustrations, hypothetical or factual. *Is it clearly related to the idea it is intended to support?* If the connection is difficult to show, the illustration will not accomplish its goal. *Is it a fair example?* An audience can be quick to notice unusual circumstances in an illustration; if you have focused on the exceptional case, your illustration will not be convincing. *Is it vivid and impressive in detail?* If this quality is absent, the advantage of using an illustration is lost. So, be sure your illustrations are pointed, fair, and vivid.

Specific Instance

A specific instance is an *undeveloped* illustration or example. Instead of describing a situation in detail, it merely mentions the person or event in question. Speakers use specific instances to clarify ideas. You might use a specific instance by saying, "You're all familiar with the pop machine that stands just inside this building's front door; half of you stop after class for a soda or can of juice. It suggests the topic of my speech today—the impact of machined fast food on the American diet." Or, you can use a series of specific instances to help establish a point. Arthur H. Goldberg, former U.S. Secretary of Labor and now President of Integrated Resources, Inc., used several specific instances to demonstrate how widespread interest in his topic was:

> Over the past year or so there has been a great deal of criticism of tax shelters. Here are headlines of some recent articles: "Billions Diverted from Government are Distorting the U.S. Economy." "The Fellow Who Sold the Brooklyn Bridge to Tourists Might Have Done Better Packaging Syndications." "Syndicators Load Real Estate Bases."
> What I'd like to address today is whether these criticisms are justified, or are tax shelters misunderstood?[6]

If the names, events, or situations you cite are well known or believable to your listeners, specific instances can aid comprehension or generate proof for an idea. However, on subjects with which listeners are not familiar or on which there are marked differences of opinion, specific instances must be supplemented with other forms of support.

Statistics

Not all figures are statistics; some numbers are used merely for counting. Statistics are figures that show *relationships* among phenomena; they emphasize largeness or smallness (magnitudes), describe subclasses or parts (segments), and establish direction (trends). Because statistics reduce great masses of information into general categories, they are useful both in clarifying a situation and in substantiating a potentially disputable claim.[7]

Magnitudes

Statistics can be used to describe the seriousness of a problem in a relatively brief space. Paul Tippett, Chairman and Chief Executive Officer, American Motors Corporation, when answering charges of excessive profits in the automobile industry, used magnitudes in that way:

> With the prospect of billion-dollar profits this year, people seem to have forgotten not only that we lost more than $4 billion in 1980 alone . . . but that our combined investments in retooling and product development for that *same* year came to *eleven-and-a-half* billion dollars. For 1981, we lost $1.3 billion and invested another twelve-and-a-half billion.

We still haven't broken even against those losses and investment outlays. Total *losses* and *investments* for the Big Four companies during the years 1980–83 came to $42 billion. That's $42 billion in the accounts payable column, versus six-and-a-half billion in the earnings column for the first six months of this year.[8]

Segments

Statistics also can be used to isolate the parts of a problem or to show aspects of a problem caused by discrete factors. In discussing sources of income for a college or university, for example, you might segment the income by indicating what percentage comes from tuition and fees, how much from state and federal money, how much from gifts and contributions, how much from special fees such as tickets, and how much from miscellaneous sources. Then you would be in a position to talk reasonably about next year's proposed tuition hike. Similarly, in arguing that there is a connection between the American way of life and profit making, Charles Wohlstetter, Chairman of Continental Telecom, Inc., wanted to destroy the myth that rich people do not pay taxes. In a speech to the International Platform Association, which had just named him "Business Speaker of the Year," Mr. Wohlstetter said:

> The top 10% [of the U.S. taxpayers], 9.5 million income earners, paid 48.7% of all individual taxes.
> There were 95 million individual tax returns filed, so that equates to 10% of the income earners paying almost 50% of the taxes:
> —The upper 50% in income paid 92.6% of all the personal income taxes.
> —The lower 50% of income earners—those with income of $14,499 or less—paid only 7.4% of the individual Federal income tax bill.
> Unfortunately, you are more likely to be caressed by "Mr. T" than you are to find such facts reported.[9]

Note Mr. Wohlstetter's strategic use of segments to make a point. He focuses on individual taxes rather than corporate taxation (where, of course, most recent agitation for reform has been occurring). And, he focuses on the top 10 percent of the taxpayers (average income of $48,500 and higher), who make much, much more *above* the average U.S. income—$15,000—than the lower 10 percent makes *below* it. Naturally, then, one would expect their tax burden to be considerably greater than those below the poverty line. He even adds a comparison—the reference to being caressed by Mr. T—to give his segmentation a little humorous reinforcement. Overall, Mr. Wohlstetter uses segments very effectively to support his point.

Finally, statistics often are used to describe directions, or trends, indications of where we have been and where we are going. Worrying about deficit financing in the United States, James L. Clayton, Dean of the Graduate School, University of Utah, coordinated trends in "structural deficits," federal deficit borrowing, and federal debts as a percentage of Gross National Product to show that three major indicators of debt all agreed that we are in trouble:

> First, federal debt has been increasing rapidly in recent years no matter how it is measured. [1] Structural deficits, i.e., what the deficit would be assuming the level of unemployment is at or below 6 percent, average 1 percent in the 1960s, 2 percent in the 1970s, and more than 3 percent since 1980. [2] Federal borrowing consumed about 30 percent of private savings in the 1970s and consumes about 50 percent today. Moreover, most of the major forecasts place the federal deficit in the $150–$200 billion range for the next 3 years, which is about as far as anyone can see, assuming current policies and realistic growth rates. [3] Federal debt levels are now rising as a percentage of GNP, whereas they fell from World War II to the mid 1970s. Federal debt was 35 percent of GNP in 1974. It is 45 percent of GNP today, and is forecast by the Office of Management and Budget to rise to 50 percent of GNP by 1987, assuming current policies continue.[10]

In using statistics, keep the following cautions in mind:

1. *Translate difficult-to-comprehend numbers into more immediately understandable terms.* In a speech on the mounting problem of solid waste, Carl Hall pictured the immensity of 130 million tons of garbage by indicating that trucks loaded with that amount would extend from coast to coast.[11]

2. *Round off complicated numbers.* "Nearly 400,000" is easier to comprehend than "396,456"; "over 33 percent" usually is preferable to "33.4 percent" and "over one third" probably is better than either of them in most situations.

3. *Whenever possible, use visual materials to clarify complicated statistical trends or summaries.* Hand out a mimeographed sheet of numbers, draw graphs on the chalkboard, or prepare a chart in advance. Then you can concentrate on explaining the significance of numbers rather than using all of your time merely reporting them.

4. *Use statistics fairly.* Arguing that professional women's salaries increased 12.4 percent last year may sound impressive to listeners, until they realize that women still are generally paid almost a quarter less than men for equivalent work. Provide fair contexts for your data.

Testimony

When you cite the opinions or conclusions of others, you are using *testimony*. Sometimes testimony merely adds weight or impressiveness to an idea, as when you quote a witty saying from *Bartlett's Dictionary of Familiar Quotations*. At other times it lends credibility, or believability, to an assertion, especially when it comes from an expert witness. Donald N. Dedmon, President of Radford University in Virginia, uses testimony in this way to underscore the fact that fewer students these days are interested in developing a philosophy of life than there were ten years ago:

> [A]ccording to Jon D. Miller, director of the Public Opinion Laboratory at Northern Illinois University, "The social and political attitudes of college students change surprisingly little during their college years." According to Alexander Astin last year, "about 44 percent of the freshmen believe(d) it (was) important to develop a meaningful philosophy of life, down from about 70 percent a decade ago."[12]

Tests of Authority

All testimony should meet the twin tests of pertinence and audience acceptability. When used to strengthen a statement, rather than merely to amplify or illustrate, testimony also should satisfy four more specific criteria:

1. The person quoted should be qualified, by training and experience, to speak on the field being discussed.

2. Whenever possible, the authority's statement should be based on firsthand knowledge. An Iowa farmer is not an authority on a South Carolina drought unless he or she has personally observed the conditions.

3. The judgment expressed should not be unduly influenced by personal interest. Asking a political opponent to comment on the current president's job performance will likely yield biased opinion.

4. The listeners should realize that the person quoted actually *is* an authority. In President Dedmon's statement, we found out who Jon D. Miller is, but he neglected to tell us the qualifications of Alexander Astin.

When citing testimony, do not use big names simply because they are well known. A TV star's opinion on the nutritional value of a breakfast cereal is less reliable than the opinion of a registered dietician. The best testimony comes from subject-matter experts whose qualifications your listeners recognize.

Finally, always acknowledge the source of an idea or particular phrasing. Do not be guilty of *plagiarism*—claiming someone else's ideas, information, or phraseology as your own. That is stealing—hardly a way to bolster your credibility. When you are caught, your trustworthiness rating drops off the bottom of the scale; an audience likely will never trust you again. So, cite your sources; give them credit for the material and yourself credit for taking the time to look something up.

SOURCES OF SUPPORTING MATERIALS

For most speeches, you will have to do some research to get sufficient supporting materials. Several sources are available to you: interviews with experts, letters and questionnaires, publications of all kinds, broadcasts, and computerized library searches.

Interviews

Beginning speakers often fail to recognize that useful and authoritative information may be gathered merely by asking questions of the right people. Are you talking about interplanetary navigation? Then interview a member of your college's astronomy department. If you are interested in the growth of the T-shirt industry, talk with the proprietor of a local shop. Brief interviews, especially if they are well planned, frequently yield valuable factual data and authoritative pieces of testimony. For some tips on how to handle an interview, see Chapter 15.

Letters and Questionnaires

If you are unable to talk with an expert directly, you sometimes can obtain the information you need through correspondence. You might, for example, write to your senator for information regarding a pending bill in the legislature or to the Kellogg Company in Battle Creek, Michigan, for data on the amounts of sugars and sodium in its products. When you use this method, be sure that you make clear exactly what information you want and why you want it. Moreover, be reasonable—do not expect a busy person to spend hours or days gathering facts for you. Above all, do not ask for information that you could find if you searched for it.

On other occasions, you may wish to discover what a group of people knows or thinks about a subject. If, for example, you wanted to give a speech on a proposed nuclear power plant, you could sample public opinion in the vicinity with a questionnaire. You might wish to send it to people

AVOIDING PLAGIARISM

"The band for which the grandstand roots,
is not made up of substitutes . . ."

—Burma Shave billboard

One of the saddest things an instructor has to do on occasion is to cite a student for plagiarism. In the beginning speech class, students occasionally take articles from *Reader's Digest, Newsweek* or *Time, Senior Scholastic,* or other easy-to-reach source, not realizing how many speech teachers habitually scan the library periodicals section. Even if the teacher has not read the article, it soon becomes apparent to most of the class that something is wrong—the wording is not similar to the way the person usually talks (see the section on "Oral Style" in Chapter 8), the speech doesn't have a decent introduction or conclusion, and the organizational pattern is not one normally used by speakers. Often, too, the person who plagiarizes an article usually reads it aloud badly, another sign that something is wrong.

Plagiarism includes more, too, than simply undocumented verbatim quotation. Because "plagiarism is the unacknowledged inclusion of someone else's words, ideas, or data as one's own" ("Academic Honesty & Dishonesty" pamphlet, Louisiana State University, adapted from LSU's *Code of Student Conduct,* 1981), it includes (1) undocumented paraphrases of others' ideas and (2) undocumented use of others' main ideas. So, for example, if you paraphrase a movie review from *Newsweek* without acknowledging that David Ansen had those insights, or if you use the motivated sequence to analyze a speech without giving credit to Alan Monroe for setting it up, you're guilty of plagiarism.

Suppose you ran across the following quotation from Kenneth Clark's *Civilisation: A Personal View* (New York: Harper & Row, 1969), speaking of eighteenth-century England: "It was the age of great country houses. In 1722 the most splendid of all had just been completed for Marlborough, the general who had been victorious over Voltaire's country: not the sort of idea that would have worried Voltaire in the least, as he thought of all war as a ridiculous waste of human life and effort. When Voltaire saw Blenheim Palace he said, 'What a great heap of stone, without charm or taste,' and I can see what he means. To anyone brought up on Mansart and Perrault, Blenheim must have seemed painfully lacking in order and propriety. . . . Perhaps this is because the architect, Sir John Vanbrugh, although a man of genius, was really an amateur. Moreover, he was a natural romantic, a castle-builder, who didn't care a fig for good taste and decorum" (p. 172). The following examples illustrate plagiarism and suggest ways to avoid it:

    1. *Verbatim quotation of a passage:* (read it aloud word for word).

    To avoid plagiarism: "Kenneth Clark, in his 1969 book, *Civilisation: A Personal View,* said the following about the architecture of great country estates in eighteenth-century England: [then quote the paragraph]."

2. *Undocumented use of the main ideas:* "In eighteenth-century England there was a great flurry of building. Country estates were built essentially by amateurs such as Sir John Vanbrugh, who built the splendid Blenheim Palace for General Marlborough. Voltaire didn't like war and he didn't like Blenheim, which he called a great heap of stone without charm or taste. He preferred the order and variety of houses designed by French architects Mansart and Perrault."

To avoid plagiarism: "In his book *Civilisation: A Personal View,* Sir Kenneth Clark makes the point that eighteenth-century English country houses were built essentially by amateurs. He uses as an example Sir John Vanbrugh, who designed Blenheim Palace for the Duke of Marlborough. Clark notes that when Voltaire saw the house he said, 'What a great heap of stone, without charm or taste.' Clark can understand that reaction from a Frenchman who was raised on the neoclassical designs of Mansart and Perrault. Clark explains the English style as arising from what he calls 'natural' romanticism."

3. *Undocumented paraphrasing:* "The eighteenth century was the age of wonderful country houses. In 1722 the most beautiful one in England was built for Marlborough, the general who had won over France. When Voltaire saw the Marlborough house, called Blenheim Palace, he said it was a great heap of stone. . . ."

To avoid plagiarism: use the same kind of language noted under example 2, giving Clark credit for his impressions.

So, do not plagiarize. Avoid the risk of being caught and the suspicion that you are untrustworthy. Plagiarizing may get you expelled from school, and it will destroy your reputation.

TO READ: Read your school's "student life" or "code of conduct" publication or other source that discusses ethical conduct. If none is published, then check with the Dean's office (Dean of Students or Dean of Academic Affairs, whichever is appropriate) to find out how plagiarism cases are handled at your school.

randomly chosen from the town's phone directory, circulate it through a dorm or classroom, or even administer it in person to passersby on a street corner. In this way, you could construct your own statistical segments and magnitudes from your own school and community. When developing a questionnaire, be sure it has an introduction that explains the exact purpose and the procedures to be followed in answering the questions. Keep it short, or people will throw it away. If you mail it, include a self-addressed, stamped envelope to help guarantee returns to you. And, when conducting the survey in person, be polite and ask for only a small amount of time.

Printed Materials

The most common source of supporting materials is the printed word—newspapers, magazines, pamphlets, and books. Through the careful use of a library—and with the help of reference librarians—you can discover an almost overwhelming amount of materials relevant to your speech subject and purpose.

Newspapers

Newspapers are obviously a useful source of information about events of current interest. Moreover, their feature stories and accounts of unusual happenings provide a storehouse of interesting illustrations and examples. You must be careful, of course, not to accept as true everything printed in a newspaper, for the haste with which news sometimes must be gathered makes complete accuracy difficult. Your school or city library undoubtedly keeps on file copies of one or two highly reliable papers, such as *The New York Times, The Observer, The Wall Street Journal,* or the *Christian Science Monitor,* and probably also a selection from among the leading newspapers of your state or region. If your library has *The New York Times,* it is likely to have the published index to that paper. By using this resource, you can locate accounts of people and events from 1913 to the present. Yet another useful and well-indexed source of information on current happenings is *Facts on File,* issued weekly since 1940.

Magazines

An average-sized university library subscribes annually to hundreds of magazines and journals. Some—such as *Time, Newsweek,* and *U.S. News and World Report*—summarize weekly events. *The Atlantic* and *Harper's* are representative of a group of monthly publications that cover a wide range of subjects of both passing and permanent importance. Such magazines as *The Nation, Vital Speeches of the Day, Fortune, Washington Monthly,* and *The New Republic* contain comment on current political, social, and economic questions. For more specialized areas, there are such magazines as *Popular Science, Scientific American, Sports Illustrated, Field and Stream, Ms., Better Homes and Gardens, Today's Health, National Geographic,* and *American Heritage.*

This list is, of course, merely suggestive of the wide range of materials to be found in periodicals. When you are looking for a specific kind of information, use the *Readers' Guide to Periodical Literature,* which indexes most of the magazines you will want to refer to in preparing a speech. Or,

Materials for Verbally Supporting an Idea

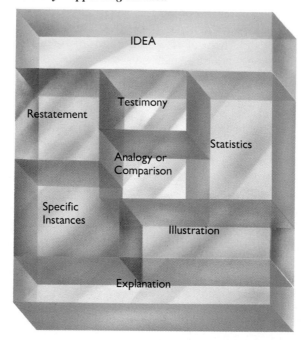

if you wish more sophisticated material, consult the *Social Science Index* and the *Humanities Index*. Similar indexes also are available for technical journals, publications from professional societies, and the like; a reference librarian can show you how to use them.

Yearbooks and Encyclopedias

The most reliable source of comprehensive data is the *Statistical Abstracts of the United States*, which covers a wide variety of subjects ranging from weather records and birth rates to steel production and election results. Unusual data on Academy Award winners, world records in various areas, and the "bests" and "worsts" of almost anything can be found in the *World Almanac, The People's Almanac, The Guinness Book of World Records, The Book of Lists*, and *Information Please*. Encyclopedias such as the *Encyclopaedia Britannica* and *Americana Encyclopedia*, which attempt to cover the entire field of human knowledge, are valuable chiefly as an initial reference source or for background reading. Refer to them for important scientific, geographical, literary, or historical facts; for bibliographies of authoritative books on a subject; and for ideas you will not develop completely in your speech.

Documents and Reports

Various governmental agencies—state, national, and international— as well as many independent organizations publish reports on special subjects. Among governmental publications, those most frequently consulted are the hearings and recommendations of congressional committees or those of the United States Departments of Health and Human Services and of Commerce. Reports on issues related to agriculture, business, government, engineering, and scientific experimentation are published by many state universities. Such endowed groups as the Carnegie, Rockefeller, and Ford Foundations and such special interest groups as the Foreign Policy Association, the Brookings Institution, the League of Women Voters, Common Cause, and the United States Chamber of Commerce also publish reports and pamphlets. Though by no means a complete list of all such pamphlets and reports, *The Vertical File Index* does offer you a guide to some of these materials.

Books

There are few subjects suitable for a speech on which someone has not written a book. As a guide to these books, use the subject-matter headings in the card catalog of your libraries. Generally, you will find authoritative books in your school library and more popularized treatments in your city's public library.

Biographies

The Dictionary of National Biography (deceased Britishers), the *Dictionary of American Biography* (deceased Americans), *Who's Who* (living Britishers), *Who's Who in America, Current Biography,* and more specialized works organized by field contain biographical sketches especially useful in locating facts about famous people and in documenting the qualifications of authorities whose testimony you may quote.

Radio and Television Broadcasts

Lectures, discussions, and the formal public addresses of leaders in government, business, education, and religion are frequently broadcast over radio or television. Many of these talks are later mimeographed or printed by the stations or by the organizations that sponsor them. Usually, as in the case of CBS's *Meet the Press* or National Public Radio's *All Things Considered,* copies may be obtained for a small fee. If no manuscript is available, you may want to audiotape the program (as long as you make no public use of that tape) or to take careful notes. When taking notes, listen with particular care in order to get an exact record of the speaker's words and meaning. Just as you must quote items from printed sources accurately and honestly, so are you obligated to respect the remarks someone has made on a radio or television program and to give that person full credit.

Computerized Searches

Finally, your library may subscribe to one or more computerized data bases. These function much like a printed index. To access a data base, you will need to work with a reference librarian in determining what *descriptors* (key words) to enter. An average-sized university library probably will have access to upward of two hundred data files, such as ERIC, BIOSIS, PsychInfo, AGRICOLA, Datrex, and MEDLINE.

You also might be able to use one or more of the available public data bases. For example, BRS/After Dark is available by subscription to those with personal computers and a modem (a communication device that links computers through phone lines); CompuServe, The Source, and Dow Jones News/Retrieval are other major consumer-oriented data base services that can be accessed through a modem and computer hookup.

These sources can be valuable time-savers, as they will search for and print lists of articles available in your specific research area. However, data bases involve expense. Libraries often charge for computer time spent in searching and printing your information, and public data bases charge an initial fee plus per-hour charges for online time. Yet, in an age of information explosion, they can save you a tremendous amount of time and put you in contact with far more material than you could reasonably assemble using only a card catalog and a few reference works.

> 66 *Computerized searches can yield a tremendous amount of information—sometimes, in fact, too much. David decided to search the Social Science/Humanities Index data base for information relevant to a speech on TV news rating systems. As one of his descriptors, he chose the word 'television.' When he ran the search, the program came up with thirty-*

two single-spaced pages of references from the last eight years. Not only did the data search cost David almost fifty dollars, it provided so much extraneous material that he asked to delay his speech a period so he could sort through his search. David should have chosen his descriptors more carefully. Had he used 'news' and 'television ratings' as coordinated descriptors, he would have had to deal with less information, and it would have been relevant.

Obviously, you will not have to investigate all of the foregoing sources of materials for every speech you make. Again, as in audience analysis, the key concept is *relevance:* Go to the sources that will yield relevant materials. Historical statistics are more likely to be found in print materials than in a television program; a viewpoint on a local problem, in an interview rather than a computer search. Use your head in selecting sources of materials to investigate, and then carry out the search carefully. If you do, you will minimize the time needed to find solid materials and yet make your speech authoritative and interesting.

RECORDING INFORMATION

When you find the information you have been looking for, either make a photocopy of it or take notes. Whether you keep your notes on 4×6 cards or in a notebook, it is helpful to have an accurate and legible record of the materials you wish to consider using in your speech. An incomplete source citation makes it difficult to find the information again, which can drive you crazy; hurried scribbles, too, are hard to decipher later. Many people find that notecards are easier to use than a notebook because they can be shuffled by topic area or type of support. If you do use a notebook, however, try to record each item on half of each page. Since most of your information will not fill a page, this will save paper; cutting the sheets in half will make it easier to sort your data or adopt a classification scheme and record information in accordance with particular themes or subpoints of your speech. When preparing notecards, place the appropriate subject headings at the top of the card and the complete source citation at the bottom. This way, the card can be classified by general subject (top right heading) and by specific information presented (top left heading).

Sample Notecards

Specific
Information

General Subject —— HOW LANGUAGE CHANGES   How words find new meaning
                                                and are placed in dictionaries

"The first cite for streaking [in the files of the Webster's
dictionary editors] dated February 24, 1974, comes from a
piece in the Springfield Sunday Republican about shenanigans
at the University of Massachusetts at Amherst. (Until then,
streaking had been what sixties-era hairdressers were doing
to the tresses of young women in white lipstick and mini-
skirts.) The word hit the New York Times in March, and in
May an editor found it in a Newsweek article describing
how in 1776 a giddy bunch of Continental Army soldiers
mortified Brooklyn ladies by racing around out of uniform.
But not until 1981, when streaking made the addendum to the
[Webster's] Third International, did this new definition of
the word don respectable garb."

Source —— Karen Donovan, "No Word Surprises Me," New England Monthly
(October 1984): 14.

Specific Information —— THE DISCOVERY OF LASER LIGHT

General Subject ——
                                                The inventor speaks

"The laser was born early one beautiful spring morning
on a park bench in Washington, D.C. As I sat in Franklin
Square, musing and admiring the azaleas, an idea came
to me for a practical way to obtain a very pure form of
electromagnetic waves from molecules. I had been doggedly
searching for new ways to produce radio waves at very
high frequencies, too high for the vacuum tubes of the day
to generate. This short wave-length radiation, I felt,
would permit extremely accurate measurement and analysis,
giving new insights into physics and chemistry. As it
turned out, I was much too conservative; the field has
developed beyond my imagination and along paths I
could not have foreseen at the time. . . . But in the
Spring of 1951, as I sat on my park bench, it was all
yet to come."

Source —— Charles H. Townes, "Harnessing Light," Science 84
(November 1984): 153.

USING SUPPORTING MATERIALS

Once you have searched out potential materials for your speech, you must decide when to use them and which types to employ.

Generally, supporting materials should be used when listeners will not accept an idea just because it is presented. Listeners reject what they have trouble believing. You should ask yourself if each idea needs to be clarified, amplified, or strengthened before listeners will accept it. If your answer is "yes," you need to use supporting materials. Sometimes two or more types of support are combined, as when statistics are used to develop an illustration or when the testimony of an authority is given to strengthen or verify an explanation. At other times they may be used singly. Remember that if the audience will not accept your supportive ideas, they will reject the central idea or claim of your speech. Rather than risk rejection, use supporting materials for each main statement.

- Which form of support to use depends on the complexity of the idea and on the kind of audience you are addressing. Any of the forms of support may be used to clarify, to amplify, or to strengthen. However, some forms tend to accomplish those purposes better than others and are more effective with particular audiences.

- Explanation, comparison, contrast, specific instance, and segment statistics are especially helpful in clarifying an idea. These materials allow the speaker to present information that simplifies an idea for the audience, and they are useful when listeners have little background or knowledge about the topic or when the subject matter is complex.

- Explanation, comparison, contrast, hypothetical and factual illustration, and magnitude and trend statistics may help the speaker amplify an idea, expanding on it so the audience can better examine the concept. These forms of support may be especially useful when the audience has only a slight knowledge of the concept.

- To strengthen or lend credibility to a point, you may want to use factual illustration, specific instances, statistics, and testimony. These forms strengthen the idea by making it vivid and believable. These techniques are beneficial when the audience is hostile or when acceptance of a particular idea is critical to the overall purpose of the speech.

- Finally, be sure that the forms of support you select do *support* the ideas. If the materials used as supports do not clarify, amplify, or strengthen, they may not be applicable to the point being developed. Test the relevancy of each supporting unit to be sure it contributes to the acceptance of the idea being developed.

Following are two outlines that illustrate how supporting materials can be used. In the first outline, note how the speaker has combined verbal and visual material to establish and develop the main point. In this speech, the supportive materials are used to amplify the idea.

. . . . **S**ample **O**utline *for an Informative Speech* . . . . . .

HOW WE BREATHE

Explanation   I. The human breathing mechanism may be likened to a bellows which expands to admit air and contracts to expel it.
    A. When we inhale, two things happen.
       1. Muscles attached to the collarbone and shoulder bones pull upward and slightly outward.
       2. Muscles in the abdominal wall relax, allowing the diaphragm—a sheet of muscle and tendon lying immediately below the lungs—to fall.
    B. This permits the spongy, porous material of which the lungs consist to expand.
       1. A vacuum is created.
       2. Air rushes in.
    C. When we exhale, two things happen also.
       1. Gravity causes the rib cage to move downward.
       2. Muscles in the abdominal wall contract, squeezing the diaphragm upward.
    D. The space available to the lungs is thus reduced.
       1. The lungs are squeezed.
       2. Air is emitted.

Comparison   E. The similarity between the breathing mechanism and a bellows is represented in this diagram:

Visual aid   *Show "How We Breathe" Diagram*

Restatement of main idea   F. In summary, then, to remember how the human breathing mechanism works, think of a bellows.
       1. Just as increasing the size of the bellows bag allows air to rush in, so increasing the space available to the lungs allows them to admit air.
       2. Just as squeezing the bellows bag forces air out, so contracting the space the lungs can occupy forces air to be emitted.

Visual Aid: How We Breathe

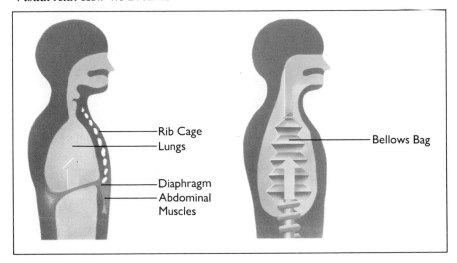

Study the following outline. Notice that the supporting materials are used to strengthen each of the points in the speech. The audience would be unlikely to accept these ideas without further development. Although the proof of a single point may not require the use of supportive materials as numerous or varied as those used in this outline, they are presented here to show how a number of different forms may be combined.

Sample Outline *for a Persuasive Speech*

CABLE TELEVISION—AT YOUR SERVICE!

Claim	I. Cable television soon will revolutionize your everyday life.
First supporting statement: hypothetical illustration	A. Suppose, on a rainy day a few years from now, you decide to "run" your errands from your living room.
	1. You turn on your two-way communication unit and begin your round of errands:
Specific instances within the illustration	a. On Channel 37, your bank's computer verifies the amount of a recent withdrawal.
	b. On Channel 26, you ask the telephone company to review last month's long-distance charges.

c. On Channel 94, a supermarket lets you scan products, prices, and home-delivery hours.

d. On Channel 5, you study a list of proposed changes in the city charter.

1. You can "call in" for further information.

2. You can vote from your own home.

e. Channel 106 gives you access to resource personnel at the public library.

Restatement of supporting statement

2. Thus—with "cable television at your service"— you have accomplished your day's errands with minimum expenditure of time, gas, and parking-meter money.

Second supporting statement
Specific instances

B. These possibilities, once thought of only as dreams, are becoming actualities across the United States.

1. Most cities have public-access channels filled with local talent and ethnic programming.

2. Ann Arbor, Michigan, and Columbus, Ohio, have been leasing channels to private firms and public utility companies.

Third supporting statement

C. Cable television soon will be available to virtually every household in the United States at a reasonable cost.

Comparison

1. Because the cost is shared by licensee and house-holder alike, no one bears an excessive burden.

Statistics

a. Commercial users find that leasing a channel costs little more than their computer-accounting systems and print/electronic advertising services.

b. Studio facilities for the public-access channels are made available at cost in most cable television contracts—normally about $30 per hour.

c. Current installation charges range from $15 to $50.

d. Monthly rental fees per household seldom exceed $15 for basic cable service.

Explanation combined with specific instances

2. The technical characteristics of cable television render it inexpensive.

a. Some existent telephone lines and equipment can be used.

b. The conversion box mounts easily on a regular television set.

c. Studio costs are minimal.

1. Relatively inexpensive 1/2″ videotape and broadcasting equipment can be used.

	2. Engineering and production personnel need minimal training for cable systems.
Restatement of claim	D. Given actual and potential uses, plus the positive cost-benefit ratio, cable television will revolutionize your daily life.
Comparison	1. Just as the wheel extended our legs and the computer our central nervous system, so will cable television extend our communicative capabilities.
Testimony used as restatement of main idea	2. In the words of Wendy Lee, communication consultant to new cable-television franchises: "We soon will be a nation wired fully for sight and sound. We will rid ourselves of the need for short shopping trips; we will cut the lines in doctors' offices; and we will put the consumer and the constituent into the front offices of his or her corporate suppliers and political servants. The telephone and the motor car will become obsolete."

● ●

CHAPTER SUMMARY

The primary forms of supporting materials are *explanation, comparison and contrast, illustration* (hypothetical and factual), *specific instance, statistics* (magnitudes, segments, and trends), and *testimony.* Those materials can be gathered through *interviews* or *letters and questionnaires* or by searching *printed materials* (newspapers, magazines, yearbooks and encyclopedias, documents and reports, books, and biographies); *radio and television broadcasts;* and *computer data bases.* Record the information you find either on notecards or on notebook pages, and use it as supporting material to *clarify, amplify,* and *strengthen* your presentation. Supporting materials should be used in both informative and persuasive speeches.

Oral Activities

1. Prepare and deliver a four- to five-minute informative speech, including at least three different kinds of supporting materials. If your instructor wishes, also turn in an outline for the speech, identifying the kinds of supporting materials used and including a bibliography of sources consulted. You may be asked, as well, to turn in notecards documenting your supporting materials.

2. Working in groups of five, meet in the reference room of your library. Each member is to locate two of the items in the left-hand column of the following list. First, determine which of the sources listed in the right-hand column contains the material you need. When you locate your items, show your group the source, indicate where it is shelved, and record the information to be turned in to your instructor.

a. Weekly summary of current national news

b. Brief sketch of the life of Henry Ford

c. Description of a specific traffic accident

d. Explanation of major Native American tribes

e. Text of Ronald Reagan's latest State of the Union address

Congressional Record

Time

Vital Speeches of the Day

Book Review Digest

Oxford English Dictionary

local newspaper

Who's Who

Statistical Abstracts

Encyclopedia Americana

The New York Times

Reference Notes

1. From "Cost Containment of Health Care: The Responsibility of Employers and Doctors" by Richard J. Hanley, from *Vital Speeches of the Day,* Volume L, November 15, 1984. Reprinted by permission of Vital Speeches of the Day.
2. From "The Unknown Orphan" by George A. Biesel. Reprinted from *Winning Orations,* by special arrangement with the Interstate Oratorical Association, Larry Schnoor, Executive Secretary, Mankato State College, Mankato, Minnesota.
3. From "Adolescents: Their Needs and Problems" by Joseph A. Califano, Jr., from *Vital Speeches of the Day,* Volume XLIV, August 15, 1978. Reprinted by permission of Vital Speeches of the Day.
4. From "Coming to Grips with the Underlying Problem" by Carl E. Bagge, from *Vital Speeches of the Day,* Volume LI, February 15, 1985. Reprinted by permission of Vital Speeches of the Day.
5. From "Leadership in the Creative Process" by P. L. Smith, from *Vital Speeches of the Day,* Volume L, October 15, 1984. Reprinted by permission of Vital Speeches of the Day.
6. From "Tax Shelters: Their Economic and Social Role" by Arthur H. Goldberg, from *Vital Speeches of the Day,* Volume L, November 15, 1984. Reprinted by permission of Vital Speeches of the Day.

7. For a technical yet rewarding introduction to statistical analysis, see John Waite Bowers and John A. Courtright, *Communication Research Methods* (Glenview, IL: Scott, Foresman and Company, 1984).

8. From "'If I Am Not for Myself . . .'" by Paul Tippett, from *Vital Speeches of the Day*, Volume L, October 15, 1984. Reprinted by permission of Vital Speeches of the Day.

9. From "The Urge to Self-Destruct" by Charles Wohlstetter, from *Vital Speeches of the Day*, Volume L, November 1, 1984. Reprinted by permission of Vital Speeches of the Day.

10. From "Why Can't We Hear the Distant Thunder?" by James L. Clayton, from *Vital Speeches of the Day*, Volume L, November 15, 1984. Reprinted by permission of Vital Speeches of the Day.

11. From "A Heap of Trouble" by Carl Hall. Reprinted from *Winning Orations,* by special arrangement with the Interstate Oratorical Association, Larry Schnoor, Executive Secretary, Mankato State College, Mankato, Minnesota.

12. From "Scrutinizing Education in the U.S." by Donald N. Dedmon, from *Vital Speeches of the Day*, Volume L, November 1, 1984. Reprinted by permission of Vital Speeches of the Day.

ARRANGING

and

OUTLINING RELATED POINTS

6

If a speech, whatever its type or purpose, is to communicate your thoughts to an audience, it must satisfy at least five general criteria:

1. *The plan of the speech must be easy for the audience to grasp and remember.* If listeners have difficulty seeing how your ideas fit together or if the ideas are joined in ways that do not immediately make sense to them, their attention will wander from your ideas and will focus instead on untangling your remarks.

2. *The pattern must provide for a full and balanced coverage of the material.* You must use a pattern that will complement the ideas and their supporting materials, one that will enhance your ability to clarify your central idea or defend your claim.

3. *The structure of the speech should be appropriate to the occasion.* As we noted in Chapter 1, there are some occasions or settings where speakers are expected to observe group traditions. Presidential inaugural addresses, for example, tend to follow a particular format originally created by our first presidents. Likewise, eulogies and speeches of introduction normally consider themes in an order that members of our culture have come to expect.

4. *The structure of a speech should be adapted to the audience's needs and level of knowledge.* Some of the patterns we will describe are particularly well suited to listeners who have little background on a subject, while others are useful when the audience is interested and knowledgeable about the subject under discussion. Thus, as you review the patterns that follow, select one that matches your audience's needs and informational background.

5. *The speech must move forward steadily toward a complete and satisfying finish.* As you structure this substantive portion of your speech, give the audience a sense of forward motion—of moving through a series of main points with a clear idea of where your ideas are heading and how you are going to arrive at a termination point. Repeated backtracking to pick up "lost" points will confuse your audience, and you will lose the sense of momentum your structure was intended to convey.

These are the major elements that any substantive portion of a speech must satisfy in conveying a coherent, planned message to an audience. Failure to meet any one of the criteria will weaken the impact of the entire speech.

TYPES OF ARRANGEMENT

Bearing in mind these five criteria, let us consider some of the options available as you begin packaging your ideas for your listeners. Generally, these options fall into four categories: (1) sequential patterns, (2) causal patterns, (3) topical patterns, and (4) special patterns.

Sequential Patterns

Sequential patterns reflect the order in which events actually occur or systematically trace the physical relationships among the parts of a whole. In the first case, the sequence is called *chronological;* in the second, *spatial.*

Chronological Sequence

When using the chronological sequence, you begin at a certain point in time and move forward—or backward—in a systematic way. For example, you might describe last year's weather by considering conditions as they existed in the spring, summer, fall, and winter or the manufacture of an automobile by following the assembly line process from beginning to end. A chronological pattern is useful when you want listeners to have a strong sense of *development* or *forward locomotion*. Here is an example of an outline using the chronological, or time, sequence:

> Central Idea: The development of paper paralleled the development of technology.
>
> I. In A.D. 105, Chinese Emperor Ts'ai Lun conceived the idea of making paper by hand from tree bark.
>
> II. In the period A.D. 618–907, the Chinese created laid transfer molds to make paper more efficiently.
>
> III. In 1694, the Bank of England not only printed money but built a machine for watermarking and engraving its bills.
>
> IV. In 1798, the first paper-making machine was invented by Nicholas-Louis Robert, finally moving paper making into the modern era.

Spatial Sequence

In the spatial (or *geographical*) sequence, the major points of the speech are arranged in terms of their *physical proximity* to or *direction* from each other. Descriptions of the migration patterns of Norwegian immigrants into the Midwest, for instance, would trace geographical movements into Iowa and Wisconsin and, from there, into Minnesota, the Dakotas, and Montana. In another example, the aspects of a public service building can seem confusing and so, are usefully discussed spatially:

> Central Idea: Knowing how the local hospital is arranged floor by floor will help you gain access to its primary services.
>
> I. You will find the information desk just inside the main entrance.
>
> II. Beyond the desk is another public area, the gift shop.
>
> III. The emergency room and other outpatient services are toward the back of the building, still on the first floor.
>
> IV. The operating theaters and critical cure units are on the second floor.
>
> V. The third floor houses most internal specialty patients—those with cancer, gastrointestinal disorders, and respiratory ailments.
>
> VI. The fourth floor houses the obstetrics and gynecology units.
>
> VII. Most of the smaller units are on the fifth floor.

Causal Patterns

As their name implies, causal patterns of speech organization move either (1) from an analysis of present causes to a consideration of future effects or (2) from a description of present conditions to an analysis of their apparent causes. Causal patterns give audience members a sense of *physical coherence* or even a sense of control, for, if one knows causes, one probably can stop or increase undesirable or desirable effects. When using a cause-effect pattern, you might first point to your college's increasing number of closed courses each semester and then predict that, as a result, students will take longer and longer to complete school. Or, reasoning in the other direction, you could argue that the increasing time students are taking to complete school is the result, at least in part, of the increasing number of closed courses. Compare the following outlines:

> Claim: Acid rain (cause) is a rising problem because it threatens our health and economy (effects).
>
> I. Manufacturing plants across the United States emit harmful acid-forming sulfur dioxide and nitrogen oxides into the air.
>
> II. The effect of these emissions is damage to important ecological structures.
>   A. Lakes and forests are threatened.
>   B. The productivity of vital croplands is reduced.
>   C. Acid particles in the air and drinking water supplies cause 5 to 8 percent of all deaths in some parts of the United States.

> Claim: Acid rain (effect) is primarily the result of modern technologies (causes).
>
> I. If we are going to control acid rain, we must learn about and deal with its causes.
>
> II. Human activities cause acid rain.
>   A. One primary cause is energy production; acids are given off by power plants.
>   B. A second main cause is motorized transportation, especially trucks and auto emissions.

Notice a characteristic of these outlines: Each starts with the aspect of the situation *better known* to audience members, and then proceeds to develop the *lesser known* facets of the problem. Therefore, use cause-effect if listeners are better acquainted with the cause; use effect-cause if the opposite is true.

Topical Patterns

Some speeches on familiar topics are best organized in terms of subject-matter divisions that have become standardized. Financial reports customarily are divided into assets and liabilities; discussions of government into legislative, executive, and judicial functions; and comparisons of kinds of telescopes into celestial and terrestrial models. Thus, topical patterns are most useful for speeches that *enumerate* aspects of persons, places, things, or processes. Occasionally, a speaker tries to enumerate all aspects of the topic, as in a sermon on the Ten Commandments. More often, however, a partial enumeration of the primary or most interesting aspects is sufficient. For example, a speech on volleyball shots, for an audience of beginners, probably would concentrate only on the three main types of shots:

Central Idea: Knowing the basic volleyball shots can increase the playing ability of amateur or backyard players.

    I. There are three main shots.
      A. A "bump" is performed by bringing your shoulders together and clasping your hands under the ball.
      B. To "set" a ball, bring your hands above your head and hit the ball near your forehead with your palms open.
      C. A "spike" is a quick power shot executed with one hand, driving the ball over the net and down to the opponent's court area.

Topical patterns are among the most popular and the easiest to use. However, take care to justify the aspects of the situation or problem you discuss, especially when doing a partial enumeration. If someone asks, "But why didn't you talk about X?" then perhaps you have not made your range of topics seem coherent and logical.

The types of speech organization thus far discussed, although they do not disregard the audience, are shaped principally by the nature of the subject matter. Some subjects, such as the historical development of a nation or a person's rise from obscurity to prominence, lend themselves readily to the chronological pattern. Subjects of a geographical nature—discussions of the world's stock of natural resources or of its chronic famine areas—fit more easily into the spatial structure. Still other matters—the reasons for the success of a given economic policy or an account of recent rule changes in football—call, respectively, for the causal or special topical plan.

Special Patterns

At times, however, rather than using any of these subject-oriented speech structures, you may decide that, for psychological or rhetorical reasons, it would be better to impose a special or more strongly audience-oriented pattern on your material. Many special patterns have been used successfully by resourceful speakers. Four of them, however, are so generally useful that they warrant mention here. We shall call them (1) *familiarity-acceptance order,* (2) *inquiry order,* (3) *question-answer order,* and (4) *elimination order.*

Familiarity-Acceptance Order

When using this order in an informative speech, you work from the familiar to the unfamiliar—from that which the audience already knows or understands to that which is new or strange. Similarly, if your aim is to persuade or actuate, you build on the facts or values the listeners already accept and show how the beliefs or actions you urge follow logically from them.

Relating new or unfamiliar material to what is already known or understood has long been recognized by teachers as one of the most effective methods of classroom instruction. Indeed, it has often been argued that all of our knowledge is derived "analogically" in the sense that we learn not by adding unrelated bits of information to our prior knowledge but by comparing or contrasting the new with the old. Provided you appraise your audience's existing knowledge correctly and do not move on to new matters too rapidly, an informative speech structured on this principle will usually succeed.

Persuasive speeches based on audience-accepted facts or values are especially suited to doubting or hostile audiences. Of course, your reasoning must be valid and your conclusion must not overstep the evidence. When you meet these standards, your audience cannot deny your central idea without denying the underlying facts or values. Here is an example of an outline of a persuasive speech using the pattern just described.

Claim: Mary Campagna embodies the values our party stands for and, therefore, should be our nominee.

I. We all agree, I am sure, that experience, ability, and integrity are prime requisites for a holder of high public office.

II. Mary Campagna has these qualities.
   A. She has experience.
      1. She has served two terms as mayor of one of our largest cities.
      2. She has been in the state senate for twelve years.
   B. She has ability.
      1. She has successfully reorganized the cumbersome administrative machinery of our city government.
      2. She has become a recognized leader in the senate.
   C. She has integrity.
      1. She has never been suspected of any sort of corruption.
      2. Her word is as good as her bond.

III. Because Mary Campagna clearly has the qualities we demand of a holder of high public office, she deserves our support in her bid to be elected governor of this state.

Inquiry Order

When using inquiry order, you retrace step-by-step the way in which *you* acquired the knowledge or arrived at the proposal you are now communicating to the audience. You may, for example, show listeners how to grow prize-winning dahlias by describing how the success and failure of your own experiments with various kinds of seeds, fertilizers, and garden locations eventually led to the recommendations you now offer. Or, if the purpose of your speech is to persuade or actuate, you may recount how you first became aware of the existence of a problem, searched for its causes, and weighed possible solutions until the one you now advocate emerged as the best.

An arrangement of this kind has a double advantage. First, it enables listeners to judge more accurately the worth of the information or policy being presented. Second, because all facts and possibilities are laid out for critical examination, it results in a more complete understanding or a firmer conviction than that produced by other methods.

Question-Answer Order

When following question-answer order in a speech, you determine in advance the questions most likely to arise in the listeners' minds about your subject or proposal, and then you deal with these questions in a way that favors your conclusion. For example, often on first hearing of a new development in medical science, people immediately want to know how it relates to their own health problems or to the needs of their loved ones. On first being told of a pending piece of legislation, they wonder how it will affect their taxes or whether it will curb their freedom. By skillfully structuring your material to address these questions early in the speech, you will be assured of a high degree of audience interest and will pave the way for the rest of your material.

Elimination Order

Whereas the sequential, causal, and topical patterns of organization are applicable to both informative and persuasive speeches, elimination order is best suited to speeches designed to influence belief or secure action.

In this order, you first survey all of the available solutions to a recognized problem or all of the courses of action that could reasonably be pursued in a given situation. Then, proceeding systematically, you show that all of the possibilities except one would be unworkable, excessively costly, or in some other way undesirable. By these means, you lead the audience, in effect, to agree with the belief or behavior you advocate.

If elimination order is to be used effectively, two requirements are important. First, your survey must be all-inclusive. If one or more options are overlooked, the logic of the process will be defective, and the listeners will not be obliged to accept the conclusion you desire. (See a discussion of "false division," page 301.) Second, the possibilities must be mutually exclusive; otherwise, one or more of the characteristics that render a rejected possibility impracticable or undesirable may also be present in the preferred point of view. Consider this example:

Claim: Building an outdoor volleyball/basketball court is the most practical plan for using our Student Council's recreation fund.

I. Three options have been proposed.
  A. A video arcade area
  B. A running/obstacle course
  C. An outdoor volleyball/basketball court

II. A video arcade area is impractical.
  A. Students would waste money.
  B. The cost of renting the machines is prohibitive.

III. A running/obstacle course is too expensive.
  A. The cost of the land cannot be met from our current treasury.
  B. We would also have to pay for maintenance.

IV. Therefore, an outdoor cement or asphalt court is the most practical choice.
  A. It is the least expensive.
  B. It could be used by any student.
  C. Its maintenance costs are minimal.

CONSISTENCY OF ARRANGEMENT

Sometimes you may want to choose one method of arrangement for the main points of your message and another method for the subordinate ideas. On no condition, however, should you shift from one method to another in the presentation of the main points themselves, because it would confuse your listeners. The following outline illustrates how spatial, special topical, and time sequences might be combined in a speech on the major cities of India.

Central Idea: The complexities of Indian culture are nowhere more evident than in India's cities.

I. The major cities of *western* India include Bombay and Ahmadabad.
  A. Bombay
    1. Early history
    2. Development under the British
    3. Condition today
  B. Ahmadabad
    1, 2, 3 *(Develop as above)*

II. The major cities of *central* India include Delhi and Hyderabad.
   A. Delhi
      1. Early history
      2. Development under the British
      3. Condition today
   B. Hyderabad
      1, 2, 3 *(Develop as above)*

III. The major cities of *eastern* India include Calcutta and Madras.
   A. Calcutta
      1. Early history
      2. Development under the British
      3. Condition today
   B. Madras
      1, 2, 3 *(Develop as above)*

Note that in this outline spatial sequence is used for the main points, special topical sequence for subpoints A and B, and time sequence for sub-subpoints 1, 2, and 3.

PHRASING OF MAIN POINTS

For reasons of emphasis as well as clarity, you should word your main points carefully. While illustrations, explanations, quotations, and the like comprise the bulk of any speech, the main points tie these supporting details together and, therefore, most directly convey the message you wish to communicate. In order to achieve maximum effectiveness in the statement of your main points, keep in mind these four characteristics of good phrasing: (1) *conciseness,* (2) *vividness,* (3) *immediacy,* and (4) *parallelism.*

Conciseness

State your main points as briefly as you can without distorting their meaning. A simple, straightforward declaration is easy to grasp; a long, complex statement tends to be vague and confusing. Avoid clumsy modifying phrases and distracting subordinate clauses. State the essence of your idea in a short sentence that can be modified or elaborated as you subsequently present the supporting material. Say "Our state taxes are too high," not "Taxes in this state, with the exception of those on automobiles, motor boats, and trucking lines, are higher than is justified by existing economic conditions." The second statement may express your idea more completely than the first, but it contains nothing that your supporting material could not clarify, and its greater complexity makes it less crisp and emphatic.

Vividness

Whenever possible, state the main points of your speech in attention-provoking words and phrases. If your principal ideas are drab and colorless, they will not stand out from the supporting materials that surround them, nor will they be easy to remember. Because they are your main points, you should make them the punch lines of your speech. Notice how much more vivid it is to say "We must cut costs!" than to say "We must reduce our current operating expenditures." Vivid phrasing should not, of course, be overdone or used to distort the truth; nor should the sort of language suitable for a pep rally or political meeting be used on a more dignified occasion. Within these limits, however, vivid phrasing is desirable. (Note: The quality of vividness—and other matters pertaining to the wording of the speech—will be examined more extensively in Chapter 8.)

Immediacy

Try to word your main points so they will appeal directly to the immediate interests and concerns of your listeners. Remember that you are speaking not merely *about* something but *to* somebody. Instead of saying "Chemical research has helped improve medical treatment," say "Modern chemistry helps the doctor make you well." Rather than saying "Air travel is fast," say "Air travel saves you time." (In this connection, review the discussion of audience interests and desires, pages 86–92.)

Parallelism

Whenever possible, use a uniform type of sentence structure and similar phraseology in stating your main points. In print, as in some outlines in this textbook, you often will vary your phraseology. However, in a speech, where audiences have only one chance to catch what you are saying, parallelism in sentence structure is very important. Avoid unnecessary shifts from active to passive voice or from questions to assertions. Use prepositions, connectives, and verb forms that provide balance, rhythm, and direction of thought. Suppose your central idea is "Different sports demand different physical and physiological characteristics." Compare two outlines:

Ineffective

I. Weight lifters depend mainly on strength.

II. Cardiovascular endurance is important to distance runners.

III. When sailing, balance and body awareness are major factors.

Effective

I. Strength is most important to weight lifters.

II. Cardiovascular endurance is most important to distance runners.

III. Balance and body awareness are most important to sailors.

Notice that in this series "is (are) most important" is repeated, with the subjects and prepositional phrases ("to . . . ") changing in parallel fashion. Repetition and parallel structure help your listeners remember the major ideas in your speech.

ARRANGING SUBORDINATE IDEAS AND SUPPORTING MATERIALS

When you have selected, arranged, and phrased the main points of your speech, you are ready to organize your subordinate ideas and supporting materials in a way that will provide substance and clear order to the whole message.

Subordinating the Subordinate Ideas

A "string-of-beads" speech, in which every bit of information seems to have equal weight—tied together by "and-uh," "and then," and "so"—not only lacks purposive form but obscures meaning. Because all points receive equal emphasis, none seems important. The speech soon becomes tiresome. Regardless of how well you have chosen, arranged, and worded the main points, they will not stand out unless your lesser ideas are properly subordinated. Avoid emphasizing your subpoints; list under your main thoughts only the ideas that are subordinate to them.

Types of Subordinate Ideas

Subordinate ideas commonly fall into one of five classes: (1) *parts of a whole,* (2) *lists of functions,* (3) *series of causes or results,* (4) *items of logical proof,* and (5) *illustrative examples.* While other types might also be listed, these five are certainly among the most important.

Parts of a Whole

If a main point concerns an object or process with a number of parts or refers to a total of many items, the subpoints identify and treat those parts or items. For example, the grip, shaft, and head are the parts you would discuss in describing the manufacture of a golf club. The number of television stations in England, Scotland, Northern Ireland, and Wales are the subtotals you would refer to in showing that the number of television stations in the British Isles has increased.

Lists of Functions

If a main point suggests the purpose of a mechanism, organization, or procedure, the subordinate ideas may list the specific functions it performs. The purpose of a municipal police department, for example, may be clarified by discussing its responsibilities for traffic control, crime detection, and safety education.

Series of Causes or Results

If a main point states that a cause has several effects or that an effect results from a number of causes, the various effects or causes may be listed as subordinate ideas. For example, the causes of crop failure may be enumerated as drought, frost, and blight, or its effect as high food prices, deprivation, and possible riots.

Items of Logical Proof

In a speech designed to influence belief, the subordinate ideas under a main point may consist of a group of separate but related arguments or of the successive steps in a single, coordinated line of reasoning. In either case, you should be able to relate the subordinate ideas to the main point by the word *because* (i.e., the main point is true because the subordinate ideas are true). You might support a plea for a new high school in your community with this series of separate but related arguments: "We need a new high school *(a)* because our present building is too small, *(b)* because our present building lacks essential laboratory and shop facilities, and *(c)* because the growth of our city has made it difficult for many students to get to our present building." Conversely, you should be able to proceed from the subpoints to the main point by using the word *therefore*. For example: "Our present high-school building *(a)* is too small, *(b)* lacks necessary facilities, and *(c)* is not centrally located; *therefore,* we should construct a new building." (The use of sound reasoning will be discussed in more detail in Chapter 13.)

Illustrative Examples

If a main point consists of a generalized concept or assertion, the subordinate ideas may illustrate it with specific cases or examples. You may use this method in both exposition and argument, the examples providing clarification in the first case and proof in the second. For instance, you may explain the theory of reciprocal trade agreements by showing your listeners how such agreements work in actual cases involving specific goods and products. Or you may, by citing the results obtained in communities that have added fluoride to their water supply, support the contention that fluoride in a community's drinking water helps prevent or reduce tooth decay.

Subordinate ideas and supporting materials should be arranged in a way that provides substance and order to your message. For instance, a general assertion that appears as a main point in your speech can be illustrated with specific examples that clarify or prove your point.

Coordinating the Subordinate Ideas

Subordinate ideas not only should be directly related to the main point under which they fall, but they should also be coordinated with each other—that is, they should be equal in scope or importance. To list poor teachers, the lack of adequate textbooks, and a broken soft drink machine as the reasons for poor scholarship among the students in a large high school would indicate that your analysis of your subject is faulty: you are treating as equal three items that obviously are not equally important. Either the broken soft drink machine is symptomatic of a greater evil—careless administration or a dilapidated school building—and therefore should be placed *under* this heading, or it is irrelevant and should be eliminated from the speech altogether. To treat it as a factor equal to poor teaching and the lack of textbooks is to confuse a less important idea with more important ones and to create an unconvincing, incongruous effect.

Arranging the Subordinate Ideas

Subordinate ideas, no less than main points, must be arranged in an orderly, purposeful fashion. Parts of a whole, functions, or causes—even items of proof or illustrative examples—often can be listed according to the patterns already discussed for ordering the main headings. You can put your subordinate ideas in a sequential, causal, or topical arrangement—whichever pattern seems most appropriate. You may want to use one pattern for the items under one main point and a different pattern for those under another; do not, however, alter the pattern of the subordinate ideas *within* the same coordinate series, for this may seriously confuse your listeners. Above all, be sure to use a systematic order; do not crowd in the subordinate ideas haphazardly just because they are subordinate. Moreover, be careful not to let the process of subordination become too intricate or involved, or your listeners will not be able to follow you; however far you go, keep your subordination consistent and logical.

Supporting the Subordinate Ideas

The important role of supporting materials in effective speechmaking was discussed in Chapter 5. The general rule should be: *Never make a statement in a speech without presenting some facts or reasoning to clarify, illustrate, or substantiate it.* Too often speakers think that if they divide every main point into two or three subordinate ideas, they have done enough. In reality, however, such divisions add only to the skeleton of the speech. They do not supply the supporting materials on which understanding or belief ultimately depends. The real *substance* of a speech lies in explanations, statistics, illustrations, instances, comparisons, and testimony. Within reasonable limits, the more such materials you have, the stronger your speech will be.

We have now considered the principles that should govern the arrangement of ideas within a speech and have surveyed several patterns by which the main points may be ordered and the subordinate points coordinated. Even with a thorough grasp of these principles and patterns, however, you probably will be unable to work out all of the details of a speech entirely in your mind. To develop a tangible, overall view of the structure as well as the content of a talk, you will find it necessary to follow an orderly procedure for setting ideas and facts down on paper. For this purpose, most speakers find it best to prepare an outline.

REQUIREMENTS OF GOOD OUTLINE FORM

The amount of detail you include in an outline will depend on your subject, on the speaking situation, and on your previous experience in speech composition. Regardless of these factors, any good outline should meet the following basic requirements:

Each unit in the outline should contain only one idea. If two or three ideas are run together under one symbol, the relationships they bear to one another and to the other ideas in the outline will not stand out clearly. Notice the difference between the following examples:

Wrong

I. You should ride a bicycle because bicycling is an ideal form of convenient and inexpensive transportation and because it is also an excellent form of healthful recreation and is fun.

Right

I. You should ride a bicycle.
   A. Bicycling is an ideal form of transportation.
      1. It is convenient.
      2. It is inexpensive.
   B. Bicycling is an excellent form of recreation.
      1. It is healthful.
      2. It is fun.

Less important ideas in the outline should be subordinate to more important ones. Because a subordinate idea is a subdivision of the larger heading under which it falls, it should rank *below* that heading in scope and importance. It should also directly support or amplify the statement made in the superior heading.

Wrong

I. The cost of medical care has skyrocketed.
   A. Operating-room fees may be as much as $1000 or $1200.
      1. Hospital charges are high.
      2. A private room may cost as much as $800 a day.
   B. X rays and laboratory tests are extra.
   C. Complicated operations may cost several thousand dollars.
      1. Doctors' charges constantly go up.
         a. Office calls usually cost between $15 and $40.
      2. Drugs are expensive.
      3. Most antibiotics cost $1.25 per dose.
   D. The cost of nonprescription drugs has mounted.

Right

I. The cost of medical care has skyrocketed.
   A. Hospital charges are high.
      1. A private room may cost as much as $800 a day.
      2. Operating-room fees may be as much as $1000 or $1200.
      3. X rays and laboratory tests are extra.
   B. Doctors' charges constantly go up.
      1. Complicated operations may cost several thousand dollars.
      2. Office calls usually cost between $15 and $40.
   C. Drugs are expensive.
      1. Most antibiotics cost $1.25 per dose.
      2. The cost of nonprescription drugs has mounted.

The logical relationship between units of the outline should be shown by proper indentation. Normally, your main points will be the most general as well as the most important statements in your speech. As such, they should be placed nearest the left-hand margin of your outline, with less important statements ranged beneath and to the right of them in the order of increasing specificity. In your finished outline, therefore, the broadest and most central statements will lie farthest to the left; the narrowest and most particular ones will lie farthest to the right. If a statement is more than one line in length, the second line should be aligned with the first. (For example, see item II in the full-content outline later in this chapter.)

A consistent set of symbols should be used throughout the outline. An acceptable set of symbols is exemplified in the outlines printed in this chapter, but whether you use this system or another, be consistent. Items comparable in importance or scope always should be assigned the same type of symbol.

The four requirements just named apply to any outline. An additional requirement, however, applies to the final draft of a complete, formal outline: *All main points and subordinate ideas in such an outline should be written as full sentences.* Especially as you prepare outlines for your classroom speeches, you will find that putting the items of the outline into sentence form will help clarify the meaning of each point and will show its exact relation to the other points. You will also find that a carefully framed statement of each point and a recognition of its place in the overall structure of your speech are valuable aids in helping you remember what you want to say when it is time to speak.

STEPS IN PREPARING AN OUTLINE

An outline, like the speech it represents, should be developed gradually through a series of stages. While the process of preparing an outline may vary from person to person and occasion to occasion, certain steps should always be taken:

1. Develop a *rough outline* that identifies your topic, your purpose, and aspects of the topic you will treat.
2. Prepare a *technical outline* in order to arrange your materials and to evaluate the sufficiency of your speech-building effort.
3. Finally, recast that material into a *speaking outline,* that is, into a form you will actually use when delivering your speech.

Developing a Rough Outline

Suppose that your instructor has asked you to prepare an informative speech on a subject in which you are interested. You decide that you will talk about drunk driving because a close friend of yours was recently injured by a drunk driver and your classmates appear to be blasé about the whole question. Your broad topic area, therefore, is:

Drunk Driving

In the six to eight minutes you have to speak, however, you obviously cannot cover the subject. Therefore, recalling what you learned in Chapter 4 about adapting your material to your audience and to time limits, you decide to focus on two organizations in the news and in TV ads—Mothers Against Drunk Driving and Students Against Drunk Driving (MADD and SADD). You think they could use some background on the organizations and more thorough information on their goals and accomplishments. So, you limit your topic as follows:

MADD and SADD (A description of background and current operations of two activist anti–drunk driving organizations)

In thinking about the limits of your subject, you already have made a preliminary selection of topics to be dealt with in your speech. Now you jot them down more systematically:

Founders of MADD and SADD

Accomplishments of the organizations

Reasons the organizations were deemed necessary

Goals of MADD and SADD

MADD's and SADD's action steps

Ways listeners can help

This list covers a number of points you may want to include, but the order appears random. As you think about organizing these items, you review various arrangement patterns: A chronological pattern would enable you to organize the history of MADD and SADD, but it really would not let you feature their current activities. Either of the causal patterns would work well for a persuasive speech, but, as this is primarily an informative speech, you do not want to talk only about the organizations as "causes" for the "effects" of reduced alcohol-related accidents. Among the special patterns, an inquiry order might work, but you discard it because you do not really know enough about audience members' questions to use it effectively. So, you settle on a topical pattern, because you want to present three kinds of information—information on the founding, operations, and local programs of MADD and SADD:

Background of MADD and SADD—information about the founders, why the organizations were founded

Description—goals, steps in action plans, results

Local applications—how parents work with their teenagers and with local media to accomplish MADD and SADD goals

All of this means that you will probably have three main points in your speech. As you subdivide each one, you come up with the following general outline:

I. Background on MADD and SADD
   A. Information about the founders
   B. Reasons the organizations were founded

II. Description of the organizations
  A. Their goals
  B. The steps they take when acting
  C. Their accomplishments so far
III. Methods to use on a local level
  A. "Project Graduation"
  B. Parent-student contracts
  C. Local public service announcements

You now have prepared a *rough outline*. You have identified your topic, clarified your purpose, considered various subtopics and settled on a reasonable number of them, and decided on a method for organizing and developing your speech. Notice that the result is a complete topical pattern: The three main points are arranged topically, as are the subpoints for each of the main points. That should be a signal to you that you will have to be extra careful so that the speech does not turn into a string of beads (see pages 172–73).

When you have arranged your main points, or heads, proceed to phrase them more precisely and then place under each major head the subordinate ideas by which it is to be explained and amplified. Executing those tasks allows you to see more clearly what kinds of information and evidence you need to find.

Developing a Technical Outline

You are now ready to assemble a full-content outline. This is normally done in two steps. First, draft the speech as completely as possible, using standard outline form. You may have to combine or rearrange certain points as they appear in your rough draft or perhaps even drop several of them because of overdevelopment or time pressures. Cast all of the items as complete sentences that convey your meaning clearly and exactly. Arrange the sentences so that they adhere to the following principles of good outline form:

1. each unit in the outline contains only one idea;
2. less important ideas are subordinated to the more important ones;
3. logical relationships between units are illustrated through proper identation; and
4. a consistent set of symbols is used throughout the outline.

Each of these principles is illustrated in the sample full-content outline.

In analyzing the completed outline to discover possible gaps or weaknesses, it is frequently helpful to work out a *technical plot* of your speech. To make such a plot, lay the completed outline beside a blank sheet of paper; on this sheet, opposite each unit, write a statement of the materials or devices used in developing it. Where you have used statistics in the outline, write the word *statistics* in the technical plot, together with a brief statement of their function. In like manner, indicate all of the forms of support and methods of development you have used.

As a testing device, a technical plot can help you determine whether your speech is structurally sound, whether there is adequate supporting material, whether you have overused one or two forms of support, and whether the appeals you plan are adapted to the audience and occasion. Many speeches, of course, do not need to be tested this thoroughly. Experienced speakers can often make an adequate analysis without drafting a complete technical plot. For the beginner, however, there is no more effective way of checking the structure of a speech and testing the methods used to develop it.

. . . Sample Full-Content Outline . . . .

The following example shows both the complete content of an outline and its technical plot. For illustrative purposes, all items in the outline are stated as complete sentences. Such completeness of detail may be desirable if the occasion is especially important or if you sometimes have difficulty framing thoughts extemporaneously. Frequently, however, it will be sufficient to write out only the main ideas as complete sentences and to state the subordinate ideas and supporting materials as key phrases. Check with your instructor.

FRIENDS DON'T LET FRIENDS DRIVE DRUNK[1]

(The introduction and conclusion for this speech will be developed in detail in Chapter 7, "Beginning and Ending the Speech," pages 166–68.)

Technical Plot	Full-Content Outline

First topic: background on founders, helping create a sense of emotional identification	I. MADD and SADD were founded in tragic circumstances.
	  A. MADD was founded in 1980 by Candy Lightner.
	    1. One of her daughters was killed by a drunk driver.
	    2. She wanted to protect other families from a similar tragedy.
	  B. SADD was founded by Lightner's other daughter.
	    1. The loss of her sister hurt deeply.
	    2. She knew the importance of peer pressure in stopping teenage drinking and driving.

Second topic: II. You can understand MADD and SADD better if you know
description   something about their goals, operations, and effectiveness.
First subtopic: A. MADD and SADD were organized the way they were
goals   because the Lightners had specific goals they wished
to achieve.

    1. They wanted the general public to carry out the
agitation for changes.

Specific instances   a. Members of the public can put pressure on
government officials.

    b. They can write letters-to-the-editor.

    c. They can campaign for state and local task
forces.

    d. They can do all this for minimal investment of
money.

    2. They wanted to expose the deficiencies in current
legislation and drunk driving control systems.

Statistics   a. They wanted to toughen the laws on operating
(segments)   a motor vehicle when intoxicated (statistics on
variations in state laws).

Specific instances   b. They wanted to pressure judges to hand down
maximum instead of minimum penalties (specific instances of light sentences).

Statistics   c. They wanted to see more drunk driver arrests
(segments)   from city, county, and state law enforcement
agents (statistics on arrest rates).

    3. They wanted to help the families of other victims.

    a. Most MADD and many SADD members have
been victims themselves.

Testimony   b. In addition to mourning, families are taught to
put their energy into getting something done
(quotations from pamphlets).

    4. And finally, MADD and SADD want to educate
the general public.

    a. They want to make people conscious of the
tragedies of drunk driving.

    b. They want to focus media attention on the
problem.

Second subtopic: B. MADD's steps for action demonstrate the thoroughness with which the organization understands the
action steps   processes of public persuasion.

Throughout, extended hypothetical illustration   1. First, a local chapter sets its goals.

    2. Second, it educates its organizers goal by goal so
that everyone knows the reasons behind each step.

exemplifies the   3. It then sets research priorities.
steps   a. One group might check on local arrest records.

         b. Another might examine drunk driving conviction rates for various judges.

         c. A third could work with local media to find out how to secure time and space for a public service announcement on drunk driving.

         d. A fourth might talk with local schools and churches about safe prom nights.

    4. Once the research is done, the local chapter can formulate its plans of action.

    5. Then, it can "go public" with action teams and task forces.

Testimony   6. This five-step process parallels the campaign model for public persuasion devised by Herbert W. Simons in his book, *Understanding Persuasion*.

Third subtopic: C. Although still young organizations, MADD and SADD
results of MADD already have had significant effects.
and SADD work
Statistics   1. As of 1984, there were 320 MADD chapters across
(magnitude) the country.

    2. About 600,000 volunteers are now working on MADD projects.

    3. State laws already are changing.

Specific instances   a. In 1982 alone, twenty-five different states enacted thirty pieces of drunk driving legislation in the face of MADD's lobbying.

Specific instance   b. After petitions, Congress raised the mandatory legal drinking age to twenty-one.

Specific instance   c. In Florida, convicted drunk drivers must have red bumper stickers on their cars reading "CONVICTED DUI."

Statistics   4. Fatalities from drunk driving have decreased (quote
(trends) before- and after-1980 statistics).

    5. MADD also takes credit for increasing the popularity of low-alcohol beer, wines, and wine coolers.

Third topic: III. You, too, can work with MADD and SADD on local
local projects projects.

  A. Set up a workshop in local high schools for parent-child contracts.

Explanation   1. In such a contract (which has no legal status), the teen agrees not to drive drunk and to call the parent for a ride, while the parent agrees to ask no questions and to impose no special penalties.

    2. The contract both reinforces the importance of not driving drunk and makes the commitment to safety a mutual one.

B. Set up a SADD "Project Graduation."
Example   1. With the cooperation of the schools and, sometimes, local youth organizations or churches, a community can sponsor nonalcoholic postprom parties.
                            2. They allow prom-goers a chance to stay up late, have fun, and celebrate without alcohol.
                        C. Work with local media to use public service announcements (PSA's) to halt teen and adult drunk driving.
                            1. MADD chapters can order ads you may have seen on TV.
Specific instances   a. Some go after drunk driving.
                                b. Some tell you to keep one member of your group sober.
                                c. Others are aimed at hosts of parties, urging them to not let drunk guests drive.
Specific instances   2. SADD chapters also can order ads and school posters, nonalcoholic party kits, and the like (show sample items).

Developing a Speaking Outline

In Chapter 7 we will complete the technical outline by adding introductory and concluding materials: quotations, appeals to the audience's interests and curiosity, and the like. But enough details have been offered thus far to indicate the virtues of full, technical outlines.

As you probably realize, however, the outline just built would be difficult to work from were you to actually deliver a speech on MADD and SADD. Because it is a full-sentence outline, it is "too dense" to be manageable from a lectern. Moreover, because all of the details are included, you probably would be tempted simply to read it to your auditors. If you did that, you would lose vital audience contact.

Therefore, you must compress the technical outline into a form more convenient for use during the presentation of the message. This may involve rewording the main heads in phrase or key-word form on a sheet or notecard, putting statistics or quotations on other notecards, and the like. The actual method you use, of course, will depend on personal preference; some people like to work from sheets of paper, others from notecards. Whatever your choice, your speaking outline should serve two functions while you are addressing the audience: (1) it should provide you with reminders of the direction of your speech—main points, subordinate ideas, etc., and (2) it should record material of a technical or specific nature that must be carefully or precisely worded. A key-word speaking outline might look like this:

FRIENDS DON'T LET FRIENDS DRIVE DRUNK

I. Background
   —MADD = 1980, Candy Lightner
   —SADD = her other daughter for hi-school kids

II. Description
   A. Goals
      1 = public agitation (gov't. officials, letters-to-editor, task forces, all for little money)
      2 = expose deficiencies in current legis. & control
         —tougher laws state by state (STATISTICS)
         —pressure judges (JUDGE NORTON, SANDERS, HANKS)
         —more arrests (STATISTICS)
      3 = public education
         —more conscious
         —media attention
   B. MADD's action steps
      1 = goals (what community needs most)
      2 = educate organizers
      3 = set research priorities (arrest records, conviction rates, PSA's, prom nights)
      4 = formulate plans of action
      5 = go public!
         (note on Simons' *Understanding Persuasion*)
   C. Results
      1 = 320 MADD chapters by 1984
      2 = 600,000 volunteers
      3 = state laws changing
         —1982: 25 states, 30 pieces of legis.
         —Congress: drinking age to 21
         —Florida, red bumpersticker, CONVICTED DUI
      4 = fatalities down (STATISTICS)
      5 = popularity of low-alc beer, wines, coolers

III. Local projects
   —contracts
   —prom night (Operation Graduation)
   —PSA's and publicity
      1 = MADD TV ads
         —after drunk driving
         —sober group member
         —host/guest—*Friends don't let friends d.d.*
      2 = SADD projects
         —school posters (SHOW POSTER)
         —non-alc party kits
         —ads

Notice four characteristics of this speaking outline:

1. Most points are noted only with a key word or phrase. If you have practiced the speech from the full, technical outline, a word or two should be enough to trigger your memory at these points.
2. Do not be afraid to write down a full sentence when you want to say something in a precise way, as illustrated in the slogan "Friends don't let friends drive drunk."
3. You may wish to include some directions to yourself, as we have done here with references to "STATISTICS" or "SHOW POSTER."
4. Emphasis can be indicated in a number of ways—all capital letters, underlining, indentation, dashes, and the like. Find methods of emphasis that catch your eye easily and will help you remember what is subordinated and/or related to what.

CHAPTER SUMMARY

The four types of arrangement patterns are *sequential* (chronological and spatial), *causal* (effect-cause and cause-effect), *topical* (enumerative), and *special* (familiarity-acceptance, inquiry order, question-answer, and elimination). Be *consistent* in using arrangement patterns in combination with each other. When phrasing main points, aim at *conciseness, vividness,* and *immediacy.* When subordinating ideas to others, you can use five classes— *parts of a whole, lists of functions, series of causes or effects, items of logical proof,* or *illustrative examples*—being sure to coordinate them. Arrange coherently and support clearly all subordinate ideas. There are four requirements for good outline form: (1) *Each unit should contain only one idea,* (2) *less important ideas should be subordinate to more important ones,* (3) *the logical relationship between units should be shown by proper indentation,* and (4) *a consistent set of symbols should be used throughout the outline.* In outlining a speech, first do a *rough,* then a *technical,* and finally a *speaking outline.*

Oral Activities

1. For each of the topics listed below, suggest two ways that materials might be ordered. Discuss which of the two ways, in general, would be more effective.
   a. Directions for driving in snow

    b. An explanation of why foreign students in the United States are demonstrating against the leadership in their home country
    c. A rationale for including women in a revised draft system
    d. The effect that the influx of tourists from the West will have on China
    e. A description of the proposed route for a highway bypass
2. For a speech entitled "The Investigator as Resource," discussing why a lawyer may want to hire a private detective on a case-by-case basis, rearrange the following points and subpoints in proper outline form:
    a. Investigative services can save the lawyer time.
    b. Investigative reports indicate areas where the lawyer should concentrate in building a case.
    c. It is advantageous for a lawyer to employ an investigator on a case-by-case basis.
    d. The investigator performs two basic services.
    e. Known witnesses must be interviewed and other witnesses sought out.
    f. The detective examines reports from the FBI or other governmental and private agencies and evaluates them for reliability and to determine what has to be done.
    g. The investigator examines, collects, preserves, and analyzes physical evidence.
    h. The investigator compiles information in an effort to reconstruct an incident.
    i. Lawyers may need only occasional detective assistance on especially critical cases.
    j. Investigative reports can be used in out-of-court settlements.

Reference Notes

1. The material for this speech, including the statistics we have not included, was drawn from the following sources: "Glad to be SADD," *Listen Magazine* (October 1982); "War Against Drunk Drivers," *Newsweek* (September 13, 1982); "They're Mad as Hell," *Time* (August 3, 1981); "How to Get Alcohol Off the Highway," *Time* (July 1, 1981); "Health Report," *Prevention Magazine* (June 1984); "Water Water Everywhere," *Time* (May 20, 1985); L. B. Taylor, *Driving High* (Watts, 1983); Sandy Golden, *Driving the Drunk Off the Road* (Washington, DC: Acropolis Books, Ltd., 1983); and a pamphlet, *How to Save Lives and Reduce Injuries—a Citizen Activist Guide to Effectively Fight Drunk Driving* (U.S. National Highway Traffic Safety Administration; Washington, DC: U.S. Government Printing Office, 1982).

BEGINNING
and ENDING
the SPEECH

7

Every speech, whether long or short, needs a beginning and an end. You must lead your audience clearly and surely into the subject matter and introduce your viewpoint to them. Your listeners also need to know when you are ending—what your final points are and in what state you are trying to leave your audience. Unfortunately, speakers often spend considerable time developing the body of the speech but neglect the equally important tasks of acclimating the audience to the talk and expertly exiting the event.

'That was embarrassing,' Yangsoo noted. 'I was a little hurried this morning as I was putting the finishing touches on my speech, and I figured I would wing the conclusion. I couldn't. I did manage to summarize the three main points, but then I still didn't know what to do. I can't believe I said "I guess I'm done and . . . I'd better sit down." '

'Did you notice, too,' replied his teacher, 'that your audience was as embarrassed as you were? They felt for you; they wanted you to have something to say at the end, to finish

strong. Many of them actually dropped their heads so they wouldn't have to watch you suffer. Next time, get ready to stop.' 99

If you plunge headlong into a speech in helter-skelter fashion, you will probably succeed only in confusing the audience and making yourself nervous. And, if you come to the end of your remarks without a prepared conclusion, you will get flustered, both you and the audience will be embarrassed, and the speech will end on a negative note. Well-prepared introductions and conclusions, therefore, (1) allow you and the audience to enter into and then depart from a clear relationship, (2) orient the audience to your purposes and ideas and clarify both at the end, and (3) signal clearly when a speech starts and ends so as to keep the audience as comfortable as possible. These are not trivial aspects of public speaking. If you do them poorly, your credibility—and, hence, your effectiveness—will suffer. If you do them well, you will significantly improve your chances for rhetorical success.

In this chapter, we will review the purposes of introductions and conclusions, discuss and examine examples of various types of introductory and concluding strategies, and then complete the full-content outline we began in Chapter 6 by adding its beginning and ending.

BEGINNING THE SPEECH

If the beginning of a speech is to complement the main idea or claim, the introduction must: (1) gain listeners' attention, (2) secure goodwill and respect for the speaker, and (3) prepare the audience for the discussion to follow.

As a speaker you want the listeners to attend to all of your speech, but you must first *gain their attention*. You must capture their attention during the first few moments of the speech—unless they are prepared to attend to what you say, your most interesting, useful information and most persuasive appeals will be wasted. By demonstrating the vitality of the topic and showing how important it may be for the audience, you can turn audience attention into a more developed interest. (You may want to review the factors of attention, pages 33–38.)

The audience will probably have begun to form opinions about you and your topic even before you begin to speak. Obviously, you want those opinions to be favorable. You have an opportunity to enhance them during the first few moments of your speech. Your confidence in your topic and general presence on the platform may serve as nonverbal cues for the audience. In many situations, your own reputation or the chairperson's introduction will help *generate goodwill*. However, there may be times when the audience is opposed to you or your topic. In these instances, it is important to deal with opposition openly so that your topic will receive a fair hearing. By commenting on the differences between your views and those of the listeners, you can let them know that you are aware of differences but are seeking areas of consensus. When confronted by indifference, distrust, or skepticism, you must take steps to change these attitudes early in the speech so that your position will be received openly.

Finally, you should lead your listeners' thinking naturally into the subject of your speech. You must *prepare the audience* by stating your purpose early; audiences that are forced to guess the thrust and purpose of the speech soon lose interest.

An introduction that secures the audience's attention and goodwill and prepares them to listen lays a solid foundation for the central idea or proposition of your speech. There are a number of established means for tailoring your introduction to achieve these ends:

1. Referring to the subject or occasion
2. Using a personal reference or greeting
3. Asking a rhetorical question
4. Making a startling statement of fact or opinion
5. Using a quotation
6. Telling a humorous anecdote
7. Using an illustration

Referring to the Subject or Occasion

If the audience already has a vital interest in your subject, you may only need to state that subject before presenting your first main point. The speed and directness of this approach suggest alertness and eagerness to address your topic. Professor Russell J. Love used this approach when discussing rights for people with severe communication problems:

> My talk tonight is concerned with the rights of the handicapped—particularly those people with severe communication disabilities. I will be presenting what I call a bill of rights for the severely communicatively disabled.[1]

Although such brevity and forthrightness may strike exactly the right note on some occasions, you should not begin all speeches this way. To a skeptical audience, a direct beginning may sound immodest and tactless; to an apathetic audience, it may sound dull or uninteresting. When listeners are receptive and friendly, however, reference to the subject often produces a businesslike and forceful opening.

Sometimes, instead of referring to the subject, you may want to refer to the occasion that has brought you and your audience together. This is especially true on a significant occasion, as it was when historian Arthur M. Schlesinger, Jr., appeared at a Joint Session of Congress to commemorate the one hundredth anniversary of Franklin D. Roosevelt's birth:

> Mr. Speaker, Mr. President, Members of Congress, friends, it is a high honor for me to share with such doughty warriors for liberty and justice as Averell Harriman, Claude Pepper, and Jennings Randolph the opportunity to address this most eminent legislative body in the world.
>
> It is, indeed, a most special occasion that brings us together. We have heard all our lives about the first hundred days of Franklin Delano Roosevelt. We gather today to celebrate his first hundred years.[2]

A reference to the occasion is a good way to begin a speech when audience members have been brought together for a special event.

Using a Personal Reference or Greeting

At times, a warm, personal salutation from the speaker or a pleasurably recalled earlier association with the audience or the scene serves as an excellent starting point. This is particularly the case if the speaker occupies a high-status position and has considerable prestige in the eyes of the audience. President John R. Silber of Boston University took advantage of this position, in a somewhat lighthearted way, when he delivered the 1986 commencement address at his school:

> This Commencement marks the fifteenth anniversary of my inauguration as seventh president of Boston University. By contemporary standards, my fifteen years as president have brought me almost to the threshold of venerability, within striking range of such epithets as "kindly old President Silber." Indeed, in the last issue of this year's *Daily Free Press,* an editorial consigned me to the dustbin of history with the words: "the long afternoons seem to be fading quietly into the twilight of John Silber's tenure at Boston University."
>
> Fifteen years ago I arrived here, without roots in Boston. I had roots, but they had been left in my native state, which, as some of you may know, is Texas. I did not feel a stranger in Boston—no one with a sense of American history can ever feel a stranger in Boston—but neither did I feel at home. Today I find myself very much at home in Boston and rooted in the history of this University. I am honored to be addressing the class of 1986 on my fifteenth anniversary.[3]

The way in which a personal-reference type of introduction can be used to gain a hearing from a hostile or skeptical audience was shown by Anson Mount, Manager of Public Affairs for *Playboy* magazine, in a talk presented to the Christian Life Commission of the Southern Baptist Convention:

> I am sure we are all aware of the seeming incongruity of a representative of *Playboy* magazine speaking to an assemblage of representatives of the Southern Baptist Convention. I was intrigued by the invitation when it came last fall, though I was not surprised. I am grateful for your genuine and warm hospitality, and I am flattered (though again not surprised) by the implication that I would have something to say that could have meaning to you people. Both *Playboy* and the Baptists have indeed been considering many of the same issues and ethical problems; and even if we have not arrived at the same conclusions, I am impressed and gratified by your openness and willingness to listen to our views.[4]

If the personal reference or greeting used in the introduction is modest and sincere, it may establish goodwill as well as gain attention. However, avoid effusiveness and hollow compliments. Audiences are quick to sense a lack of genuineness on the part of the speaker, and they always react unfavorably toward feigned or falsified sentiments. At the other extreme, avoid apologizing. Do not say "I don't know why I was picked to talk on this subject when others could have done it so much better," or "Unaccustomed as I am to public speaking . . ." Apologetic beginnings suggest that your speech is not worth listening to. Be cordial, sincere, and modest, but do not apologize.

Asking a Rhetorical Question

A third way to open a speech is to ask a question or a series of questions to start the audience thinking about your subject. Jacqueline Jackson, a student at Regis College, used this approach to introduce a speech on "Why Johnny Can't Read":

> Johnny can't read. Johnny can't write. Johnny doesn't know how to spell. Johnny's not good with numbers. Johnny has a hard time remembering. Johnny lost the football game. Maybe Johnny's retarded and we're not doing enough for him. Maybe Johnny's gifted and we're holding him back. Johnny can't get along with others; Johnny can't get along with his teachers either. Johnny can't seem to do anything right. But why can't Johnny read, write, spell, play football, or get along with others? Could it be the fault of the schools? That seems to be the answer that the mass media have been promoting for years. Is the American school system responsible for the unbalanced, semi-literate children of today? Should the school system be responsible to educate every unbalanced semi-literate? Are schools being asked to do too much? Are schools being asked to do the right things?[5]

Making a Startling Statement

On certain occasions you can open a speech with what some writers have referred to as the "shock technique," making a startling statement of fact or opinion. This approach is especially useful when listeners are distracted or apathetic. The following shows how a speech on weight control might be introduced:

> There's a disease sweeping our country. None of us is immune. There are no miracle drugs to combat it, although Americans spend millions of dollars each

year to try to deal with the illness. The disease can affect all ages, all economic classes, all ethnic groups. It can cause permanent bodily damage, shorten life span, and may even cause death. Some of you may already be affected; most of you will in some way be touched by this disease. The disease is obesity; the cure, you. Today I will examine some of the causes of obesity and suggest some preventative measures.

Using a Quotation

If carefully selected, a quotation may be an excellent means of introducing a speech, because it usually forces an audience to think about something important, and it often captures an appropriate emotional tone. Hoping to get his audience to keep an open mind on this topic—ethics in education— John R. Hogness, President of the Association of Academic Health Centers, quoted a poet to get his speech started on the right foot:

> "Education," according to Robert Frost, "is the ability to listen to almost anything without losing your temper or your self-confidence." Since I may, inadvertently, touch on a topic that could raise a few tempers, it helps *my* self-confidence considerably to have such an educated audience [at the University of Oklahoma].
>
> Before treading softly where angels fear to go, however, I want to thank you . . . . [6]

Here, then, the quotation is not really used for proof, as it would be were it *testimony* (see Chapter 5), but it captures a sentiment Mr. Hogness hopes his audience accepts so that, after one more personal thank-you, he can get into his sensitive material on ethics.

Telling a Humorous Anecdote

You can begin a speech by telling a funny story or relating a humorous experience. When doing so, observe three communication rules:

1. Be sure the story is at least amusing, if not absolutely funny. If it is not, or if you tell it badly, you will embarrass yourself and your audience.
2. Be sure the anecdote is relevant to your speech. If its subject matter or punch line is not directly related to you, your topic, or at least your next couple of sentences, the story will appear to be a mere gimmick.
3. Be sure it is in good taste. In a public gathering, an off-color or doubtful story violates accepted standards of social behavior and can

undermine an audience's respect for you. This means that you should generally avoid sexual, racial, antireligious, ageist, and sexist humor.

All three of these standards were observed by David T. Kearns, Chair and Chief Executive Officer of Xerox Corporation, when talking to the Graduate School of Business at the University of Chicago about "Economics and the Student":

> There's a story about a Frenchman, a Japanese and an American who face a firing squad. Each gets one last request. The Frenchman asks to hear The Marseillaise. The Japanese asks to give a lecture on the art of management. The American says, "Shoot me first—I can't stand one more lecture on Japanese management."
>
> You'll be glad to hear that I'm not going to talk about Japanese management today.
>
> In fact, if we keep on the right road, we may wind up listening to the Japanese give lectures on American management.[7]

With that, Mr. Kearns was ready to talk about the importance of higher educational institutions in training today's managers of American companies.

Using an Illustration

One or more real-life incidents, a story taken from literature, or a series of hypothetical illustrations also can get a speech underway. As in the case of the humorous anecdote, any illustration you use should not only be interesting to the audience but also should be connected to your central idea or claim. When Judd H. Alexander, Executive Vice-President of the James River Corporation, spoke to the Association of American Colleges in 1986, he wanted to make sure his audience understood that his praise of a liberal arts education was genuine. He used the following illustration to underscore his primary theme:

> Two thousand three hundred years ago, a wise father chose the greatest scholar of his age to tutor his young son in the liberal arts. Aristotle instructed the boy in architecture, music, literature, politics and the natural sciences.
>
> A few years later, the youth, now barely in his twenties, set out to conquer the world. He did. It took him just eleven years. He became the greatest leader, the most visionary strategist, the finest administrator the world has ever known. He became Alexander [the Great].
>
> Two and one half centuries [sic] later and a half a world away, the liberal arts are still doing an outstanding job of preparing young people for leadership.[8]

Sometimes one of the approaches we have discussed can be used alone; at other times, two or more of them can be combined. Whether used singly or in combination, however, the materials comprising your introduction should always be aimed at the same objective: arousing the attention and winning the goodwill and respect of your listeners. Moreover, those materials should be relevant to the purpose of your speech and should lead naturally into the first of the major ideas you wish to present. That is, the introduction should be an integral part of the speech. It should not be, for example, a "funny story" told merely to make an audience laugh but should be thematically and tonally tied to the body of the speech. Many speakers use a *forecast*—"In this speech, I will first . . . and then will . . . "—in order to complete the task of orienting an audience before moving on to the substance of the discourse. A forecast is a relatively easy and yet effective way to make the transition from introductory notions to main concerns.

To establish a common ground of interest and understanding and to point the audience toward the conclusion you hope to reach—these are the functions your introductory remarks should perform.

ENDING THE SPEECH

Just as the introduction to the speech accomplishes specific purposes, so too does the ending, or conclusion. A suitable conclusion should: (1) focus the thought of your audience, (2) establish a concluding mood, and (3) convey a sense of finality.

The principal function of the conclusion of a speech is to *focus the thought of the audience on your central theme and purpose.* If your speech has one dominant theme or idea, you will usually restate that point at the end in a manner that makes your meaning clear and forceful. If your speech is more complex, you may bring its most important points together in a condensed and uniform way; or, you may spell out the action or belief these points suggest.

In addition to bringing the substance of the speech into final focus, your conclusion should *aim at leaving the audience in the proper mood.* If you want your listeners to express vigorous enthusiasm, you should stimulate that feeling in your closing remarks. If you want them to reflect thoughtfully on what you have said, you should encourage a calm, judicious attitude. Therefore, you should decide whether the response you seek requires a mood of serious determination or lighthearted levity, of warm sympathy or utter disgust, of thoughtful consideration or vigorous desire for action. Then you should plan to end your speech in a way that will create that mood.

Finally, a good ending should *convey a sense of completeness and finality*. Listeners grow restless and annoyed when they are given reason to feel that the speaker has finished, only to hear him or her ramble on. Therefore, avoid false endings. Tie the threads of thought together so that the pattern of your speech is brought clearly to completion:

1. Tell your listeners what you are going to say.
2. Say it.
3. Tell them what you said.
4. Sit down.

Much truth lies in those classic pieces of advice for speakers. *Orientation* is the key to introductions, while *summary* is the corresponding heart of conclusions. The last point, too, deserves reinforcement. Speakers who cannot quite bring themselves to "sit down," who go on and on and on at the end with just "one more" story or "one more" pithy quotation, drive an audience to distraction.

> *A distinguished college professor brought down the house one evening at the University of Iowa Theatre's production of Hedda Gabler. It was a long, slow production on a hot evening. It seemed interminable, as the clock struck ten, then eleven, and then threatened midnight. Finally, Hedda moved backstage and pulled a curtain. We heard the suicidal gunshot. The exhausted professor, under his breath but audibly, said, 'Thank God!' The spell was broken, and the audience burst into a combination of laughter and applause. A director who did not know how to quit had received his comeuppance.*

Some of the means most frequently used to conclude speeches are:

1. Issuing a challenge or appeal
2. Summarizing
3. Using a quotation
4. Using an illustration
5. Supplying an additional inducement to belief or action
6. Stating a personal intention

Issuing a Challenge or Appeal

A speaker can conclude by openly appealing for support or action or by reminding listeners of their responsibilities in furthering a desirable end. Such an appeal should be clear and compelling and should include a suggestion of the principal ideas or arguments presented in the speech. Judd Alexander, whose introduction to a speech on the liberal arts we examined earlier, built a challenge to his audience into his final sentences:

> I believe Henry Adams was correct when he wrote: "What one knows is, in youth, of little moment; they know enough who know how to learn." Some students can gain that ability from a specialist education. They will develop faster and further with a passion for a narrow field of study and the comfort of an early career choice. Thank God. Society needs specialists and industry needs a variety of educational backgrounds from which to choose its executives of the future.
>
> There are other students, however—bright, inquisitive, versatile—whose thirst for knowledge cannot be quenched by drinking from a single bowl. These students' talents, social value and self-satisfaction will best develop through the mind expanding, horizon lifting, vision broadening experience of liberal arts.
>
> It appears to me that our job, yours and mine, is to be sure that students with this special aptitude for the liberal arts are not denied its pleasures and rewards for reasons that are false. We must offset the bad advice from peers and parents that liberal studies close career doors when the opposite is true. We must communicate to all the publics out there the eternal value of a classic education. We must defend the liberal arts.[9]

Summarizing

A summary conclusion reviews the main ideas that have been presented and draws whatever inferences may be implicit in the speech as a whole. In a speech to inform, a summary ending is nearly always appropriate because it restates the points you want remembered. In a speech to persuade, a summary provides a final opportunity to reiterate—and reinforce—your primary arguments. Neal E. Carter, Vice-President, Battelle Memorial Institute, and Director, Columbus Division, faced a doubting audience. A summary conclusion allowed him one more chance to set his claims in their minds and to depict the "good" scientist:

> Therefore, my concern is that if we fail in this nation to meet the challenge of communication between the scientist and the public and political sectors of the nation, then severe consequences will occur. That is,
> —Significant dollars will be wasted when we provide standards for environ-

mental effluents which are far beyond what is required to protect the environment or public health. This directly affects our international competitiveness.

—Technical solutions will not be implemented. We will not be able to apply biomedical applications or nuclear waste disposal solutions or chemical waste disposal solutions because we could not gain the public acceptance of these technological developments.

—Significant research which is of long-term value to the nation will be terminated, such as breeder technology, fusion technology, solar power, [and] advanced coal research, and aerospace technology will not be implemented because the public support was not developed.

This is, in summary, the changing world of the scientist and technologist. He definitely no longer lives in an ivory tower. He must of necessity deal with social and political forces that are not only looking over his shoulder but in some cases telling him how he must go about accomplishing his goal. In such areas as nuclear energy, nuclear and hazardous chemical waste disposal, toxicological assessments of chemical substances ingested by humans, acid rain and air pollution, and management of major projects, the technical person must work with the socially oriented person, the politically oriented person, and in some cases, financially oriented persons to accomplish his technological objective.

And, as Walter Cronkite used to say, "That's the way it is."[10]

Using a Quotation

A quotation, either in poetry or prose, is often used to end a speech. Frequently, poetry can capture the essence of your message in uplifting language. Quoted prose, if the author is known to be wise and/or knowledgeable, can go further, adding additional credibility to your central ideas or claims. Notice former President Richard M. Nixon's use of Winston Churchill's *ethos* in urging his audience to seek improvement of U.S.-Soviet relations:

> Let our legacy be not just that we saved the world from communism, but that we helped make the world safe for freedom.
>
> What would Churchill's message [he was quoted also at the beginning of the speech] be if he were addressing you today? Listen to his words:
>
> "The United States stands at this time at the pinnacle of world power. It is a solemn moment for the American democracy. For with primacy in power is also joined an awe-inspiring accountability for the future."
>
> "The Stone Age may return on the gleaming wings of science, and what might shower immeasurable material blessings on mankind may bring about its total destruction."

"Our fortunes are still in our hands. We have the power to save the future."

Let this generation of Americans be remembered not for presiding over the twilight of an old civilization, but for helping to usher in the dawn of a new era in which the bloody twentieth century was followed by a peaceful twenty-first century—an era in which people everywhere had a chance to enjoy the blessings of freedom, justice, and progress which have made America such a good and great country.[11]

Using an Illustration

Just as an illustration may be used to set the tone and direction of a speech, so may it also be used to close off your conversation with an audience. It should be both *inclusive* and *conclusive:* inclusive of the main focus or thrust of your speech and conclusive in tone and impact. Sometimes the *same* illustration can be used to tie up the whole speech. This is what Michael Twitchell, a student at a speaking contest, did when talking about the causes and effects of depression:

Opening

Have you ever felt like you were the little Dutch boy who stuck his finger in the leaking dike? You waited and waited but the help never came. The leak became worse and the water rushed around you and swept you away. As you fought the flood, gasping and choking for air, you realized that the flood was inside yourself. You were drowning and dying in your own mind. According to the *American Journal of Psychiatry,* as many as half the people in this room will be carried away by this devastating flood. What is this disaster? Mental depression.

Closing

Let's go back to my illustration of the little Dutch boy. He was wise to take action and put his finger in the dike, preventing the flood. In the case of depression, each one of us must be like the little Dutch boy—willing to get involved and control the harmful effects of depression.[12]

Supplying an Additional Inducement to Belief or Action

Sometimes a speech may be concluded by quickly reviewing the leading ideas presented in the body and then supplying one or more additional reasons for endorsing the belief or taking the proposed action.

All in all, you will find an annual checkup by a competent physician to be a wise investment, no matter what your age or how well you may feel at the moment. As I have pointed out, in their early stages a number of potentially serious diseases have no symptoms of which the victim is in any way aware. Many other ills if caught in time can be eliminated or brought under control. Finally, the time and money a good checkup will cost you are only a tiny fraction of the time and expense a serious illness entails.

Here, as in other aspects of life, be guided by the old but still pertinent adage, "A stitch in time saves nine." Remember that even though you may be foolish enough to take chances with your own well-being, you owe it to your loved ones and to those dependent on you to take no chances with the most precious of all things—your own good health. Make an appointment for a checkup today!

Stating a Personal Intention

A statement of the speaker's intention to act as his or her speech recommends is particularly valuable when the speechmaker's prestige with the audience is high, or when a concrete proposal needing immediate action has been offered. If the speaker can indicate an intention to take immediate action, that lends credibility both to the speaker and to the ideas presented. When asking the audience to give blood, the following conclusion might be appropriate:

> Today I have illustrated how important healthy blood is to human survival and how blood banks work to ensure the possibility and availability of blood for each of us. It is not a coincidence that I spoke on this vital topic on the same day that the local Red Cross Bloodmobile is visiting campus. I want to urge each of you to ensure your future and mine by stopping at the Student Center today or tomorrow to make your donation. The few minutes that it takes may add up to a lifetime for a person in need. To illustrate how firmly I believe in this opportunity to help, I'm going to the Student Center to give my donation as soon as this class is over. I invite any of you who feel this strongly to join me.

Regardless of the means you choose for closing your speech, remember that your conclusion should focus the thought of your listeners on the central theme you have developed. In addition, a good conclusion should be consistent with the mood or tenor of your speech and should convey a sense of completeness and finality.

FITTING THE BEGINNING AND ENDING TO THE BODY
OF THE SPEECH

In Chapter 6 we considered various patterns for developing the body,
or substance, of a speech and the principles to be followed in outlining
that part. When the introduction and conclusion are added to the outline,
the completed structure should look something like this:

Introduction

I. _____ .
    A. _____ .
    B. _____ .

Body

I. _____ .
    A. _____ .
    B. _____ .
        I. _____ .
        2. _____ .

II. _____ .

III. _____ .

Conclusion

I. _____ .
    A. _____ .
    B. _____ .

• • • • • Sample Outline *for an Introduction and a Conclusion* • •

*An introduction and conclusion for the classroom speech on MADD and SADD,
outlined in Chapter 6 (pages 145–48), might take the following form. Notice the
speaker uses one of the factors of attention—suspense—together with startling
statements to lead the audience into the subject and concludes by combining a final
illustration with a statement of personal intention.*

Introduction

I. Many of you have seen the "Black Gash"—the Vietnam War memorial in
Washington, DC.
    A. It contains the names of more than 40,000 Americans who gave their lives
in Southeast Asia between 1961 and 1973.
    B. We averaged over 3000 war dead a year during that anguishing period.

II. Today, another enemy stalks Americans.
   A. The enemy kills, not 3000 per year, but over 20,000 citizens every twelve months.
   B. The enemy is not hiding in jungles but can be found in every community in the country.
   C. The enemy kills, not with bayonets and bullets, but with bottles and bumpers.

III. Today, I want to talk about organizations that are trying to contain and finally destroy the killer.
   A. Every TV station in this town carries a public service ad that says "Friends Don't Let Friends Drive Drunk."
   B. Those ads are trying to rid our streets of that great killer, the drunk driver.
   C. In response to that menace, two national organizations—Mothers Against Drunk Driving and Students Against Drunk Driving—have been formed and are working even in this community to make the streets safe for you and me.

IV. (Central Idea) MADD and SADD are achieving their goals with your help.

V. To help you understand what these familiar organizations do, first I'll tell you something about the founders of MADD and SADD; then, I'll describe their operations; finally, I'll mention some of the ways community members get involved with them.

(Body)

Conclusion

I. Today, I've talked briefly about the Lightners and their goals for MADD and SADD, their organizational techniques, and ways you can get involved.

II. The work of MADD and SADD volunteers—even on our campus, as I'm sure you've seen their posters in the Union—is being carried out to keep you alive.
   A. You may not think you need to be involved, but remember, after midnight one in every five or fewer drivers on the road is probably drunk.
   B. You could be involved whether you want to be or not.
   C. That certainly was the case with Julie Smeiser, a member of our sophomore class, who just last Friday was hit by a drunk driver when going home for the weekend.

III. If people don't take action, we could build a new "Black Gash"—this time for victims of drunks—every two years, and soon fill Washington, DC, with monuments to needless suffering.
   A. Such monuments would be grim reminders of our unwillingness to respond to enemies at home with the same intensity with which we attacked enemies abroad.

B. Better would be a positive response to groups such as MADD and SADD, who are attacking the enemy on several fronts at once in a war on motorized murder.

IV. If you're interested in learning more about SADD and MADD, stop by Room 324 in the Union tonight at 7:30 to hear the president of the local chapter of SADD talk about this year's activities—I'll be there; please join me.

• •

CHAPTER SUMMARY

Introductions should *gain attention, secure goodwill,* and *prepare an audience* for what you will be saying. Types of introductions include *referring to the subject or occasion, using a personal reference or greeting, asking a rhetorical question, making a startling statement of fact or opinion, using a quotation, telling a humorous anecdote,* and *using an illustration.* In concluding a speech, you should attempt to *focus the thoughts of your audience, establish a concluding mood,* and *convey a sense of finality.* Useful techniques for ending a speech involve *issuing a challenge or appeal, summarizing, using a quotation, using an illustration, supplying an additional inducement to belief or action,* and *stating a personal intention.* Once you have prepared your introduction and conclusion, you should fit them to the body of your speech with appropriate transitions and then move on to your remaining preparatory tasks.

Oral Activities

1. In small class groups, decide what might be *two* excellent introductory strategies for the following people to use in the situations noted:

Speaker	Situation
Phyllis Schlafly	Opening session of a Pro-Life conference
Roger Staubach	Banquet sponsored by Fellowship of Christian Athletes
Jimmy Carter	Seminar on peace in the Middle East
Ralph Nader	Keynote for a National Association of Business conference

2. For your next speech, write out completely a proposed introduction and conclusion, indicate also your central idea or claim, and list the main

(first-level) headings for the rest of your speech. Turn that material in to your instructor for critique and suggestions before you deliver the speech.

Reference Notes

1. From "The Barriers Come Tumbling Down" by Russell J. Love. Given at the Harris-Hillman School Commencement, Nashville, Tennessee, May 21, 1981. Reprinted by permission.
2. Arthur M. Schlesinger, Jr., "In Memory of Franklin D. Roosevelt," in *Representative American Speeches,* Owen Peterson, ed., (New York: H. W. Wilson, 1982), 161.
3. From "Of Mermaids and Magnificence: Heroism" by John R. Silber, from *Vital Speeches of the Day,* Volume LII, July 15, 1986. Reprinted by permission of Vital Speeches of the Day.
4. Excerpt from a speech presented to the Christian Life Commission of Southern Baptist Convention by Anson Mount, Manager of Public Affairs for *Playboy* magazine, from *Contemporary American Speeches,* 5th ed., Wil A. Linkugel et al., eds., (Dubuque, IA: Kendall/Hunt, 1982).
5. From "Why Johnny Can't Read" by Jacqueline Jackson. Reprinted from *Winning Orations,* 1981, by special arrangement with the Interstate Oratorical Association, Larry Schnoor, Executive Secretary, Mankato State College, Mankato, Minnesota.
6. From "The Essence of Education: Ethics and Morality" by John R. Hogness, from *Vital Speeches of the Day,* Volume LII, July 1, 1986. Reprinted by permission of Vital Speeches of the Day.
7. From "Economics and the Student: Business Must Be Involved in Education" by David T. Kearns, from *Vital Speeches of the Day,* Volume LII, July 1, 1986. Reprinted by permission of Vital Speeches of the Day.
8. From "Liberal Learning: The World of Management" by Judd H. Alexander, from *Vital Speeches of the Day,* Volume LII, March 1, 1986. Reprinted by permission of Vital Speeches of the Day.
9. Ibid.
10. From "The Political Side of Science: Communication Between Scientists and the Public" by Neal E. Carter, from *Vital Speeches of the Day,* Volume LII, July 1, 1986. Reprinted by permission of Vital Speeches of the Day.
11. From "The Pillars of Peace: Soviet-American Relations" by Richard M. Nixon, from *Vital Speeches of the Day,* Volume LII, July 15, 1986. Reprinted by permission of Vital Speeches of the Day.
12. From "The Flood Gates of the Mind" by Michael A. Twitchell. Reprinted from *Winning Orations,* 1983, by special arrangement with the Interstate Oratorical Association, Larry Schnoor, Executive Secretary, Mankato State College, Mankato, Minnesota.

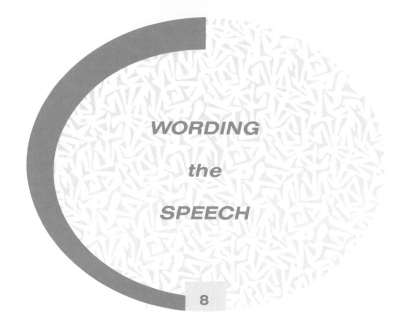

WORDING
the
SPEECH

8

So far, we have focused on the process of creating speeches: preparing, organizing, and adapting messages to their intended audiences. We shall turn our attention in the next three chapters to the *encoding* of these messages—that is, to the means by which public speakers give expression and form to their ideas, attitudes, feelings, and values. These means include the choice of language, the use of visual aids, and the control of bodily and vocal behaviors.

We will begin the discussion of channels, or modes, of communication by examining language—the choices of wording and style you make when you put your ideas and feelings into language for others. To put your ideas into language publicly is to *stylize* them. Language is both a *referential* and a *relational* medium of communication. Through its direct, or denotative, aspects, it allows you to refer to persons, places, and things, and, through its indirect, or connotative, aspects, it signals relationships between you and your audience. A *speaking style,* therefore, is a communicative impression that results when a series of denotative word choices are combined with verbal signals to establish a social-psychological relationship between the speaker and audience members. Thus, in this chapter we will be concerned with both particular word choices and larger units of style.

ESSENTIALS OF EFFECTIVE WORD CHOICES

Communicating with precision is not easy. Yet, rhetorical and communication theorists have known for centuries that speakers can help listeners understand their message better if they keep certain virtues of oral language in mind. The virtues of *accuracy, simplicity, coherence, language intensity,* and *appropriateness* are primary features of effective word choices.

Accuracy

Careful word choice is an essential ingredient in transmitting your meaning to an audience. The man who tells a hardware store clerk that he has "broken the hickey on my hootenanny and needs a thingamajig to fix it" had better have the hootenanny in his hand to procure the right thingamajig. When you speak, your goal should be precision. Leave no doubt as to your meaning. Words are symbols that represent concepts or objects. Your listener may attach to a symbol a meaning quite different from the one you had intended to convey. "Democracy," for example, does not mean the same thing to a citizen of the United States as it does to a citizen of the Soviet Union, or, in fact, to one American citizen and another. The term "democracy" will elicit different meanings in those belonging to the Moral Majority and those belonging to the American Communist party.

It is also imprecise to discuss people or objects in a particular class as though they were no different from other members of the same class. Asian-American A differs from Asian-Americans B and C; one Oldsmobile may be an excellent car and another may be a lemon. Students of General Semantics continually warn us that many errors in thinking and communication arise from treating words as if they were the actual conditions, processes, or objectives and were fixed and timeless in meaning. From their perspective, the phrase "once a thief, always a thief" is an imprecise and inaccurate reference to all persons convicted of theft; a person is more than a label.[1]

To avoid vagueness in definition and elsewhere, choose words that express the exact shade of meaning you wish to communicate. While the verb "shine" may refer to, or denote, a ray of light to speakers of the English language, you may wish to indirectly communicate other aspects (connotations) of that light; such verbs as "glow," "glitter," "glisten," "gleam," "flare," "blaze," "glare," "shimmer," "glimmer," "flicker," "sparkle," "flash," and "beam" are familiar enough to be used in your speech. They will allow you to communicate more precise features of the ray.

Simplicity

"Speak," said Lincoln, "so that the most lowly can understand you, and the rest will have no difficulty." This advice is as valid today as when Lincoln offered it, and because modern electronic media create audiences that are vaster and more varied than any Lincoln dreamed of, there is even more reason for contemporary speakers to follow it. Say "learn" rather that "ascertain," "try" rather than "endeavor," "use" rather than "utilize," "help" rather than "facilitate." Never use a longer or less familiar word when a simpler one is just as clear and accurate. Billy Sunday, the famous evangelist, gave this example:

> If a man were to take a piece of meat and smell it and look disgusted, and his little boy were to say, "What's the matter with it, Pop?" and he were to say, "It is undergoing a process of decomposition in the formation of new chemical compounds," the boy would be all in. But if the father were to say, "It's rotten," then the boy would understand and hold his nose. "Rotten" is a good Anglo-Saxon word, and you do not have to go to the dictionary to find out what it means.[2]

Simplicity does not mean that your language must be simplistic or that you should talk down to your audience; it does suggest that you consider the advantages of short, easily understandable words that convey precise, concrete meanings.

Coherence

Transmitting ideas orally requires attention to the perceived *coherence* of your message. Audiences do not have the luxury of going back over your points as they do in reading an essay; nor do they have punctuation marks to help them distinguish one idea from another. Hence, speakers use *signposts* in the form of carefully worded phrases and sentences to help listeners follow the movement of ideas within a speech and perceive the overall message structure.

Summaries are useful signposts in ensuring that your audience is able to see the overall structure: *preliminary* and *final summaries* are especially helpful in laying out or pulling together the major divisions or points of the speech:

Preliminary Summaries	*Final Summaries*
Today I am going to talk about three aspects of. . . .	I have talked about three aspects of. . . .
There are four major points to be covered in. . . .	These four major points—(restate them)—are the. . . .
The history of the issue can be divided into two periods. . . .	The two periods just covered—(restate them)—represent the significant. . . .

In addition to these summarizing strategies, signposts may be *connectives* that move an audience from one idea to another within the speech. The following are typical *transition* statements you might use:

In the first place. . . . The second point is. . . .
In addition to . . . notice that. . . .
Now look at it from a different angle. . . .
You must keep these three things in mind in order to understand the importance of the fourth. . . .
What was the result? . . .
Turning now. . . .

The preceding signposts are *neutral*—they tell the audience that another idea is coming but do not indicate the more subtle relationships that exist between the points being made. You can improve the clarity and coherence of your message by being precise about such relationships as *parallel/hierarchical, similar/different,* and *coordinate/subordinate.* Expressing these relationships requires *connectives* such as:

Not only . . . but also. . . . *(parallel)*
More important than these. . . . *(hierarchical)*
In contrast. . . . *(different)*
Similar to this. . . . *(similar)*
One must consider X, Y, and Z. . . . *(coordinated)*
On the next level is. . . . *(subordinated)*

Your use of preliminary or final summaries and signposts is important to your audience. The summaries—elements of *macrostructure*—give listeners an overall sense of your entire message; if they can easily see the structure, they will better understand and remember your speech. The signposts are elements of *microstructure,* and, hence, lead your listeners step-by-step through the speech, signaling specific relationships between ideas.

Language Intensity

As a speaker, your word choice is partially determined by the way you feel about the object you are describing and by the strength, or intensity, of that feeling. That is, through your choice of words or phrasing you communicate your *attitude* toward the object. Consider, for example, the following "attitudinally weighted" terms:

Highly Positive
{
"savior"
"patriot"
"defender"
}

Relatively Neutral
{
"G.I."
"soldier"
"mercenary"
}

Highly Negative
{
"enemy"
"murderer"
"foreign devil"
}

These nine terms are roughly rank-ordered according to their intensity, ranging from the highly positive "savior" to the highly negative "foreign devil." Notice that we tend to add even religious connotations when

---

Language Intensity Chart

	Subject	Verb	Predicate
Positive	A Doctor of Philosophy at an institution of higher learning	discussed	dialectical perspectives on life and living.
Neutral	The philosophy professor at State U	outlined	Karl Marx' economic and social theories.
Negative	An effete intellectual snob at the local haven for draft-dodgers	harangued our children with	Communist drivel.

getting to the extremes of language intensity. Generally, then, such language choices signal to your listeners the intensity of your feelings toward your subject.

How intense should your language be? John Waite Bowers has suggested a useful rule of thumb: Let your language be, roughly, one step more intense than the position or attitude of your audience.[3] If your audience already is committed, say, to your positive position on academic reform, then you can afford to make your language quite intense. If not, you had better use comparatively neutral language. Intense language can help create intense reactions, but only if you suit your word choices to auditors' beliefs and tastes.

'I sure don't understand why people didn't vote for my proposal for a take-home final exam in this class yesterday.' 'You don't understand? Haven't you learned anything in here yet?' Toni replied. 'Look, Dick, first you insulted Marlena by saying her ideas for an in-class test "stunk"—hardly the kind of language you use to talk about a friend. Then you called our instructor a Nazi for having a final at all. And, finally, you insulted the intelligence of nearly everybody when you said, "All of you loafers should favor a take-home because you can get help with your exam if we do them on our own." Really, Dick, you have the finesse and sensitivity of a dump truck!' 'I was just trying to be funny!' said Dick. 'Maybe so, but you'd better check out your audience's beliefs and sensitivities to figure out when jokes turn into jabs.'

Appropriateness

Besides being accurate, clear, and properly intense, your language should be appropriate to the topic and to the situation. Solemn occasions call for diction that is restrained and dignified; joyful occasions, for word choices that are informal and lively. Just as you would never use slang in a speech dedicating a memorial, so you should never phrase a humorous after-dinner speech in a heavy style, unless you are using irony. Suit your language to the tone of the occasion. And, be sure, as well, that your language is appropriate to the audience you are addressing. Your slang, for example, differs in many ways from that of your parents, so even if the occasion allows for informal language, you will want to see whose informal verbal constructions are appropriate by noting who is in the audience. "Gee whiz,"

"Wow," "Good grief," "Far out," and "Awesome" are pieces of slang that came into English in different eras; if you use any of them, be sure that people from that era comprise a major segment of your audience and, of course, that you can say the expression without laughing.

SELECTING AN APPROPRIATE STYLE: STRATEGIC DECISIONS

Thus far, we have discussed the general qualities of an effective style, such as accuracy, simplicity, coherence, language intensity, and appropriateness. Those qualities are necessary for clear, understandable oral communication. Next we will consider the aspects of speaking style that more particularly control audience members' impressions of you as a person, the nature of your message, and even the occasion itself. The combination of these aspects of oral communication is generally called *tone*. Are you basically an informal, happy-go-lucky person or someone talking seriously and formally about important matters? Are you presenting an argument to the audience members or telling them stories? Are you principally concerned with yourself and what the audience thinks of you, or are you trying to focus their attention primarily on your ideas?

While tone is an elusive quality of speech, nevertheless it is possible to identify some of its primary aspects, or dimensions. Three dimensions will receive special attention here: *written vs. oral style, serious vs. humorous atmosphere,* and *propositional vs. narrative form.*

Written vs. Oral Style

Oral speech developed long before written language. That may appear to be a simple and obvious fact, but its implications are far reaching. Oral speech, we presume, sprang directly from early humanity's contact with a harsh environment, and it still retains features of its origin. Generally, spoken language, because we use it more in informal settings (at the grocery store, over the back fence, around the supper table, in the street) than we do written language, is looser and less complicated. While you might write someone a note requesting them to "please depart from this area," the spoken version might be an order to "Get outta town!" Such words as "honey," "sweetie," and "dear" look terrible on the printed page, yet when spoken by intimates can elicit highly positive reactions. And, of course, the stereotyped waitress' "Whutkinahgitcha?" makes no sense in this book, yet it certainly does the job at 7:25 A.M. in the local greasy spoon.

Because we are usually tense about speaking in public, we often err in the direction of formality. This is especially likely to be true if we have written out the whole speech. Because we are used to composing on paper for the eye (for a reader) rather than for the ear (for a listener), most of us compose speeches in a written rather than oral style. The speeches sound stilted and stiff. They are likely to have sentences such as these:

> I am most pleased that you could come this morning. I would like to use this opportunity to discuss with you a subject of inestimable importance to us all— the impact of inflationary spirals on students enrolled in institutions of higher education.

Translated into the kind of oral style preferred in most speaking situations, those sentences would run something like this:

> Thanks for coming. I'd like to talk today about something that everyone here has had experience with—the rising costs of going to college.

Notice the differences in the two versions: the first is wordy, filled with prepositional phrases, larded with complex words, and formal in addressing the audience. The second contains shorter sentences, a more direct address of the audience, and a simpler vocabulary. The first is in a written style; the second, in an oral style.

On most occasions, you will want to cultivate an oral style. To be sure, there are some highly ceremonious occasions and situations, such as news conferences, in which you will read from a prepared text, but even at those times, you will want to strive for oral style.[4]

Serious vs. Humorous Atmosphere

Related to the matter of written vs. oral style is another variable: the seriousness with which a speaker expects an audience to take a speech and a speaking situation. You convey your impressions to the atmosphere of the occasion—and even the degree to which *you* expect to be taken seriously— largely by your speaking style.

Sometimes the speaking occasion dictates an appropriate atmosphere. We do not expect a light, humorous speaking style to be used, for example, during a funeral. This is not to say that jokes are never told during a funeral; often a minister, priest, or rabbi will tell a heart-warming, even humorous, story about the deceased. Yet, the overall tone of a funeral speech or sermon is somber, meditative, and serious. In contrast, a speech after a football victory, election win, or successful fund drive is seldom heavy, philosophical, or penetrating in its analysis of the human condition. Victory speeches are times for celebration, humor, warmth, joy, applause, and a feeling of unity with others who have worked on the cause.

Again, this is not to say that *humorous* means there are no audience-centered, nonfrivolous purposes for speaking involved here. As we will note in Chapter 14, even speeches to entertain have worthy purposes; they can be persuasive in their goals, and they can be given in grave earnestness. The political satirist who throws humorous but barbed comments at pompous, silly, or corrupt politicians is very concerned about political reform.

We are not talking here about serious or humorous speaking *purposes,* but, rather, serious or humorous linguistic *atmospheres*—the mind-set or mental attitude a speaker attempts to create in audiences. A speech urging individuals to be and think for themselves, cast in a serious atmosphere, might contain a section such as: "Be yourself. Trust in your own decision-making powers. Whenever you turn over your decision-making powers to a group, you become a dependent human being." That same section of a speech offered within a humorous atmosphere might sound like this: "Remember that a camel is a horse built by a committee. And when God put the universe together, she didn't consult with the angels and the archangels, the cherubim, seraphim, and the other folks hanging around heaven. If God had done that, they'd all still be arguing to this day, trying to figure out who should be in charge of stars, and of planets, and of moons—and you and I would still be dustballs in the back pocket of God. Socrates said, 'Know thyself,' and he could have added, 'Get off your duff and do something with that knowledge!' "

Sometimes, you will want to create a serious, sober atmosphere, a time for personal reflection and commitment on the part of your listeners. At other times, you will wish to loosen them up, to penetrate their defenses, and to share humor and joy with them. Make sure that the atmosphere you attempt to create is appropriate to the speaking situation and to your purposes.

Propositional vs. Narrative Form

Finally, speaking styles can differ greatly in another important way: Some styles are highly *propositional*—that is, they involve the presentation of arguments; other styles are highly *narrative*—that is, they are dominated by storytelling. When using a propositional form of speaking, the speaker offers a series of claims or assertions and supports each one with evidence. When using a narrative form, the speaker offers a story that contains a compelling message or "moral."

Suppose, for example, that you wished to persuade your classmates to make appointments to see their academic advisers regularly. Such a speech, in propositional form, might run something like this:

I. You ought to see your adviser regularly because he or she can check on your graduation requirements.
   A. Advisers have been trained to understand this school's requirements.
   B. They also probably helped write the departmental requirements for your major, and so they know them, too.

II. You ought to see your adviser regularly because that person usually can tell you something about careers in your field.
   A. Most faculty members at this school regularly attend professional meetings and find out what kinds of schools and companies are hiring in your field.
   B. Most faculty here have been around a long time and, thus, have seen what kinds of academic backgrounds get their advisees good jobs after school.

III. You ought to see your adviser regularly so that you can check out your own hopes and fears with someone.
   A. Good advisers help you decide whether you want to continue with a major.
   B. And, if you do decide to change majors, they often will help you find another adviser, in another department, who can work with a person like you.

This same speech, cast into narrative form, would come out as a story about someone's successes and difficulties:

I. I thought I could handle my own advising around this school, and that attitude got me into trouble.
   A. I could read, and I thought I knew what I wanted to take.
   B. I decided to steer my own course, and here's what happened.

II. At first, I was happy, taking any old course I wanted to.
   A. I skipped the regular laboratory sciences (chemistry, biology, physics) and took "Science and Society" instead.
   B. I didn't take statistics to meet my math requirement but instead slipped into remedial algebra.
   C. I piled up the hours in physical education so I could have a nice grade-point average to show my parents.

III. When I was about half done with my program, however, I realized that:
   A. I hadn't met about half of the general educational graduation requirements.
   B. I wanted to go into nursing.

IV. Therefore, I had to go back to freshman- and sophomore-level courses even though I was technically a junior.
   A. I was back taking the basic science and math courses.
   B. I was still trying to complete the social science and humanities requirements.

V. In all, I'm now in my fifth year of college, with at least one more to go.
   A. My classmates who used advisers have graduated.
   B. I suggest you follow their examples rather than mine if you want to save
      time and money.

Most of the time, speakers rely on propositional forms of speaking—most audiences expect them. But, in situations where a story or a personal illustration will allow you to make all of your points, you might wish to use a narrative form. It naturally catches up an audience in a situation—if you are a good storyteller—and usually is easier for people to remember than a bundle of arguments.

Ultimately, selecting an appropriate style is a matter of assessing yourself, your audience, the situation or context, and your purposes as a speaker. Thinking through those aspects of the communication model will help you select an appropriate style—formal or informal, serious or humorous, and propositional or narrative in form.

RHETORICAL STRATEGIES

By selecting an appropriate speaking style, you can not only help listeners comprehend and retain what you are saying, but also control the general atmosphere. Now it is time to get a good deal more specific about *rhetorical strategies*—the particular words you choose to use when you talk and how you can use different sorts of words and phrases to increase the comprehensibility and impact of your speeches.

There are countless rhetorical strategies available to speakers. We will review four of the most common and discuss ways they are used by effective speakers. These categories are: *definitions, restatements, imagery,* and *metaphor.*

Definitions

In most speaking situations, audience members need fundamental definitions of concepts. Your cannot expect them to understand ideas if the words are unfamiliar or if you are using words in a manner different from their generally accepted definition. Eight sorts of definitions are useful to speakers.

Defining from Dictionaries

A dictionary definition is a *reportive definition,* which indicates how people in general use a word. Dictionary definitions categorize an object or concept and specify its characteristics: "An orange is a *fruit* (category) which is *round, orange* in color, and a member of the *citrus family* (characteristics)."

John F. Kennedy was a master of rhetorical strategy. When he spoke, listeners not only understood and remembered his message; they felt the intensity of his words.

Dictionary definitions sometimes help you learn an unfamiliar or technical word, but they are seldom helpful to speakers because they tend to describe meanings in fairly general terms. So, dictionary definitions normally must be followed by other kinds of definitions that more precisely clarify a concept.

Defining in Your Own Words

Occasionally, a word has so many meanings that speakers have to indicate which one they wish to use. In that case, you must use a *stipulative definition*—one that stipulates the way you will use a word: "By *speech* I mean the act of offering a series of ideas and arguments to a group of hearers in a face-to-face situation." Such a definition orients the audience to your subject matter. Furthermore, if you think an audience respects an authority or expert, you can use that person's stipulative definition (an *authoritative definition*): "Hyman Smith, president of this school, defines a *liberal arts education* as one in which students are taught not merely technical operations and job-related skills but also ways of thinking and reasoning. Today, I want to explore that definition and what it means to you in your four years here."

Defining Negatively

Further clarity can be added by telling an audience how you are *not* going to use a term or concept—by using a *negative definition*. Along with the stipulative definition of speech, for example, we could have said: "By *speech* I do not mean to refer to the production of the 'correct' sounds and words of the English language, even though that is a common meaning of the word; rather, I will mean . . . ." Defining negatively can clear away possible misconceptions. Using a negative definition along with a stipulative definition is a technique that is especially useful when you are trying to treat a familiar concept in a new or different way.

Defining from Origins

Sometimes you can reinforce a series of feelings or attitudes you wish an audience to have about a concept by telling them where the word came from: "*Sincere* comes from two Latin words: *sine,* meaning 'without,' and *ceres,* meaning 'wax.' In early Rome, a superior statue was one in which the artisan did not have to cover his mistakes by putting wax into flaws. That statue was said to be *sine ceres*—'without wax.' Today, the term *a sincere person* carries some of that same meaning." This is called an *etymological definition* when you trace a word's meaning back into its original language. It is termed a *genetic definition* when you explain where the idea rather than the word comes from. You could, for instance, explain the American concept of freedom of speech by looking at important discussions of that idea in eighteenth-century England, and then showing how the American doctrine took its shape from our ancestors' British experiences. Defining from original sources, either of the word or of the idea, gives an audience a sense of continuity and at times explains certain nuances of meaning we cannot explain in any other way.

Defining by Examples

Particularly if a notion is unfamiliar or technical, one of the best ways to define is by an *exemplar definition*—one that simply points to a familiar example: "Each day, most of you stroll past Old Capitol on your way to classes. That building is a perfect example of what I want to talk about today—Georgian architecture." Be careful to pick only defining examples that your audience members will be familiar with.

Defining by Context

You also can define a word or concept by putting it in its usual context— through a *contextual definition*. This can be done verbally, as when a speaker says, "The difference between the words *imply* and *infer* is best understood in this way: The person generating a message *implies* a meaning; an observer *infers* an interpretation. Thus, *you* imply some idea or feeling in what you say, while *I* draw inferences about what you meant." A contextual definition also can go beyond such verbal descriptions, and, like a definition that uses examples, can point to a "real" context: "While there are many possible meanings to the word *revolution,* today I want to use it to describe the events that produced the American Revolution." You then would go on to specify those events. Defining by context gives an audience a sense of meaningfulness and is a good tactic for making certain kinds of concepts concrete.

Defining by Analogy

Still another means for making technical or abstract notions easier to understand is the *analogical definition.* An analogy compares a process or event that is unfamiliar or unknown with something that is familiar or known:

> Remember when you were a kid and you got into shouting matches with other kids? You'd begin with an "am, too/are not" argument: "I'm a better baseplayer than you." "You are not." "Am, too." "Are not." "Am too." Then you would up the ante by making it an "are, too/are not" match. "Well, your parents aren't as rich as mine." "They are, too!" "Are not." "Are, too." "Are not." And, finally, the argument would reach its peak with an "-ist" section: "Yeah, well, Methodists aren't real Christians." "They are, too—you're just a Communist." "Am not—I'm a Congregationalist." Those children's shouting matches are analogous to what we see in our country today. We are playing games very much like we did when we were kids, arguing over people's places in society. And today, as well, the strongest arguments in those struggles are "-ist" arguments, centered on such words as "racist," "sexist," "Americanist," "Communist," "Rightist," and "ageist." I want to discuss the destructive power of "-ist" accusations, and . . . .

By relying on a familiar experience or process, the analogical definition can make the new or abstract much easier to grasp. Just make sure that the analogy fits.

Defining by Describing Operations

Some words or concepts are best defined by reviewing the operations or procedures used in making or measuring something—by offering an *operational definition.* Scientists do this often so that they can translate abstract verbal concepts into observable or measurable things. Thus, a social scientist is most comfortable when defining *intelligence,* not abstractly but operationally: "*Intelligence quotient* is a person's performance on the Wechsler-Bellevue Intelligence Test compared with the performance of other members of the population." Along with exemplar and analogical definitions, operational definitions are especially good for making an audience "see" an idea or process.

> *Hank and Juan were discussing their speeches of definition after class. 'You know, Juan, I just don't think people were fair with me today. I found a neat definition of "socialism" and told them about Sweden and all that. I think you all came down too hard on me.' 'I don't, Hank. I think you deserved what you got. First, you just took a general dictionary defini-tion—what was it again?' Hank sorted through his notes until he came to the definition: 'Socialism: Any of various social-political theories advocating collective ownership and admin-istration of the means of production and control of the distribution of goods.' 'Right,' replied Juan. 'Listen to those words: What do they mean? They're too abstract. And besides, given that definition, you could be referring to countries as different as Russia and the United States—for after all, we have collective ownership and administration of power utili-ties, right? You're sure referring to more than Sweden. Why didn't you define subtypes of socialism? Why didn't you give a larger number of examples? Why didn't you distinguish between "socialism" and "communism"? Why didn't you . . . ' 'All right, all right!' interrupted Hank. 'I get the point.' 'And also, why didn't you use more than one type of definition, to really hit home? And . . . ' 'Enough, enough,' protested Hank. 'I'll work on it next time.' 'Do that. We'll listen better.'*

Restatement

If accuracy and simplicity were your only criteria as a speaker wishing to convey clear meanings, messages might resemble a famous World War II bulletin: "Sighted sub, sank same." But, because you are working face-to-face with listeners in oral, not written, language, another criterion is important. *Restatement,* as we use the term, is intentional repetition of two kinds: (1) *rephrasing* of ideas or concepts in more than one set of words or sentences, and (2) *reiteration* of ideas or concepts from more than one point of view. Because words literally disappear into the atmosphere as soon as you speak them, as an oral communicator you do not have the writer's advantage when transmitting ideas to others. Instead, you must rely heavily on rephrasing and reexamination.

Rephrasing

The effect of skillful rephrasing to clarify a message and make it more specific can be seen in the following passage from John F. Kennedy's inaugural address:

> Let the word go forth from this time and place, to friend and foe alike, that the torch has been passed to a new generation of Americans—born in this century, tempered by war, disciplined by a hard and bitter peace, proud of our ancient heritage—and unwilling to witness or permit the slow undoing of those human rights to which this nation has always been committed, and to which we are committed today at home and around the world.
>
> Let every nation know, whether it wishes us well or ill, that we shall pay any price, bear any burden, meet any hardship, support any friend, oppose any foe to assume the survival and the success of liberty.[5]

Reiteration

Reiterating an idea from a number of perspectives can usually be done by reforming the elements that make it up or by redefining the basic concept. You can see this principle of reiteration at work in the following excerpt from a student speech. Note how the speaker defines and redefines *political image* in a variety of ways, thereby providing metaphorical, psychological, and sociological perspectives:

> A "politician's image" is really a set of characteristics attributed to that politician by an electorate *[formal perspective]*. A political image, like any image which comes off a mirror, is made up of attributes which reflect the audience's concerns *[metaphorical perspective]*. An image is composed of bits and pieces of information and feelings which an audience brings to a politician *[psychological perspective],* and therefore it represents judgments made by the electorate on the bases of a great many different verbal and nonverbal acts a politician has engaged in *[sociological perspective]*. Therefore, if you think of a political image only in terms of manipulation, you are looking only at the mirror. Step back and examine the beholder, too, and you will find ways of discovering what a "good" image is for a politician.

If carefully handled, restatement in the form of rephrasing or reiteration can help you clarify your ideas and can help your listeners remember them more readily. However, be careful of mindless repetition; too many restatements, especially of ideas already clear to any alert member of your audience, are sure to be boring.

Imagery

We receive our impressions of the world through sensations of sight, smell, hearing, taste, and touch. If your listeners are to experience the object or state of affairs you are describing, you must appeal to their senses. But you cannot punch them in the nose, spray exotic perfume for them to smell, or let them taste foods that are not present. The primary senses through which you can reach your listeners *directly* are the visual and the auditory: they can see you, your movements, your facial expressions, and objects you use as "visual aids," and they can hear what you say.

Despite this limitation, however, you can *indirectly* stimulate all of their senses by using language that has the power to produce imagined sensations or causes them to recall images they have previously experienced. Through image-evoking language, you can help your listeners create many of the sensory pictures and events that you have experienced. Through vivid words, you can project the desired image swiftly into the mind's eye of your listeners. The language of imagery is divided into seven classes, or types, each related to the particular sensation that it seeks to evoke:

1. Visual *(sight)*
2. Auditory *(hearing)*
3. Gustatory *(taste)*
4. Olfactory *(smell)*
5. Tactual *(touch)*
   a. Texture and shape
   b. Pressure
   c. Heat and cold
6. Kinesthetic *(muscle strain)*
7. Organic *(internal sensations)*

Visual Imagery

Try to make your audience "see" the objects or situations you are describing. Mention *size, shape, color,* and *movement.* Recount events in vivid visual language. For example, in a time of cold war between the United States and Russia, General of the Army Douglas MacArthur knew he had to steel the cadets of the United States Military Academy for their uncertain future. His central theme—"duty, honor, and country"—was a refrain through the speech. To give that theme life, however, General MacArthur relied on a variety of visual images, as well as many of the other types of imagery we shall discuss. Note particularly his stress on images of size, shape, color, and movement:

In twenty campaigns, on a hundred battlefields, around a thousand campfires, I have witnessed that enduring fortitude, that patriotic self-abnegation, and that invincible determination which have carved his statue in the hearts of his people.

From one end of the world to the other, he has drained deep the chalice of courage. As I listened to those songs in memory's eye I could see those staggering columns of the First World War, bending under soggy packs on many a weary march, from dripping dusk to drizzly dawn, slogging ankle deep through mire of shell-pocked roads; to form grimly for the attack, blue-lipped, covered with sludge and mud, chilled by the wind and rain, driving home to their objective, and for many, to the judgment seat of God.

. . . Always for them: Duty, honor, country. Always their blood, and sweat and tears, as they saw the way and the light. And twenty years after, on the other side of the globe, again the filth of dirty foxholes, the stench of ghostly trenches, the slime of dripping dugouts, those boiling suns of relentless heat, those torrential rains of devastating storms, the loneliness and utter desolation of jungle trails, the bitterness of long separation of those they loved and cherished, the deadly pestilence of tropical disease, the horror of stricken areas of war.

Their resolute and determined defense, their swift and sure attack, their indomitable purpose, their complete and decisive victory, always through the bloody haze of their last reverberating shot, the vision of gaunt, ghastly men, reverently following your password of duty, honor, country.[6]

Auditory Imagery

To create auditory imagery, use words that help your listeners "hear" what you are describing. Auditory imagery may be used to project an audience into a scene. Author Tom Wolfe, for example, described a demolition derby by recounting the chant of the crowd as it joined in the countdown, the explosion of sound as two dozen cars started off in second gear, and finally "the unmistakable tympany of automobiles colliding and cheap-gauge sheet metal buckling."[7]

Gustatory Imagery

Sometimes you may even be able to help your audience "taste" what you are describing. Mention its saltiness, sweetness, sourness, or spiciness. Remember that foods have texture as well as taste. In a speech demonstrating how to make granola, you might mention the mealiness of rolled oats, the firmness of whole-grain wheat and flax seeds, and the stringiness of coconut. Such descriptions allow your audience to make positive or negative judgments about the experience.

Olfactory Imagery

Help your audience "smell" the odors connected with the situation you describe. Do this not only by mentioning the odor itself but also by describing the object that has the odor or by comparing it with more familiar ones. If you grew up in the country, think of the confusion of contrasting smells on a spring day—the fragrance of lilacs or cherry blossoms on the breeze, mingled with the odor of decaying manure as the barn is cleaned out. If you are a city person, what about the variety of smells that assault your nose as you stroll past a row of ethnic restaurants: Greek, Italian, East Indian, and Mexican?

Tactual Imagery

Tactual imagery is based on the various types of sensation that we get through physical contact with objects. In particular, it gives us sensations of texture and shape, pressure, and heat or cold.

Texture and shape: Let your audience "feel" how rough or smooth; dry or wet; or sharp, slimy, or sticky a thing is.

Pressure: Let them "sense" the pressure of physical force on their bodies: the weight of a heavy laundry bag, the pinch of jogging shoes that are too tight, the blast of a high wind on their faces.

Heat or cold: Sensations of heat or cold are aroused by what is sometimes called *thermal imagery.* Review the excerpt from Douglas MacArthur's speech for some vivid examples of all of these types of tactual imagery.

Kinesthetic Imagery

Kinesthetic imagery describes the sensations associated with muscle strain and neuromuscular movement. Phrase your speech on the agonies and joys of jogging in such a way that your listeners "feel" for themselves the muscle cramps, the constricted chest, the struggle for air—and the magical serenity of getting a second wind and thinking they will be able to "fly like this forever."

Organic Imagery

Hunger, dizziness, nausea—these are a few of the feelings organic imagery calls forth. There are times when an image is not complete without the inclusion of specific details likely to evoke these inner feelings. The sensation of dizziness as you struggled through the rarefied mountain air to reach the summit is one example. Another is the way the bottom dropped out of your stomach when the small plane dropped sharply, then righted itself. Be careful, however, not to offend your audience by overdoing this type of

Types of Imagery

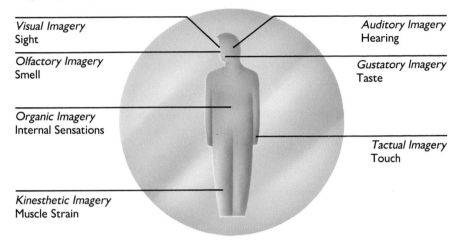

Visual Imagery
Sight

Auditory Imagery
Hearing

Olfactory Imagery
Smell

Gustatory Imagery
Taste

Organic Imagery
Internal Sensations

Tactual Imagery
Touch

Kinesthetic Imagery
Muscle Strain

imagery. Develop the sensitivity required to measure the detail necessary for creating vividness without making the resultant image gruesome, disgusting, grotesque.

The seven types of imagery we have considered—*visual, auditory, gustatory, olfactory, tactual, kinesthetic,* and *organic*—may be referred to as "doorways to the mind."[8] They open the audience to new levels of awareness in understanding and believing speakers and acting on their messages. Because people differ in their degrees of sensitivity to different types of imagery, you should try to build into your messages as many appeals to their senses through these perceptual "doorways" as possible.

In the following example, note how the speaker has combined various sensory appeals to arouse listener interest and reaction:

The strangler struck in Donora, Pennsylvania, in October of 1948. A thick fog billowed through the streets enveloping everything in thick sheets of dirty moisture and a greasy black coating. As Tuesday faded into Saturday, the fumes from the big steel mills shrouded the outlines of the landscape. One could barely see across the narrow streets. Traffic stopped. Men lost their way returning from the mills. Walking through the streets, even for a few moments, caused eyes to water and burn. The thick fumes grabbed at the throat and created a choking sensation. The air acquired a sickening bittersweet smell, nearly a taste. Death was in the air.[9]

In this example, college student Charles Schaillol uses vivid, descriptive phrases to affect the senses of his listeners: *visual*—"thick sheets of dirty moisture"; *organic*—"eyes to water and burn"; *olfactory, gustatory*—"sickening bittersweet smell, nearly a taste."

To be effective, such illustrations must appear plausible: The language must convey an impression that what is being described did or could happen in the way the speaker chooses to relate it. The speaker who describes the "strangler" that struck Donora offers a plausible account of the event. More importantly, he does so in a fashion that arouses feelings. Audiences would not be as likely to share the experience if the speaker had simply said, "Air pollution was the cause of death in Donora."

Metaphor

The images created by appealing to the various senses are often the result of using *metaphors*—words that compare two dissimilar things. Charles Schaillol's "fog . . . thick sheets" is one example of a metaphor used to illuminate the image he wished to create of the fog's effect. To be successful, as Michael Osborn notes, the metaphor should "result in an intuitive flash of recognition that surprises or fascinates the hearer."[10] Furthermore, good metaphors should extend our knowledge or increase our awareness of a person, object, or event. A reference to a table's "legs" may illuminate the object, but it lacks fascination. When they are fresh or vivid, metaphors can be powerful aids in evoking feelings (for example, "balanced on four obese toothpicks, the antique table swayed under the heavy load").

While vividness and freshness can make metaphors highly appealing to audiences, on other occasions you will want to use metaphors drawn from everyday experiences. In almost every public speech he delivered, for example, Martin Luther King, Jr., appealed to our experiences of light and darkness, as he did in the following quotation:

> With this faith in the future, with this determined struggle, we will be able to emerge from the bleak and desolate midnight of man's inhumanity to man, into the bright and glittering daybreak of freedom and justice.[11]

This simple light-dark metaphor was important to King's thinking and speechmaking because it allowed him to suggest *(1)* sharp contrasts between inhumanity and freedom and *(2)* the inevitability of social progress (as "daybreak" always follows "midnight"). In other words, the metaphor worked—it communicated King's beliefs about justice and injustice and urged his followers to act.

In summary, words are not neutral conduits for thought. Words not only reflect the "real" world outside your mind, but they also, as theoretical critic Kenneth Burke suggests, help *shape* our perceptions of people, events, and social contexts. It is clear that language has a potent effect on people's willingness to believe, to feel, and to act.

. . . $Sample$ $Speech$ . . . .

William Faulkner (1897–1962) presented the following speech on December 10, 1950, in accepting the Nobel Prize for Literature. As he had no reputation as a lecturer, the public might have expected a lesser speech filled with the kind of pessimism so characteristic of his novels. Instead, he greeted his listeners with a stirring challenge to improve humankind.

Notice in particular Mr. Faulkner's use of language. Although known for the tortured sentences of his novels, here he expresses his ideas clearly and simply. His tone is closer to a written than to an oral language, yet his use of organic imagery and powerful metaphors keep the speech alive. The atmosphere is generally serious, befitting the occasion. While one might expect a Nobel Prize-winner to talk about himself, Mr. Faulkner did just the opposite, stressing his craft—writing—and what audience members must be committed to in order to practice that craft; this material emphasis led naturally to an essentially propositional rather than narrative form. Overall, in 1950 William Faulkner offered a speech that meets today's oral language requirements and challenges.

ON ACCEPTING THE NOBEL PRIZE FOR LITERATURE[12]
William Faulkner

I feel that this award was not made to me as a man, but to my work—a life's work in the agony and sweat of the human spirit, not for glory and least of all for profit, but to create out of the materials of the human spirit something which did not exist before. So this award is only mine in trust. It will not be difficult to find a dedication for the money part of it commensurate with the purpose and significance of its origin. But I would like to do the same with the acclaim too, by using this moment as a pinnacle from which I might be listened to by the young men and women already dedicated to the same anguish and travail, among whom is already that one who will some day stand here where I am standing.   /I

Our tragedy today is a general and universal physical fear so long sustained by now that we can even bear it. There are no longer problems of the spirit.

There is only the question: When will I be blown up? Because of this, the young man or woman writing today has forgotten the problems of the human heart in conflict with itself which alone can make good writing because only that is worth writing about, worth the agony and the sweat.   /2

He must learn them again. He must teach himself that the basest of all things is to be afraid; and, teaching himself that, forget it forever, leaving no room in his workshop for anything but the old verities and truths of the heart, the old universal truths lacking which any story is ephemeral and doomed— love and honor and pity and pride and compassion and sacrifice. Until he does so, he labors under a curse. He writes not of love but of lust, of defeats in which nobody loses anything of value, of victories without hope and, worst of all, without pity or compassion. His griefs grieve on no universal bones, leaving no scars. He writes not of the heart but of the glands.   /3

Until he relearns these things, he will write as though he stood among and watched the end of man. I decline to accept the end of man. It is easy enough to say that man is immortal simply because he will endure: that when the last ding-dong of doom has clanged and faded from the last worthless rock hanging tideless in the last red and dying evening, that even then there will still be one more sound: that of his puny inexhaustible voice, still talking. I refuse to accept this. I believe that man will not merely endure: he will prevail. He is immortal, not because he alone among creatures has an inexhaustible voice, but because he has a soul, a spirit capable of compassion and sacrifice and endurance. The poet's, the writer's, duty is to write about these things. It is his privilege to help man endure by lifting his heart, by reminding him of the courage and honor and hope and pride and compassion and pity and sacrifice which have been the glory of his past. The poet's voice need not merely be the record of man, it can be one of the props, the pillars to help him endure and prevail.   /4

• •

CHAPTER SUMMARY

Successful speeches generally are characterized by *accurate, simple, coherent, properly intense,* and *appropriate* language choices. In selecting a speaking style appropriate to you, the occasion, your subject matter, and the audience, you must make decisions about *written vs. oral language,* a *serious vs. humorous atmosphere,* and *propositional vs. narrative forms* of presentation. So far as rhetorical strategies are concerned, consider: (1) *definitions* (in your own words, negatively, from original sources, by examples, by context, by analogy, and by describing operations);

(2) *restatement* (both rephrasing and reiteration); (3) *imagery* (visual, auditory, gustatory, olfactory, tactual, kinesthetic, and organic); and (4) *metaphor.* Language choices, and the resulting speaking styles, are speakers' most crucial channels of substantive communication.

Oral Activities

1. Individually or in groups, construct a two- to three-minute speech narrative, using as many clichés, mixed metaphors, and pieces of slang as you can. Present the narrative to your class, asking audience members to suggest even more overused and misused expressions relating to your topic.
2. Prepare a three- to four-minute speech narrating your feelings about a particular location—for instance, the town in which you grew up, a building you have dreamed of touring, or a place made famous by a favorite author. If your instructor allows it, deliver the speech from manuscript. Turn in that manuscript after delivering the speech so that your instructor can comment on your language—accuracy, simplicity, coherence, intensity, appropriateness, oral style, definitions, restatements, imagery, and metaphors.
3. As a take-home assignment, rewrite a complicated message (e.g., an insurance policy, agreement for a credit card or loan, income tax instruction, or difficult passage from this textbook) in simpler yet still-accurate language. Present the material as a short speech in your class, turning it in later for your instructor's comments.

Reference Notes

1. For more extended treatments of this subject, see Doris B. Garey, *Putting Words in Their Places* (Glenview, IL: Scott, Foresman and Company, 1957); and Roger Brown, *Words and Things* (Glenview, IL: Scott, Foresman and Company, 1968).
2. Quoted in John R. Pelsma, *Essentials of Speech* (New York: Crowell, Collier, and Macmillan, 1934), 193.
3. John Waite Bowers, "Language and Argument," in *Perspectives on Argumentation,* G. R. Miller and T. R. Nilsen, eds., (Glenview, IL: Scott, Foresman and Company, 1966), esp. 168–72.
4. For a summary of several technical studies distinguishing between oral and written styles and for a discussion of sixteen characteristics of oral style, see John F. Wilson and Carroll C. Arnold, *Public Speaking as a Liberal Art,* 5th ed. (Boston: Allyn and Bacon, 1983), 227–29.

5. From *Public Papers of the Presidents of the United States: John F. Kennedy* (Washington, DC: U.S. Government Printing Office, 1961).
6. Excerpts from "Duty, Honor and Country" by Douglas MacArthur in *The Dolphin Book of Speeches,* edited by George W. Hibbitt. Copyright © 1965 by George W. Hibbitt. Reprinted by permission of Doubleday & Company, Inc.
7. A selection from *The Kandy-Kolored Tangerine-Flake Streamline Baby* by Tom Wolfe. Copyright © 1963, 1965 by Thomas K. Wolfe, Jr. Copyright © 1963 by New York Herald Tribune, Inc. Reprinted with the permission of Farrar, Straus & Giroux, Inc. and International Creative Management.
8. Victor Alvin Ketcham, "The Seven Doorways to the Mind," in *Business Speeches by Business Men,* William P. Sandford and W. Hayes Yeager, eds. (New York: McGraw-Hill Book Company, 1930).
9. From "The Strangler" by Charles Schaillol. Reprinted from *Winning Orations* by special arrangement with the Interstate Oratorical Association, Larry Schnoor, Executive Secretary, Mankato State College, Mankato, Minnesota.
10. Michael Osborn, *Orientations to Rhetorical Style* (Chicago: Science Research Associates, 1976), 10.
11. From "Love, Law and Civil Disobedience" by Martin Luther King, Jr. Copyright © 1961, 1963 by Martin Luther King, Jr. Reprinted by permission of Joan Daves.
12. "On Accepting the Nobel Prize for Literature" by William Faulkner. Reprinted from *The Faulkner Reader.* Copyright 1954 by William Faulkner, Random House, Inc.

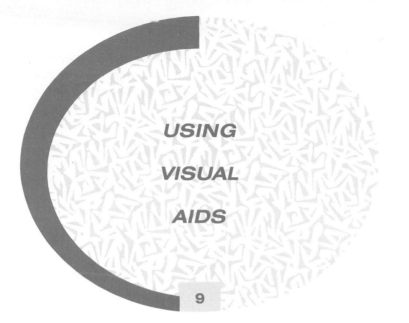

USING

VISUAL

AIDS

9

Television, film, transparencies, VCRs and videotape, overhead projections, billboards, banners trailing from airplanes, sidewalk tables with samples from a hardware store's "today only" sale—your world is filled with visual communication media. Ours is a visual age second to none, and the United States undoubtedly is the most visually oriented society in the world today. Entire companies—from such famous ones as the major television and film studios down to small-town graphics production shops in people's basements—feed off your willingness to pay for good pieces of visual communication.

Likewise, the public speaker is in the business of visually communicating. Your presence in front of an audience is a visual act (we will deal with the matter of nonverbal, or body, communication in Chapter 10). Your use of visual aids—from objects a second grader brings to school for "show and tell" to the flipcharts sales trainers use, to the slides you show from your vacation—makes visual communication an essential part of the oral communication transaction.

Research on visual media, learning, and attitude change has told us something about the impact of visual aids on audiences.[1] Yet, much advice you receive is still a matter of veteran speakers' passing on their experiences to novices. In this chapter, we will mix advice from social-scientific research with wisdom from the "old pros." First, we will deal with the functions of visual aids, then describe the various types you can use, and finally offer some advice on how to use them effectively.

THE FUNCTIONS OF VISUAL AIDS

Visual materials enhance your presentation in two important ways: (1) they aid listener comprehension and memory and (2) they add persuasive impact to your message.

Comprehension and Memory

The truth of the old saying "A picture is worth a thousand words" depends on whether the picture adds information that is more easily understood visually than aurally. Visual research has demonstrated that bar graphs, especially, make statistical information more accessible to an audience. Similarly, simple drawings enhance recall, and charts and such human interest visuals as photographs help listeners process and retain data.[2] Pictures accompanying a story being read aloud to children have significant effects on listener recall and comprehension.[3] Thus, visuals can be of immense value if your purpose is to inform or teach an audience.

Persuasiveness

In the process of enhancing comprehension and memory, visuals will save you precious time in persuasive situations. Visuals can heighten the persuasive impact of your ideas. Lawyers, for example, have taken advantage of the dramatic effects that accompany the visual evidence of injuries or crimes in order to elicit a favorable response from juries. Some lawyers are experimenting with the use of video technology to create dramatic portrayals of events—the condition of a road in an involuntary manslaughter case, or a parent's evident sense of caring and loving in a custody battle—in order to influence jury decisions. Undeniably, your credibility as a speaker, as well as the credibility of the message, is positively affected by the effective use of appropriate visuals.[4] Visual materials satisfy the "show-me" attitude that is prevalent within many audiences; in this sense, they provide one more crucial means of meeting listener expectations.[5]

TYPES OF VISUAL SUPPORT

Visual materials can be divided into two broad classes: real objects and symbolic representations of actual objects. As we discuss both broad groupings, we will examine specific tips on how you can use them to supplement your oral presentation of ideas.

Actual Objects

The objects you bring to a presentation, including your own body, can be discussed under two headings: animate objects and inanimate objects.

Animate Objects

Live animals or plants can, with appropriate discretion, be brought into a speaking situation. If you are demonstrating the "care and feeding of laboratory mice," bringing one or two in a cage may be useful in clarifying points of your speech. Describing the differences between two varieties of plants may be easier if you use real plants. However, you might be stretching your luck a bit by bringing a real horse into class and showing how one is saddled (it happened), although it is a useful way of making the procedure clear. Discretion and common sense about what is possible and in good taste will help make such visuals work for you rather than against you.

As is true of other visuals, you will want to maximize audience attention on your commentary *about* the actual object, rather than allowing the audience to become absorbed *by* the object. A registered Persian cat may be perfect for a speech illustrating what judges look for in cat shows, but if it gets loose or is passed around the class, your message may be lost in the process. Keeping the animal restrained and firmly in your possession will help.

Speeches on yoga positions, various ways of loosening up before running, ballet steps, or tennis strokes gain concreteness and vitality from speakers who illustrate such subjects personally. The entire speech need not be devoted to a "physical" subject in order to effectively use your body in illustrating action. A yoga position may be well executed, but it will not help if you are on the floor and the members in the back rows cannot see you (use the top of a sturdy table). Slow the tempo so that the audience can see discrete movements; fast tennis swings will not help the audience understand what is being done. One advantage to such visual action is that you *can* control the audience's attention to the demonstration.

Inanimate Objects

Demonstrations often are enhanced by the presence of the actual object being discussed. Telling an audience how to string a tennis racket will be aided by bringing one in to illustrate the process. Showing the best means of repairing rust holes in a car is made easier if you have samples of the work required in the separate stages. As in television cooking shows, you do not have the time to do the actual work. By preparing samples before the presentation, you save valuable time and illustrate what must be done.

As noted above, you will want to keep audience attention focused on the message and not solely or completely on the object. Moving objects to "center stage" and then removing them will help you control the flow of attention from the object to your narrative. Keeping the object between you and the audience, to the extent possible, also will allow greater visual contact. If you stand in front of the object or to the side, you run the risk of blocking the audience's view.

Symbolic Representations

When you cannot actually bring the object in or use your own movement to clarify your meaning, you may resort to symbolic representations of the objects or the concepts being discussed. These representations may be relatively *concrete,* as in the use of pictures, slides, films, or videotapes. *Abstract* drawings, graphs, charts, and models can also depict the object or concept.

Concrete Representations

Photographs can give the audience a visual sense of what you are talking about. You can illustrate flood damage by using photos of ravaged homes and land, for instance, or depict the beauty of an area threatened by a new dam. One problem with photographs is that audiences may not be able to see what is being shown as you hold a picture in front of them. If you need to pass pictures around, try to limit the number and hand out each one after discussing the point that the photo helps you make. This will minimize audience distraction as photos are passed from one person to another. If you can enlarge a small photograph so that people can see it more easily, this, too, will help control audience attention.

Slides (35-mm transparencies) also allow you to depict color, shape, texture, and relationships. If you are presenting a travelogue, slides are virtually a necessity in discussing buildings and landscape. A speech on the days of the steam engines can be more interesting and informative if you can obtain appropriate slides of various machines in operation. The persuasive impact of a speech against the construction of a dam can be enhanced by slides depicting the white water that will be destroyed. Slides of the work of famous artists will enable you to illustrate differences in their work.

Slides do require some familiarity with projection equipment and some forethought about how to set up the presentation so that people can see. Attention to small, seemingly inconsequential details will make a major difference in how smoothly the presentation goes. Do you know how to change the projection lamp (and did you bring a spare bulb along just in case)? Will you need an extension cord, or will the projector's cord reach the outlet? Do you know how to remove a jammed slide? If you operate on the assumption "Whatever can go wrong, will," you will be prepared for most circumstances.

Videotapes and *films* also can be useful in illustrating the point you want to make. Segments from several current sitcoms can dramatically illustrate your claim that child stars are forced into adult roles. Taping two or three political ads can help you illustrate the packaging of a candidate. Again, familiarity with the operation of a videocassette recorder and monitor will help ensure a smooth presentation, and, if you are using films, be sure that you can thread the machine. Too often, speakers bring films with them, assuming that a projector and a skilled technician will be provided, only to find that no one can get the machine running properly. Such delays increase your nervousness and make it more difficult to get the audience to concentrate on your presentation once the equipment problems have been solved. Again, knowing how to change a projection lamp will help you avoid a crisis.

Abstract Representations

If you need to illustrate the growth or decline of inflation or show how revenue will be spent in the next six months, you will find yourself resorting to more abstract representations than those discussed above. The form and style of the representation—drawings, charts, graphs—will depend on the formality of the situation. If you are discussing a building plan for a prospective client, a quick sketch may suffice. However, if you are meeting with the client's board of directors, the same rough drawing will be inadequate. The board will expect a polished presentation, complete with a professionally prepared prospectus. Similarly, a chalkboard drawing may be sufficient in explaining the process of cell division to a group of classmates, but when presenting the same information as part of a formal project, you will want to refine the visual support materials. The care with which you prepare these visuals will convey to the audience an attitude of indifference or concern.

Chalkboard drawings are especially valuable when you want to unfold an idea step-by-step. By drawing each stage as you come to it, you can control the audience's attention to your major points. Coaches often use this approach in showing players how a particular play will work. Time lines and size differences also can be depicted with rough sketches on a chalkboard. The relatively short history of life forms can be shown visually by a time line showing approximations of when life began, when recorded history began, and the time elapsed since Columbus discovered America.

Overhead projectors are often used like chalkboards; although it can be somewhat distracting to see such movement across a light source, some speakers draw with a grease pencil on an acetate sheet while they talk. Better is the practice of preparing transparencies beforehand. One advantage of an overhead projector is that you can turn it off when you have made your point, thereby removing a competing stimulus from the environment.

> *Benj decided to save a little time and money on visual aids for his speech. He ordered an opaque projector, which projects pages of a book directly onto a screen. The problems began as soon as he arrived at the classroom on the day of his speech. First, he almost herniated himself carrying the projector into the room; he had had no idea how heavy it would be. When he turned it on after the introduction to his speech, he could barely make himself heard over its noisy cooling fan. Then, as he inserted the book with the first graph he wanted to project, there was a ripple of laughter because the image was upside down. Finally, he discovered that the magnification on an opaque projector is minimal, so people in the back row could not read the graph at all. After that experience, Benj and his classmates decided to leave opaque projectors alone and take the time to make other, easier-to-use visual aids for their speeches.*

When using either a chalkboard or an overhead projector, make your drawings large enough to be clear to the audience. You can continue to talk to the audience as you draw, so long as you are brief; attention will wander if you talk to the board or the light source for three or four minutes while drawing. Also, consider the visual field while you draw: Where should you stand to avoid blocking the audience's view? And finally, when you are through talking about the illustration, either erase the board or turn off the projector.

Graphs require more attention than quick drawings, as they normally are used to show relationships among various parts of a whole, or between variables across time. In these cases, accuracy is critical in visually illustrating the degree of difference. Graphs can take several forms:

1. *Bar graphs* show the relationships between two or more sets of figures. If you are indicating the discrepancy between income earned by various groups of professionals, or between men and women in the same occupations, a bar graph would be an appropriate visual support for your oral presentation.

Bar Graphs

Bar graphs visually illustrate relationships. Changing spacing and size of bars can affect the visual message.

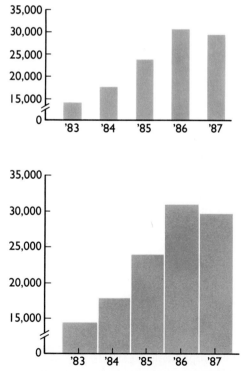

Line Graphs

Line graphs can reveal relationships; they also can deceive the unwary. These graphs show the same data but use different spacing along one or both axes to change the visual image.

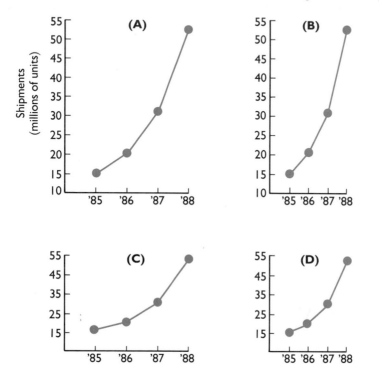

2. *Line graphs* show relations between two or more variables. If you are trying to explain a complex economic relationship involving supply and demand, a line graph will be a useful tool.

3. *Pie graphs* show percentages by dividing a circle into the proportions being represented. A charity may use a pie graph to show how much of its income is spent on administration, research, and fund-raising campaigns. Town governments use pie graphs to show citizens what proportion of their tax dollars go to municipal services, administration, education, recreation, and so on.

4. *Pictographs* signify size or number through the use of symbols. A representation of the U.S. and Soviet missile strength would use drawings of missiles (one symbol represents 1000 actual missiles), allowing a viewer to see at a glance the disparity between the two countries.

Pie Graphs

$ Support for Intercollegiate Athletics

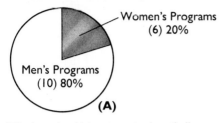

(A)

This pie graph, with two segments, dramatically illustrates a perceived imbalance in funding for intercollegiate athletics. Shading one segment also helps draw attention to the difference.

Cost of Major Men's Sports

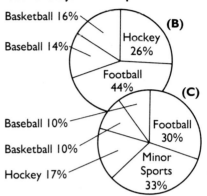

A speaker can break down one segment of graph A in two ways: to show the costs of four major sports (graph B) and to contrast the costs of major sports and the "minor" sports of tennis, golf, wrestling, and so on (graph C).

Male-Female Athletics

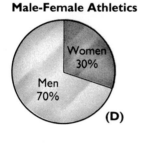

(D)

Having illustrated what appears to be an imbalance in the funding of intercollegiate athletics, a speaker may offset some of the argument by discussing the male/female ratio of total players funded. (graph D). When used in conjunction with graph A, the disparity is lessened: 80 percent of the money supports 70 percent of the participants.

Taken alone or together, the data in these graphs *do not* provide compelling evidence that women's sports are treated fairly or unfairly. Nevertheless, using such visual aids heightens interest and dramatizes points made orally.

Your choice of bar, line, pie, or pictorial graphs will depend on the subject and the nature of the relationship you wish to convey. A pie graph, for example, will not illustrate discrepancies between two groups, nor will it show effects of change over time. To visually represent these relations, a bar graph or a line graph might be used. A bar graph can, however, create a misleading impression of the difference between two items if one bar is short and wide while the other is long and narrow. Line graphs can distort time if the units of measurement are not the same for each time period. These problems can be avoided by using consistent measurements in creating the graphs.

Charts and *tables* also lend support and clarity to your ideas. If you are trying to indicate the channels of communication or lines of authority in a large company, your presentation will be much easier to follow if each

Pictographs

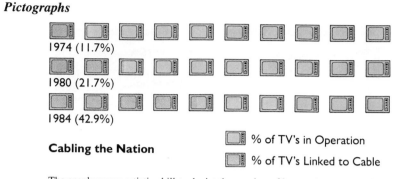

Cabling the Nation

⬛ % of TV's in Operation

⬛ % of TV's Linked to Cable

The speaker uses artistic skill to depict the number of houses (represented by television sets) being accessed by cable systems. The artistry draws attention to the information.

Source: *USA Today*, January 28, 1985.

listener has an organizational chart to refer to. If the organization is large and complex, you may want to develop a series of charts, each one focusing on a smaller subset of the original. A dense chart showing all the major and minor offices may simply overwhelm the listeners as they try to follow you through the maze.

Unveiling successive charts (through the use of a *flipchart*) also will focus audience attention on specific parts of the speech. If you hand an audience a complete chart, they will tend to stray from your order of explanation as they read parts of the chart. A *flow chart* can help indicate the actions that might be taken across time; planners can indicate what will be done by whom and in what order. If you are explaining a fund-raising campaign, a flow chart will allow audiences to visualize the stages of the campaign. As long as the information is not too complex or lengthy, *tables* can indicate changes in inventory over time. They also can be used to rank lists of items and their cost, frequency of use, or relative importance. As with charts, tables should be designed so that they can be seen and so that they convey data in a simple, clear form; too much information will force the audience to concentrate more on the visual support than on your oral explanation.

Models of real objects that cannot be brought into a room or cannot be seen because of their small size can assist in dramatizing your explanation. Architects construct models of new projects to show to clients. Developers of shopping malls, condominiums, and business offices use models when persuading zoning boards to grant needed rights-of-way or variances. An explanation of the complexity of the DNA molecule would be aided by a

Flipcharts allow a speaker to control the pace and sequential flow of information to the audience. The same effect can be achieved with chalkboard drawings or slide transparencies projected onto a screen.

model. Models need to be manageable and visible to the audience. If you are using a model that will come apart so that different pieces can be explained, practice removing and replacing the parts beforehand.

SELECTING AND USING VISUAL AIDS: STRATEGIES AND DETERMINING FACTORS

Your decisions of which visual materials to use, and to your best advantage, should be based on three considerations: (1) the communicative potential of various visual materials, (2) your ability to integrate verbal and visual materials effectively, and (3) the characteristics of the audience and occasion.

Consider the Communicative Potential of Various Visual Aids

Keep in mind that each type of visual material has certain potentials for communicating particular kinds of information, and that each type interacts with your spoken presentation as well as your audience's state of mind. In general, primarily pictorial or photographic visuals can make an audience *feel* the way you do. Slides, movies, sketches, or photographs often can be used effectively to accompany travelogues or reports of personal experiences because they illustrate or reproduce in others the kinds of feelings you experienced in another place, situation, or time.

> Molly was giving an informational speech on types of relaxation techniques available in the university community. As she got up to speak, she darkened the room, turned on a colored, oil-filled, lighted motion machine and played a tape of random, gentle electronic music. Within a minute, the audience visibly sagged, and some students put their heads down on their books. Molly began speaking quietly over the music in tones reminiscent of a nighttime FM announcer. Within another minute, two kids fell asleep. She then turned everything off and had the class stand up, telling everyone to jump up and down a few times to wake themselves up. Molly then moved into the rest of her introductory remarks. Her visual-aural aids had not only set a tone for the talk but captured the mood of her central idea. Molly's instructor and classmates agreed that her presentation was one of the most effective uses of sensual visual-aural aids they had ever seen (and heard).

Visuals containing descriptive or verbal materials, on the other hand, can help an audience *think* the way you do. Such aids as models, diagrams, charts, and graphs frequently add rational support to claims you are attempting to defend. Your topic and communicative purpose, therefore, play large roles in determining the best kinds of visuals to use in a given circumstance. A speech informing listeners of your experiences in Indonesia should probably be accompanied by slides or films and even some household artifacts. A speech to persuade your listeners that the United States ought to sever all association with the Southeast Asia Treaty Organization probably should be supported by maps, charts, and chalkboard drawings.

Integrate Verbal and Visual Materials Effectively

To be effective, visual aids should be relevant to your topic and your communicative purpose. You use visuals in order to save time, to enhance the impact of your message, to clarify complex relations, and to generally enliven your presentation. The following suggestions build on, and in some cases reinforce, those already presented in our discussion of specific aids.

1. *Design abstract symbolic representations with care.* Use contrasting colors (red on white, black on yellow) to highlight the information in an organizational chart or table. Segments of a pie graph can be differentiated by using contrasting colors. A bar graph can use the same color for two or more bars, or it can be designed so that each bar is highlighted by using a new color.

2. *Keep charts and other graphic aids clear and simple.* Research has demonstrated that plain bar graphs—probably because they offer not only numbers but also a visualization of those numbers—are the single most effective method for displaying statistical comparisons.[6] Make sure that the essential information you want your audience to focus on stands out clearly from the background. Let simplicity be your watchword in the preparation of all visual aids.

3. *Make your visuals—especially those with materials that must be read or scrutinized closely—large enough to be seen clearly and easily.* Listeners get frustrated when, in the middle of the speech, they find themselves having to lean forward and squint in order to see a detail on a sketch or graph. Make your figures and lettering large enough so that, as John Hancock noted in connection with the Declaration of Independence in 1776, they "can be seen by the King of England without his glasses."

4. *Take enough time in preparing visuals to make them presentable.* Draw neatly; spell correctly; make bar graph lines proportional; make all letters the same size. Such advice may seem juvenile, but the fact remains that beginning speakers often throw together visual materials at the last minute, forgetting that *everything* they present to an audience contributes to its assessment of their credibility. You may be sure that misspelled words and sloppy graphs lower listeners' estimation of your competence.

5. *Decide well in advance whether to bring animate or inanimate objects with you and, if you do, how you will handle them.* This is especially true for so-called "demonstration" speeches, in which you show listeners how to do something. For example, if you do tombstone dabbing (making paper casts of old tombstone faces), do you bring one in? (Tombstones are heavy.) How much of the process do you show? (It is time consuming and messy.) How detailed should you get? (Should you include discussions of the chemicals used for cleaning stone surfaces, of the different kinds of paper, or of various dabbing techniques? Or, should you just describe the basic processes?) Unless you think through such questions in advance, you are liable to find yourself making hasty decisions in midspeech, when you have other things to worry about.

6. *Be prepared to compensate orally for any distraction your visual aid may inadvertently create.* If you pass around a sample of your work—a leather purse or silver ring you have made—remember that an actual object or detailed model is a complex, potent visual stimulus. This makes it a message maker in its own right, and you must compete with it for your listeners' attention. So, tell your audience what aspects of the object to examine closely and which ones to ignore. If, despite your cautions, the object or full-scale model is likely to prove distracting, build enough reiteration into your speech to make reasonably certain your listeners can follow your train of thought even while they are studying the object and passing it around. As added insurance, you might also provide a rough sketch of it on the chalkboard, visually reinforcing the verbal message you are trying to communicate.

7. *When using slides, films, overhead projectors, or videotapes, be prepared to make the verbal and physical adjustments necessary to coordinate the visual materials with the spoken materials.* With these aids, you often darken the room, thereby compelling your audience to concentrate on a source of light: the silver screen in the case of slides and films, the 19-inch screen in the case of a TV monitor. At such times, you—the *oral* communicator—must compete with the *mechanical* or *electronic* communicator. If, as often happens, your audience begins to concentrate harder on the flow of light than on the flow of words, you defeat your own purpose. Therefore, when using projected materials as visual support, either *(a)* talk more loudly and move more vigorously when communicating simultaneously with the machine or *(b)* refuse to compete with it at all. That is, show the film or the slides either *before* or *after* you comment on their content. Whatever strategy you use, however, make sure that the projected visual materials are well integrated into the rest of your presentation.

8. *Hand your listeners a copy of those materials you wish them to think back on or carry away from your speech.* If, for example, you are making recommendations to a student council, you may provide copies of a proposal for the council's subsequent action. Or, if you are reporting the results of a survey, the most pertinent statistics will be better understood and remembered if you give each listener a copy of them. Few people can recall the seven warning signs of cancer, but they could keep a list of them in a handy place if you gave a copy to each member of your audience. Remember that we are referring here only to speech material that is a legitimate *visual aid*. Obviously, you will not put everything you have to say on a photocopied page. Select only elements or items that will have lasting value.

Although more could be said about choosing and using the various types of visual media to which we have referred, the foregoing suggestions should enable you—with careful planning—to take advantage of their communicative potential. Good visual material is not distracting. It "fits," it is essential to the verbal message, and it leaves an audience with a feeling of completeness.

Consider the Audience and the Occasion

In choosing the types and content of the visual supporting materials you will use, common sense will tell you that you must also consider the *status* of the subject in the minds of your audience. Ask yourself: Do I need to bring a map of the United States to an audience of American college students when discussing the westward movement of population in this country? Or, if I am going to discuss offensive and defensive formations used by a football team, should I provide diagrams of such formations? And, can I really expect an audience to understand the administrative structure of the federal bureaucracy without an organizational chart?

How much an audience *already knows, needs to know,* and *expects to find out* about you and your subject are clearly determinants that weigh heavily when you choose the types and numbers of visual supports you will use in a speech. How readily that audience can comprehend *aurally* what you have to say is another. Granted, it is not always easy to assess any of these conditions or capabilities. It may be exceedingly difficult, in fact, to decide how much an audience of college freshmen and sophomores knows about college or governmental structures, and, certainly, you cannot easily judge how well acquainted a Rotary Club audience is with football plays. That being the case, probably the best thing you can do is to check out your speculations by asking around among your potential listeners well ahead of the time you are scheduled to deliver your speech. In other words, before making any final decisions about visual supporting materials, do as much audience research and analysis as you possibly can.

As a part of your advance planning for the use of visuals, also take into account the nature of the occasion or the uniqueness of the circumstances in which you will be speaking. You will find that certain kinds of occasions seemingly cry out for certain types of graphic supporting materials. The corporate executive who presents a projective report to the board of directors without a printed handout or diagrams probably would find his or her credibility questioned. The military adviser who calls for governmental expenditure for new weapons without offering pictures or drawings of the proposed weapons and printed technical data on their operations is not likely to be viewed as a convincing advocate. At halftime, an athletic coach without a chalkboard may succeed only in confusing team members, not helping them. In classroom settings, students who give demonstration speeches without visuals frequently feel inadequate, even helpless—especially when they realize that most of the other speakers are well fortified with such support. In short, if you are to speak in a situation that demands certain kinds of visual media, plan ahead and enhance your message by taking full advantage of them. If the speech occasion does not appear to require visual supports, analyze it further for possibilities anyway. Use your imagination. Be innovative. Do not overlook opportunities to make your speech more meaningful, more exciting, and more attention holding in the eyes of your listeners.

CHAPTER SUMMARY

Visual aids, as a discrete mode, or channel, of communication, can *aid listener comprehension and memory* and *add persuasive impact* to a speech. There are two main types of visual aids—*actual objects* and *symbolic representations*. Actual objects include both *animate and inanimate objects*. Types of symbolic representations include concrete representations *(slides or transparencies, videotapes, films)* and abstract representations *(chalkboard drawings, graphs, charts and tables,* and *models)*. In selecting and using visual aids, consider the *communicative potential* of each kind, find ways to *integrate verbal and visual materials effectively,* and adapt them to *the audience and occasion.*

Oral Activities

1. Prepare a short speech explaining or demonstrating a complex process. Use two different types of visual aids and ask the class to evaluate their effectiveness.
2. Work in small groups to develop at least three different types of visual aids for three of the following topics. A representative of each group will report to the class as a whole, telling about or showing the proposed visual aids.
   a. How to play a musical instrument
   b. How to splint a broken arm or leg
   c. How to assemble a disassembled product
   d. How to do the drownproof swimming technique
   e. How to cut your utility bill

Reference Notes

1. The general theories of Gestalt psychology are reviewed understandably in Ernest R. Hilgard, *Theories of Learning* (New York: Appleton-Century-Crofts, 1956). Their applications in areas of visual communication can be found, among many other places, in Rudolph Arnheim, *Visual Thinking* (Berkeley: University of California Press, 1969); John M. Kennedy, *A Psychology of Picture Perception* (San Francisco: Jossey-Bass, 1974); Sol Worth, "Pictures Can't Say Ain't," *Versus* 12 (December 1975): 85–108; and Leonard Zusne, *Visual Perception of Form* (New York: Academic Press, 1976). For a discussion of research on media and learning, see Gavriel Salomon, *Interaction of Media, Cognition, and Learning* (San Francisco: Jossey-Bass, 1979); E. Heidt, *Instructional Media and the Individual Learner* (New York: Nichols, 1976).
2. William J. Seiler, "The Effects of Visual Materials on Attitudes, Credibility, and Retention," *Speech Monographs* 38 (November 1971): 331–34.
3. Joel R. Levin and Alan M. Lesgold, "On Pictures in Prose," *Educational Communication and Technology Journal* 26 (1978): 233–44. See Marilyn J. Haring and Maurine A. Fry, "Effect of Pictures on Children's Comprehension of Written Text," *Educational Communication and Technology Journal* 27 (1979): 185–90.
4. For more specific conclusions regarding the effects of various sorts of visual materials, see F. M. Dwyer, "Exploratory Studies in the Effectiveness of Visual Illustrations," *AV Communication Review* 18 (1970): 235–40; G. D. Feliciano, R. D. Powers, and B. E. Kearle, "The Presentation of Statistical Information," *AV Communication Review* 11 (1963): 32–39; William J. Seiler, "The Effects of Visual Materials on Attitudes, Credibility, and Retention," *Speech Monographs* 38 (November 1971): 331–34; M. D. Vernon, "Presenting Information in Diagrams," *AV Communication Review* 1 (1953): 147–58; and L. V. Peterson and Wilbur Schramm, "How Accurately Are Different Kinds of Graphs Read?" *AV Communication Review* 2 (1955): 178–89.
5. For a clear exploration of the relationships between ideas and visuals, see Edgar B. Wycoff, "Why Visuals?" *AV Communications* 11 (1977): 39, 59.
6. See Feliciano et al., Vernon, and Peterson and Schramm (note 4).

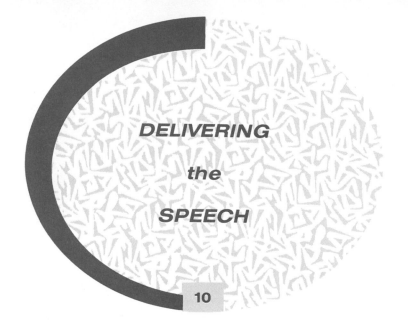

DELIVERING the SPEECH

10

History records that many famous speakers had to overcome severe problems of delivery before others would listen to their ideas. Abraham Lincoln suffered from extreme speech fright; Eleanor Roosevelt appeared awkward and clumsy. John F. Kennedy had a strong regional dialect and repetitive gestures. Each of these famous speakers, and many others, realized that the effectiveness of a speech depends not only on careful research and organization, but also on the presentation of ideas. It is important to be aware that the actual presentation of the speech adds to the impact of the ideas.

As a speaker, you must be aware of all of the channels of communication—both the meaning and the delivery of your words. Your voice and bodily movements—the *aural* and *visual channels of communication*—help transmit your feelings and attitudes toward yourself, your audience, and your topic. You may see speakers who reluctantly approach the platform with downcast eyes and grimacing faces, dragging their feet and fussing with their notes. Their feelings and attitudes toward themselves, their audience, and their topic are abundantly clear even before they utter their first word. These speakers unwittingly establish audience predispositions that work

212

against them. Even if their ideas are important, the audience will have difficulty in listening to those ideas because they expect the worst.

Your speech will gain strength and vitality if you present it well. To help you better understand this capstone of the communication process, we will discuss three important aspects of presentation: selecting the method of presentation, using your voice to communicate, and using your body to communicate.

SELECTING THE METHOD OF PRESENTATION

Which method should you use to present your speech? Your choice should be based on several criteria, including the type of speaking occasion, the seriousness and purpose of your speech, audience analysis, and your own strengths and weaknesses as a speaker. Attention to these considerations will help you decide whether your method of presentation should be (1) impromptu, (2) memorized, (3) read from a manuscript, or (4) extemporized.

The Impromptu Speech

An impromptu speech is one delivered on the spur of the moment without lengthy preparation. The speaker relies entirely on previous knowledge and skill. The ability to speak impromptu is useful in an emergency, but you should limit your use of this method to situations in which you are unable to anticipate the need to speak. When using this method, try to focus on a single idea, carefully relating all significant detail to it. This strategy will help you avoid the rambling, incoherent "remarks" that the impromptu method often produces.

The Memorized Speech

As its name implies, this type of speech is written out word for word and committed to memory. Although a few speakers are able to use this method effectively, it presents certain problems. Usually memorization results in a stilted, inflexible presentation; the speaker may be either excessively formal and oratorical or may tend to hurry through the speech—pouring out words with no thought as to their meaning. Using a memorized speech makes it difficult for the speaker to take advantage of audience feedback to adjust ideas as the speech progresses. If you memorize your speech, remember that you tend to use more formal language when writing than you do when speaking. Be sure that your speech does not sound like a written essay.

The Read Speech

Like the memorized speech, the read speech is written out, but, in this method, the speaker reads from a manuscript. If extremely careful wording is required—as in the president's messages to Congress, in which a slip of the tongue could undermine domestic or foreign policies, or in the presentation of scholarly reports, where exact, concise exposition is required—the read speech is appropriate. Many radio and television speeches also are read from manuscript because of the strict time limits imposed by broadcasting schedules. The ability to read a speech effectively is valuable in certain situations, but this method should not be used unnecessarily. No matter how experienced you are, when you read your message you will inevitably sacrifice some of the freshness and spontaneity necessary for authentic communication. Again, as with the memorized speech, it is difficult to react to audience feedback. Also, the speech may sound somewhat stilted because you used more formal, written language. If you use this method, "talk through" the speech as you are writing it to ensure an oral style.

The Extemporaneous Speech

Representing a middle course between memorized or read speech and the speech that is delivered impromptu, the extemporaneous speech requires careful planning and a detailed outline. Working from an outline, practice the speech aloud, expressing the ideas somewhat differently each time you go through it. Use the outline to fix the order of ideas in your mind, and practice various wordings to develop accuracy, conciseness, and flexibility of expression. If the extemporaneous method is used carelessly, the result will resemble an impromptu speech—a fact that sometimes leads to a confusion of these two terms. A proper use of the method, however, will produce a speech that is nearly as polished as a memorized one and certainly more vigorous, flexible, and spontaneous. (Refer back to Chapter 6 for guidelines to help you phrase the main points of the speech.) With few exceptions, the speeches you deliver will probably be extemporaneous. For that reason, most of the advice in this textbook assumes the use of that method.

> **STUDENT:** *I just don't understand why I blanked out like that. I'm really embarrassed—how can I ever give another speech—my boyfriend's in that class too!*
>
> **INSTRUCTOR:** *Why do you think you had memory lapses during your speech?*
>
> **STUDENT:** *Oh, I don't know. I just couldn't remember which words came next.*
>
> **INSTRUCTOR:** *How did you get ready to give this speech? Did you write it out?*
>
> **STUDENT:** *Sure. I always write them out, then memorize them. Then I make my notecards and my outline to hand in. But I never had trouble remembering a speech before.*
>
> **INSTRUCTOR:** *Maybe you've been using the wrong approach. What do you think would happen if you made a detailed outline first and didn't write out the speech word-for-word at all?*
>
> **STUDENT:** *Gee, I suppose I could, but what if I couldn't remember the exact words I wanted to use?*
>
> **INSTRUCTOR:** *That's where the outline would be helpful. It would jog your memory, and you wouldn't be tied to your notes as much. I'll bet your eye contact and responsiveness to your audience would improve too.*

USING YOUR VOICE TO COMMUNICATE

Your voice is an instrument that helps convey the meaning of language. It can affect your listeners' perception and interpretation of your message.[1]

You can communicate your enthusiasm for your ideas to your listeners through your voice. An awareness of the characteristics of vocal quality can help you make your ideas more interesting for your listeners. Listen to a stock market reporter rattle off the daily industrial averages. Even though every word may be intelligible, the reporter's vocal expression is often so repetitive and monotonous that the ideas are not very exciting. On the other hand, recall a play-by-play account of a baseball game broadcast by Howard Cosell or Don Drysdale. The vividness of their descriptions depends in large part on the way they used their voices. Such enthusiasm is infectious.

Currently, our culture seems to prize one essential vocal quality above all others—a sense of "conversationality."[2] The most successful speakers of our time have cultivated the ability to make their listeners feel they are being directly, even intimately, addressed. Even speakers who address millions through mass media on evening newscasts or nightly talk shows speak as though they are in a personal conversation with each one of us. Such conversational quality comes primarily from the realization that you are talking "with" not "at" an audience. Your principal concern, then, as you consider the vocal channel of public speaking, should be mental rather than physical. You should adapt your voice to the public speaking situation without losing the interpersonal qualities of dialogue.

The Effective Speaking Voice

A successful speaker is able to use the voice to emotionally color the ideas captured in the words of the message. These vocal attributes contribute to the "meanings" that public speakers convey to audiences through the vocal channel. A flexible speaking voice has *intelligibility, variety,* and *understandable stress patterns.*

Intelligibility

In everyday conversations with friends, we all tend to articulate sloppily and to speak more rapidly and softly than we would in public speaking situations. We can usually get by with inadequate articulation because we know the persons we are talking with and because we are probably only three to five feet from them. However, in public speaking, you may be addressing people you do not know, often from twenty-five feet or more away. In such situations, to ensure maximum intelligibility, you must consider four independent but related factors: (1) the overall level of loudness at which you speak, (2) the rate at which you speak, (3) the care with which you enunciate important words, and (4) the standard of pronunciation you observe.

Adjust your loudness level. Probably the most important single factor in intelligibility is the loudness level at which you speak as related to the *distance* between you and your listeners and the amount of *noise* that is present.[3] Obviously, the farther away your listeners are, the louder you must talk for them to hear you well. Most of us unconsciously adjust our loudness level when projecting our voices over extended distances. What we often forget is that a corresponding adjustment is required when the listeners are only a few feet away. You must realize also that your own voice will always sound louder to you than to your listeners.

In addition to distance, the amount of surrounding noise with which you must compete has an effect on the required loudness level. Even in normal circumstances, some noise is always present. For example, the noise level of rustling leaves in the quiet solitude of a country lane (10 decibels) is louder than a whisper at six feet away. The noise in an empty theater averages 25 decibels, but with a "quiet" audience it rises to 42. In the average factory, a constant noise of about 80 decibels is characteristic. This is just about the same level as very loud speaking at a close range.

How can you determine the proper strength of voice to use in order to achieve sufficient loudness for the distance and noise conditions of a particular speech situation? You can always use your eyes to see if your auditors appear to be hearing you, or, even better, you can *ask* them. Get your instructor's advice on this point. Ask your friends to report on the loudness of your voice as you talk in rooms of various sizes and under varying noise conditions. Listen to the sound of your voice so that you can begin to correlate your own vocal production with their reports. You will soon learn to gauge the volume you must use in order to be heard.

Control your rate. In animated conversation, you may well jabber along at two hundred to two hundred fifty words a minute. This rate is especially characteristic of people raised in the North, Midwest, Southwest, or West. As words tumble out of your mouth in informal conversational situations, they usually are intelligible because the distance they must travel is short. In large auditoriums or outdoors, however, rapid delivery can impede intelligibility. Echoes can distort or destroy sounds in rooms. In outdoor situations, words often seem to drift and vanish into the open air.

When addressing larger audiences, then, most of us must slow down to an average of one hundred twenty to one hundred fifty words a minute. Obviously, you do not go around timing your speaking rate, but you can remind yourself of potential rate problems as you rise to speak. You can also get feedback from your instructors and classmates regarding their perceptions of your speaking rate.

All of this is not to say, of course, that you should never speak rapidly. Undoubtedly, there are situations when a quickened delivery will help you stir and intensify the emotions of your auditors. If you find yourself in such a situation, you will have to learn to compensate. As your rate increases, for example, you must often adjust your volume and take more care in your enunciation of sounds and words.

Enunciate clearly. Enunciation refers to the crispness and precision with which we form words vocally. Most of us are "lip lazy" in normal conversation: we tend to slur sounds, drop syllables from words, and skip over beginnings and endings of words. Careless enunciation may not inhibit communication between intimate friends, but it can seriously undermine a speaker's intelligibility for an audience.

When speaking publicly, you may have to force yourself to say "go*ing*" instead of "go-*in*," "*just*" instead of "*jist*" (which can aurally be mistaken for "gist"), and *govern*-ment instead of· "*guv*-ment." Physiologically, this means opening your mouth a bit more widely than usual and forcing your lips and tongue to form the consonants firmly. If you are having trouble making your vocal mechanism enunciate well, ask your instructor for some exercises to improve your performance.

Meet standards of pronunciation. Pronunciation and dialect depend on enunciation, or articulation. To be intelligible, you must form sounds carefully and meet audience expectations regarding acceptable pronunciation. If your words cannot be understood because they are slurred, garbled, or otherwise inarticulate, your listeners will not be able to grasp what you say. And, even if your words are recognizable, any peculiarity of pronunciation is almost sure to be noticed by some of your listeners. This may distract their attention from your ideas and may undermine your credibility as a speaker.

Standards of pronunciation, or *dialects,* differ among geographic regions and among cultural groups. A dialect is a language use—including vocabulary, grammar, and pronunciation—that sets a group apart. Your pronunciation of words, together with the ways in which you arrange them grammatically, or syntactically, determines your dialect. You may have a "foreign accent," a white Southern or black Northern dialect, a New England "twang," or a Hispanic trill. Since dialects have unique rules for vocabulary, grammar, and pronunciation, a clash of dialects can result in confusion and frustration for both speaker and listener. Recall trying to understand the words and meanings of someone from another region of the country. You are distracted from the message by the way the words sounded.

Unfortunately, dialects may produce not only misunderstandings and frustrations but *negative judgments.* These negative impressions may seriously affect listeners' perceptions of a speaker's credibility—that is, the speaker's education, reliability, responsibility, and capabilities for leadership.[4] Such judgments of credibility occur because dialects and even professional jargon contribute heavily to what paralinguists call "vocal stereotypes."[5] All of this means that you, as a speaker, have to make decisions regarding your accent: Should you learn to use the grammar, vocabulary, and vocal patterns of "middle America" when addressing such audiences? Many speakers are forced to become "bilingual," using their own dialects when facing local audiences but switching to Midwestern American when addressing more varied audiences. You will notice, if you listen carefully, that many network television newscasters have adopted a Midwestern American dialect but sometimes slip momentarily into their natural dialect.

Variety

As you move from intimate conversation to the enlarged context of public speaking, you may discover that listeners accuse you of monotony of pitch or rate. When speaking in a large public setting, you should compensate for the greater distance that sounds travel by varying certain characteristics of your voice. You must learn to vary *rate, pitch, force,* and *pauses.*

Vary the rate. Earlier we discussed the overall rate at which we normally speak. Consider ways to alter your speaking rate in accordance with the ideas you are expressing. The emotional character of your subject matter, likewise, should affect variations in rate. So, you should consider slowing down to add emphasis to a particular point or to indicate your own thoughtfulness, and you will quicken the pace when your ideas are emotionally charged. Observe, for example, how a sports announcer varies speaking rate from play to play, or how an evangelist changes pace regularly. A variable rate helps keep an audience's attention riveted on the speech.

Change the pitch. Three aspects of pitch (the musical "notes" in your speaking voice) are relevant to effective vocal communication. First, your *pitch level*—your habitual pitch, whether in the soprano, alto, tenor, baritone, or bass range—is normally adequate for most of your daily communication needs.

However, people who frequently speak in public should use a broader *pitch range.* In normal conversation, you may use only a few notes, sometimes even less than an octave. However, if you use such a limited range from a podium, you may sound monotonous. Given the distances that sounds must travel between speaker and audience and the length of time speakers talk, you should exaggerate your range of sounds in order to communicate effectively. Raise your pitch "highs" and lower your "lows." Usually, the more emotionally charged your ideas, the more you should vary your pitch range. Obviously, you can get carried away. Just as a narrow pitch range communicates boredom, an extremely wide pitch range can communicate artificiality or uncontrolled excitement or fear.

The key to successful control of pitch ultimately depends on understanding the importance of *pitch variation.* As a general rule, use higher pitches to communicate excitement and lower pitches to create a sense of control or solemnity. Use different parts of your range, in other words, for different kinds of emotions. And, as a second rule, let the sense of a particular sentence control pitch variations. Thus, move your voice up at the end of a question; change to higher or lower notes to add emphasis within a particular sentence. An abrupt change in pitch is called a *step*. When a more gradual or continuous pitch inflection accompanies the production of the sound, it is termed a *slide*. Television announcer Ed McMahon uses both of these techniques in his famous introduction of Johnny Carson:

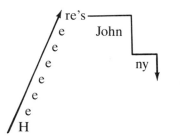

Ed successively slides his voice up until he reaches a high pitch level on the end of the first word "Here's"; then, he steps down the scale on the word "Johnny." Such vocal slides and steps add emphasis to the words. By mastering their use, you can call attention to your word choices, making your meaning clearer and more precise.

Stress

A third significant aspect of vocal behavior is stress—the ways in which sounds, syllables, and words are accented. Without vocal stress, everything in a speech would sound the same, and the resulting message would be both incomprehensible and emotionless. Without vocal stress, you would sound like a computer. Vocal stress is achieved in two ways—through vocal emphasis and through the judicious use of pauses.

Add emphasis. Emphasis refers to the points in a sentence where, principally through increased vocal energy (loudness), changes in intonation (pitch), or variations in speed (rate), one vocally makes particular words or phrases stand out. By emphasis, we mean the way you accent or "attack" words. Emphasis is most often achieved through changes in loudness or energy; variations in loudness can affect the meanings of your sentences. Consider the sentence "Tom's taking Jane out for pizza tonight." Notice how the meaning varies with the word being emphasized:

1. TOM's taking Jane out for pizza tonight. (not John or Bob)

2. Tom's taking JANE out for pizza tonight. (not Sue or Wanda)

3. Tom's taking Jane OUT for pizza tonight. (rather than staying home as usual)

4. Tom's taking Jane out for PIZZA tonight. (not seafood or hamburgers)
5. Tom's taking Jane out for pizza TONIGHT. (not tomorrow or next weekend)

Without careful control of vocal force, a speaker is liable to utter messages subject to a great many possible meanings. A lack of vocal stress, therefore, not only creates an impression of boredom but can also cause needless misunderstandings.

Emphasis is also fostered through changes in pitch and rate. Relatively simple changes in pitch, for example, can be used to "tell" an audience where you are in an outline, as when a speaker says,

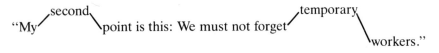

In this sentence, the audience can hear that the speaker has completed one idea and has moved on to the next, and that temporary workers will be the principal concern of that section. Variations in rate can operate in the same way. Consider the following sentence:

> We are a country faced with . . . [moderate rate] balance of payments deficits, racial tensions, an energy crunch, a crisis of morality, unemployment, government waste . . . [fast rate] and-a-stif-ling-na-tion-al-debt. [slow rate]

This speaker has built a vocal freight train. The ideas pick up speed through the accelerating list of problems and then come to an emphatic halt when the speaker's main concern—the national debt—is mentioned. Such variations in rate essentially communicate to an audience what is and what is not especially important to the speech. Emphasis has been achieved through the control of speaking rate.

Use helpful pauses. Pauses are intervals of silence between or within words, phrases, or sentences. Pauses punctuate thought by separating groups of spoken words into meaningful units. When placed immediately before a key idea or the climax of a story, they can create suspense; when placed immediately after a major point or central idea, they add emphasis. Introduced at the proper moment, a dramatic pause can express your feeling more forcefully than words. Clearly, silence can be a highly effective communicative tool *if* used intelligently and sparingly, and if not embarrassingly prolonged.

Sometimes, speakers fill silences in their discourse with sounds— "umms," "ahs," "ers," "well-ahs," "you-knows," and other meaningless fillers. You have probably heard speakers say, "Today, ah, I would like, you know, to speak to you, umm, about a pressing, well-uh, like, a pressing problem facing this, uh, campus." Such vocal intrusions convey feelings of hesitancy and lack of confidence to an audience. You should make a concerted effort to remove these intrusions from your speaking behavior.

On the other hand, do not be afraid of silences. Pauses allow you to achieve stress for important ideas, as when the audience waits for the "punch line" in a story or argument. Pauses also intensify listeners' involvement in emotional situations, as when Barbara Walters or William F. Buckley, Jr., pauses for reflection. However, avoid too many pauses or those that seem artificial, which can make you appear manipulative or over-rehearsed. Use strategic silence as an important weapon in your arsenal as an effective communicator.

Controlling the Emotional Quality

A listener's judgment of a speaker's personality and emotional commitment often centers on that speaker's vocal quality—the fullness or thinness of the tones, whether it is harsh, husky, mellow, nasal, breathy, or resonant. Depending on your vocal quality, an audience may judge you as being angry, happy, confident, fearful, sincere, or sad.

Fundamental to an audience's reaction to your vocal quality are *emotional characterizers*—their sense of a speaker's laughing, crying, whispering, inhaling or exhaling, etc.[6] They combine in various ways with the words you speak to communicate different shades of meanings to a listener. Consider, for a moment, a few of the many ways you can say the following sentence:

I can't believe I ate that entire pizza.

You might say it as though you were *reporting* a fact, as if you *cannot believe* you just ate it all, or, as though it were an *impossible* achievement. Finally, you might say it as though you were *expressing doubts* about the truth of the action. As you say the sentence to express these different meanings, you not only vary your pitch and loudness, but probably also alter your emotional characterizers. Such changes are important determiners of how meaning is communicated to listeners.

In sum, your vocal qualities are of prime importance in determining the impression you make on an audience. While you cannot completely control such qualities, you can be alert to the effects they are likely to produce in your listeners. Keep in mind your repertoire of vocal qualities as you decide how to express key ideas for an audience.

Read the following fictitious broadcast of a horse race several times. Each time, vary your rate, loudness, pitch, stress, and pauses to add realism to the scenario:

A-a-a-a-and they-r-r-r-r off, Ladies and Gentlemen. It's Sinbad and Dusk Rose in the lead with Champagne Taste and the pack following. Lucky Lou's trailin' on the inside—problems breakin' at the gate.

They're inta the first turn—Sinbad and Dusk Rose, nose-ta-nose. Double Risk, Champagne Taste, Whirligig . . . Lucky Lou.

Rodrigues goes ta tha whip and Lucky Lou gains anose but what's this? Lucky Lou's coming up ontha inside. Whatdayaknow . . . . It's Lucky Lou inta tha lead by a nose. Now itsa head and he's movin' away from the pack. They're roundin' the Clubhouse turn inta tha final stretch. Can ya believe it, folks? Wow whatafinish. It's Lucky Lou by a length.

Lucky Lou is paying $14.50. You may redeem your tickets on Level A. Thank you.

Practicing Vocal Control

Do not assume that you will be able to master in a day all of the vocal skills that have been described. Take time to review and digest the ideas presented. And above all, *practice.* Ask your instructor to provide exercises designed to make your vocal apparatus more flexible—breathing; phonation; resonance; articulation; and control of rate, pause, and inflection. When you are able to control your vocal mechanism to make it respond to your desires, then you will be able to achieve vocal intelligibility, variety, and stress. You will be able to add the emotional coloring of a well-tuned vocal instrument. Remember that any vocal skill, before it can be natural and effective with listeners, must be so much a habit that it will work for you with little conscious effort when you begin to speak and will continue to do so throughout your oral message. Once your voice can respond as you want it to in the enlarged context of public speaking, you will be able to achieve the sense of conversationality so highly valued in our society.

USING YOUR BODY TO COMMUNICATE

Just as your voice gives meaning to your message through the aural channel, your physical behavior carries meaning through the visual channel. While the audience is using the aural channel to grasp your ideas, it is simultaneously using the visual message you send to add clarity. You can use these two complementary channels to help create a better understanding of your presentation.[7] To help you explore ways of enhancing your use of the visual channel, we will examine the speaker's physical behavior on the platform.

Dimensions of Nonverbal Communication

In recent years, research has re-emphasized the important roles of physical, or nonverbal, behaviors in effective oral communication.[8] Basically, those roles can be reduced to three generalizations:

1. Speakers reveal and reflect their emotional states by their nonverbal behaviors in front of audiences. Your listeners read your feelings toward yourself, your topic, and your audience from your facial expressions; from the way you stand and walk; and from what you do with your head, arms, shoulders, and hands. Summarizing a good deal of research into nonverbal communication processes, communications scholar Dale G. Leathers has noted: "Feelings and emotions are more accurately exchanged by nonverbal than verbal means. . . . The nonverbal portion of communication conveys meanings and intentions that are relatively free of deception, distortion, and confusion."[9]

2. The speaker's nonverbal cues enrich or elaborate the message that comes through words. A solemn face can reinforce the dignity of a funeral eulogy. The words, "Either you can do this or you can do that," can be illustrated with appropriate arm-and-hand gestures. Taking a few steps to the left or right tells an audience that you are moving from one argument to another.

3. Nonverbal messages create a reciprocal interaction sent from speaker to listener and from listener back to speaker. Listeners frown, smile, shift nervously in their seats, and engage in many types of nonverbal behavior already noted in Chapter 2. In this chapter, we will concentrate on the speaker's control of "body language." There are four areas of nonverbal communication that concern every speaker: (1) *proxemics* (the use of space), (2) *movement and stance,* (3) *facial expressions,* and (4) *gestures.*

DRESS FOR SUCCESS

dress n ... **3:** *covering, adornment, or appearance appropriate or peculiar to a particular time* **4:** *a particular form of presentation:* GUISE

—Webster's Ninth Collegiate Dictionary

The complexities of thinking about dressing for public speaking situations are found in the definitions of the word "dress" quoted above. On the one hand, "dressing" is a matter of covering oneself *appropriately,* in accordance with the norms of social propriety and style. On the other hand, "dressing" can be thought about *rhetorically,* as, in our terms, a communication message you want others to receive and react to. Hence, dressing is simultaneously *position* and *power*— reflecting who one is in the world and the effect one wishes to have on others.

While such matters as dress codes, fashion and personal morality, and the power of uniforms have been discussed through most of our recorded history, in 1975 the questions of position and power came sharply into focus on talk shows as well as in board rooms and personnel departments because of the publication of John T. Molloy's book *Dress for Success.* It became an overnight phenomenon, and dozens of books as well as hundreds of articles followed in its wake. Why?

Dress for Success combined several virtues: (1) It was based on loose-but-grounded research—interviews with clients from numerous professions—as Molloy styled himself "America's first wardrobe engineer," dealing with "the socioeconomic value of a man's clothing" (his first book was followed in 1978 by *The Women's Dress for Success Book*). (2) For all his references to "experiments," however, Molloy stressed practical advice—how to dress in order to get ahead. (3) And finally, the book was right for our times. In an age of careerism and upward mobility, Molloy sought to analyze particular subcultures in a complex society and to find the underlying cultural rules at work. It can be a useful and interesting study for the student of communication.

What, then, are you as a speaker to make of the "dress for success" phenomenon? At a basic level, the central message—"People's impressions of you as a human being and as an expert on something are in part dependent on your appearance"—is one you should make neither too much nor too little of. That is, don't assume that clothing can be a *substitute* for expertise, skills, and an open and accessible personality. Yet, don't *underestimate* people's tendency to use all available clues—including your dress—to judge your abilities. Scraggly hair, blue jeans and sandals, dirty clothing *do* provide clues to a slovenly, uncaring, insensitive individual.

At a more specific level, you may find Molloy's advice about specific items of clothing and grooming (even haircuts and eyeglasses) useful in particular situations. His comments, for example, on interviewing in the South or on dressing

225

in ways appropriate to your product (or subject matter, in the case of a speech) may help you in ways that his more general advice may not. Much of his advice can be translated into hints that will help you feel more competent and self-assured before your audience.

Finally, remember the central issue as you plan your costuming is the one we started with: It is one thing to dress to meet social expectations, but another to assume you can beat people into submission with your appearance. There is a fine line between conforming to social expectations and thinking there are tricks to success. Do not get drawn into gossip magazines' mindless chatter on power: you could end up not gaining power but losing face.

TO READ: See, of course, John T. Molloy, *Dress for Success* (New York: Warner Books, 1975) and *The Women's Dress for Success Book* (New York: Warner Books, 1978). For a readable theoretical discussion of dress/fashion in terms of perception and effect, see Loretta A. Malandro and Larry Barker, *Nonverbal Communication* (Reading, MA: Addison-Wesley Publishing Company, 1983), esp. Chapter 3, "Clothing and Personal Artifacts." Even broader views can be found in Aaron Wolfgang, ed., *Nonverbal Behavior: Perspectives, Applications, Intercultural Insights* (New York: C. J. Hogrefe, Inc., 1984).

Proxemics

One of the most important but perhaps least recognized aspects of nonverbal communication is proxemics, or the use of space by human beings. Two components of proxemics are especially relevant to public speakers:

1. *Physical arrangements*—the layout of the room in which you are speaking, including the presence or absence of a podium, the seating plan, the location of chalkboards and similar aids, and any physical barriers between you and your audience.

2. *Distance*—the extent or degree of separation between you and your audience.[10]

Both of these components have a bearing on your message. Most public speaking situations involve a speaker facing a seated audience. Objects in the physical space—the lectern, a table, several flags—tend to set the speaker apart from the listeners. This "setting apart," you must remember, is both *physical and psychological.* Literally as well as figuratively, objects can stand in the way of free communicative exchange. If you are trying to create a more informal and direct atmosphere, you will want to reduce the physical barriers in the setting. You might stand beside or in front of the lectern instead of behind it. In very informal settings, you might even sit on the front edge of a table while talking.

A formal stance behind a lectern puts physical and psychological distance between a speaker and the audience.

There is no single rule for using space. However, there are several guidelines for helping you determine your use of space in creating a particular physical and psychological impact:

1. The *formality* of the occasion affects your impact—the more solemn or formal the occasion, the more distance and barriers. Lectures, prepared reports, and the like are better suited to presentations from behind the lectern.

2. The *nature of the material* may require the use of a lectern, such as when you have extensive quoted material or statistical evidence. The use of visual aids often demands special equipment, such as an easel, table, or overhead projector.

3. Finally, your *personal preference* can be considered. You may feel more at ease speaking from behind rather than in front of the lectern.

Some speaking situations call for a less formal relationship between a speaker and the audience. A speaker can "reach out" to audience members by reducing the barriers of space between them.

The distance component of proxemics adds a second set of considerations. Speakers in most situations are talking over what Edward T. Hall has termed a "public distance"—twelve feet or more away from their listeners.[11] To communicate with people at that distance, you obviously cannot rely on your normal speaking voice or minute changes in posture or muscle tone. Instead, you must *compensate* for the distance by using larger gestures, broader shifts of your body from place to place, and increased vocal energy. Perhaps the necessity to communicate in larger terms, with bigger-than-usual movements, is one of the qualities that make public speaking such a new and strange experience to some people. With practice, however, you can acquire and refine the techniques of effective nonverbal delivery and can overcome these fears and feelings of strangeness.

Movement and Stance

How you move and stand provides a second set of nonverbal cues for your audience. *Movement* includes shifts you make from one spot to another during the delivery of a speech; *posture* refers to the relative relaxation or rigidity of your body, as well as to your overall stance (erect, slightly bent forward or backward, or slumping).

Purposive movements can communicate ideas about yourself to an audience. The speaker who stands stiffly and erectly may, without uttering a word, be saying either (a) "This is a formal occasion" or (b) "I am tense, even afraid, of this audience." The speaker who leans forward, physically reaching out to the audience, is saying silently but eloquently, "I am interested in you. I want you to understand and accept my ideas." Sitting casually on the front edge of a table and assuming a relaxed posture communicate informality and a readiness to engage in a dialogue with your listeners.

Movements and postural adjustments *regulate* communication. As a public speaker, you can, for instance, move from one end of a table to the other to indicate a change in topic, or you can accomplish the same purpose simply by changing your posture. At other times, you can move toward your audience when making an especially important point. In each case, you are using your body to signal to your audience that you are making a transition in your subject or are dealing with a matter of special concern.

Along with all of this, an equally important point to remember is that your posture and movements can not only work for you but also against you. Aimless and continuous pacing is distracting. A nervous bouncing or swaying will make the audience tense and uneasy, and if you adopt an excessively erect stance, you may lose rapport with your listeners. Your movements, in other words, should be *purposive*. Only then will stance and movement help your communicative effort and produce the sense of self-assurance and control you want to exhibit.[12]

Facial Expressions

Your face is another important nonverbal message channel. When you speak, your facial expressions function in a number of ways: First, they communicate much about yourself and your feelings. What Paul Ekman and Wallace V. Friesen call *affect displays* are given to an audience through the face. That is, an audience scans your face to see how you feel about yourself and how you feel about them.[13] Second, facial details provide listeners with cues that help them *interpret the contents* of your message: Are you being ironic or satirical? How sure are you of some conclusion you have stated? Is this a harsh or a pleasant message? Psychologists tell us that a high percentage of the information conveyed in a typical message is communicated nonverbally. Psychologist Albert Mehrabian has devised a formula to account for the emotional impact of a speaker's message. Words, he says, contribute 7 percent, vocal elements 38 percent, and facial expressions 55 percent.[14] And third, the "display" elements of your face—

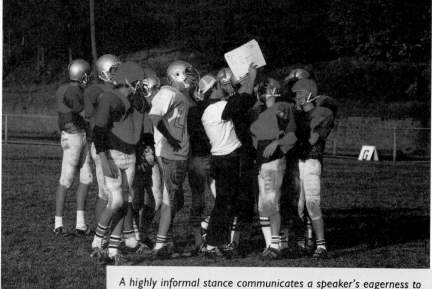

A highly informal stance communicates a speaker's eagerness to engage in a dialogue and encourages immediate feedback from the audience.

your eyes, especially—establish a *visual bonding* between you and your listeners. The speaker who looks down at the floor instead of at listeners, who reads excessively from notes or a manuscript, or who delivers a speech to the back wall has severed visual bonding. Our culture has come to expect eye-to-eye contact from speakers who are deemed "earnest," "sincere," "forthright," and "self-assured." In other words, it is in part through regular eye contact with individuals in your audience that you establish your *credibility.*[15]

Of course, you cannot control your face completely, which is probably why listeners search it so carefully for clues to your feelings, but you can make sure that your facial messages do not belie your verbal ones. In practical terms, this means that when you are uttering angry words, your face should be communicating anger; when you are sincerely pleading with your listeners, your eyes should be looking at them intently. In short, use your face to maximum communicative advantage.

Gestures

Gestures are purposive movements of the head, shoulders, arms, hands, or other areas of the body. They support and illustrate the ideas you are expressing. Fidgeting with your clothing and notecards or clutching the sides of the lectern are not gestures because they are not purposive. They distract from the ideas you are communicating. The effective public speaker commonly uses three kinds of gestures:

1. *Conventional gestures*—physical movements that are symbols to which specific meanings have been assigned by custom or convention. These gestures *condense* ideas. They are shorthand movements for things or ideas it would take many words to describe fully. The raised-hand "stop" gesture of the police officer directing traffic, the manual sign language of deaf persons, and the arm signals of football referees are examples of conventional gestures.

2. *Descriptive gestures*—physical movements that describe the idea to be communicated. Speakers often depict the size, shape, or location of an object by movements of the hands and arms. Such gestures function through *pictorialization*. That is, they "draw pictures" for listeners. A speaker might use thumb and fingers to describe the "O" rings of a space shuttle, for example. Or, an upraised arm can indicate the height of a stranger.

3. *Indicators*—movements of the hands, arms, or other parts of the body that express feelings. Thus speakers may throw up their arms when disgusted, pound the podium when angry, shrug their shoulders when puzzled, or point a threatening finger when issuing a warning. Such gestures encourage listeners' feelings through *arousal;* that is, they communicate your state of mind to your listeners and encourage similar responses in them. Your facial expressions and other body cues usually reinforce such gestures.[16]

Characteristics of Effective Gestures

Once you understand their purposes, you can perfect your gestures through practice. As you practice, you will obtain better results if you keep in mind three characteristics of effective gesturing: (1) *relaxation,* (2) *vigor and definiteness,* and (3) *proper timing.*

If your muscles are tense, your movements will be stiff and your gestures awkward. You should make a conscious effort to relax your muscles before you start to speak. You might "warm up" by taking a few unobtrusive steps, rearranging your notes, or even breathing deeply.

Good gestures are lively, vigorous, and definite. They communicate the dynamism associated with speaker credibility. You should put enough force into your gestures to show your conviction and enthusiasm. However, avoid exaggerated or repetitive gestures, such as pounding the table or chopping the air, for minor ideas in your speech. Vary the nature of your gestures as the ideas in your speech demand.

Timing is crucial to effective gestures. Try making a gesture after the word or phrase it was intended to reinforce has already been spoken and observe the ridiculous result. The *stroke* of a gesture—that is, the shake of the fist or the movement of the finger—should fall exactly on, or should slightly precede, the point the gesture is used to emphasize. If you practice making gestures until they have become habitual and then use them spontaneously as the impulse arises, you will have no trouble on this score. Poor timing is often the result of an attempt to use "canned," or preplanned, gestures.

Adapting Nonverbal Behavior to Your Presentations

Although you can never completely control your body language, you can gain skill in orchestrating your gestures and other movements. You can consciously make *some* decisions about how you will use your body to communicate.

1. *Plan a proxemic relationship with your audience that reflects your own needs and attitudes toward your subject and your listeners.* If you feel

Public speakers commonly use three kinds of gestures. *Conventional gestures* represent customary group or cultural meanings; *descriptive gestures* illustrate such information as size, shape, and location; and *indicators* express personal feelings.

more at home behind a lectern, plan to have it placed accordingly. If you want your whole body to be visible to the audience yet feel the need to have notes at eye level, stand beside the lectern and arrange your notecards on it. If you want to relax your body (and are sure you can compensate for the resulting loss of action by increasing your vocal volume), sit behind a table or desk. If you feel free physically and want to be wholly "open" to your audience, stand in front of a table or desk.

2. *The farther you are from your listeners, the more important it is for them to have a clear view of you.* The speaker who crouches behind a lectern in an auditorium of three hundred people soon loses contact with them. The farther away your audience is, the harder you must work to project your words, and the broader your physical movements must be. Think about the large lecture classes you have attended, sermons you have heard in large churches, or political rallies you have attended. Recall the behaviors and techniques of speakers who worked effectively in such situations, choosing and adapting those that might also work for you.

3. *Insofar as practical, adapt the physical setting to your communicative needs and desires.* If you are going to use such visual aids as a chalkboard, flipchart, or working model, remove the tables, chairs, and other objects that might obstruct the listeners' view and therefore impair their understanding of your message.

4. *Adapt the size of your gestures and amount of your movement to the size of the audience.* Keeping in mind what Edward Hall noted about public distance in communication (page 228), you should realize that subtle changes of facial expression or small movements of the fingers cannot be seen clearly when you are twenty-five feet or more from your listeners. Although many auditoriums have a raised platform and a slanted floor to allow a speaker to be seen more clearly, you should, nevertheless, adjust by making your movements and gestures larger.

5. *Continuously scan your audience from side to side and from front to back, looking specific individuals in the eye.* This does not mean, of course, that your head is to be in constant motion; "continuously" does not imply rhythmical, nonstop bobbing. Rather, it implies that you must be aware—and must let an audience know you are aware—of the entire group of human beings in front of you. Take them all into your field of vision periodically; establish firm visual bonds with them occasionally. Such bonds enhance your credibility and keep your auditors' attention from wandering.

6. *Use your body to communicate your feelings about what you are saying.* When you are angry, do not be afraid to gesture vigorously. When you are expressing tenderness, let that message come across your face. In other words, when you communicate publicly, use the same emotional indicators as when you talk to another individual on a one-to-one basis.

7. *Use your body to regulate the pace of your presentation and to control transitions.* Shift your weight from one idea to another. Move more when you are speaking more rapidly. When you are slowing down to emphasize particular ideas, decrease bodily and gestural action accordingly. Avoid arbitrary, preplanned movements, because they are not usually effective.

8. *Finally, use your full repertoire of gestures while talking publicly.* You probably do this in everyday conversation without even thinking about it, so re-create that behavior when addressing an audience. Here, physical readiness is the key concern. Keep your hands and arms free and loose enough so that you can call them into action easily, quickly, and naturally. Let your hands be comfortably at your sides—relaxed but ready. Occasionally, rest them on the lectern. Then, as you unfold the ideas of your speech, use descriptive gestures to indicate size, shape, or relationship, making sure the movements are large enough to be seen in the back row. Use conventional gestures also to give visual dimension to your spoken ideas. Keep in mind, of course, that there is no "right" number of gestures to use. However, during the preparation of your talk, you can think of the kinds of bodily and gestural actions that would most appropriately and effectively complement your delivery.

Selecting the appropriate method of presentation and using your voice and body productively will enhance the chances of gaining support for your ideas. *Practice* is the key to the effective use of these elements. Through practice, you can judge your method of presentation. You will also have an opportunity to see how your voice and body complement or detract from your ideas. The more confident you feel about presenting the speech, the more comfortable you will be, and confidence is built through careful preparation and practice. Remember that the nonverbal channel of communication creates meaning for your audience.

CHAPTER SUMMARY

Every speaker should effectively use the *aural and visual channels* of communication. This begins with choosing an appropriate method of presentation, such as *impromptu, memorized, read,* or *extemporaneous* delivery. Regardless of the method of presentation, a good voice enables a speaker to present a clear message. A flexible speaking voice has *intelligibility, variety,* and *understandable stress patterns. Loudness, rate, enunciation,* and *pronunciation* interact to determine intelligibility. Varying standards of pronunciation create regional speech differences known as *dialects.* Changing *rate, pitch, stress,* and *pauses* influence the variety of presentation and help eliminate monotonous delivery. *Emotional character-izers* communicate shades of meaning to listeners.

Physical movements complement vocal quality to add clarity to the message. Speakers can use space, or *proxemics,* to create physical and psychological intimacy or distance. *Movement* and *stance* regulate communication. *Facial expressions* communicate feelings, provide important clues to meaning, establish visual bonding with listeners, and influence perceived speaker credibility. Finally, *gestures* enhance listener responses to messages, if the gestures are relaxed, definite, and properly timed.

Selecting the appropriate method of presentation and using your voice and body to communicate will enhance your chances of gaining support for your ideas and communicating meaning to your listeners.

Oral Activities

1. Divide the class into teams and play "charades." (Those needing rules for classroom games should read David Jauner, "Charades as a Teaching Device," *Speech Teacher* 20 [November 1971]: 302.) A game of charades will not only loosen you up psychologically but should help sensitize you to the variety of small but perceptible cues your "read" when interpreting messages.

2. Meet briefly in task groups to determine which of the four methods of speaking would be most appropriate in each of the following situations. Choose a reporter to convey the group's justification for their selections to the class.
   a. A college president addressing her faculty on the goals of the college for the school year
   b. A student's response to his speech professor when asked what he hoped to learn in the course
   c. A president of a large company reporting to all administrative personnel on the success/failure of the company for the past year
   d. A student participating in the national oratorical contest
   e. An alumna of a local high school attending a reunion and being asked to comment on the adequacy of her high-school training for college
   f. A sales representative attempting to get the board of directors of a business chain to use his advertising agency

Reference Notes

1. R. Geiselman and John Crawley, "Incidental Processing of Speaker Character-istics: Voice as Connotative Information," *Journal of Verbal Learning and Verbal Behavior* 22 (1983): 15–23.
2. W. Barnett Pearce and Bernard J. Brommel, "Vocalic Communication in Persuasion," *Quarterly Journal of Speech* 58 (1972): 298–306.
3. The term *loudness* is used synonymously with *intensity* here because the former term is clearer to most people. Technically, of course, loudness—a distinct function in the science of acoustics—is not strictly synonymous with intensity. To explain the exact relationship between the two terms is beyond the scope of this textbook because the explanation involves many complicated psychophysical relationships. For a full discussion of these relationships, see Giles W. Gray and Claude M. Wise, *The Bases of Speech*, 3rd ed. (New York: Harper, 1959), Chapter 3.
4. Mark L. Knapp, *Essentials of Nonverbal Communication* (New York: Holt, 1980).
5. Klaus R. Scherer, H. London, and Garret Wolf, "The Voice of Competence: Paralinguistic Cues and Audience Evaluation," *Journal of Research in Personality* 7 (1973): 31–44; Jitendra Thakerer and Howard Giles, "They Are—So They Spoke: Noncontent Speech Stereotypes," *Language and Communication* 1 (1981): 255–61.
6. Bruce L. Brown, William J. Strong, and Alvin C. Rencher, "Perceptions of Personality from Speech: Effects of Manipulations of Acoustical Parameters," *Journal of the Acoustical Society of America* 54 (1973): 29–35.
7. Haig Bosmajian, ed., *The Rhetoric of Nonverbal Communication* (Glenview, IL: Scott, Foresman and Company, 1971).
8. Much of this research is summarized in Mark L. Knapp, *Nonverbal Communication in Human Interaction,* 2nd ed. (New York: Holt, 1978).
9. Dale G. Leathers, *Nonverbal Communication Systems* (Boston: Allyn & Bacon, 1975), 4–5.
10. For a fuller discussion of each of these components, see Leathers, 52–59.
11. Hall divides interhuman communication distances into four segments: *intimate distance*—up to 1 1/2 feet apart; *personal distance*—1 1/2 to 4 feet; *social distance*—4 to 12 feet; and *public distance*—12 feet or more. On the basis of these distinctions, he has carefully noted how people's eye contact, tone of voice, and ability to touch and observe change from one distance to another. See Edward T. Hall *The Hidden Dimension* (New York: Doubleday, 1969), Chapter X.
12. Albert E. Scheflen, "The Significance of Posture in Communication Systems," *Psychiatry* 27 (1964), 321.
13. Paul Ekman, Wallace V. Friesen, and P. Ellsworth, *Emotion in the Human Face: Guidelines for Research and an Integration of Findings* (New York: Pergamon, 1972).

14. Robert Rivlin and Karen Gravelle, *Deciphering the Senses: The Expanding World of Human Perception* (New York: Simon and Schuster, 1984), 98; Flora Davis, "How to Read Body Language," *Glamour Magazine,* (September 1969).

15. For a difficult but rewarding essay on the management of demeanor, see Erving Goffman, *Interaction Ritual: Essays on Face-to-Face Behavior* (New York: Doubleday, 1967), 5–46.

16. For a more complete system of classifying gestures, see Paul Ekman and Wallace V. Friesen, "Hand Movements," *Journal of Communication* 22 (1972): 360.

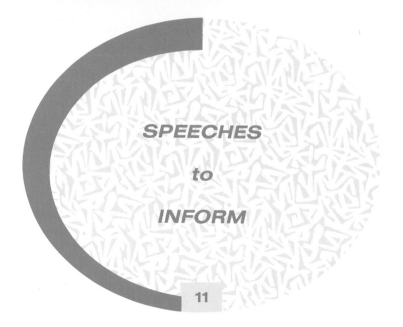

SPEECHES to INFORM

11

Ours is a society that almost worships "facts." Particularly because of such technological developments as electronic media, photostatic printing, miniaturized circuitry, and computerized data storage and retrieval systems, a staggering amount of information is available. Mere information, however, does nothing, "tells" us nothing; information is simply there until human beings shape, interpret, and act on it. That is why public speakers often are called on to assemble, package, and present information to other human beings.

A theme will be sounded throughout this chapter: *"Mere information" is useless until someone has put it together in ways that make it clear and relevant to the lives of others.* That is why there are such things as informative speeches. In this chapter, we will discuss various types of informative speeches, outlining their essential features and reviewing easy ways of structuring them.

TYPES OF INFORMATIVE SPEECHES

Informative speeches take many forms, depending on the situation, the level of knowledge possessed by audience members, and your own abilities as a presenter of data. Four of these forms—*speeches of definition, instructions and demonstrations, oral reports,* and *lectures*—occur so frequently, however, that they merit special attention. They represent four ways people package or interrelate information.

Speeches of Definition

"Mommy, what is a 'knucklehead'?" "Professor Martin, could you please stop a moment and tell us what a 'quark' is?" "Joanne, before we can decide whether to buy this house, you are going to have to answer a dumb question for us: What's 'earnest money'?" You have been asking these sorts of questions all of your life. As you can see, a speech of definition is not something that merely asks for a dictionary definition of something; you could look up the word if that were all that is involved. Rather, a speech of definition seeks to define concepts or processes in ways that make them *relevant* to a situation or problem an audience faces. Once five-year-old Sarah knows what a "knucklehead" is, she will know she has a human relations problem she had better work on; once you know what a "quark" is, Professor Martin's lecture will make a good deal more sense; and, once you know that "earnest money" is simply a sign of good faith in a purchase agreement, your anxiety will disappear.

Instructions and Demonstrations

Throughout your life, classroom instructions, job instructions, and instructions for the performance of special tasks have played vital roles. Not only have you gone through many "tell" sessions with others, but you have also had people "show" you how to execute desired actions—how to implement a special procedure in chemistry class, how to conduct a voter registration drive, how to make a never-fail soufflé. In general, then, instructions are verbal communications that explain complex processes, while demonstrations are verbal and nonverbal messages explaining and illustrating those processes. Both involve the *serial presentation* of information, usually in steps or phases, and demand *utter clarity,* simply because your listeners are expected to repeat or reproduce those steps themselves after you have instructed them.

Oral Reports

Academic reports, committee reports, and executive reports are typical kinds of oral reports. Scientists and scholars announce their research findings at professional conventions. Committees in business, industry, and government carry out special research or advisory tasks and then present oral reports to their parent organizations or constituencies. Board chairpersons report annually to the stockholders on the past year's activities. Thus, an oral report is a speech in which one assembles, arranges, and interprets information gathered in response to a request made or a goal set by a group.

Lectures

Characteristic types of lectures include talks on travel and public affairs, classroom lectures, and talks at club meetings, study conferences, and institutes. The purpose of a lecture is to increase the audience's understanding or appreciation of a particular field of knowledge or activity. Lectures usually involve some sort of *explanation*. Lecturers are called on to define unclear or new concepts but also to indicate how a certain situation arose, or to point out the implications of an old or new policy. For instance, a business executive might not only define "management by objectives" but then go on to show how it can modernize even a small business; a historian might tell a group of students what social-cultural forces converged to create the American Revolution; and a social worker could lecture an audience of government officials on the local impact of the Gramm-Rudmann Act and tax reform.

Group decisions are often based on information that an individual member has compiled, interpreted, and presented in an oral report.

ESSENTIAL FEATURES OF INFORMATIVE SPEECHES

Four qualities should characterize any speech to inform: (1) *clarity,* (2) *the association of new ideas with familiar ones,* (3) *coherence,* and (4) *motivational appeal.*

Clarity

The quality of clarity is largely the result of effective organization and the careful selection of words. Informative speeches achieve maximum clarity when your listeners can follow you and understand what you are saying.

In organizing your speech, observe the following rules:

1. Do not try to cover too many points. Confine your speech to three or four principal ideas, grouping whatever facts or ideas you wish to consider under these headings. Even if you know a tremendous amount about your subject matter, remember that you cannot make everyone an expert in a single speech.

2. Clarify the relationship between your main points by observing the principles of coordination. Word your transitions carefully—"*Second,* you must prepare the chair for caning by cleaning out the groove and cane holes"; "The Stamp Act Crisis was *followed by* an *even more important* event—The Townshend Duties"; "To test *these* hypotheses, we set up the *following* experiment." Such transitions allow auditors to follow you from point to point.

3. Keep your speech moving forward according to a well-developed plan. Do not jump back and forth between ideas, charging ahead and then backtracking; that creates more smoke than light.

In selecting your words, follow the advice we offered in Chapter 8:

1. Use a precise, accurate vocabulary without getting too technical. In telling someone how to finish off a basement room, you might be tempted to say, "Next, take one of these long sticks and cut it off in this funny-looking gizmo with a saw in it, and try to make the corners match." An accurate vocabulary will help your listeners remember what supplies and tools to get when they approach the same project: "This is a ceiling molding; it goes around the room between the wall and the ceiling to cover the seams between the paneling and the ceiling tiles. You make the corners of the molding match by using a mitre box, which has grooves that allow you to cut 45-degree angles. Here's how you do it."

2. Simplify when possible, including only as much technical vocabulary as you need. Do not make a speech on the operation of a two-cycle internal combustion engine sound as if it came out of a lawn mower mechanic's operational manual. An audience bogged down in unnecessary detail and vocabulary can become confused and bored.

3. Use reiteration when it clarifies complex ideas, but avoid simply repeating the same words. Rephrase to help solidify ideas for those who had trouble getting them the first time: "Unlike a terrestrial telescope, a celestial telescope is used for looking at moons, planets, and stars; that is, its mirrors and lens are ground and arranged in such a way that it focuses on objects thousands of miles, not hundreds of feet, away from the observer."

Association of New Ideas with Familiar Ones

Audiences grasp new facts and ideas more readily when they can associate them with what they already know. Therefore, in a speech to inform, try to connect the new with the old. To do this, of course, you need to have done enough solid audience analysis so that you know what experiences, images, analogies, and metaphors to use in your speech.

Sometimes the associations you ought to make are obvious. A college dean talking to an audience of manufacturers on the problems of higher education presented his ideas under the headings of raw material, casting, machining, polishing, and assembling. He thus translated his central ideas into an analogy his audience, given their vocations, would be sure to understand and appreciate. At other times, if you cannot think of any obvious associations, you may have to rely on common experiences or images. For instance, you might explain the operation of the human eye pupil by comparing it to the operation of a camera lens aperture.

Coherence

Coherence is in part a matter of organization—of finding a pattern that fits your subtopics together in a meaningful manner. Sometimes it is relatively easy to create a sense of coherence, as when giving a speech on the structure of the federal government, for there are only three branches. At other times, especially when you are not covering all components of a subject, you have to manufacture coherence.

Occasionally, you may have to do a little forcing. Suppose you decided to give a speech on the Nielsen television program rating system. You might decide to discuss only three aspects of the system—what it is, how it works, and how it is used by network executives to determine which programs to continue and which to drop. To give the speech coherence, you could use a question-answer organizational pattern and move into the body of your speech in this fashion: "People who worry about the effect of the Nielsen ratings on what they watch usually ask three questions: 'What *is* a Nielsen rating, anyway?' 'How is the rating done?' 'Why do the networks rely on it for making decisions on shows?' To answer these common questions, and to explain the 'what,' 'how,' and 'why' of television ratings, today I first will . . . . " Notice that the speaker has taken a common trio of words— *what, how, why*—and used them as an organizing principle to give coherence to this explanatory speech.

Motivation of the Audience

Finally, and perhaps most important, you must be able to motivate the audience to listen. Unfortunately, many people ignore this essential feature of good informative speeches. Many of us blithely assume that because *we* are interested in something, our audience also will want to hear about it. To you, stamp collecting may be an interesting, relaxing, and profitable hobby, but until your listeners are likewise convinced, they will yawn through your speech on American commemoratives.

Keep in mind, therefore, what we have said about attention and motivation even when preparing informative speeches: *(a)* Use the factors of attention to engage the members of your audience, to draw them into your speech. *(b)* Once you have captured them initially, be sure to build in motivational appeals, reasons why they should want to know what you are about to tell them. If you indicate that your talk will increase their interpersonal effectiveness, provide them with additional income, reduce their confusion about important matters, and the like, you will be making your speech relevant and compelling.

STRUCTURING INFORMATIVE SPEECHES

Now that we have described the various types of informative speeches and treated their essential features, it is time to examine ways to structure each of those types. Of course, it is possible to use any of the organizational patterns we have described earlier, but some patterns are better suited to particular types than others.

Speeches of Definition

Introduction

Because speeches of definition treat either unfamiliar or familiar concepts in a new light, their introductions must create *curiosity* and *need* in listeners. Curiosity is a special challenge in speeches on unfamiliar concepts, for we are all tempted to say, "Well, if I've made it this far through life without knowing anything about black holes or carcinogens or trap blocking, why should I bother with learning more about these ideas now?" The answer, to a large extent, depends on your ability to make people wonder about the unknown. You may want to concentrate part of your introduction to a definitional speech, therefore, on making listeners desire to know more about unknown aspects of their everyday environment or of far-away segments of life.

Speeches on both unfamiliar and familiar concepts must be attentive to the needs or wants of the listeners. This means that their introduction should include motivational materials—explicit statements that indicate how the information can affect the audience. Thus, one often hears statements such as the following: "Understanding the dynamics of trap blocking will help you better appreciate line play in football and therefore increase your enjoyment of the game every Saturday afternoon in our stadium."

Body

Most speeches of definition use a topical pattern (discussed earlier in the book) because such speeches usually describe various aspects of a thing or idea. It seems natural, for example, to use a topical pattern when giving a speech on a career in computer programming and to organize the body of the speech around such topics as "the duties of a computer programmer," "skills needed by a computer programmer," and "training you will need to become a computer programmer."

There are occasions, too, when other patterns may serve your specific purpose well. You might use an effect-cause pattern, for example, when preparing an informative speech on the laws of supply and demand. You could enumerate a series of effects with which people are already familiar—soaring prices coupled with seemingly fantastic sales, interest rates that apparently change every other week—and then discuss the laws of supply and demand that account for such confusing fiscal patterns in society.

A speech on cancer could be outlined as follows:

WHAT DOES CANCER MEAN?[1]

I. "You have cancer" is a phrase that can strike fear into the hardiest among us. Fear of the unknown is the most difficult to accept. Thus, if we are to understand *cancer*, we must know more about what the term means.
   A. My intent is to acquaint you with several terms that, together, will give us a better understanding of cancer.
   B. By knowing more about what is involved in cancer, hopefully we will have less fear.

II. There are several terms used in the scientific discussion of cancer. Not all are clearly understood.
   A. *Carcinogen:* Chemicals from various products (for example, cigarette smoke) may lead to cancer.
   B. *Activation:* The carcinogen must be chemically changed in order to start the cancer process.
   C. *Detoxification enzymes:* These are naturally occurring chemicals in the body that detoxify—take the poison out of substances ingested into the body.
      1. Most carcinogens entering the body are detoxified and can cause no harm.
      2. In some cases, the detoxification process goes wrong, and the carcinogen is rendered capable of entering a cell's nucleus and attaching itself to DNA.
   D. *DNA attachment:* The DNA is the central "code" that determines the function of the cell, the central operating system of the human computer.
      1. The "second line of defense" occurs when "scavenger molecules" attack the activated carcinogen and render it harmless.
      2. Unfortunately, this line of defense sometimes fails.
      3. DNA has a third line of defense, as invading activated carcinogens can be isolated by DNA "repair molecules."
      4. Unfortunately, this line of defense can also fail.
   E. *Cell mutation and division:* Remember your junior-high biology? Cells divide and create exact replicas.
      1. If the defenses have failed, an active carcinogen is attached to DNA inside a cell.
      2. Cell division will produce two new cells with the carcinogen-affected DNA.
      3. Mutation is not an automatic sign of cancer, for the alteration may only cripple one cell.
   F. *Promoter chemicals.* These are chemicals near the mutated cell that foster its multiplication, to the detriment of other nonmutants nearby.
      1. The mutant cell may also be attacked by a second carcinogen.
      2. If all of the defenses fail again, a second mutation occurs.
      3. After several cycles of mutation and promotion, a group of cells may begin to form a tumor.
III. I hope this review of the major terms and their meanings gives you a better understanding of the term *cancer.*

Conclusion

Conclusions for speeches of definition frequently have two characteristics: (1) They usually include a summary, especially if a good many facts, figures, and ideas have been covered, and (2) they often stress the kinds of

Verbal and nonverbal "how to" messages teach listeners the steps involved in performing complex tasks. Thus, an "instructor" must present information with utter clarity so that listeners understand and can perform such tasks themselves.

applications people can make of the ideas they have been given. For example, a speech on your campus' aerobics classes could conclude with a review of the main features of aerobics exercise and a list of campus buildings where noon and evening classes are held. As with all good conclusions, the ending of a speech of definition should not come abruptly, as a dictionary definition does. Rather, round it off for your listeners, tying it up in ways useful to them.

Instructions and Demonstrations

Introduction

In most situations where you will be called on to give instructions or offer a demonstration, you will need to spend little time piquing curiosity or motivating people to listen. After all, if you are instructing your listeners in a new office procedure or giving a workshop on how to build an ice boat, they already have the prerequisite interest and motivation; otherwise, they would not have come. If your listeners' attendance is not voluntary (as can be the case in speech communication classrooms), then you will have to pay attention to motivational matters. Normally, however, you must concentrate your introduction on two other tasks:

1. *Preview* your speech. If, say, you are going to take the members of your audience through the seven steps involved in making a good tombstone rubbing, give them an overall picture of the process before you start describing each operation in detail.

2. *Encourage* them to follow along, even through some of the more difficult steps. A process like tombstone rubbing, for example, looks easier than it is; many are tempted to quit listening and give up somewhere along the way. If, however, they are forewarned and are promised special help with the difficult techniques, they are more likely to bear with you.

Body

As we suggested earlier, most speeches of demonstration and instruction are packaged in a chronological and/or spatial pattern, simply because you are teaching people a serial process you want them to be able to carry out on their own. A nonsequential organizational pattern would be very confusing.

In other words, speakers usually have little trouble organizing the body of a speech of demonstration or instruction. Their problems are more likely technical ones:

1. *The problem of rate.* If the glue on a project needs to set before you can go on to the next step, what do you do? You cannot just stand there and wait for it to dry. You need to have preplanned some material for filling the time—perhaps additional background or a brief discussion of what problems one can run into at this stage. Preplan your remarks carefully for those junctures; otherwise, you are likely to lose your audience.

2. *The problem of scale.* How can you show various embroidery stitches to an audience of twenty-five? When dealing with minute operations, you often must increase the scale of operation. In this example, you might use a large piece of poster board or even a 3′ by 4′ piece of cloth stretched over a wooden frame. By using an oversized needle, yarn instead of thread, and stitches measured in inches instead of millimeters, you could easily make your techniques visible to all audience members. At the other extreme, in a speech on how to make a homemade solar heat collector, you probably would want to work with a scaled-down model.

3. *The coordination of verbal and visual materials.* Both instructions and demonstrations usually demand that speakers "show" while "telling." To keep yourself from becoming flustered or confused, be sure to practice talking while doing—demonstrating your material while explaining aloud what you are doing. Decide where you will stand when showing a slide so that the audience can see both you and the image; practice talking about your aerobic exercise positions while you are actually doing them; work a dough press in practice sessions as you tell your mythical audience how to form professional-looking cookies. If you do not, you will inevitably get yourself into trouble in front of your real audience.

Thinking through such procedural and technical problems you can face might lead to a speaking outline like the following one on planting tomatoes:

HOW TO PLANT TOMATOES

Coordinate verbal and visual materials

I. First, you must select a variety of tomato seed that is suited to various geographical, climatological, agricultural, and personal factors. (*display chart, showing varieties in columns along with their characteristics*)
   A. Some tomatoes grow better in hard soils; some, in loose soils.
   B. Some varieties handle shade well; some, direct sunlight.
   C. Some are well suited to short growing seasons; others, to long seasons.
   D. Each variety tends to resist certain diseases, such as blight, better than others.

II. Once you have selected a variety (or maybe even two, so that they mature at different times), next you must start the seeds.

Coordinate verbal and visual materials

   A. Prepare a mixture of black dirt, peat moss, and vermiculite as I am doing. (*do it, indicating proportions*)
   B. Fill germination trays, pots, or cut-off milk cartons with the germination soil, and insert seeds. (*do it*)

Reduce time delay (rate)

   C. With watering, sunlight, and patience, your plants will grow. I can't show you that growth here today, but I can use these seedlings to illustrate their care along the way. (*bring out half-grown and fully grown seedlings*)

Coordinate verbal and behavioral actions

      1. When the seedlings are about an inch or two tall, thin them. (*demonstrate*)
      2. At about six inches (*show them*), you can transplant them safely.
      3. But, you'll know more about which plants are strong if you wait until they are ten to twelve inches tall. (*show them plants of different strengths*)

D. Now you are ready to transplant the seedlings to your garden.

1. Carefully unpot the seedlings, being sure not to damage the root network. *(demonstrate)*

Coordinate visual and verbal materials; enlarge materials

2. Put each seedling in a hole already prepared in your plot; this diagram shows you how to do that. *(show an enlarged drawing that illustrates hole size and depth, a mixture of peat moss and vermiculite in the bottom, and spacing of plants)*

3. Pack the garden soil firmly but not so hard as to crush the roots.

4. Water it almost every day for the first week.

Coordinate verbal and visual materials; reduce size of materials

5. Put some sort of mulching material—grass clippings, hay, black sheets of plastic—between the rows if weeds are a problem. *(another drawing or picture)*

E. Once you know your plants are growing, cage or stake each plant. *(show sketches of various styles of cages or stakes, discussing the advantages of each)*

Conclusion

Conclusions for demonstration speeches usually have three parts:

1. First, *summaries* are offered. Most audiences need this review, which reminds them to ask questions about procedures or ideas they do not fully understand.

2. Second, some *bolstering* has to take place. People trying their hands at new processes or procedures usually get in trouble the first few times and need to be reassured that this is natural and can be overcome.

3. Finally, *future help* should be offered. What sounded so simple in your talk can be much more complicated in execution. If possible, make yourself available for later assistance: "As you fill out your registration form, just raise your hand if you're unsure of anything and I'll be happy to help you." Or point to other sources of further information and assistance: "Here's the address of the U.S. Government Printing Office, whose pamphlet X1234 is available for only a dollar; it will give you more details"; "If you run into a filing problem I haven't covered in this short orientation to your job, just go over to Mary McFerson's desk, right over here. Mary's experienced in these matters and is always willing to help." Such statements not only offer help, but assure your audience members that they will not be labeled as dull-witted if they actually have to ask for it.

Oral Reports

Introduction

Oral reports are requested by a group, committee, or class; the audience, therefore, generally knows what it expects and why. In introducing oral reports, then, you need not spend much time motivating your listeners— they already are motivated. Rather, you should concentrate on *(1)* reminding them of what they asked for, should their memories be short; *(2)* describing carefully the procedures you used in gathering the information; *(3)* forecasting the development of various subtopics so the audience can follow you easily; and *(4)* pointing ahead to any action they are expected to take in light of your information. Thus, the key to a good introduction for an oral report is *orientation*—reviewing the past (their expectations and your preparations), the present (your goal now), and the future (their responsibilities once you are done). Remember that you give the report to an audience for a purpose.

Body

The principle for organizing the body of an oral report can be stated simply: *Select the organizational pattern best suited to the audience's needs.* Have you been asked to provide them with a history of a group or problem? Use a chronological pattern. Do they want to know how a particular state of affairs came to be? Try a cause-effect format. Have you been asked to discuss an organizational structure for the group? A topical pattern allows you to review the constitutional responsibilities of each officer. If you were asked to examine the pros and cons of various proposals and to recommend one to the group, the elimination pattern is the way to go, as in the following example:

REPORT FROM THE FINAL EXAMINATION COMMITTEE

    I. My committee was asked to compare and contrast various ways of structuring a final examination in this speech class and to recommend a procedure to you. *(the reporter's "charge")*

        A. First, we interviewed each one of you.

        B. Then, we discussed the pedagogical virtues of various exam procedures with our instructor.

        C. And next, we deliberated as a group, coming to the following conclusions. *(orientation completed)*

    II. Like many students, we first thought we should recommend a take-home essay examination as the "easiest" way out.

        A. But, we decided our wonderful textbook is filled with so much detailed and scattered advice that it would be almost impossible for any of us to answer essay-type questions without many, many hours of worry, work, and sweat.

   B. We also wondered why a course that stresses oral performance should test our abilities to write essays.

III. So, we next reviewed a standard, short-answer, in-class final.

   A. Although such a test would allow us to concentrate on the main ideas and central vocabulary, which has been developed in lectures, readings, and discussion, it would require a fair amount of memorization.

   B. And, we came back to the notion that merely understanding communication concepts will not be enough when we start giving speeches outside this classroom.

IV. Thus, we recommend that you urge our instructor to give us an oral examination this term.

   A. Each of us could be given an impromptu speech topic, some resource material, and ten minutes to prepare a speech.

   B. We could be graded, in this way, on both substantive and communicative decisions we make in putting together and delivering the speech.

   C. Most important, such a test would be consistent with this course's primary goal—and could be completed quickly, almost painlessly.

Conclusion

Most oral reports end with a conclusion that mirrors the introduction. The report's purpose is mentioned again; the main points are reviewed; committee members (if there are any) are thanked publicly; and then either a motion to accept the committee recommendations (if there are any) is offered or, in the case of more straightforwardly informative reports, questions from the audience are called for. Conclusions to reports—when done well—are quick, firm, efficient, and pointed.

Lectures

Introduction

Introductions to lectures can use many of the techniques we have described thus far. You might have to raise curiosity in some instances (how many of your classmates wonder about the causes of the American Revolution at ten o'clock in the morning?). You might also have to generate a need or desire to listen, especially if your topic seems distant or irrelevant. Also, if the explanation will be somewhat complex, a forecast of coming ideas is almost mandatory. Finally, you may need to encourage your listeners to follow along, telling them you will go into greater detail later, especially in the sections of greatest difficulty.

*'How on earth can I make this speech relevant to my class?'
Jeremy sat, crestfallen, in his instructor's office. He knew a
lot about the Vietnam War, and he really wanted his classmates to know more about its causes and its effects on
American life. 'Well,' his instructor replied, 'what are some of
the things that really interest them?' 'Beer drinking, football,
movies, and television,' replied Jeremy. 'Then that's it, that's
your key,' said his teacher. 'What is? Bar hopping?' 'No, no,'
said the instructor, 'television!' 'Television?' 'Yes, television.
And movies. Think of all of the television programs and films
dealing with Vietnam. For movies, there are* Coming Home,
Apocalypse Now, The Deer Hunter, Platoon, *and all the* Rambo
*films. There have been a number of documentaries about
Vietnam recently, and even such prime time shows as
"Magnum P.I." and "Hill Street Blues" have shown Vietnam
vets reliving the war. Use those movies and TV programs as
ways to reach your audience.'*

Body

Most lectures fit well into causal and topical organizational patterns. If you are trying to explain how or why something operates the way it does, either cause-effect or effect-cause order works very well. Or, if you are attempting to show how a problem can or should be solved, a straightforward problem-solution format is effective, especially if your listeners are unsure of what the solution might be. These patterns work well because, as we saw earlier, lectures usually seek to interrelate things and/or ideas.

Conclusion

Typically, the conclusion of a good lecture develops additional implications or calls for particular actions. If, for example, you have explained how contagious diseases spread through geographical areas, you should probably conclude by discussing some actions listeners can take to halt the process of contagion. Or, if you have explained the concept of "children's rights" to a parent-teacher organization, close by asking your listeners to consider what these rights *should* mean to them—how they should change their thinking and their behaviors toward six-year-olds.

Suppose you are a theater buff, and you decide to give a lecture on Shakespeare's Globe Theater for an assignment calling for an explanation. Consider the following outline to see how some of this advice can be put to work for you.

LECTURE ON THE GLOBE THEATER[2]

General Purpose: *To inform*

Specific Purposes: *To increase audience interest in performances of Shakespeare by explaining how characteristics of his plays were shaped by the physical structure of the Globe Theater and vice versa.*

Introduction

Curiosity: Raise their curiosity by noting how odd some of the special effects and stage directions are in Shakespearean plays. *(show sketches or a model of the Globe)*

Desire: Indicate that increasing their knowledge of Shakespearean play production will not only make them more liberally educated college students but should help them improve their performance in literature class.

Body

Organizational Pattern: Use a kind of problem-solution pattern to capture listeners up in the dynamics of theater construction, e.g.:

I. External characteristics of the Globe
  A. Shakespeare wished the audience to see better, so a round (20- or 24-sided) theater was constructed.
  B. Shakespeare wished to accommodate both wealthy and poor patrons, so the good seats were elevated and covered, while the "groundlings" stood in the pit (open semicircle in front of the stage).

II. Internal characteristics of the Globe
  A. Shakespeare needed elevations to stage such scenes as the balcony scene in *Romeo and Juliet*.
    1. A half-roof over the upper stage could be the balcony or castle top.
    2. It also could house musicians who played drums and wind instruments to represent thunder and wind.
  B. Because the stage was rounded, actors could not move into the wings, yet Shakespeare's plays needed to move actors on and off easily and to "hide" some actors from others, as when Polonius in *Hamlet* or Iago in *Othello* overhears someone talking.
    1. Multiple rear exits into so-called "tiring rooms" were built.
    2. Some exits led backstage, while others were covered with curtains as hiding places.
  C. Elizabethan plays were filled with ghosts, angels, devils, and other apparitions that needed to appear suddenly.
    1. Shakespeare accommodated the ghosts and devils by The Heavens, the upper stage noted before.
    2. For the lower spirits and disappearing magicians, he filled the main stage with trap doors, so that actors could suddenly sink away in a burst of smoke.
    (Other points having to do with costumes, banners, dueling, etc., could be made.)

Conclusion

Implications: Point out that we usually read plays as "literature," but, in reality, they ought to be read as "performance guides"; also indicate that plays from ancient Greece, the Restoration period, and even contemporary dramatists are designed in part to fit the stage mechanisms and styles of an era.

Overall, informative speeches are greater challenges than most people realize. Information is not useful to listeners until it has been carefully selected, structured, and cast into motivational appeals that draw them in. "The facts" are seldom enough for human beings; as an informative speaker, you must supply the rest.

. . . **Sample Speech** *to Inform* • • • • • • • • • • •

The following speech, "The Geisha," was delivered by Joyce Chapman in her freshman year at Loop College, Chicago. It illustrates most of the virtues of a good informative speech: (1) It provides enough detail and explanation to be clear. (2) It works from familiar images of geishas, adding new ideas and information so as to enlarge audience members' conceptions. (3) Its topical pattern of organization makes it both easy to follow and coherent. (4) It includes the sorts of motivational appeals that make audiences want to listen.

THE GEISHA[3]

Introduction

Personal reference

As you may have already noticed from my facial features, I have oriental blood in me and, as such, I am greatly interested in my Japanese heritage. One aspect of my heritage that fascinates me the most is the beautiful and adoring Geisha. /1

I recently asked some of my friends what they thought a Geisha was, and the comments I received were quite astonishing. For example, one friend said, "She is a woman who walks around in a hut." A second friend was certain that a Geisha was, "A woman who massages men for money and it involves her in other physical activities." Finally, I received this response, "She gives baths to men and walks on their backs." Well, needless to say, I was rather surprised and offended by their comments. I soon discovered that the majority of my friends perceived the Geisha with similar attitudes. One of them argued, "It's not my fault, because that is the way I've seen them on TV." In many ways my friend was correct. His misconception of the Geisha was not his fault, for she is often portrayed by American film producers and directors as: a prostitute, as in the movie, *The Barbarian and the Geisha,* a streetwalker, as seen in the TV series, "Kung Fu," or as a showgirl with a gimmick, as performed in the play, *Flower Drum Song.* /2

Central idea

A Geisha is neither a prostitute, streetwalker, or showgirl with a gimmick. She is a lovely Japanese woman who is a professional entertainer and hostess. She is cultivated with exquisite manners, truly a bird of a very different plumage. /3

Orientation

I would like to provide you with some insight to the Geisha, and, in the process perhaps, correct any misconception you may have. I will do this by discussing her history, training, and development. /4

Body

First point: The Geisha has been in existence since 600 A.D., during
history   the archaic time of the Yakamoto period. At that time the
Japanese ruling class was very powerful and economically rich.
The impoverished majority, however, had to struggle to survive.
Starving fathers and their families had to sell their young
daughters to the teahouses in order to get a few yen. The
families hoped that the girls would have a better life in the
teahouse than they would have had in their own miserable
homes.   /5

During ancient times only high society could utilize the
Geisha's talents because she was regarded as a status symbol,
exclusively for the elite. As the Geisha became more popular,
the common people developed their own imitations. These
imitations were often crude and base, lacking sophistication
and taste. When American GIs came home from World War
II, they related descriptive accounts of their wild escapades
with the Japanese Geisha. In essence, the GIs were only
soliciting with common prostitutes. These bizarre stories
helped create the wrong image of the Geisha.   /6

Second point: Today, it is extremely difficult to become a Geisha. A
training   Japanese woman couldn't wake up one morning and decide, "I
think I'll become a Geisha today." It's not that simple. It takes
sixteen years to qualify.   /7

At the age of six a young girl would enter the Geisha
training school and become a Jo-chu, which means housekeeper.
The Jo-chu does not have any specific type of clothing, hairstyle,
or make-up. Her duties basically consist of keeping the
teahouse immaculately clean (for cleanliness is like a religion
to the Japanese). She would also be responsible for making
certain that the more advanced women would have everything
available at their fingertips. It is not until the girl is sixteen
and enters the Maiko stage that she concentrates less on
domestic duties and channels more of her energies on creative
and artistic endeavors.   /8

The Maiko girl, for example, is taught the classical Japanese
dance, Kabuki. At first, the dance consists of tiny, timid steps
to the left, to the right, backward and forward. As the years
progress, she is taught the more difficult steps requiring
syncopated movements to a fan.   /9

The Maiko is also introduced to the highly regarded art
of floral arrangement. The Japanese take full advantage of the
simplicity and gracefulness that can be achieved with a few
flowers in a vase, or with a single flowering twig. There are

three main styles: Seika, Moribana, and Nagerie. It takes at least three years to master this beautiful art. /10

During the same three years, the Maiko is taught the ceremonious art of serving tea. The roots of these rituals go back to the thirteenth century, when Zen Buddhist monks in China drank tea during their devotions. These rituals were raised to a fine art by the Japanese tea masters, who set the standards for patterns of behavior throughout Japanese society. The tea ceremony is so intricate that it often takes four hours to perform and requires the use of over seventeen different utensils. The tea ceremony is far more than the social occasion it appears to be. To the Japanese, it serves as an island of serenity where one can refresh the senses and nourish the soul. /11

One of the most important arts taught to the Geisha is that of conversation. She must master an elegant circuitous vocabulary flavored in Karyuki, the world of flowers and willows, of which she will be a part. Consequently, she must be capable of stimulating her client's mind as well as his esthetic pleasures. /12

Third point: development   Having completed her sixteen years of thorough training, at the age of twenty-two, she becomes a full-fledged Geisha. She can now serve her clients with duty, loyalty, and most important, a sense of dignity. /13

The Geisha would be dressed in the ceremonial kimono, made of brocade and silk thread. It would be fastened with an obi, which is a sash around the waist and hung down the back. The length of the obi would indicate the girl's degree of development. For instance, in the Maiko stage the obi is longer and is shortened when she becomes a Geisha. Unlike the Maiko, who wears a gay, bright, and cheerful kimono, the Geisha is dressed in more subdued colors. Her make-up is the traditional white base, which gives her the look of white porcelain. The hair is shortened and adorned with beautiful, delicate ornaments. /14

As a full-fledged Geisha, she would probably acquire a rich patron who would assume her sizable debt to the Okiya, or training residence. This patron would help pay for her wardrobe, for each kimona can cost up to $12,000. The patron would generally provide her with financial security. /15

The Geisha serves as a combination entertainer and companion. She may dance, sing, recite poetry, play musical instruments, or draw pictures for her guest. She might converse with them or listen sympathetically to their troubles. Amorous advances, however, are against the rules. /16

Conclusion

> So, as you can see the Geisha is a far cry from the back-rubbing, streetwalking, slick entertainer that was described by my friends. She is a beautiful, cultivated, sensitive, and refined woman. /17

• •

CHAPTER SUMMARY

Speeches to inform include all messages that attempt to assemble, package, and interpret raw data, information, or ideas. Four common types of informative speeches are *speeches of definition, instructions and demonstrations, oral reports,* and *lectures.* No matter what type of informative speech you are preparing, you will need to strive for *clarity, ways to associate new ideas with familiar ones, coherence,* and *methods to motivate an audience.* Finally, think carefully through the various organizational structures available to you and select one that best suits your purpose and message.

Oral Activities

1. Prepare a three- to four-minute speech in which you give instructions. For example, you might explain how to calculate your life insurance needs, how to canvass a neighborhood for a political candidate, or how to make a charter or group flight reservation. To put some pressure on your oral instruction abilities, use no visual aids.
2. How would you explain rabies vaccinations for pets to each of the following audiences? Work with three or four classmates to formulate specific purposes, to suggest organizational patterns, and to identify some key kinds of supporting materials needed for each:
   a. A junior 4-H Club studying the grooming and training of dogs
   b. A city council meeting at which a new vaccination ordinance for cats is to be discussed
   c. Members of your speech class
   d. A group of preveterinary science majors
3. Give one of the following types of speeches in your next round:
   a. A *demonstration* speech, wherein you coordinate verbal speech and nonverbal materials to illustrate or explain a device, product, or steps in a process

b. An *opposing positions* speech, wherein you clearly and impartially present two sides of a controversial topic

c. An *unfamiliar* or *complex concept* speech, wherein you explain to your class some such thing as marriage contracts, est, charismatic religious experiences, or the wholesale price index using visual aids when appropriate

Reference Notes

1. Material for this outline drawn from Boyce Rensberger, "Cancer—The New Synthesis: Cause," *Science 84* 5 (September 1984): 28–33.
2. Material for this outline drawn from Stanley Wells, *Shakespeare* (London: Kaye & Ward Ltd., 1978); and John Russell Brown, *Shakespeare and His Theatre* (New York: Lothrop, Lee & Shepard Books, 1982).
3. "The Geisha" by Joyce Chapman, *Communication Strategy: A Guide to Speech Preparation* by Roselyn L. Schiff et al. Copyright © 1981 by Scott, Foresman and Company.

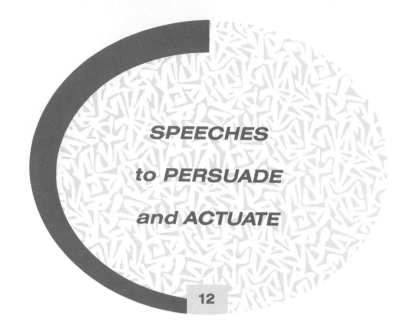

SPEECHES
to PERSUADE
and ACTUATE

12

Speeches to persuade and actuate are attempts to cause changes in people's psychological states or behaviors. In comparison, a successful informative speech affects listeners in some way, altering their conceptions of the world or, in the case of instructions and demonstrations, the way they do things. Yet, the central focus of informative speeches is always on "information" and its successful (clear) transmission. In contrast, the heart of persuasion is psychological change or, in the case of actuative speeches, actions you wish listeners to take as a result of their altered mental states.

Think back to our discussion of beliefs, attitudes, and values in Chapter 4. You could offer informative speeches on the American two-party political system, describing two-party vs. multiparty (coalition) politics, comparing two-party democracies with one-party totalitarian governmental systems, or even tracing the history of two-party confrontations in various epochs of U.S. history. But, were you to engage in persuasion, you probably would attempt to convince people that one party is *better* than the other or that a particular election had been *misinterpreted* by some historians. An actuative speech might urge that everyone vote on the second Tuesday in November.

Thus, the persuader/actuator is making quite a different demand on an audience than is the informer. The informative speaker is satisfied when listeners understand what has been said. However, the persuader is never happy until the audience *internalizes* (adopts as its own credo) or *acts on* the speech. The demand is for personal change.

> *The biggest persuader of them all today is television's all-pervasive 'ad' or 'spot.' Ads can cost nearly half-a-million dollars for a half-minute, as they did during the 1986 Super Bowl, reaching over 100 million people at once. TV spots, in a sense, have made your job as a persuader more difficult, for audience members have become conditioned to bells and whistles, slick editing and professional actors—all done within a few seconds and costing the product or political advertiser $100,000 to $200,000 to make. You're lucky if you've got enough money to photoduplicate a couple of visual aids. So, how do you, the public speaker, compete with the advertising power of ads? Simple. You don't. You may not have bells and whistles, electronic editing, professional makeup artists, and high-paid talent at work, but you have you. The physical presence of a human being can persuade millions—just consider Jesus of Nazareth; Adolph Hitler; Winston Churchill; Martin Luther King, Jr.; Golda Meir; and Ronald Reagan. The spot ad hits you quick and slick, over and over, beating you into submission. The persuasive speech seizes your whole mind and body and can change your life in ways far greater than a 15-second appeal to ring-around-the-collar.*

Although the purpose of these speeches is to win belief or produce action, an unwilling decision is of little value. Beliefs people are forced to accept may soon be abandoned; actions done unwillingly are usually done inefficiently and without any sense of reward or accomplishment. To change them successfully, therefore, not only must you make your listeners believe or do something, but you also must make them *want* to believe or do it. For this reason, two subsidiary purposes of persuasive and actuative speaking must be kept in mind: (1) to provide the audience with motives for believing by appealing to certain of their basic needs or desires and (2) to satisfy their

Societies attempt to overcome their shortcomings and conquer collective problems through the various methods of persuasion.

understanding by convincing them that the proposition you recommend will make the satisfaction of these desires possible.

We will begin this chapter, therefore, with a discussion of motive needs and the motivational appeals speakers can use to tap those needs. Then, we will examine the motivated sequence as an organizational pattern that helps you efficiently combine motivational appeals with claims to belief, attitude, value, and action to persuade the audience or move them to action.

ANALYZING THE NEEDS AND DESIRES OF LISTENERS

As we have said, a speech must be related to listeners' interests and desires. For your purposes as a public speaker, it is helpful to think of these interests and desires as *motive needs*.

The Concept of Motive Needs

We may think of a *need* as a desire, want, or uneasiness that individuals become aware of when considering their own situation. That need may arise from physiological considerations—pain, lack of food, or an uncomfortable temperature in a room—and it may come about for sociocultural reasons, as when you feel left out of a group or wonder whether your peers judge you to be a "good" person. If that need is deeply felt, it may impel you to do something about your situation, for example to eat, to adjust the thermostat, or to seek membership in a group. In these sorts of situations, you have been motivated to act. A motive need, then, is a tendency to move or act in a certain direction, an impulse to satisfy a psychological-social want or a biological urge.

A Classification of Motive Needs

The classification of fundamental human needs often cited today is the one developed by psychologist Abraham H. Maslow.[1] Maslow presented the following categories of needs and wants that impel human beings to think, act, and respond as they do:

1. *Physiological Needs*—for food, drink, air, sleep, sex, etc.—the basic bodily "tissue" requirements.
2. *Safety Needs*—for security, stability, protection from harm or injury; need for structure, order, law, and predictability; freedom from fear and chaos.
3. *Belongingness and Love Needs*—for abiding devotion and warm affection with spouse, children, parents, and close friends; need to feel a part of social groups; need for acceptance and approval.
4. *Esteem Needs*—for self-esteem based on achievement, mastery, competence, confidence, freedom, independence; desire for esteem of others (reputation, prestige, recognition, status).
5. *Self-Actualization Needs*—for self-fulfillment, actually to become what you potentially can be; desire to actualize your capabilities; being true to your essential nature; what you *can* be you *must* be.[2]

These needs, according to Maslow, function as a *prepotent hierarchy;* that is, lower-level needs must be largely fulfilled before higher-level needs operate. Persons caught up in the daily struggle to satisfy physiological and safety needs will, for example, have little time and energy left to strive for "esteem" or "self-actualization." Once these basic requirements of living are satisfied, however, higher-level drives take over. We should note, moreover, that, as individuals, we tend to move upward or downward from one level to another as our life progresses or regresses.

Finally, it should be noted that motives do not always automatically produce certain courses of action. Physiologically, you may feel a sharp pain from not having eaten for two days; yet, because of higher-level needs or pressures, you will not tear into a plate of food with your bare hands but rather will sit politely with fork and napkin. Thus, for example, the need

Maslow's Hierarchy of Needs

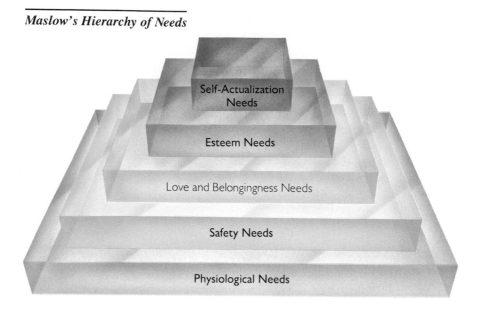

for social approval may control the way one satisfies physiological needs. Nevertheless, the hierarchy of prepotency is of considerable use in conceptualizing human motivation, even if individuals vary in the ways they manifest those needs.

Motivational Appeals in Public Speaking

Once you recognize the power of motive needs to impel human action, you may ask "How can I as a public speaker go about creating and satisfying such needs? How can I use these basic needs, wants, and desires as the basis for effective public communication?" The answer to both of these questions is: With the use of motivational appeals.

A *motivational appeal* is either (1) a *visualization* of a desire and a method for satisfying it or (2) an *assertion* that an entity, idea, or course of action holds the key to fulfilling a particular motive need.

Suppose, for example, that you want your parents to pay for a trip to London over the winter break. How do you prepare to ask them? Usually, you try out scenarios in your head, psychologically creating mini-movies: Will I be suave, casual, plaintive, stubborn, or adult? Will I find the words, the looks, the behaviors to move them to action? Will they respond with anger or sympathy, flippantly or seriously? In preparing these scenarios, you use visualization to work out motivational appeals: Is your parents' *fear* of losing an older child's support strong enough to move them? Are appeals to *love and respect* the best ways to go? How about appeals to *companionship* and to the *educational experiences* one gets in foreign countries? Thus, through the process of intrapersonal visualization you assemble a group of motivational appeals and organize them into little stories you can tell.

At other times, instead of visualizing courses of action for yourself or your listeners, you more simply attach motivational concepts directly to other concepts. Technically, this verbal process is called *attribution*.[3] Suppose, for example, that you had avoided going to church because you thought of churches as *conformist, authoritarian, dominating, repulsive,* and *destructive* institutions. One night, however, you went to a religious meeting, one where the preacher talked about the *adventure* of living a God-based life, the *beauty* of God's creation, the *reverence* one must feel in living a full life, and the *endurance* one must have in overcoming doubts. On reflection, you decided that you had misconstrued the church's motivation and even misanalyzed yourself. You became a devout churchgoer. What happened? You changed the attributes of "churchness" in your own mind. Instead of attributing conformity/authority/dominance/etc., to that institution and ideal, you began attributing adventure/beauty/reverence/etc., to personal religion. Conversion took place; your behavior changed.

Motivational appeals, therefore, are verbal attempts to activate certain motives within audience members relevant either to the idea or proposal under discussion or to factors making the audience reluctant to accept that idea or proposal. Such appeals may be made through images (verbal depiction) or assertion (verbal association).

Some Common Motivational Appeals

Following is a list of motivational appeals speakers can use to arouse in their listeners a particular feeling, emotion, or desire in an attempt to stimulate one or more of the primary motive needs. This list is, of necessity, incomplete, because there is an infinite number of human wants, needs, and motives—and combinations thereof. This list does, however, include some of the specific desires, drives, feelings, and sentiments to which practiced speakers often appeal in order to effectively motivate their listeners toward a given belief or action.[4]

Achievement and Display

"The successful business executive knows . . . ." "To make maximum use of your talents, act today to . . . ." Such appeals depend on people's interest in making a mark, in developing or actualizing themselves.

Only one person knows how much AT&T's full service means to you. You.

Be sure to send in your ballot.

You're the only one who knows exactly what you need from a long distance company. Only you know how important AT&T's full service long distance operators and customer service representatives are. Only you know how much AT&T's instant long distance connections and unbeatable sound clarity can mean.

But you can make your feelings clear. Right now, some of you are being asked to choose a long distance company. If you don't, one will be chosen for you. And since this decision won't be based on your needs, it might not be the right one for you.

AT&T Long Distance. For over a hundred years, when you reached out, we were there. And you can keep it that way. If you're asked to choose, mail in your ballot.

© AT&T 1986

AT&T
The right choice.

Testimony from a celebrity spokesman is one of the persuasive techniques used in this magazine ad. Can you identify the ad's motivational appeals to audience needs?

Acquisition and Saving

In this era of "me-ism," as seen in the growth of assertiveness training workshops, investment clubs, and special savings plans offered by banks, the appeal to personal savings and reward is potent. Rewards can be described in materialistic, social, spiritual, or personal terms.

Adventure and Change

"Taste the High Country!" cries the beer commercial. "Join the Navy and see the world," says the local recruiter. The human soul yearns for release; the human body seeks risk as a way of validating human worth. The appeal works.

Companionship and Affiliation

Yet we all need others—their presence, their touch, and their recognition of who we are. Thus, we all on occasion listen and respond to such appeals as "We care about you," "Join our group and find fellowship with kindred souls," and "You are one of a select group we're extending this invitation to."

Creativity

As Maslow noted, the height of self-actualization is a sense of individualized abilities and talents. The ads that urge you to "Draw Me" so as to get a "scholarship" to a correspondence school art course and the cookbooks that insist you become a "gourmet chef" by following step-by-step recipes appeal to your sense of creativity.

Curiosity

Children tear open alarm clocks to find out where the tick is, and adults crowd the sidewalks to gaze at a celebrity. Curiosity is often "idle," yet it is also the driving force behind such "high achievers" as experimenters, scholars, and explorers.

Deference

When we perceive that others have wisdom, experience, or expertise superior to our own, we defer to their knowledge and judgment. The successful use of testimony as a form of supporting material depends on listeners' deference.

Destructiveness

In times of high agitation and anger, we often respond to appeals that ask us to tear apart, to batter, to destroy. In times of war, "the enemy" must be destroyed; in times of interpersonal argument, ideas suffer the same fate. If you think through the moral implications of urging destruction and use it in conjunction with more positive appeals, you will find that this appeal can be a potent weapon.

Endurance and Tradition

We are all sensitive to our own relatively short span of earthly existence and to all of the others who came before us, building the great social and physical monuments to life. Hence, we are all susceptible to appeals to our family, group, and social traditions as (1) entities for which we have responsibility and (2) guides to our own behavior.

Fear

People have a broad range of fears—of failure, of death, of speechmaking, of inadequacy, of triumph by another. Fear is powerful and productive of both good (as when an individual is driven to achievement and bravery) and evil (as when fear-based prejudice produces bestial behavior toward others). Use it carefully and cautiously.

Fighting and Aggression

Because human groups and societies tend to be hierarchical, our natural biological urge to fight for our own rights and territory becomes translated into appeals to personal and social competition. So, ad after ad tells you how to "get ahead of the crowd" or to "beat your competition to the punch," and many a group leader urges action so "we can win" or "we can beat them [competing groups] on this issue." No one wants to lose.

Imitation and Conformity

At times, people's sense of belonging becomes so strong that they feel psychological pressure to be "one of the crowd." Commercials stressing what "the prudent homeowner does," what the "successful business-woman wears," and what "all true Americans believe" contain appeals to conformity.

Independence and Autonomy

But you also frequently hear "Be your own person; don't follow the crowd." Appeals to "know yourself," "be yourself," and "stand on your own two feet"—like the appeal to adventure—draw their force from our struggles to at least occasionally stand apart from others.

Loyalty

Periodically, we all want to celebrate our membership in groups and societies. In times of crisis, therefore, speakers often call for "tests of loyalty," for extraordinary actions that visibly demonstrate individuals' adherence to group standards for belief and action. You can ask listeners to be loyal to family, friends, organizations, states, geographical regions, or their country.

Personal Enjoyment

Like appeals to creativity, curiosity, and independence, appeals to personal enjoyment depend on our "selfish" instincts. While we often act as group members, at least as often we take a course of action because it promises personal comfort and luxury, esthetic enjoyment, recreation and rest, relief from home and work restraints, and just plain fun.

Power, Authority, and Dominance

Like its first cousin, the appeal to fighting and competition, the appeal to power, authority, and dominance depends for its potency on our aggressiveness. But, unlike the appeal to fighting and competition, this appeal moves beyond "mere winning" to *control:* People with power and authority control objects or other people. Thus, when President Jimmy Carter called his energy policy "the moral equivalent of war," he was urging us to control our energy needs; when the public service announcement says that "Cancer can be beaten in your lifetime," it is asking you to act from a sense of domination.

Pride

Appeals to pride—a sense of your own or our group's worth—can drive us to collective or individual achievement. Such appeals tighten one's loyalties to groups and, when coupled with appeals to adventure, creativity, and/or independence, move individuals to great personal exertion.

Reverence or Worship

Many times in our lives we recognize our own inferiority—our inferiority to others of superior qualities, to institutions we admire, to nature and the cosmos, and to deities that humble us in their magnitude and eternity. Beyond deference, a sense of reverence or worship leads to *submission.* Such reverent submission can take three forms: *hero worship; reverence for institutions;* and *divine worship,* conceived of both religiously and philosophically (as when eighteenth-century philosophers worshipped Nature).

Revulsion

The fragrance of a flower garden attracts people; the odor of a refuse heap repels. Similarly, in symbolic terms, you can attract people by verbally depicting the esthetic pleasures they will enjoy by acquiring or doing something or by visualizing in strong images objects of disgust or loathing. (See "imagery" in Chapter 8.) So, by picturing the unsanitary conditions of slums or the horrors of war, you can often mobilize people to action.

However, beware that you do not make such descriptions so gruesome that your appeal to revulsion turns them disgustedly against you. Be impressive without offending the deeper sensibilities of your listeners.

Sexual Attraction

Sex appeal is a staple of advertising trying to sell you deodorant, hair rinse and spray, beer and liquor, and sundry other sundries. "Sex sells," note the ad agents. Actually, as you look closely at such appeals, you will find that their core lies not so much in bodily functions per se in a more general idea of "personal attractiveness." Especially over the last decade, as our masculine and feminine consciousnesses have been raised, we have come to reject most objectionally blatant appeals to libidinous appetites, but we all listen to messages that promise to enhance our personal physical and psychological attractiveness and well-being.

Sympathy and Generosity

While we often (cynically) assume that most people are selfish at root, we know that, on many occasions, we can all be shamed or drawn to reach out for others. All appeals to giving, to support of others, and to self-sacrifice in the name of the "common good" are based on the assumption that your *social self* (that part of you bonded to others) will overcome your *private self* (that part of you that is self-centered) when the right appeal is made. "Reach out and touch someone," "Give that others might live," "There but for the grace of God go I"—such appeals form the heart of many an actuative speech.

You may have noticed that this list contains certain appeals that seem to contradict each other: for example, fear against the drive for adventure, defense against the desire for power/authority/dominance, and so on. Remember, in this regard, that the human being is an inconsistent and changeable creature who, at different times, may pursue quite different goals.

Using Motivational Appeals

In practice, motivational appeals seldom are used singly; speakers usually combine them. Suppose you were selecting a new car. What factors would influence your decision? One thing would be price (*saving*); another would be your comfort and appearance (*personal enjoyment*) as a result of driving it; a third consideration might be its European styling (*imitation*) or, conversely, its uniqueness (*independence*). And finally, all of these items together would raise the question of *pride:* Will other people think the vehicle a good one for you, and will you feel good about being identified with it? Some of these influences, of course, would be stronger than others, and some might conflict, but all of them would probably affect your choice to one degree or another, and you would buy the car that made the strongest total appeal.

Because motivational appeals are interrelated, it is a good idea to package a group of them in a speech, making sure that they are not so varied that they confuse your listeners. Generally, you ought to select three or four appeals that will *target* segments of your audience, as described in Chapter 4, or that will tap multiple dimensions of any individual's life. Watch out for *conflicting appeals;* do not describe the *adventure* of spelunking (cave exploration) so vividly that you create a sense of *fear.* Review your appeals for their pertinence and consistency.

Targeting and avoiding conflicting appeals are strategies visible in the following series of main headings for a speech by a student union representative urging students to take a summer trip to Europe:

Acquisition and savings	I. The tour is being offered for the low price of $2000 for three weeks.
Independence	II. There will be a minimum of supervision and regimentation.
Companionship	III. You'll be traveling with friends and fellow students.

In the complete speech, this student also emphasized the educational value of the experience *(self-advancement)* and said that a special mountain-climbing expedition could be worked in *(adventure).*

One final piece of general advice: Do not let your motivational appeals be too obvious, because your listeners might reject your proposal. Avoid "I want you to *imitate* Jones, the successful banker" or "If you give to the anti-apartheid fund, we'll print your name in the newspapers so that your *reputation* as a caring person will be known to everybody." Instead, merely suggest these results through your descriptions and illustrations. Especially avoid overt talk about the most self-centered appeals—greed, imitation, personal pride, and fear. People rarely admit, even to themselves, that they act on the basis of these motivations.

ORGANIZING THE SPEECH: THE MOTIVATED SEQUENCE

When you have a persuasive goal, various sorts of supporting materials, a list of possible motivational appeals, and some thoughts about your audience's beliefs, attitudes, and values clearly in mind, it is time to think about organizing the materials—about "packaging." And, as we have been suggesting, a very important consideration in structuring materials is people's psychological tendencies—ways in which individuals' own motivations and circumstances favor certain kinds of frameworks for structuring ideas. Basically, we can say that people follow their own motives-to-action along one of two perceptual paths:

1. We may tend toward a *world* or *problem orientation.* Early in this century, the American philosopher John Dewey recognized this tendency when he devised his "psycho-logic"—a pattern for thought he called "reflective thinking." In Dewey's view, individuals tend to follow a systematic procedure for solving problems. First, said Dewey, people become aware of a specific lack or disorientation—a situation with which they are, for one reason or another, dissatisfied. Second, they examine this difficulty in their world to determine its nature, scope, causes, and implications. Third, they search for new orientations or operations that will solve the problem or satisfy the need. Fourth, they compare and evaluate the possible solutions that have occurred to them. And, fifth, they select the solution that, on the basis of their foregoing reflections, seems most likely to put their minds at rest and to handle the real-world dimensions of the problem.[5] Dewey, in other words, adapted the so-called "scientific method" to individual and group problem solving.

2. Our other tendency is to be more *self-centered,* more *motivation-centered.* Salespersons and advertisers began recognizing this principle in the 1920s. They realized that you and I buy a particular automobile not simply to get from here to there but also to create a certain image; we buy this or that style of clothes to identify ourselves with others who wear certain sorts of trousers or dresses; we buy furniture that is both functional and decorative. In other words, our personal motivations, hopes, fears, and desires often control the ways we act and the goods we consume.

Alan Monroe (1903–75), the original author of this textbook, knew Dewey's work well and trained sales personnel in the 1920s. As he thought about Dewey's "psycho-logic" and the various sales techniques he had taught people to use, Monroe discovered he could unite both sets of procedures—one set based on the personalized scientific method and the other rooted in an understanding of human motivation—to form a highly useful organizational pattern. Since 1935, that structure has been called "Monroe's Motivated Sequence."[6] In this, the Tenth Edition of Monroe's textbook, we will devote the rest of this chapter to it.

The motivated sequence derives its name partly from Dewey's problem-solution format for thinking. It also makes attractive analyses of those problems and their solutions by tying them to human motives. That is, in

The Motivated Sequence

Audience Response

1 **Attention**

Getting
attention

I want to listen.

2 **Need**

Showing the
need:
describing the
problem

Something
needs to be done.

3 **Satisfaction**

Satisfying the need:
presenting the solution

This is what
to do to satisfy
the need.

4 **Visualization**

Visualizing the
results

I can see myself
enjoying the
benefits of such
an action.

5 **Action**

Requesting
action or
approval

I will do this.

terms of our preceding discussion, the motivated sequence is simultaneously *problem-oriented* and *motivation-centered*.

Thus, the motivated sequence is composed of five basic steps in the presentation of verbal materials:

1. *Attention.* The creation of interest and desire.

2. *Need.* The development of the problem, through analysis of things wrong in the world and through a relating of those wrongs to individuals' interests, wants, or desires.

3. *Satisfaction.* The proposal of a plan of action that will alleviate the problem and satisfy the individuals' interests, wants, or desires.

4. *Visualization.* The verbal depiction of the world as it will look if the plan is put into action.

5. *Action.* The final call for personal commitments and deeds.

Sample Speech *to Actuate Using the Motivated Sequence* • •

The following speech, delivered to a joint session of Congress on December 8, 1941, was President Franklin Delano Roosevelt's message requesting a declaration of war against Japan. Round-the-clock negotiations with Japan had been suddenly disrupted when, on Sunday morning, December 7, the Japanese launched a massive surprise attack on Pearl Harbor, Hawaii, sinking eight American battleships and other smaller craft and leveling planes and airfields.

The nation was numbed; Congress was indignant; and the president moved quickly. The joint session was held in the House chamber. The galleries were overflowing, and the speech was broadcast worldwide.

Notice that this message contains only a short attention step (because the surprise attack created all of the necessary attention), a longer need step (paragraphs 2–11) that details the situation in the Pacific, and a short satisfaction step (paragraph 12) that only hints at American military strategy. The visualization step (paragraphs 13–17) attempts, in heroic fashion, to steel the nation for war, and it is followed by a concise, sharply drawn action step. The president's strategies seem clear. The fact that the need and visualization steps receive detailed development shows his concern for (1) providing an informational base for the action, (2) offering a psychological orientation to wartime thinking, and (3) justifying the commencement of hostilities.

FOR A DECLARATION OF WAR AGAINST JAPAN
Franklin Delano Roosevelt

Attention step   TO THE CONGRESS OF THE UNITED STATES: Yesterday, December 7, 1941—a date which will live in infamy—the

United States of America was suddenly and deliberately attacked by naval and air forces of the Empire of Japan. /1

Need step The United States was at peace with that nation and, at the solicitation of Japan, was still in conversation with its government and its Emperor, looking toward the maintenance of peace in the Pacific. Indeed, one hour after Japanese air squadrons had commenced bombing in Oahu, the Japanese Ambassador to the United States and his colleague delivered to the Secretary of State a formal reply to a recent American message. While this reply stated that it seemed useless to continue the existing diplomatic negotiations, it contained no threat or hint of war or armed attack. /2

It will be recorded that the distance of Hawaii from Japan makes it obvious that the attack was deliberately planned many days or even weeks ago. During the intervening time the Japanese government had deliberately sought to deceive the United States by false statements and expressions of hope for continued peace. /3

The attack yesterday on the Hawaiian Islands has caused severe damage to American naval and military forces. Very many American lives have been lost. In addition, American ships have been reported torpedoed on the high seas between San Francisco and Honolulu. /4

Yesterday the Japanese government also launched an attack against Malaya. /5

Last night Japanese forces attacked Hong Kong. /6

Last night Japanese forces attacked Guam. /7

Last night Japanese forces attacked the Philippine Islands. /8

Last night the Japanese attacked Wake Island. /9

This morning the Japanese attacked Midway Island. /10

Japan has, therefore, undertaken a surprise offensive extending throughout the Pacific area. The facts of yesterday speak for themselves. The people of the United States have already formed their opinions and well understand the implications to the very life and safety of our nation. /11

Satisfaction step	As Commander-in-Chief of the Army and Navy I have directed that all measures be taken for our defense. /12
Visualization step	Always will we remember the character of the onslaught against us. /13
	No matter how long it may take us to overcome this premeditated invasion, the American people in their righteous might will win through to absolute victory. /14
	I believe I interpret the will of the Congress and of the people when I assert that we will not only defend ourselves to the uttermost but will make very certain that this form of treachery shall never endanger us again. /15
	Hostilities exist. There is no blinking at the fact that our people, our territory, and our interests are in grave danger. /16
	With confidence in our armed forces—with the unbounded determination of our people—we will gain the inevitable triumph—so help us God. /17
Action step	I ask that the Congress declare that since the unprovoked and dastardly attack by Japan on Sunday, December 7, a state of war has existed between the United States and the Japanese Empire. /18

• •

Using the Motivated Sequence to Structure Actuative Speeches

The motivated sequence provides an ideal blueprint for speeches calling for some sort of action on the part of audience members. For this reason, we shall look first at some ways in which you might use Monroe's concept in structuring actuative speeches.

Step 1. Getting Attention

It has been said that all too frequently the attitude of people about to hear someone give a speech is "Ho-hum." Obviously, you must change this attitude at the very beginning if you hope to persuade your listeners to believe or to act. The methods for effecting this change are described in Chapter 7. A review of pages 153–60 will remind you how startling statements, illustrations, questions, and other supportive materials can be used to focus wide-awake attention on what you have to say. You cannot persuade an audience unless you have their attention.

Step 2. Showing the Need: Describing the Problem

When you have captured the attention of your listeners, you are ready to make clear why the policy you propose is needed. To do this, you must show that a definite problem exists; you must point out what is wrong with things as they are and, through facts and figures, make clear just how bad the situation is. For example, "Last month our plant at Littleton produced only 200 carburetors rather than the 300 scheduled. As a result we have had to shut down our main assembly line at Metropolis three times, with a loss of more than $60,000."

In its full form, a need or problem step requires a fourfold development: (1) *Statement*—a definite, concise statement of the problem. (2) *Illustration*—one or more examples explaining and clarifying the problem. (3) *Ramification*—additional examples, statistical data, testimony, and other forms of support showing the extent and seriousness of the problem. (4) *Pointing*—making clear to the listeners how the problem directly affects them. You will not, however, invariably need to use all four of these developmental elements. "Statement" and "pointing" should always be present, but the inclusion of "illustration" and "ramification" will depend on the amount of detail required to impress the audience. But whether you use the complete development or only a part of it, the need step is exceedingly important in your speech, for it is here that your subject is first definitely related to the needs and desires of your listeners.

Step 3. Satisfying the Need: Presenting the Solution

The solution or satisfaction step in a speech urging the adoption of a policy has the purpose of getting your listeners to agree that the program you propose is the correct one. Therefore, this step consists of presenting your proposed solution to the problem and proving this solution practicable and desirable. Five items are usually contained in a fully developed satisfaction step: (1) *Statement*—stating the attitude, belief, or action you wish the audience to adopt. (2) *Explanation*—making sure that your proposal is understood. (Often diagrams or charts are useful.) (3) *Theoretical demonstration*—showing by reasoning how your proposed solution meets the need. (4) *Reference to practical experience*—supplying examples to prove that the proposal has worked effectively where it has been tried. (Use facts, figures, and the testimony of experts to support this contention.) (5) *Meeting objections*—forestalling opposition by answering any objections that might be raised against the proposal.

Just as certain items can at times be omitted from the need step, one or more of these phases can be left out of the satisfaction step if the situation warrants. Nor must the foregoing order always be followed exactly. Occasionally, you can best meet objections by dealing with them as they arise in the minds of your listeners. In other situations, the theoretical demonstration and reference to practical experience can be combined. If the satisfaction step is developed properly, at its conclusion the audience will say, "Yes, you are right; this is a practicable and desirable solution to the problem you pointed out."

Step 4: Visualizing the Results

The function of the visualization step is to raise or intensify desire. It should picture for the audience how conditions will be in the future (1) if the policy you propose is adopted or (2) if the policy you propose is not adopted. Because it projects the thinking of the audience into the future, it might just as correctly be called the "projection" step.

This projection can be accomplished in one of three ways: by the *positive* method, the *negative* method, or the method of *contrast*.

The positive method: When using this method, you describe conditions as they will be in the future if the solution you propose is carried out. Make such a description vivid and concrete. Select a situation that you are quite sure will arise. Then picture your listeners in that situation actually enjoying the conditions your proposal will produce.

The negative method: This method describes conditions as they will be in the future if your proposal is *not* carried out. It pictures for your audience the evils or dangers that will arise from failure to follow your advice. Select from the need step the most undesirable aspects of the present situation and show how these conditions will be aggravated if your proposal is rejected.

The method of contrast: This method combines the two preceding ones. The negative approach is used first showing the disadvantages that arise from failure to adopt your proposal; then the positive approach is used, showing the advantages of its adoption. Thus, the desirable situation is thrown into strong contrast with the undesirable one.

Whichever method you use—positive, negative, or contrast—remember that the visualization step must stand the test of reality: the conditions you picture must be capable of attainment. Moreover, they must be made vivid. Let your listeners actually "see" themselves enjoying the advantages or suffering the evils you describe. The more clearly you can depict the situation, the more strongly the audience will react.

The following excerpt illustrates how a speaker urging you to think about all four years of college at once might develop a visualization step by the method of contrast:

Suppose that you enter the university, as nearly a quarter of our students do, with little sense of educational interests and goals. In your first two semesters, you simply take a few required courses and pass your writing and speaking skills tests. In your second year, you start experimenting with some electives on the basis of friends' recommendations—"Take Speech 101 because it's easy," "Take Photography 102 because it's cool," "Take Art 103 because it's pretty," "Take History 104 because I'm taking it," "Take Astronomy 105 because the professor is neat." Now comes your junior year. You're nowhere near a major and you're getting close to the three-quarter pole in your education. Your adviser nags you, your parents nag you, your friends nag you—even you get down on yourself. In your senior year, you sample some social work courses, finally discovering something you really like. Only then do you realize it will take three or four more semesters—if you're lucky—to complete a B.S.W. degree.

In contrast, suppose you're one of another quarter of our entering students—those who seek career and personal advising early. You enroll for the no-credit "Careers and Vocational Choices" seminar your first semester. While meeting your liberal arts requirements, you take classes in as many different departments as possible so as to get a broad sampling. Near the end of your sophomore year, you talk with people in both Career Planning and personal counseling, all the while trying courses in areas of possible interest. By your junior year, you get departmental advisers in two majors, find out you don't really like one as much as you thought, and then go only to the second after midyear. You then complete that major, taking a correspondence class to catch up because you were a little behind, but still you graduate with other freshmen who entered the year you did.

Careful planning, reasoning through choices, and rigorously analyzing your own interests and talents—these are the actions that separate the completers from the complainers at the end of your years here. So . . . *[move into the action step at this point]*

Step 5. Requesting Action

The function of the action step in an actuative speech is to translate into overt action the desires created in the visualization step. Commonly, you call for action with a challenge or appeal, a special inducement, or a statement of personal intention as described in Chapter 7. (Review the conclusions discussed there for examples.)

Do not make the action step too long. As the old adage goes, "Stand up; speak up; shut up." Finish your speech firmly and briskly, and sit down.

> " At what should have been the conclusion of her speech, Elena had motivated her classmates to charge out of the classroom and sign up to give blood at the university hospital. Instead of hitting them with a final call for action, however, she talked on and on. She read a list of eight different locations where the Bloodmobile would be over the next three weeks; she mentioned conditions that would prevent students from giving blood; she gave detailed descriptions of where to find the Blood Bank in the hospital. As she talked, first her listeners visibly relaxed, then they looked out the window, next they checked their watches, and finally most of them just quit listening completely. By overdoing her conclusion, Elena had destroyed the effectiveness of her speech. "

Overall, this description of the motivated sequence gives you a basic outline. Remember that you can be a little flexible once you gain some basic skills. Like cooks who alter good recipes to their personal tastes, you can adjust the formula to particular occasions—changing the number of main points from section to section, sometimes omitting restatement from the attention step, or not offering both positive and negative projections in the visualization step. *Like any recipe, the motivated sequence is designed to give you an almost universal formula to follow, not a rigid cell within which to imprison yourself.* It gives you an excellent pattern, but it does not remove the human element; you still have to think about what you are doing with it.

Sample Outline *for an Actuative Speech*

An abbreviated outline for an actuative speech urging students to monitor their blood pressure might take the following form:[8]

NUMBERS THAT CAN SAVE YOUR LIFE

Specific purpose: To urge students to begin checking their blood pressure even while in school

Attention step	I. Americans live in a maze of numbers:
	  A. Your student ID number identifies you on the campus.
	  B. Your telephone number lets others reach you.
	  C. Your social security number follows you from near birth to death and after.

Need step	II. A number most of you ignore, however, could kill you— your blood pressure.
(Statistics)	A. According to the Department of Health and Human Services, this year 310,000 Americans will die from illnesses where the major factor is hypertension.
(Statistics)	B. Two million will suffer strokes, heart attacks, and kidney failure as a direct result of hypertension.
(Testimony)	C. According to Dr. Theodore Cooper, Director of the Heart and Lung Institute, "Hypertension can be brought under control through proven treatment which is neither unduly hazardous, complicated or expensive."

(Explanation)	D. You must understand what high blood pressure does to your body before this will sink in.
	    1. When the pressure of your blood becomes too great for the arterial walls, it can tear a muscle, and if the artery breaks, you can die.
	    2. High pressure can also result from fatty tissues, salts, and fluid build-ups that cause the arteries to narrow and the heart to work harder, until it can't.

(Testimony)	E. Even worse, according to the National High Blood Pressure Council, "Half of those who have high blood pressure don't even know that they do. Of those who do, only half are being treated; only half again of those have their blood pressure under control. Patients and physicians alike just don't seem to take this condition seriously."

Satisfaction step	III. Thus, the public needs to be aware of these problems, health care must be improved, and hypertensives must learn that self-control is life.
	  A. Public service ads can keep the issue before the public.
	  B. Community- and business-supported hypertension clinics must be established at little or no cost to clients.
	  C. Individuals simply must monitor their own blood pressure regularly.

Visualization step	IV. The future of a significant proportion of our population depends on these programs.

(Negative)   A. Given the American diet, general lack of exercise, and tense life-styles, without these programs heart attacks will claim more and more victims annually.

(Positive)   B. With such programs, our collective health will improve measurably.

(Specific instances)   1. Drs. Andrea Foote and John Erfurt have established a Worker Health Program, which was tested at four different sites and which allowed 92 percent of the hypertensives at those jobs to control their blood pressure.
   2. The Hypertensive Education Program in Michigan and Connecticut is cutting the insurance rates in those states.
   3. In 1970, Savannah, Georgia, had the infamous title of "Stroke Capital of the World," but today, with fourteen permanent blood pressure reading stations and special clinics, the stroke rate has been cut in half.

Action step   V. Even now, in your prime, it's time for you to develop good health maintenance habits.
   A. You could be one of America's 11 million people with high blood pressure and not even know it.
   B. Even if you're not, you should monitor yourself, safe in the knowledge that your pressure is in the normal—90/70 to 140/90—range.
   C. Get your blood pressure checked today, free of charge, at the Student Health Center and save a life—your own.

Using the Motivated Sequence to Structure Persuasive Speeches

Sometimes you are not so much calling your listeners to action as seeking to bring about a change in their attitudes or values—their positive or negative judgments about people, practices, institutions, or philosophies. In such cases, you may wish to adapt the basic pattern of the motivated sequence, either ending with the visualization step or turning the action step into an appeal for accepting and/or retaining the belief or judgment you have presented. The pattern for such a speech might look something like this:

1. *Getting attention:* Capture the attention and interest of the audience.

2. *Showing the need:* Make clear that a judgment concerning the worth of the person, practice, or institution is needed. Do this by showing (a) why a judgment is important to your listeners personally or (b) why it is important to the community, state, nation, or world of which they are a part.

3. *Satisfying the need:* (a) Set forth the criteria on which an intelligent judgment may be based. (b) Advance what you believe to be the correct judgment and show how it meets the criteria.

4. *Visualizing the results:* Picture the advantages that will arise from agreeing with the judgment you advance or the evils that will result from failing to endorse it.

5. *Requesting action or approval:* Appeal for the acceptance of the proposed judgment and for a determination to retain it.

$\mathbf{S}$ample $\mathbf{O}$utline *for a Persuasive Speech*

Each of the five steps in the basic pattern of the motivated sequence, adapted as we have suggested, is illustrated in the following speech outline:

CONTRIBUTE TO CHARITIES WISELY[9]

Specific purpose: To persuade listeners to evaluate carefully the efficiency and effectiveness of the charitable organizations to which they contribute.

Attention step (Startling statement)
I. In 1975, Americans gave over 11.6 billion dollars to charitable organizations, not counting contributions to religious and educational institutions, but some experts have estimated that 116 million dollars was wasted because it went to fraudulent or poorly managed organizations.

Need step
II. There are differences in the ways charities distribute their funds.

(Example to describe the problem)
A. Example of a charity that uses 94 percent of its contributions for administration.
B. Example of a charity—United Way—that distributes ninety cents out of every dollar collected.

(Call for evaluation)
III. Unless we all simply decide to stop giving to charities, we must come up with criteria for evaluating organizations and procedures for investigating them.

Satisfaction step   IV. How, then, can you evaluate charities?
(Criteria)   A. Fund-raising and administrative costs should total less
                               than 50 percent of the total public contributions.
                            B. An effective charity should be controlled by an active,
                               unsalaried governing board, with no paid employees
                               serving as voting members of that board.
                            C. It should use reputable promotional and fund-raising
                               methods.
                            D. It should publicly disclose a complete and indepen-
                               dently audited annual financial report. *(Each of these
                               criteria could be justified by appeals to authority and
                               example.)*

(Indication of how   V. These criteria can be applied by both governmental units
criteria can be   and individuals.
applied)   A. Both Florida and Pennsylvania have laws governing
                               what percentage of their total contributions charities
                               can spend on fund raising.
                            B. The federal government similarly regulates charities
                               soliciting in more than one state.
                            C. As an individual, you also can check into charities you
                               might wish to support.
                               1. Ask for an annual report before contributing.
                               2. The Council of Better Business Bureaus publishes
                                  a rating list.
                               3. The National Information Bureau discloses perti-
                                  nent information.

Visualization step   VI. If both government and individuals do their investigative
                            jobs properly, imagine the benefits that would accrue
                            from the extra money spent on those who need it.
                            A. The number of poor that could be fed and clothed
                               would increase.
                            B. Additional medical and health care facilities could be
                               built.
                            C. Research into killing and crippling diseases could
                               proceed with more vigor.

Action step   VII. You have the power to direct your contributions to the
                            most beneficial charities.
(Summary)   A. Keep the evaluative criteria—efficiency, disinterest-
                               edness, fairness, and openness—in mind when you
                               receive a call for help.
(Appeal)   B. And when you give, open your heart, your pocket-
                               book, and, yes, your mind—give, but give wisely.

CHAPTER SUMMARY

Speeches to persuade and actuate have as their primary feature a desire for *psychological or behavioral change.* Given the human propensity to seek satisfaction of needs hierarchically, according to *Maslow,* the concept of *motive need* is central to an understanding of persuasion and actuation. Thus, keys to the achievement of persuasion are *motivational appeals,* which are verbally created *visualizations* or *assertions* that link an idea, entity, or course of action to a *motive.* Commonly used motivational appeals include appeals to: achievement and display; adventure and change; companionship and affiliation; creativity; curiosity; deference; destructiveness; endurance and tradition; fear; fighting and aggression; imitation and conformity; independence and autonomy; loyalty; personal enjoyment; power, authority, and dominance; pride; reverence or worship; revulsion; sexual attraction; and sympathy and generosity. These motivational appeals work especially well in one particular organizational pattern for persuasive and actuative speeches—*Monroe's Motivated Sequence.* The five steps in the sequence are *attention, need, satisfaction, visualization, and action,* and each step can be developed by using appropriate rhetorical devices.

Oral Activities

1. Present a five- to eight-minute actuative speech in which your primary goal is to get class members to *actually* do something. Use the motivated sequence to create attention, lay out needs, propose solutions, visualize the results, and call for the action. On a future "Actuative Speech Check-Up Day," find out how many took the actions you suggested— *signing a petition, writing letters to officials, attending meetings, giving blood, or taking some other personal action.* How successful were you? Why?
2. In a brief persuasive speech, attempt to alter your classmates' impression or understanding of a particular concept. Analyze their current attitude toward it and then prepare a speech reversing that attitude. Sample topics might include: pesticides, closed shop unions, airline or broadcasting deregulation, open housing, compulsory health insurance, the all-volunteer army, or party politics.
3. What relevant motivational appeals might you use in addressing each of the following audiences? Be ready to discuss your choices in class.
    a. A group of farmers protesting federal agricultural policy
    b. A meeting of prebusiness majors wondering about jobs

c. Women at a seminar on nontraditional employment opportunities
d. A meeting of local elementary and secondary classroom teachers seeking smaller classes
e. A group gathered for an old-fashioned 4th of July picnic

Reference Notes

1. Abraham H. Maslow, *Motivation and Personality* (New York: Harper & Row, 1954).
2. In the 1970 revision of his book, *Motivation and Personality,* Maslow identified two additional needs—the cognitive and esthetic needs—as higher need states that frequently operate as part of self-actualization.
3. For a fuller discussion of *attribution,* see Philip G. Zimbardo, *Psychology and Life,* 11th ed. (Glenview, IL: Scott, Foresman and Company, 1985), esp. 576–79.
4. For a somewhat fuller discussion of these and other motivational appeals, see Douglas Ehninger, Bruce E. Gronbeck, Ray E. McKerrow, and Alan H. Monroe, *Principles and Types of Speech Communication,* 10th ed. (Glenview, IL: Scott, Foresman and Company, 1986), Chapter 6.
5. John Dewey, "Analysis of Reflective Thinking," in *How We Think* (Boston: D. C. Heath & Company, 1910), 72.
6. Anyone interested in how Alan Monroe conceived of and first used the motivated sequence—then a revolutionary idea—should see the first edition of this book: Alan H. Monroe, *Principles and Types of Speech* (Chicago, IL: Scott, Foresman and Company, 1935), esp. vii–x.
7. Originally published in the *Congressional Record,* 77th Congress, 1st Session, Volume 87, Part 9, pp. 9504–5, December 8, 1941.
8. The outline based on a speech, "The Silent Killer," by Todd Ambs; his materials were formed into an outline by special arrangement with the Interstate Oratorical Association, Larry Schnoor, Executive Secretary, Mankato State University, Mankato, Minnesota.
9. This outline is based on a speech given by Steve Favitta, Central Missouri State University, in 1978. We have omitted the supporting materials, but most may be found in "New CT Ratings on 53 Charities," *Changing Times* (November 1976); and "United Way: Are the Criticisms Fair?" *Changing Times* (October 1977). This altered outline is used with the permission of Mr. Favitta. Text supplied courtesy of Professors Roger Conaway and Dan Curtis.

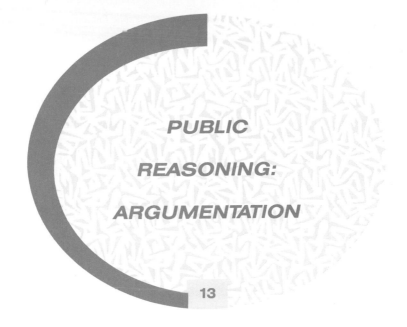

PUBLIC REASONING: ARGUMENTATION

13

Argumentation is a fundamental activity in democratic institutions. In order to reach decisions through the democratic process, advocates must be free to advance arguments for specific claims and appraise the outcomes of those arguments. This is a necessary activity because there are seldom absolute answers to the problems that confront groups and nations. Public debate encourages the examination of alternatives for enlightened decision making. The ultimate purpose of argumentation is to persuade (see Chapter 12); however, such persuasion is accomplished by providing and supporting claims.

In argumentation, a speaker offers reasons supporting particular claims in opposition to claims advanced by others. It is a give-and-take process aimed at the acceptance of one set of claims over another. In everyday use, the word "argument" has several meanings. We often confuse argumentation with fighting and attacking. We might say, for example, "I don't want to argue with you; I'm your friend," or "Now, that was a good fight [or argument]!" However, argumentation—public reasoning—is a type of communication and decision making that differs from attack and warfare. In this chapter, we will first review the characteristics of argumentation that make it distinct from fighting. Then, we will outline a unit of argument, discuss proper and improper (fallacious) reasoning, and conclude with several tips for developing arguments.

ARGUMENTATION AS A TYPE OF COMMUNICATION

Argumentation is distinct from other types of communication because it is *rule governed*. A major difference between argumentation and attacking or fighting is that argumentation proceeds according to the rules of social conventions and logic. In this chapter, we will examine those specialized rules that govern an act of arguing with other people. Instead of merely offering an opinion or just stating information, *the act of arguing commits you to communicating according to certain rules*. This requires that you understand social conventions and the anatomy of an argument.

Social Conventions

In our society, there are unstated, yet potent, *social conventions,* or habitual *expectations* that govern argumentation. When you engage in argumentation, you are probably following these four conventions:

Convention of Bilaterality

Argumentation is inherently bilateral: it requires at least two people or two competing messages. The arguer, whether he or she says so explicitly, is presenting a message that is open for others to examine and evaluate. When you engage in argumentation, you should understand that others may differ and present opposing messages. The seller of new cars seldom wishes to engage in this kind of critical exchange; Ford, General Motors, and Chrysler are hoping to persuade, not argue with, you. Their public communication is aimed at getting you to test drive only their makes and models. However, when candidates for political office present campaign platforms, they expect counteranalysis or counterarguments from opposing candidates. Usually, candidates invite reasoned responses to their ideas. Often, formalized public debates ensue.

Convention of Self-Risk

When you engage in argumentation and open up your ideas to critique and counterproposals, you assume certain risks. There is always a chance that your ideas will fail, but you face that risk any time you voice them in public. More important, in argumentation there is a risk that you will be proven *wrong*. For example, when you argue that all federal employees should be subjected to mandatory drug testing to detect the use of illegal chemical substances, you face the possibility that people who oppose this action will convince your audience that such a proposal is not only expensive but impractical. Public scrutiny can expose your own or your opponent's weaknesses. This risk is potent enough to make many people avoid public argumentation. With some understanding of argumentation and a little practice, you can develop the skill and confidence to engage in the public exchange of ideas.

The Fairness Doctrine

Arguers also commit themselves to a version of what the broadcast industry calls the "fairness doctrine." The Federal Communication Commission's fairness doctrine maintains that every viewpoint must be given equal access to the airwaves. In the same way, arguers say, in effect, "I have the right to be heard. You may reject my claims and reasons, but first you must hear me out." For this reason, most legislative bodies are reluctant to cut off debate. They are committed to upholding First Amendment rights of expression through the fairness doctrine. While we may not agree with it, we must uphold another's right to express a point of view.

Commitment to Rationality

Arguers commit themselves to proceed reasonably. When you argue, you are committed to provide good reasons for the claims you make. If you argue, for instance, that international peace is best achieved through military preparedness, someone else has the right to assert an opposing claim (the fairness doctrine). They might argue that military preparedness actually encourages aggressive behavior rather than curtails it (the convention of bilaterality). No matter what the proposition, each arguer has a right to ask, "*Why* do you believe that?" (the convention of rationality). As an arguer, you are committed to *giving reasons*. You must provide reasons to support your claim and to convince unsure listeners. Argumentation, therefore, is a rational form of communication in which all parties believe there are good reasons for the acceptance of their claims. They are obligated to provide these reasons rather than simply voicing unsupported personal opinions or feelings. The arguer meets the commitment to rationality by advancing relevant reasons to defend the claim he or she advocates.

In some cases, arguers are committed not only to generalized conventions or accepted bases of argumentation, but also to arguing in accordance with particular, formalized procedures or technical strictures. Among the most common of these technical rules is *parliamentary procedure,* as set forth in *Robert's Rules of Order* and similar systems. In many formal meetings, such systems of rules are used to enhance efficiency and fairness. Since such technical rules are important and you will undoubtedly encounter them, we have included a section on parliamentary procedure for handling meetings in Chapter 16.

The Anatomy of an Argument

You can approach the question of argumentation's "anatomy" at three levels. The overall process of arguing, with proponents and opponents taking turns addressing each other, represents the "gross anatomy" of argumentation. This process is initiated with an *argumentative,* or *constructive,* speech; it progresses when someone offers a *refutative* speech; it then continues through a series of *rebuttals* until a decision is reached by voting or consensus. This is the general level of argumentation.

At a specific level, you can examine the anatomy of a single argumentative speech, noting that:

1. Your introduction should set out the position and suggest criteria for judging your claim as supported or unsupported.

2. The body should be organized around the series of reasons that supports your claim.

3. The conclusion should summarize your position and indicate why it is superior to the opposing view.

At this level, the argumentative speech provides reasons for the claims a speaker wishes an audience to accept.

Finally, at the cellular level, you can focus on how a "unit of argument" is constructed. Each of these building blocks consists of (a) the *claim* or proposition to be defended, (b) the relevant *evidence* you provide in support of that claim or proposition, and (c) the *reasoning pattern* (sometimes called the *inference*) you use to connect the evidence to the claim. It is this level that we are primarily concerned with in this chapter.

THE ELEMENTS OF AN ARGUMENT

Every argument has three essential features. As you plan your arguments, you need to understand these important elements: (a) the types of claims common to arguments; (b) the evidence, or support, for a claim; and (c) the reasoning that connects the evidence to the claim.

Types of Claims

Most argumentative speeches assert that, in the opinion of the speaker, (1) something is or is not the case; (2) something is desirable or undesirable, or (3) something should or should not be done. Such judgments or recommendations, when formally addressed to others, are called the

The Levels of Argumentation

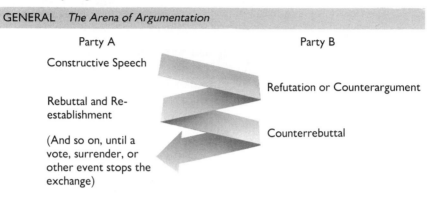

GENERAL   *The Arena of Argumentation*

Party A   Party B

Constructive Speech

                                           Refutation or Counterargument

Rebuttal and Re-
establishment

                                           Counterrebuttal

(And so on, until a
vote, surrender, or
other event stops the
exchange)

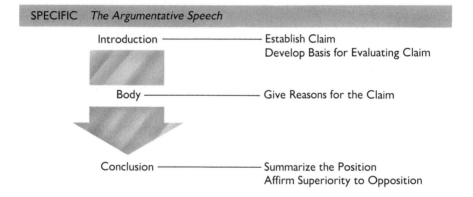

SPECIFIC   *The Argumentative Speech*

Introduction ———————— Establish Claim
                               Develop Basis for Evaluating Claim

Body ———————— Give Reasons for the Claim

Conclusion ———————— Summarize the Position
                               Affirm Superiority to Opposition

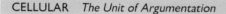

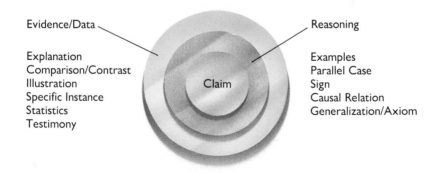

CELLULAR   *The Unit of Argumentation*

Evidence/Data   Reasoning

Explanation   Examples
Comparison/Contrast   Parallel Case
Illustration   Claim   Sign
Specific Instance   Causal Relation
Statistics   Generalization/Axiom
Testimony

speaker's *propositions,* or *claims.* The first step in constructing a successful argument is to determine the nature of the claim you wish to establish.

Claims of Fact

If you were trying to convince your listeners that "price controls on raw agricultural products result in food shortages," you would be presenting a factual claim—asserting that a given state of affairs exists or that something is indeed the case. When confronted with a claim of this sort, two questions are likely to arise in the mind of a thoughtful listener:

1. *By what criteria, or standards of judgment, should the truth or accuracy of this claim be measured?* If you were asked to determine a person's height, you would immediately look for a yardstick or other measuring instrument. Listeners likewise look for a standard when judging the appropriateness of a factual claim. In the previously mentioned example, before agreeing that price controls result in shortages, the members of your audience would almost certainly want to know what you mean by "shortages." Does it mean "the disappearance, for all practical purposes, of a given kind of food" or merely "less of that food than everyone might desire"? Against what standard, precisely, is the accuracy of the claim to be judged?

2. *Do the facts of the situation fit the criteria?* Does the amount of produce and other raw agricultural products presently on supermarket shelves fall within the limits set by your definition of "shortages"? First, get your listeners to agree to certain standards or measurements for judgment and then present evidence to show that a given state of affairs meets these standards. Then you will, in most instances, be well on your way toward winning their belief.

Claims of Value

When, instead of asserting that something is or is not so, you assert that something is good or bad, desirable or undesirable, justified or unjustified, you are advancing a claim of value—a claim concerning the intrinsic *worth* of the belief or action in question. Here, as in the case of claims of fact, it is always appropriate to ask: (1) *By what standards, or criteria, is something of this nature to be judged?* (2) *How well does the item in question measure up to the standards specified?* We may, for example, assert that the quality of a college is to be measured by the distinction of its faculty, the excellence of its physical plant, the success of its graduates in securing positions, and the reputation it enjoys among the general public and then proceed to argue that because the college we are concerned with meets each of these tests, it is indeed a good one.

Claims of Policy

A claim of policy recommends a course of action you want the audience to approve. Typical examples are: "Federal expenditures for pollution control *should be* substantially increased"; "The student senate *should have* the authority to expel students who cheat." In both instances, you are asking your audience to endorse a proposed policy or course of action. When analyzing a policy claim, four questions are relevant:

1. *Is there a need for such a policy or course of action?* If your listeners do not believe that a change is called for, they are not likely to approve your proposal.

2. *Is the proposal practicable?* Can we afford the expense it would entail? Would it really solve the problem or remove the evil it is designed to correct? Does such a policy stand a reasonable chance of being adopted? If you cannot show that your proposal meets these and similar tests, you can hardly expect it to be endorsed.

3. *Are the benefits your proposal will bring greater than its disadvantages?* People are reluctant to approve a proposal that promises to create conditions worse than the ones it is designed to correct. Burning a barn to the ground may be a highly efficient way to get rid of rats, but it is hardly a desirable one. The benefits and disadvantages that will result from a plan of action must always be carefully weighed along with considerations of its basic workability.

4. *Is the offered proposal superior to any other plan or policy?* Listeners are hesitant to approve a policy if they have reason to believe that an alternative course of action is more practicable or more beneficial.

From what has been said about the three types of claims, you should now be able to see the importance of knowing exactly the kind of claim you are seeking to establish. Is it a claim of policy, fact, or value? If it is a claim of policy, do you need to answer all four of the basic questions listed above, or is your audience likely to accept one or more of them without proof? If yours is a claim of fact or value, what criteria should you use as bases for judgment, and how well are they met by the evidence?

Finally, unless there are sound reasons for delay, you should announce early in your speech the claim you are going to support or oppose. If your listeners do not see the precise point on which they will be asked to judge, your strongest arguments and appeals probably will prove useless.[1]

Lawyers are professional advocates who work within a framework of full and structured debate. Their arguments must be fully researched and supported by evidence in order to influence legal decisions.

Evidence

As you discovered in Chapter 5, supporting materials are the items you use to clarify, amplify, and strengthen the ideas in your speech. They provide evidence for the acceptance of your central idea and its supporting points. Evidence is a crucial part of developing a clear, compelling argument. It can be presented in any of the forms of supporting materials with which you are already familiar: explanations, comparisons and contrasts, illustrations, specific instances, statistics, and testimony.

You have already engaged in the process of research required to find the supporting materials necessary to reinforce the ideas in your speeches. The *selection of relevant evidence* is particularly important in constructing good arguments. There is no single or easy rule for selecting relevant evidence. Supporting material that is relevant to one claim may not be relevant to another, or it may be relevant as logical proof but not as a compelling reason for action. You should consider both the *rational* and the *motivational* characteristics of good evidence selection.

Rationally Relevant Evidence

The type of evidence you choose should reflect the type of claim you advocate. For example, if you are defending the claim that censorship violates the First Amendment guarantee of freedom of speech, you will probably choose testimony by noted authorities or definitions of terms to

294

advance your claim. On the other hand, examples, illustrations, and statistics work better for showing that a problem exists or a change is needed. If nine out of ten Americans believe that taking adult literature off of public library shelves is a violation of their rights, there is popular support for a change. As you can see, the claim you present requires a logically relevant type of evidence. As you plan your arguments, you should ask yourself, "What type of evidence is logically relevant in support of my claim?"

Motivationally Relevant Evidence

If you hope to convince your listeners to adopt your attitudes or actions, your claim must be supported by more than logically relevant evidence. Your evidence must also create in your listeners a desire to become involved. That is, it must be motivationally relevant to them. In order to best determine what evidence works for specific audiences, you should ask two questions:

1. *What type of evidence will this audience demand?* Whenever Congress proposes a new form of taxation, taxpayers usually demand that it also supply statistical evidence, financial reports, an explanation of underlying key concepts, testimony from experts in economics, examples of the ways the new laws will affect us, and comparisons and contrasts with this law and other potential tax legislation. "Mere" examples or illustrations are not compelling enough to garner public support for higher taxes. On the other hand, if you were reviewing a recent film for a group of friends, an example from the plot, a figurative analogy, or an illustration of dialogue would be more forceful as proof than statistical counts of words, box office receipts, or testimony from published movie critics. Careful audience analysis will help you determine what type of evidence is needed psychologically to move your particular group of listeners.

2. *Which specific pieces of evidence will your listeners be most responsive to?* This is a question you should pose once you have determined the type of evidence required in your argument. For example, if you have decided to use expert testimony to support your argument, whom should you quote? Or, if you are using an illustration, should you use a factual example from the local group or develop one of your own? Will your listeners be more moved by a personalized story or a general illustration?

To answer these and similar questions about your listeners, you need to analyze them. A homogeneous audience may be suspicious of outsiders. They might react best to local experts or illustrations from their community or range of experience. A heterogeneous audience, on the other hand, will require more generally recognized authorities and geographically varied examples because such an audience does not share experience and background. While you cannot always tailor your evidence to your audience's demographic or psychological characteristics, you can at least attempt to consider them.

In sum, it is one thing to discover evidence but quite another to select it wisely. Select evidence with both your claim and audience in mind.

Reasoning (Inferences)

The third element of a unit of argumentation is that which "connects" the evidence with the claim. This is called *reasoning,* or inference. Reasoning is a process of connecting something that is known or believed (evidence) to a concept or idea (claim) you wish others to accept. *Patterns of reasoning* are habitual ways in which a culture or society uses inferences to connect that which is accepted to that which is being urged on them. Basically, there are five reasoning patterns.

Reasoning from Examples

Often called *inductive* reasoning, reasoning from instances or examples is a matter of examining a series of examples of known occurrences (evidence) and drawing a general conclusion (claim). The inference in this reasoning pattern can be stated: "What is true of particular cases is true of the whole class." This represents a kind of mental inductive "leap" from specifics to generalities. For example, the National Cancer Institute has studied hundreds of individual case histories and discovered that people whose diets are high in fiber are less prone to contract cancers of the digestive tract. With an inductive leap, they then moved to the factual claim "High fiber diets prevent certain types of cancer." Commuters use a similar pattern of reasoning every time they drive during rush hour. After trial and error, they decide that a residential street is the best route to take home between 5:00 and 5:30 P.M. and the expressway between 5:30 and 6:00 P.M. In other words, after enough instances, they arrive at a generalization and act on it.

Reasoning from Generalization or Axiom

Applying a general truth to a specific situation, sometimes called *deduction,* is essentially the reverse of reasoning from instances (induction). In high school consumer education class you may have learned that buying goods in large quantities saves money (the generalization or evidence). Now, you may shop at discount stores because they purchase goods in quantity, thereby saving money and passing that savings on to you (the claim deduced from the evidence). Or, you may believe that getting a college education is the key to a better future (the generalization or axiom). Therefore, if you get a college degree, you will get a better job (claim). This inference gathers power because of *experience* (you learned it through observation) or by *definition* (one of the characteristics of education is self-improvement). You ultimately accept this inference because of the uniformities you believe exist in the world.

Reasoning from Sign

A third reasoning pattern uses an observable mark, or symptom, as proof of the existence of a state of affairs. You reason from sign when you note a rash or spots on your skin (the evidence) and decide you have measles (the claim). The rash does not "cause" measles; rather, it is a sign of the disease. Detectives, of course, are experts at reasoning from sign. When they discover that a particular suspect had motive, access, and a weapon in his possession (the signs), they move to the claim that he might be the murderer. Your doctor works the same way every time she asks you to stick out your tongue and looks for signs of trouble. These signs, of course, are circumstantial evidence—and could be wrong. Just ask detectives and doctors. The inference "This evidence is a sign of a particular conclusion" is one you have to be careful with. This sort of reasoning works well with natural occurrences (ice on the pond is always a sign that the temperature has been below 32 degrees Fahrenheit). However, reasoning from sign can be troublesome in the world of human beings (as when we take people's skin color as a sign that they are lazy or dishonest). Yet, we often must use signs as indicators; otherwise we could not project our economy, predict our weather, and forecast the rise and fall of political candidates.

Reasoning from Parallel Case

Another common reasoning pattern involves thinking solely in terms of similar things and events. Your college or university, for example, probably designed its curriculum by examining the curricula of similar colleges or universities. These curricula functioned as evidence; the claim was that similar courses should be offered at your university. The inference that linked the evidence and the claim was probably something like this: "What worked at Eastern University will work here at Western University because they are similar institutions." Your instructors might use parallel reasoning every time they tell you, "Study hard for this exam. The last exam was difficult; this one will be too." Obviously this is not a generalization, since every exam will probably not be the same. However, your instructors are asserting that the upcoming examination and past examinations are similar cases—they have enough features in common to increase the likelihood that careful study habits will pay off.

Reasoning from Causal Relation

Finally, cause-effect reasoning is an important form for reaching conclusions. For this reason, it is frequently used as a basic pattern for organizing speeches. The assumption of causal reasoning is that events occur in a predictable, routine manner with a cause that accounts for every occurrence. Reasoning from causal relation involves associating events that come before (antecedents) with events that follow (consequents). If the drug problem, for example, appears to be increasing in this country, there is an immediate scramble to find the cause. Is it organized crime, lower moral standards, the break-up of the traditional family, the inadequacy of our schools, or another possible cause? When children have difficulty in classes, educators often look for the root of the problem in family difficulties, physical problems, or social trauma. Educators might even predict that weak performance in the classroom is the antecedent for such future problems as juvenile delinquency or underemployment. In this case, effects can become causes. The inference in causal reasoning is simple and constant: "Every effect has a cause."

These five forms of reasoning are judged "logical" or "rational" in this culture. They offer us the primary means of connecting evidence with claims.

EVALUATING ARGUMENTS

The reasoning process is the pivot on which arguments rest. It is essential, therefore, that you test your reasoning carefully in order to protect yourself as both a generator and a consumer of arguments. For each form of reasoning, there are special tests, or questions, that will help you determine the soundness of your argument.

Testing Your Reasoning

Consider the following questions as you construct your own arguments and listen to those of others.

Reasoning from Examples:

1. *Have you looked at enough instances to warrant generalizing?* (You do not assume spring is here because of one warm day in February.)

2. *Are the instances fairly chosen?* (You certainly hope your neighbors do not think you have a rotten kid just because he picked one of their flowers; you want them to judge your son only after seeing him in many different situations.)

3. *Are there important exceptions to the generalization or claim that must be accounted for?* (While it is generally true, from presidential election studies, that "As Maine goes, so goes the nation," there have been enough exceptions to that rule to keep Maine losers campaigning hard even after that primary.)

Reasoning from Generalization or Axiom:

1. *Is the generalization true?* (Remember that sailors set certain courses on the assumption that the world was flat or that for years parents in this country accepted as gospel Benjamin Spock's generalizations about child rearing.)

2. *Does the generalization apply to this particular case?* (Usually, discount stores have lower prices, but if a small neighborhood store has a sale, it may well offer better prices than discount houses. While the old saying "Birds of a feather flock together" certainly applies to birds, it may not apply to human beings.)

Reasoning from Sign:

1. *Is the sign "fallible"?* (As we have noted, many signs are merely circumstantial. Be extremely careful not to confuse sign reasoning with causal reasoning. If sign reasoning were infallible, your weather forecaster would never be wrong.)

Reasoning from Parallel Case:

1. *Are there more similarities than differences between the two cases?* (City A and City B may have many features in common—size, location, and so on—yet they probably also have many different features, perhaps in the subgroups that make up their populations, the degree of industrial development, and the like. Too many differences between two cases rationally destroy the parallel.)

2. *Are the similarities you have pointed out the relevant and important ones?* (There are two children in your neighborhood who are the same age, go to the same school, and wear the same kinds of clothes; are you therefore able to assume that one is well-behaved simply because the other is? Probably not, because more relevant similarities would include their home lives, their relationships with siblings, and so forth. Comparisons must be based on relevant and important similarities.)

Reasoning from Causal Relation:

1. *Can you separate causes and effects?* (We often have a difficult time doing this. Do higher wages cause higher prices, or is the reverse true? Does a strained home life make a child misbehave, or is it the other way around?)

2. *Are the causes strong enough to have produced the effect?* (Did Ronald Reagan's winning smile really give him the election, or was that an insufficient cause? There probably were much stronger and more important causes.)

3. *Did intervening events or persons prevent a cause from having its normal effect?* (If a gun is not loaded, you cannot shoot anything, no matter how hard you pull the trigger. Even if droughts normally drive up food prices, that might not happen if food has been stockpiled, if spring rains left enough moisture in the soil, or if plenty of cheap imported food is available.)

4. *Could any other cause have produced the effect?* (Although crime often increases when neighborhoods deteriorate, increased crime rates can be caused by any number of other changes—alterations in crime reporting methods, increased reporting of crimes that have been going on for years, or closings of major industries. We rationally must sort through all of the possible causes before championing one.)

Detecting Fallacies in Reasoning

As we have suggested, one of your jobs as a listener and as a person who will engage in argumentation is to evaluate the claims, evidence, and reasoning of others. Whether you are a listener or a participant in public debate, you must be able to think carefully about the arguments. On one level, you are looking for ways in which the ideas and reasons of others are important to your own. And, on another level, you are examining the logical soundness of their thinking. A *fallacy* is a flaw in the rational properties of an argument or inference. Although we cannot present a complete course in logic including logical fallacies, we can discuss some of the most common errors in reasoning. As you detect these fallacies in your own or in others' arguments, you should note and point them out. We can divide fallacies into three categories: *fallacies in evidence, fallacies in reasoning,* and *fallacies in language.*

Fallacies in Evidence

As the label suggests, these flaws in reasoning occur in the way we use supporting material to reach our claims. Three of them stand out: (a) hasty generalization, (b) false division, and (c) genetic fallacy.

Hasty generalization (faulty "inductive leap"): A hasty generalization is a claim made on the basis of too little evidence. You should ask "Has the arguer really examined enough typical cases to make a claim?" If the answer is "No," then a flaw in reasoning has occurred. Urging the ban of aspirin because several people have died of allergic reactions to it or the closure of a highway because of a traffic fatality are examples of hasty generalizations.

False division: A false division occurs when someone argues that there is only one way to divide a process or idea. In fact, there may be many ways to view the process or idea. Be on the lookout when someone argues that the only ways to treat the mentally handicapped are to confine them to institutions or to place them with guardians. "Only" often signals a false division; there may well be other options worth our attention.

Genetic fallacy: Many people argue for an idea by citing its origins, history, or sacred tradition (see "Definitions," pages 180–84). They assume that if an idea has been around for a long time, it must be true. Many people who defended slavery in the nineteenth century referred to the Biblical practices of slavery and to those of the earliest American settlers. However, times change; new values replace old ones. Genetic definitions may help us understand a concept, but they are hardly "proof" of its correctness or justice.

Fallacies in Reasoning

Logical flaws often occur in the thought process itself. Five fallacies of reasoning should be mentioned.

Appeal to ignorance *(argumentum ad ignoratiam)*: People sometimes argue with double negatives: "You *can't* prove it *won't* work!" Or, they may even attack an idea because our information about it is incomplete: "We can't use radio beams to signal UFOs and extraterrestrials because we don't know what languages they speak." Both of these are illogical claims because they depend on what we do not know. Sometimes, we simply must act on the basis of the knowledge we have, despite the gaps in it. In countering such claims, you often can cite parallel cases and examples to overcome this fallacy.

Appeal to popular opinion *(argumentum ad populum)*: A frequent strategy is to urge "jumping on the bandwagon." This argument assumes that if everyone else is doing or thinking something, you should too. For example: "But Christopher, everyone knows the world is flat!" or "But Dad, everyone else is going!" While these appeals may be useful in stating *valuative* claims, they are not the basis for *factual* claims. Even if most people believe or think something, it still may not be true. The world has witnessed hundreds of widely believed but false ideas, from the belief that night air causes tuberculosis to panic over an invasion by Martians.

Sequential fallacy *(post hoc, ergo propter hoc):* Literally translated from the Latin "after this, therefore because of this," the sequential fallacy is often present in arguments from causal relations. It is based on the assumption that if one event follows another, the first must be the cause. Thunder and lightning do not cause rain, although they often occur sequentially. And, even though you may usually catch colds in the spring, the two are not causally related. That is, the season of the year does not cause your cold; a virus does.

Begging the question *(petitio principii):* Begging the question is rephrasing an idea and then offering it as its own reason. It is a *tautology,* or circular thought. If someone asserts, "Abortion is murder because it is taking the life of the unborn," he or she has committed a fallacy by rephrasing the claim (it is murder) to form the reason (it is taking life). Sometimes questions can be fallacious, such as "Have you quit cheating on tests yet?" The claim, phrased as a question, assumes that you have cheated on tests in the past. Whatever your answer to the question, you are guilty. Claims of value are especially prone to *petitio principii.*

Appeal to authority *(ipse dixit): Ipse dixit* fallacies ("because he says it") occur when someone who is popular but not an expert urges the acceptance of an idea or product. Television advertisers frequently ask consumers to purchase products because famous movie stars or sports heroes endorse them. Thus, celebrities promote everything from pantyhose to beer. The familiar figure provides name recognition but not expertise. You can detect this fallacy by asking, "Is he or she an expert on this topic?"

Fallacies in Language

Finally, some fallacies creep into our arguments simply because of the ways in which we use words. Word meanings are flexible, so language can be used sloppily or manipulatively. Five linguistic fallacies are frequent in public debate.

Ambiguity: A word often has two or more meanings. Because of this, such words, used in the same context, can cause confusion and inaccurate claims. Suppose you hear: "Some dogs have fuzzy ears. My dog has fuzzy ears. My dog is SOME dog!" The problem here rests in the word "some." In its first usage, it means "not all." However, the word shifts meanings, so in the second usage it becomes "outstanding/exceptional." Such shifts of meaning can result in flawed claims.

Nonqualification: It is all too easy to drop out some important qualifications as an argument progresses. If such words as "maybe," "might," and "probably" fall by the wayside, the meaning of the argument can change. Advertisers often claim: "Our brand *may* result in fewer cavities *if* you follow a program of regular hygiene and professional dental care." When the qualifications are underplayed, the argument becomes verbally distorted.

Is-Faults: One of the trickiest verbs in English is "is." "John is a man" and "John is a radical" are grammatically equivalent sentences. However, gender is a permanent characteristic of John, while his political leanings are not. We might expect political orientation to change, but not gender. Learn to distinguish between the "is" of classification and the "is" of attribution. Condemnatory speeches and advertisements are often the sources of such fallacies.

Persuasive definition: In the heat of an argument, many advocates attempt to win by offering their own definitions of ideas or concepts. Value terms or abstract concepts are most open to special or skewed definitions. "Liberty means the right to own military weapons." "A good university education is one that leads to a good job." "Real men don't wear cologne." Each of these definitions sets up a particular point of view; each is capricious or arbitrary. If you accept the definition, the argument is over.[2] In order to challenge this fallacious argument, you can substitute a definition from a respected source.

Name calling: Name calling is the general label for several kinds of attacks on people instead of on their arguments. *Argumentum ad hominem* is an attack on the special interests of a person: "Of course, you're defending her. You voted for her." *Argumentum ad personam* is an attack on a personal characteristic of someone rather than on their ideas: "You're just a geek" (or yuppie or chauvinist). Even geeks, yuppies, and chauvinists sometimes offer solid claims. *Ideological appeals* link ideas or people with emotional labels: "Social security is really a Communist plot to overthrow America." This appeal links social security to something the listener considers sinister rather than examining it on its own merits. Claims ought to be judged on their own features, not on their sources.

These are some of the material, logical, and linguistic fallacies that creep into argumentation. A good basic logic book can point out additional fallacies.[3] Armed with knowledge of such fallacies, you should be able to construct sound arguments to protect yourself against unscrupulous demagogues, sales personnel, and advertisers.

 Todd Barker for Class President

We need a strong leader and Todd has proven that he can lead through his active participation in sports this past season. Todd holds the school record for passes completed,

*and he was instrumental in winning our last two home games.
Todd is versatile, too. He participated in track and field
competition and heads one of our intramural volleyball teams.
We need effective decision makers in student government.
Todd's just the person to do the job right.*

   Would you vote for Todd?

TIPS FOR DEVELOPING ARGUMENTS

As you begin to develop arguments for public debates, you should
consider the following practical suggestions:

1. *Organize your arguments, using the strongest first or last.*[4] This
takes advantage of the *primacy/recency effect.* That is, we know that people
more readily retain information that is presented first or last. Information
or arguments presented first set the agenda for what is to follow (the primacy
effect). If you use your strongest argument first, it is likely that your listeners
will judge what follows to be equally as strong. Or, you may want to take
advantage of the recency effect. Listeners also tend to retain the most
recently presented idea. Since your last argument is most recent in their
minds, they will probably remember it. Therefore, it makes good sense to
place a strong argument either first or last.

2. *Vary your evidence.* You should use a variety of evidence as you
construct each argument; take advantage of both relevance and motivation.
For example, if you decide to argue for capital punishment, you may use
statistics to alert your listeners to the widespread problem of premeditated
violence. However, to clinch such an argument, more than cold, hard facts
are necessary. It would be wise to provide a moving example of a victim of
crime to involve your listeners in the human drama of the problem.

3. *Avoid personal attacks on your opponent.* It is important to maintain
the argument at an intellectual level. Indirectly, this enhances your credibility. If you can argue without becoming vicious or personal, you will earn
the respect, if not the convictions, of your listeners. You may also discourage
the tendency for your opponent to attack you on a personal level.

4. *Know the potential arguments of your opponent.* Often, the best
advocates know their opponent's arguments better than their opponent
does. It is important at least to understand what your opponent might say
during an argument. This will not only enable you to prepare a response, it
will boost your confidence in your own ability to argue well.

5. *Finally, practice constructing logical arguments and detecting fallacious ones.* Ultimately, argument is a skill based on logic. The common

denominator of all arguments, despite their different content, is the patterns of reasoning people use. If you have a clear grasp of the basic building blocks of argumentation, including the material presented in this chapter, you will develop your understanding and skill.

• • • • **Sample Outlines** *for Argumentative Speeches* • • • • • •

The following outlines present the arguments for and against a new and controversial experimental surgical procedure known as radial keratonomy. Each outline provides a detailed introduction and conclusion. In addition, each shows the basic elements of a good argument: (1) It develops a claim of fact, value, or policy. (2) It establishes logical patterns of reasoning. (3) It supports claims with relevant evidence.

THE CASE FOR RADIAL KERATONOMY

Introduction

Establishing a claim of policy By the year 2000, corrective eyewear, including glasses and contact lenses, will become obsolete. As you tour museums containing artifacts of the twentieth century, you will undoubtedly run across exhibits of wire-rimmed, horn-rimmed, designer, wing-shaped, and bifocaled spectacles in exhibit cases.

Brief statement of problem The reason: radial keratonomy, a new surgical procedure, will replace the need for corrective eyewear in all of us who have less than 20/20 vision. The only reason radial keratonomy, or RK, has not yet been used extensively in this country is that the medical establishment has been dragging its feet. I'd like

Forecast of main arguments to provide you with three reasons RK will soon replace the old-fashioned pair of spectacles—simplicity, effectiveness, and cost.

Body

I. Simplicity

Explanation A. RK procedure uses sophisticated technology.
Explanation   1. Computer measures the eyeball and performs specific calculations for guiding incisions.
Analogy   2. Computer then guides laser perforations in outer eye covering much like the spokes on a wheel or segments of an orange.
Explanation   3. Eyeball is then adjusted so that light rays passing through the lens of the eye fall squarely on the optic nerves at the back of the eye.
Sign reasoning B. Little medical training needed—second-year medical student can safely perform RK.

Causal reasoning   C. RK procedure completed on outpatient basis in fifteen
                            minutes.

                    II. Effectiveness

Statistics   A. RKs are 94 percent effective in curing myopia; 100
                            percent of patients report significantly improved
                            vision.

Expert testimony   B. According to physicians who have performed the
                            procedure, RKs can eliminate the need for glasses
                            forever.

Reasoning from   C. Individuals with unsightly "pop-bottle-bottom" len-
example (specific   ses, who cannot wear contact lenses, can be spared
instances)   the need to wear eyeglasses.

                    III. Cost

Comparison/   A. Currently, RKs are approximately $1500—no more
contrast   than the lifetime cost of wearing eyeglasses or contact
                            lenses.

Reasoning from   1. As the procedure becomes more popular, the cost
generalization/   will go down.
axiom   2. Eyeglass frames go out of style; the results of an
                               RK will not.

Comparison/   B. RKs save the time and expense of yearly eye exami-
contrast   nations or lens prescription changes.

                        Conclusion

Superiority of   Imagine yourself wandering through a museum of twentieth
claim   century artifacts in the year 2000. Your child points to a set
                        of odd glass orbs held together by wire and asks, "What are
                        those?" You answer, remembering the old days—squinting
Use of hypotheti-   through fogged lenses and the soreness of the bridge of your
cal example   nose—"Don't worry, honey, you'll never need them."

THE CASE AGAINST RADIAL KERATONOMY

                        Introduction

Establishing a   Among your senses, your eyes are most precious. You greet
value   morning sunrises and the wonders of your world with this
                        sense. You can study diligently and participate in our complex
                        world because you can see well. Good eyesight is one of those
                        gifts you often take for granted. It would be ludicrous,
                        considering how precious your eyesight is, to trust it to an
                        experimental, perhaps only temporary solution, for myopia.
Claim of policy   We need to consider carefully the risks and costs of radial
                        keratonomy, an experimental surgical technique for treating
Forecast of main   myopia, before we allow it to be used on literally thousands
arguments   of Americans.

Body

I. Risks

Explanation	A. There has not been enough research performed in connection with RK to really understand the limitations of the procedure or the extent of the risk involved.
Argument from generalization/ axiom	B. As with any surgical procedure, there is always the potential of infection or a surgical blunder even under the most sterile, clinical conditions.
Specific instances	C. Individuals with unusual eye conditions, such as astigmatism or cataracts, can suffer eye damage as a result of corneal incisions.
	D. Nearsighted individuals can be made farsighted as the curvature of the eye is changed through RK.
Expert testimony	E. According to optometrists, we do not yet know if there is regression to the presurgical condition over time after an RK.

II. Costs

Argument from generalization/ axiom	A. Most major health insurance policies will not cover such "experimental surgical procedures" as RKs.
Explanation and specific instances	B. There may be hidden costs of corrective surgery or even eye damage resulting from RK.

Conclusion

Superiority of claim *Comparison/contrast and appeal to value*	Your world would be drastically altered if you lost the use of your eyes. We have many ways of correcting vision difficulties. Why trust your most precious sense to what is, at best, a new surgical procedure in its experimental stages and, at worst, a dangerous fad?

CHAPTER SUMMARY

Argumentation is a persuasive activity in which a speaker offers reasons and support for claims in opposition to claims advanced by others. It is governed by *social conventions,* including: *the convention of bilaterality, the convention of self-risk, the fairness doctrine,* and *the commitment to rationality.*

Basically, an argument consists of (a) the *claim* or proposition to be defended, (b) the *evidence* relevant to the claim, and (c) the *reasoning pattern,* or inference, used to connect the evidence to the claim. *Claims of fact* assert that something is or is not the case, *claims of value* propose that something is or is not desirable, and *claims of policy* attempt to establish that something should or should not be done. Evidence is chosen to support these claims because it is *rationally* or *motivationally relevant.*

There are five basic inferences, or patterns of reasoning: *reasoning from examples, reasoning from generalization or axiom, reasoning from sign, reasoning by parallel case,* and *reasoning from causal relation.* A flaw in the reasoning or other rational properties of an argument is called a *fallacy.*

Oral Activities

1. Bring several magazine and newspaper advertisements to class. Discuss them with your classmates, identifying their fallacies of reasoning and fallacies of language.
2. With a classmate, prepare a ten-minute argumentative exchange on a particular topic. Divide the available time equally; one of you will advocate a claim and the other will oppose it. Or, adopt another format you both feel comfortable with. You may choose: (a) a Lincoln/Douglas format—the first person speaks four minutes; the second, five; and then the first person returns for a one-minute rejoinder; (b) an issue format— you both agree on several key issues and then each speaks for two and a half minutes on each issue; (c) a debate format—each speaker talks twice alternatively, three minutes in a constructive speech and two minutes in rebuttal; and (d) a heckling format—each of you has five minutes, but during the middle of each speech, the audience or your opponent may ask you questions.

Reference Notes

1. A full discussion of the logical grounding of claims in evidence and reasoning is presented in Douglas Ehninger and Wayne Brockriede, *Decision by Debate,* 2nd ed. (New York: Harper & Row, 1978).
2. For a fuller discussion of persuasive definitions, see Charles L. Stevenson, *Ethics and Language* (New Haven: Yale University Press, 1944), Chapter 9.
3. An excellent logic textbook is Irving M. Copi, *Introduction to Logic,* 5th ed. (New York: Macmillan Publishing Co., Inc., 1978), esp. Chapters 2 and 3.
4. See Robert N. Bostrom, *Persuasion* (Englewood Cliffs, NJ: Prentice-Hall, 1983), 177–78.

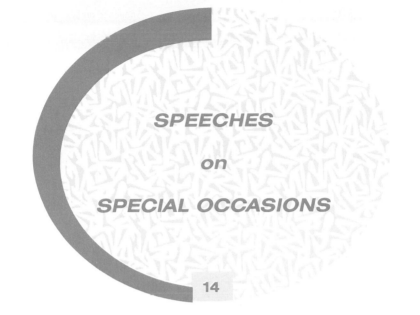

SPEECHES

on

SPECIAL OCCASIONS

14

Speeches to inform and persuade are the two kinds of talk you most often will be called on to make. Many occasions, however, require special types of speeches. Such occasions call in part for information and in part for persuasive efforts, yet they require more as well: They are occasions for demonstrating and even celebrating *group solidarity or membership.* You are familiar with many such occasions—funeral speeches for relatives and fallen heroes; tributes paid to outstanding humanitarians, artists, and professionals; and after-dinner and other entertaining speeches.

These occasions can stretch speakers' rhetorical skills to their fullest because of the pomp and ceremony associated with some events, and because of special expectations of the audience. Indeed, *audience expectations* are especially important in special-occasion speeches: The audience expects to hear something profound in retirement speeches, something forceful in nomination speeches, something honorary in introductions of guest speakers, and something funny yet relevant in after-dinner speeches.[1]

Such expectations put extraordinary social-psychological pressures on speakers at special occasions. Yet, if you know something about those expectations, you can reduce much of that pressure, and your preparing well can deflate the rest. The purpose of this chapter is to review the particular audience expectations you face when presenting three types of special-occasion speeches: speeches of introduction, speeches of courtesy, and speeches to entertain. We will look at some examples that show clearly how those expectations can be met.

SPEECHES OF INTRODUCTION

Speeches of introduction are usually given by the chairperson. Some-times, however, they are presented by another person who is especially well acquainted with the featured speaker.

Purpose

If you are invited to give a speech of introduction, remember that your main object is to create in the listeners a desire to hear the speaker you are introducing. Everything else should be subordinate to this aim. Do not bore the audience with a long recital of the speaker's biography or with a series of anecdotes about your acquaintance with him or her. Above all, do not air your own views on the subject of the speaker's message. You are only the speaker's advance agent; your job is to "sell" that person to the audience. Therefore, you must try (1) to arouse curiosity about the speaker and the subject in the minds of the listeners so that it will be easy to capture their attention and (2) to motivate the audience to like and respect the speaker so they will tend to respond favorably to the forthcoming information or proposal.

Formulating the Content

Usually the better known and more respected a speaker is, the shorter your introduction can be; the less well known he or she is, the more you will need to arouse interest in the speaker's subject and to build up his or her prestige. When presenting a speech of introduction, observe these principles:

1. *Be brief.* To say too much is often worse than to say nothing at all. For example, if you were to introduce the president, you might simply say, "Ladies and gentlemen, the President of the United States." The prestige of the person you introduce will not always be great enough for you to be so brief, but it is always better to say too little than to speak too long.

2. *Talk about the speaker.* Who is he? What is her position in business, education, sports, or government? What experiences has he had that qualify him to speak on the announced subject? Build up the speaker's identity, tell what he knows or what she has done, but do not praise his or her ability as a speaker. Let speakers *demonstrate* their own skills.

3. *Emphasize the importance of the speaker's subject.* For example, in introducing a speaker who will talk about the oil industry, you might say:

"All of us drive automobiles in which we use the products made from petroleum. A knowledge of the way these products are manufactured and marketed is, therefore, certain to be valuable to our understanding and our pocketbooks."

4. *Stress the appropriateness of the subject or of the speaker.* If your town is considering a program of renewal and revitalization, a speech by a city planner is likely to be timely and well received. If an organization is marking an anniversary, the founder may be one of the speakers. Reference to the positions these people hold is obviously in order and relates the speaker more closely to the audience.

5. *Use humor if it suits the occasion.* Nothing better puts an audience at ease and creates a friendly feeling than congenial laughter. Take care, however, that the humor is in good taste and does not come at the expense of someone else. In particular, do not risk offending the speaker whom you are introducing or detract from his or her prestige.

• • • Sample Speech of Introduction • • • • • •

Under all circumstances, remember that the four primary virtues of a speech of introduction are tact, brevity, sincerity, and enthusiasm. These virtues are illustrated in the following introduction.

INTRODUCING A CLASSMATE
Benita Raskowski

We've all come to know Sandy Kawahiro in this class. When we introduced ourselves during the first week of the semester, you learned that Sandy was raised in Hawaii, later moving to the West Coast to live with an uncle. Sandy's first speech dealt with his experiences in California's Sonoma Valley as a minority person for the first time in his life and of the pressures those experiences put upon his values and behavior. In his second speech, Sandy offered an explanatory speech on his post-collegiate career, industrial relations.

Today, Sandy's going to combine his personal and his professional life. If you followed the state legislature's recent public hearings on discrimination on the job, or saw CBS's special report on work environments in Japan two nights ago, you know how important human relations training can be to a successful business operation. This morning, Sandy will continue some of those ideas in a speech arguing for further development of human relations programs in executive training packages. The speech is entitled "Human Relations Training on the Job: Creating Color Blindness."

SPEECHES OF COURTESY: WELCOMES, RESPONSES, ACCEPTANCES

Most speakers will have occasion to give a speech of courtesy either on behalf of themselves or on behalf of an organization they represent.

Typical Situations

Speeches of courtesy are given to fulfill one of three obligations:

1. *Welcoming visitors.* When a distinguished guest is present, some-one—usually the presiding officer—should extend a public greeting.

2. *Responding to a welcome or a greeting.* An individual so welcomed must express appreciation.

3. *Accepting awards.* An individual who is presented an award for a special accomplishment is obligated to acknowledge this honor. Sometimes

An individual who is publicly rewarded for an accomplishment is expected to acknowledge that honor in an acceptance speech.

the award is made to an organization rather than to an individual, in which case someone is selected to respond for the group.

Purpose

The speech of courtesy has a double purpose. The speaker not only attempts to express a sentiment of gratitude or hospitality but also to create an aura of good feeling in the audience. Usually the success of such a speech depends on satisfying the listeners that the appropriate thing has been said. Just as courtesies of private life put people at ease, so public acts of courtesy create good feeling in the recipient and the audience.

Formulating the Content

The scope and content of a speech of courtesy should be guided by the following principles:

1. *Indicate for whom you are speaking.* When you act on behalf of a group, make clear that the greeting or acknowledgment comes from everyone and not from you alone.

2. *Present complimentary facts about the person or persons to whom you are extending the courtesy.* Review briefly the accomplishments or qualities of the person or group you are greeting or whose gift or welcome you are acknowledging.

3. *Illustrate; do not argue.* Present incidents and facts that make clear the importance of the occasion, but do not be contentious. Avoid areas of disagreement. Do not use a speech for courtesy as an opportunity to air your own views on controversial subjects or to advance your own policies. Rather, express concretely and vividly the thoughts that are already in the minds of your listeners.

These virtues are illustrated in William Faulkner's "On Accepting the Nobel Prize for Literature," reprinted in Chapter 8, pages 191–92. Faulkner clearly indicates he is speaking *as* a writer *to* future writers. He honors those young writers in taking their compositional problems seriously; his own difficulties as a writer, which come out in the flood of metaphors and images that make up the bulk of his speech, stand not as arguments but as illustrations of the struggle he finds at the core of all good writing.

Speeches of courtesy, therefore, are more than merely courteous talk. The courtesies expended in welcoming someone into your midst or in thanking someone for work done are really statements of your group's rules for living—its guiding principles. In extending courtesies to others, you are acknowledging the culture you share with them.

SPEECHES TO ENTERTAIN

To entertain an audience presents special challenges to speakers. As you may recall, we identified "to entertain" as an independent type of speech in Chapter 3 because of the peculiar force of humor in speechmaking. Discounting slapstick humor (of the slipping-on-a-banana-peel genre), most humor depends primarily on a listener's *sensitivities to the routines and mores of one's society,* which is obvious if you have ever listened to someone from a foreign country tell a series of jokes. Much humor cannot be translated, in part because of language differences (puns, for example, do not translate well) and in even larger measure because of cultural differences.

Purposes and Manner of Speaking to Entertain

Like most humor in general, speeches to entertain usually work within the cultural frameworks of a particular group or society. Such speeches may be "merely funny," of course, as in comic monologues of certain types, but most are serious in their force or demand on audiences. After-dinner speeches, for example, usually are more than dessert; their topics normally are relevant to the group at hand, and the anecdotes they contain usually are offered to make a point. That point may be one as simple as *deflecting an audience's antipathy toward the speaker,* as group-centered as *making the people in the audience feel more like a group,* or as serious as *offering a critique of one's society.*

Speakers seeking to deflect an audience's antipathy often use humor to ingratiate themselves. For example, Henry W. Grady, editor of the *Atlanta Constitution,* expected a good deal of distrust and hostility when, after the Civil War, he journeyed to New York City in 1886 to tell the New England Society about "The New South." He opened the speech not only by thanking the Society for the invitation but also telling stories about farmers, husbands and wives, and preachers. He praised Abraham Lincoln, a Northerner, as "the first typical American" of the new age; told another humorous story about shopkeepers and their advertising; poked fun at the great Union General Sherman—"who is considered an able man in our hearts, though some people think he is a kind of careless man about fire"; and assured his audience that a New South, one very much like the old North, was arising from those ashes.[2] Through the use of humor, Henry Grady had his audience cheering every point he made about The New South that evening.

Group cohesiveness also can be created through humor. Politicians, especially when campaigning, spend much time telling humorous stories about their opponents, hitting them with stinging remarks. In part, of

USING HUMOR THERAPEUTICALLY

Humour ... n. ... *b.* spec. *In ancient and mediaeval physiology, one of the four chief fluids (cardinal humours) of the body (blood, phlegm, choler, and melancholy or black choler), by the relative proportions of which a person's physical and mental qualities and dispositions were held to be determined ... temperament ...* **Humour** ... v. ... *l.* trans. *To comply with the humour of; to soothe or gratify by compliance; to indulge.*

—Oxford English Dictionary

It is at least interesting, and perhaps important, that "humor" as a noun draws etymologically on physiology, a bodily or personal theory of personality, while "humor" used as a verb is social in origin. Joining psychological and social conceptions together is never easy, but such thinking can give us insights into the use of humor in public speaking.

A key area of concern in contemporary psychology is the relationship between stress and humor (see Zimbardo). Stress reduction is an important part of personal survival in a complex world, and a primary strategy of contemporary stress reduction therapy is *emotion regulation.* Some people attempt to regulate their emotions through such physiological palliatives as tranquilizers or alcohol, others, through avoidance (e.g., evading an unpleasant situation by escaping to a movie or a friend), and others, through the introduction of humor into their lives.

Many comedians, for example, report that they developed and used their talents while children as ways of coping with stress or panic (Janus). Carol Burnett has been on talk shows around the dial, discussing her youth as a child of alcoholic parents. In addition, Norman Cousins, former editor of *Saturday Review,* used humor as part of his health and hypertension therapy. Faced first with a disease of the connective tissue ("incurable") and then with a heart attack, Cousins altered his diet, changed a hospital bed for his own pleasant home environment, and watched old *Candid Camera* films and other funny movies, which caused him to laugh deeply. He completely recovered from both the disease and the heart damage.

What has all this to do with public speaking? To understand something about the relationships between stress and humor is to understand a dimension of using humor in speeches. We've noted that humor deflects an audience's antipathy, makes audience members feel they are a part of a group, and provides an excellent vehicle for sociopolitical critique. More than even that, however, this discussion of stress suggests that humor, at *both* a psychophysical and a social level of existence, is *therapeutic:*

● The successful use of humor in a speech probably significantly reduces a speaker's level of psychophysical stress, or speech fright.

315

- The successful use of humor in a speech, because it can reduce the threatening aspects of social situations, helps integrate speakers "into" their audiences.

- Likewise, audience members equally should find successful humor stress reducing; hence, as the *OED* definition of the verb "humor" suggests, they should feel soothed or gratified by the speaker and, thus, feel a close bond with the speaker.

Humor, therefore, not only calms the wild beast in its natural environment, but may well calm the beasts in our minds, facilitating more free-flowing human interactions.

TO READ: For an introduction to the topic of therapeutic humor, see Philip G. Zimbardo, *Psychology and Life,* 11th ed. (Glenview, IL: Scott, Foresman and Company, 1985), esp. 476–77. See also W. F. Fry and M. Allen, *Make 'Em Laugh* (Palo Alto, CA: Science and Behavior Books, 1975); and S. S. Janus, "The Great Comedians: Personality and Other Factors," *American Journal of Psychoanalysis, 3* (1975): 169–74.

course, biting political humor degrades the opposition candidates and party; however, such humor also can make one's own party feel more cohesive, more unified. So, Democrats collected Nixon's 1972 bumperstickers, which said "Nixon Now," so they could cut off the "w" and put them on their own autos. Republicans likewise were not above calling the 1984 Democratic presidential candidate "Walter *Mono-dull*" during that campaign. Such zingers allow political party members to laugh at their opponents and to celebrate their membership in a "better" party.

And finally, speeches to entertain can be used not merely to poke fun at outsiders but even to critique one's society. Humor can be used to urge general changes and reform of social practices. You can see this purpose in Dick Cavett's graduation address on pages 317–22.

Formulating the Content

When arranging materials for speeches to entertain, develop a series of illustrations, short quotations or quips, and stories, each following another in fairly rapid succession. Most important, *make sure that each touches on a central theme or point.* An entertaining speech must be more than a comic monologue; it must be cohesive and pointed. The following sequence works well for speeches to entertain:

1. Relate a story or anecdote, present an illustration, or quote an appropriate passage.

2. State the essential idea or point of view implied by your opening remarks.

3. Follow with a series of additional stories, anecdotes, quips, or illustrations that amplify or illuminate your central idea. Arrange those supporting materials so that they are thematically or tonally coherent.

4. Close with a striking restatement of the central point you have developed. As in Step 1, you may use another quotation or one final story that clinches and epitomizes your speech as a whole.

The following speech by television's Dick Cavett illustrates many of the ideas we have been discussing. Although Mr. Cavett was concerned with the ceremonial demands of a commencement speech (see his comments in paragraphs 1–4), he also knew that, given his usual speaking style and reputation, the audience expected him to be "funny." To some speakers, these audience expectations would have appeared to be contradictory in light of our discussion. Not to Mr. Cavett. He chose to use an entertaining speech to make a serious point about American society; that point dealt with the personal and social uses of the English language. The resulting speech was appropriate for the special occasion, for the speaker's reputation, and for his audience of college students.

IS ENGLISH A DYING LANGUAGE?[3]
Dick Cavett

Mrs. Villard, President Smith, members of the faculty, students of Vassar, and friends: /1

The last college commencement I attended was my own. That, as President Smith mentioned, was at Yale in 1958. So if I get rattled here this morning, don't be surprised if I suddenly take out my handkerchief and launch into a chorus of "Bright College Years."   /2

Actually, that was not only the last commencement I attended, but the only other one I've ever attended; so my whole sense of these affairs comes from that single experience. I gather that the speaker in my position is expected to address himself to some vaguely uplifting topic that has a bearing on the academic career you graduates are leaving behind you, but also looks ahead to some problem that awaits you, some challenge that will be put to you to try to make the world a better place. In 1958 I seem to remember being urged to go out and do something about the Cold War. And, as you can see, the results speak for themselves.   /3

Anyway, those are the requirements as I understand them. And I'm sorry to tell you I have a topic that meets them perfectly. But don't worry—I don't think I'll use it. After all, the world would little note nor long remember what I might say here about "Ethical Dilemmas in Ecology During a Nuclear Age." /4

Instead, let me begin on what, for me, is firmer ground: humor, or at least a humorist. James Thurber was talking at a party with an actress he knew. She was telling him about the troubles of a mutual friend. The friend, she said, had had her apartment broken into so many times that she finally had to have it "burglarized." Thurber thought about that for a moment and said, "Wouldn't it have been simpler for her just to have it alarmed?"   /5

Now, there's more than a joke here, as Thurber was quick to point out when he told this story in one of his essays. "Ours is a precarious language," he said, "in which the merest shadow line often separates affirmation from negation, sense from nonsense, and one sex from another." In his later years, when he was blind, Thurber took in the world mostly through his hearing, and what he heard, acutely, was how our language was being mangled. He wrote often about "The Spreading You-Know" and other blights that he wished would pass "from the lingo into limbo." Even the sound and the fury, he said, had become the unsound and the fuzzy.   /6

Thurber was one of a long line of people who have confirmed what George Orwell wrote nearly 35 years ago—that "most people who bother about the matter at all would admit that the English language is in a bad way." We can confirm it ourselves, every day.   /7

We can confirm it when we take an airplane, and the pilot doesn't tell us he expects a bumpy ride; he says he anticipates experiencing considerable turbulence. Or we open a newspaper and read that a government office isn't going broke; it's undergoing a budget shortfall situation. Or we hear a policeman who doesn't say the suspect got out of the car; he relates that the alleged perpetrator exited the vehicle.   /8

We can confirm it when we encounter viable, meaningful, beautiful, "in" buzz-words; for example, "input," "interface," and "thrust," which, as somebody said, shouldn't be used in public but might be all right in private among consenting adults.   /9

We can confirm it when we hear people using "disinterested" as if it meant the same thing as "uninterested"; or "infer" as if it meant the same thing as "imply." To confuse any such pair is to take two distinct, useful words and blur them into a single, useless smudge. Every time it happens the language shrinks a little.   /10

Of course, I work in television, which is one of the designated disaster areas of language. In the past 11 years I've conducted thousands of hours of interviews, during which I've probably been an accessory to, or committed myself, all the known violations. I shouldn't even talk about this subject unless I'm granted complete immunity. Television is, among other things, a machine for turning nouns into verbs. I "host" a show. It's "funded" by the Chubb Corporation and "aired" by PBS. And naturally I always hope it will be "successed." /11

I could go on and on. The phrase "between you and I" appears, like an upraised pinkie, whenever people who should know better try for refinement. We seem to be stuck with that barbarous abbreviation "Ms.," which doesn't abbreviate anything, except common sense. The "you-know" is still spreading. /12

Worst of all is the fact that the very authorities we might expect to shore up these collapsing standards—the experts in linguistics, the dictionary makers, the teachers of English—are in many cases leading the onslaught. It's as if, in the middle of a coup, we turned to the palace guard for help and saw them coming at us with bayonets. /13

I had several linguistics professors on a series of shows about language earlier this season. They assured me that things like grammar, syntax and spelling were mere superficial details that shouldn't be allowed to interfere with the deeper importance of self-expression. In fact they suggested that, in matters of language, rules and standards of any kind were snobbish, authoritarian and downright undemocratic. Most of them were apostles of a group called the Council on College Composition and Communication, which a few years ago put out a policy statement advocating "the student's right to his own language," no matter what dialect, patois, slang or gibberish it might be. This idea could revolutionize education. I keep waiting for other departments to pick it up: the student's right to his own math, the student's right to his own history, and so on. /14

In Browning's poem "The Grammarian's Funeral," the grammarian himself was dead, obviously. Today the grammarian is underground in a different sense. A man named Richard Mitchell, who teaches English at Glassboro State College in New Jersey, publishes a monthly broadside called *The Underground Grammarian,* which is his one-man guerrilla war on jargon, cliches and fuzziness. The point is, his chief target is not the Philistine outside the ivied wall, but his own colleague, the English teacher sitting in the library—excuse me, I mean the language skills instructor sitting in the learning resources center. /15

Yes, the English language *is* in a bad way. In my business there's a famous phrase characterizing the Broadway theater as a "fabulous invalid." To me, that's exactly what the language has become. My late friend, the writer Jean Stafford, once described its symptoms in the following clinical terms: /16

"Besides the neologisms that are splashed all over the body... like the daubings of a chimpanzee turned loose with finger paints, the poor thing has had its parts of speech broken to smithereens... and upon its stooped and aching back it carries an astounding burden of lumber piled on by the sociologists and the psychologists, the Pentagon, the admen, and, lately, the alleged robbers and bug planters of Watergate. The prognosis for the ailing language is not good. I predict that it will not die in my lifetime, but I fear that it will be assailed by countless cerebral accidents and massive strokes and gross insults to the brain and finally will no longer be able to sit up in bed and take nourishment by mouth." /17

Members of the class of 1979, I can imagine you saying to yourself, "I'm sorry the language is ailing, but there's nothing I can do. It doesn't affect me anyway, since that's not my field. I can still get through the day. I can always get my meaning across." /18

At this point the sharper students among you will recognize that I have come around the back way and snuck up on my subject. For I am here this morning to say it *does* affect you, and there *is* something you can do. No matter what you majored in, you're still English majors. We're all English majors, willy-nilly, until the day we join Browning's grammarian. The breakdown of language isn't just something that happens to language. It's something that happens to us, and to our lives. /19

Let's go back for a moment to Thurber and the actress at the party. They were, as Thurber put it, on the shadow line, close to losing rational touch with each other. Of course, it wouldn't have mattered all that much if they had. There are many occasions when it doesn't matter all that much if words and meaning part company—if an undertaker advertises coffins with a "lifetime guarantee," for example; or if the *New York Times* prints this sentence about Nelson Rockefeller: "He was chairman of the Museum of Modern Art, which he entered in a fireman's raincoat during a recent fire, and founded the Museum of Primitive Art." /20

But E. B. White, who found that sentence in the *Times,* reminds us that muddiness of meaning isn't always such harmless fun. "Muddiness," White says, "is not merely a disturber of prose, it is a destroyer of life, of hope: death on the highway caused by a badly worded roadsign, heartbreak among lovers caused by a misplaced phrase in a well-intentioned letter, anguish of a traveler not being met at a railroad station because of a slipshod telegram." /21

You will live a lot of your lives on this mundane, practical level, exchanging gossip at a party, giving and taking directions, making and breaking plans. If your language is faulty, then these transactions will be faulty. Each of you literally will be in danger of not knowing what the other is talking about. Reconsider for a minute: can you really get through the day? Can you really always get your meaning across? When the gravedigger catches Hamlet out in a bit of muddiness, Hamlet says to his friend Horatio, "We must speak by the card, or equivocation will undo us." E. B. White believes it, and so do I. /22

Beyond this practical level, there are two other levels on which the breakdown of language affects you. One is moral and esthetic. Language is "the defining mystery of man," in George Steiner's phrase. It is the index to our civilization, the history of our race, the living web of our shared values and emotions. But it doesn't only define man generally and culturally. Specifically and personally it defines *men,* or rather, persons. The cardinal virtues of language are: clarity; simplicity; precision; vigor, if possible; and, on good days, gracefulness. What you ask of yourselves in each of those categories will define the terms by which you perceive things, by which you think, by which you register on the world around you. It will also define the terms by which other people judge you. /23

I'm not talking about language as an ornament, or about having a good prose style the way you might have a good backhand. I don't mean something external like Gucci stripes. I mean some outward sign of an inner dimension. Come to think of it, Gucci stripes probably are an outward sign of an inner dimension. But anyway, consider the phrase, "I could care less." It means exactly the opposite of what it's intended to mean. If you could care less, then you *do* care. But people use the phrase as a corruption of "I *couldn't* care less," which apparently is now too much trouble to say. And I judge their inner dimensions accordingly. The woman who says to me, "I could care less," is numb to logic and meaning. She simply isn't thinking about what she's saying, and I don't want to have anything to do with her—even if she *is* my wife. /24

Finally, the breakdown of language affects you politically, and I'm using the word in the broad sense that George Orwell used in the essay I quoted at the beginning, "Politics and the English Language." By politics I think Orwell meant that whole way we order our public life and common welfare. When politics in this sense is decayed, language tends to be decayed too. This was true in Nazi Germany. It's true today in Soviet Russia. Part of what Solzhenitsyn and other Russian dissidents are protesting is the repression of the mother tongue, the debasement of words like "truth" and "freedom" into Newspeak, the twisting of a term like "insane" until it means any thought that departs from the Party line. /25

Alas, we have more of that kind of decay in the West, specifically here in America, than we like to think. Vietnam taught us that, if nothing else. When soldiers bombard a village, drive the peasants into the countryside, burn their huts, machine-gun their cattle and then call it "pacification," how different is that from Newspeak? /26

Orwell wasn't sure whether politics debased the language, or vice versa, or whether it was a cycle. Our language "becomes ugly and inaccurate because our thoughts are foolish," he said, "but the slovenliness of our language makes it easier for us to have foolish thoughts." What Orwell *was* sure of was that the condition was curable, that we could shake off dead verbiage and mindless orthodoxy.   /27

If one simplifies one's English, he said, "one can think more clearly, and to think clearly is a necessary first step towards political regeneration . . . When you make a stupid remark its stupidity will be obvious, even to yourself. Political language . . . is designed to make lies sound truthful and murder respectable, and to give an appearance of solidity to pure wind. One cannot change this all in a moment, but one can at least change one's own habits, and from time to time one can even, if one jeers loudly enough, send some wornout and useless phrase . . . into the dustbin where it belongs."   /28

"If one jeers loudly enough . . . ." That takes me back, again, to Thurber. What appeals to me about that moment at the party is that Thurber not only skewered the actress's verbal absurdity, but he did it with humor. If I've raised any laughter here this morning, it hasn't been to reconcile you to the follies and abuses I've been talking about. It's been to hold them up to ridicule, to shame the people who commit them, and to render them so silly and contemptible that you won't commit them yourselves.   /29

There are other ways to achieve the same ends. There are a thousand ways. Humor is mine. The important thing is for you to find yours.   /30

Thank you.   /31

CHAPTER SUMMARY

Speeches for special occasions tend to celebrate *group solidarity or membership*. They recognize a person's presence in, contributions to, or departure from the audience-community. While there are many types, three—*speeches of introduction, speeches of courtesy,* and *speeches to entertain*—occur often enough to deserve careful examination. In this chapter, we have examined the purposes underlying, the content appropriate to, and the forms generally used by speakers giving each type of special-occasion talk.

Oral Activities

1. Your instructor will give you a list of special-occasion, impromptu speech topics, such as:
   a. Student *X* is a visitor from a neighboring school; introduce him or her to the class.
   b. You are Student *X;* respond to this introduction.

   c. Dedicate your speech-critique forms to the state historical archives.

   d. You have just been named Outstanding Classroom Speaker for this term; accept the award.

   e. You are a representative for a Speechwriters-for-Hire firm; sell your services to other members of the class.

You will have between five and ten minutes in which to prepare and then will present a speech on a topic assigned or drawn from the list. Be ready also to discuss the techniques you used in putting the speech together.

  2. Giving speeches to entertain is quite difficult because humor is a delicate art that few can master. However, many audiences, as well as speakers, have come to expect the inclusion of jokes and funny stories in even the most serious of presentations. Make a collection of jokes, anecdotes, and cartoons that fit a certain genre, such as ethnic, religious, or sex-role related. Analyze your collection with audience adaptation in mind. How might these jokes be offensive to some groups? How might they be modified so they are no longer offensive? How useful is material that is offensive even though it may seem funny to you? Also collect jokes, anecdotes, and cartoons that are not offensive and suggest how they might be useful in speaking situations. Be prepared to share your observations with your classmates.

Reference Notes

1. On the importance of people's expectations within various situations, see Lloyd Bitzer, "The Rhetorical Situation," *Philosophy & Rhetoric* 1 (Winter 1968): 1–14.

2. Henry W. Grady, "The New South," reprinted in *American Public Addresses; 1740–1952,* A. Craig Baird, ed., (New York: McGraw-Hill Book Co., 1956), 181–85.

3. "Is English a Dying Language?" by Dick Cavett. Given at Vassar College Commencement, May 27, 1979. Reprinted by permission of Dick Cavett.

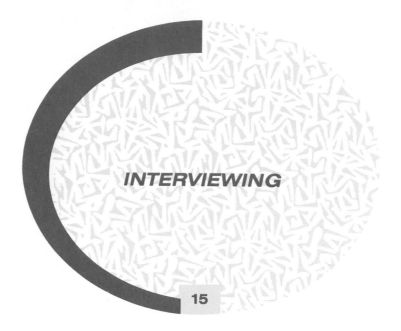

INTERVIEWING

15

You may be surprised to find a chapter on interviewing, a one-on-one type of communication transaction, in a book devoted to public speaking. Basic interviewing skills are relevant to this book for two reasons:

1. As we noted in Chapter 5, interviews of varying degrees of formality often are important sources of ideas, information, and expert testimony for speakers. *Informative interviews* save you time and frequently shed light on up-to-date, locally relevant issues for your speeches.

2. *Evaluative* and *persuasive interviews* will be important aspects of your postschool professional life. Almost everyone goes through such evaluative experiences as employment and on-the-job appraisal interviews, and we all run into sales representatives selling everything from candy to new careers.

While there are many specific kinds of interviews, generally all interviews fall into one of three categories. An informative interview is one in which the parties exchange concepts, ideas, or information. For example, polling agencies conduct survey interviews to find out how people assess the performance of the president or what they think about a new line of products. Almost all companies, too, conduct employment (also termed "selection" or "entrance") interviews of prospective employees to discover their qualifications, personalities, talents, and desires, in turn telling them about the company. Similarly, school administrators, faculty members, and admissions officers interview would-be students for much the same reasons. And, architects, lawyers, doctors, and engineers conduct interviews to see if their services match a prospective client's or patient's needs.

In an evaluative interview, one party seeks to interpret and judge the performance of another or of an object. You may have had an "oral test" in school, for example. Or, in the case of businesses, employees periodically are called in by their supervisors for an "appraisal" interview on their job performance or the company's image, or on a new office procedure needing examination. Likewise, most other professionals must periodically evaluate their progress with clients and patients by using evaluative interviews.

In a persuasive interview, one person tries to convince another, in a one-on-one situation, to use a certain product, to accept a particular idea, to vote for a candidate, and so on. Thus, faculty members sometimes try to convince you to enroll in a course, major in a discipline, or cooperate in a project. Or, you may find someone at your door trying to persuade you to attend a religious meeting, buy a vacuum cleaner, or vote for Jones in the upcoming election.

Interviewing, therefore, includes a series of communication skills with close ties to the sorts of public communication with which this textbook is primarily concerned. While we will not go into the topic in any great depth here—your school may offer another course doing that—we will discuss features common to all interviews; typical structures of informative, evaluative, and persuasive interviews; types of questions; and communication skills relevant to the interviewing process.

COMMON FEATURES OF ALL INTERVIEWS

Formally defined, *an interview is an interpersonal, usually one-on-one, communication transaction, characterized by mutually recognized goals, communicative interaction, and often specific role playing.* That is, interviews involve give-and-take between two (or sometimes more) people.

1. *Interviews are purposive.* People engaged in an interview are seeking to gather or express particular ideas, opinions, evaluations, or proposed courses of action. Each participant generally knows what the other person hopes to get out of the communication. For example, when you request an "interview" to get a grade raised, the professor knows you are seeking a *B* instead of a *C,* and you know he or she probably will resist changing a previously made judgment.

2. *Interviews are interactive processes.* There is a definite pattern of "turn taking" in interviews, which allows the parties to concentrate on one item at a time and helps guarantee that the exchange benefits both participants. The parties in an interview speak alternately, which leads to highly adapted messages; thus, when a potential employer asks you, "Why did you leave your last job?" you know it is your turn to talk, and the interviewer is seeking a satisfactory message that justifies your quitting the other job.

3. *Interviews are usually role specific.* A person who is a father, husband, Presbyterian, and softball player by night becomes a publishing company's sales representative by day, with his work-related behavior aimed toward selling books. All of those other roles are suppressed. And while you may be a single, female, Roman Catholic, Chicano piano player, when you want a grade raised, you talk from your student role.

Interviews, to say all this in a somewhat different way, are *highly rule-governed communication activities.* Some of the rules are written down; for example, federal law prohibits an interviewer from asking you about your marital status, age, or race. Most are informal communication rules; you probably know quite a few of them:

Some Common Interviewing Rules

- "If you are going to ask to have a grade raised, have some substantive reasons; plead for mercy only as a last, desperate resort."
- "When interviewing for a corporate job, dress in comparatively conservative yet comfortable suits; tank tops are out."
- "Do not chew gum at an appraisal interview."
- "When selling products, fit them to the needs and desires of the potential customer; probe those needs and desires before making the sales pitch."
- "Make a little small talk, to warm up an interviewee, before jumping into the main subject matter."
- "Clearly signal that it is time to terminate an interview before leaving so as not to startle the other party."

These and other communication rules are the kinds of directives you learn through experience. You learn some easily, while other rules will come to you only through painful failure. However you learn them, try to take positive advantage of them in future interview situations.

A difficult rule to learn for some especially skilled speakers is "Do not be too cocky in an interview." There is a fine line between self-confidence and cockiness.

> *Bob, the student government president, was participating in an in-class employment interview exercise. He was obviously experienced as a public speaker, had a fantastic résumé, had letters of recommendation from the dean and the university president, and had pat answers to every question he was asked. At the end of the class meeting, however, his class-mates voted to give the job to someone else—a student who had less experience, who handled himself much more humbly, and who had worked as a short-order cook to finance his education. Bob was dumbfounded. His classmates tried to explain their rationale: 'The job was an entry-level position. You interviewed as though you wanted to be vice-president of the company the day after tomorrow. Sam talked about his willingness and even eagerness to start where the work was. You talked as though you were superior to the interviewer; Sam talked in a straightforward, direct manner. Why should we hire you when we could get a real human being instead?' Sam had understood the rules of the particular situation, played by them, and won the job.*

FORMATS FOR INTERVIEWS

Interviews are almost always structured. Any interview has a begin-ning, a middle, and an end, whether or not these divisions are formally fixed. The beginning of an interview normally sets its purposes and limits, allows the participants to establish mutual rapport, and lets both parties know what to expect in the course of the interaction. In the middle of an interview, there is an exchange of information, opinions, values, feelings, and arguments. And, at the end, there is usually a summary, a mutual exchange of perspectives, final appeals, perhaps a projection for a future meeting, and an exchange of parting courtesies.

Interviews are structured substantively as well. That is, one or both of the parties usually come with prepared questions. Employment and appraisal interviews are instances in which both parties may have preplanned questions used to structure the transaction.

The Structure of an Interview

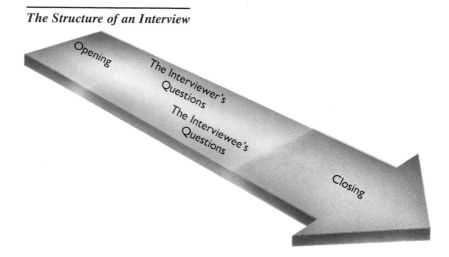

Informative Interviews

An informative interview generally has a simple, straightforward structure:

Opening:
1. Mutual greeting
2. Discussion of purposes
    a. Reason information is needed
    b. Kind of information wanted
Informational Portion:
1. Question #1, with clarifying questions if needed
2. Question #2, with clarifying questions if needed
3. (etc.)
Closing:
1. Summary by one or both parties
2. Final courtesies (promise to show interviewee any use made of the information, thanks, and good wishes)

In some situations, this structure may need to be more complicated. In an employment interview, for example, in which the exchange of information is two-way, the main portion may be subdivided. In most employment interviews, the body of the exchange is divided into two substages: interviewer questioning and interviewee questioning. Sometimes, even the closing contains another stage; in addition to summaries and final courtesies, informational interviews in the employment situation, if the rest has gone well, will include negotiations between the prospective hiree and the company regarding job conditions, follow-up interviews and visits, and the like.

When you are doing an informative interview to get some expert advice, plan well. If you start by saying, "You're the expert—tell me what issues I ought to be concerned with," not only do you communicate your own lack of preparation, but you cannot control the interaction. When you let the interviewee direct the flow of the questions and answers, you surrender your right to think to someone else.

> *Conchita interviewed a professor in the Political Science Department when she was preparing a speech on an upcoming election. The professor remarked afterward: 'That kid was prepared! She'd read up on past elections in this state, she'd read at least one of my articles, and she knew who had political clout in this district. I usually dread student interviews, because they want you to do all the work. Not her, though. She was a joy. By the end of the interview, I was asking her if she would take a work-study job as one of my assistants.'*

Finally, note that when informative interviews contain negotiations, they tend to be more like evaluative interviews.

Evaluative Interviews

Evaluative interviews, because they call for interpretation and commentary, tend to have a more complicated structure than informative interviews:

Opening:
1. Mutual greeting
2. Discussion of purposes
    a. Reason for evaluation
    b. Use to which the evaluation will be put
    c. Kinds of evaluative criteria to be used

Evaluative Portion:
1. Evaluative criterion #1, along with data on which the evaluation is based
2. Evaluative criterion #2, along with data on which the evaluation is based
3. (etc.)

Interpretive Portion:
1. Overall judgment of the person, process, or product being evaluated
2. Effect that judgment may have on the person's, process', or product's future

Closing:
1. Summary, to verify accuracy
2. Final courtesies (promise to show interviewee any use or record made of the evaluation, perhaps plan for future evaluations on a preset schedule, final thanks)

Evaluative interviews are especially sensitive exchanges. The interviewee often feels threatened by the evaluative process, especially if it is an appraisal interview carried on by a superior at work. The interviewer, too, has to take care to keep an open mind and a sympathetic demeanor, to be sure the exchange is productive and not destructive. Above all, the purpose and possible future consequences of the interview must be clear at all times to reduce hedging and fear.

Persuasive Interviews

A persuasive interview has a structure similar in many respects to the informative interview.

Opening:
1. Mutual greeting
2. Discussion of purposes
   a. Reason it is being conducted
   b. Gains the interviewee can make by participating

Informational Portion:
1. Information about the interviewee
2. Probing of needs and interests of the interviewee

Persuasive Portion:
1. Ways in which the product or course of action can meet the needs and interests of the interviewee
2. Discussion of doubts or questions the interviewee has after the presentation of the product or action

Closing:
1. Summary, with probe of the probability that the interviewee will buy the product or take the desired action
2. Final courtesies

Notice that the middle portion of the interview is split into informational and persuasive segments. This occurs because interviewers trying to sell a product (insurance, a used car, a new brand of coffee) or course of action (a trip to Europe, a political party, a religious meeting) first need to assess the personality and needs of the interviewee before trying to show the

An interview is a highly structured, interactive event in which participants seek a common goal—the exchange of useful information. Interview questions must be carefully phrased and organized in order to elicit answers that provide such information.

person that the product or action will be satisfying. Thus, an insurance agent gathers as much information as possible about a family before offering a particular policy to meet its needs; a travel agent inquires about your financial situation, preferences in transportation, and personal interests before offering you a package deal.

PHRASING AND ORGANIZING QUESTIONS

While everyone knows that answers to questions often determine one's success in achieving major goals in interviews, too often most of us forget how equally important questions are. We all must learn how to better phrase different types of interview questions and how to organize them in order to elicit the information we seek.

Types of Interview Questions

A skill you possess as both interviewer and interviewee is facility in answering questions. Six types of questions are often asked, and you must possess the ability to ask each type in appropriate situations.

Primary questions introduce a topic or area of inquiry, while *follow-up questions* probe more deeply or call for elaboration. Thus, in an employment interview, "What college courses prepared you for this job?" might be a primary question, and "Tell me more about the 'Introduction to Computer Sciences' " would signal a follow-up. One also has to be able to frame *direct questions* ("How long did you work at your last company?") as well as *indirect questions* ("What do you want to be doing in five years?"). Direct questions allow you to gather information in a hurry, while indirect probes let you see interviewees "thinking on their feet," structuring materials and responses, and exploring their own minds. Also, careful interviewers use both *open* and *closed questions*. A closed question—"Have you had experience as a clerk, a typist, a buyer, or a sales representative?"—specifies a range of responses, while an open question—"What are you looking for in a job?"—allows the interviewee to control the categories of response. Closed questions require little effort from the interviewee and are easy to "code" or record; open questions allow an interviewer to observe an interviewee's habits, to let the interviewee feel in control of the interaction. Note, of course, that these types of questions overlap: you can use a direct or indirect, an open or closed, question as your primary question; a closed question can be used in direct ways ("Are you a freshman, sophomore, junior, or senior?") or indirect ways ("Would you rather be a manager, a supervisor, or a line worker in five years?").

Overall, it is important to know that primary, direct, and closed questions tend to produce a lot of "hard" information quickly. Follow-up, indirect, and open questions produce more thought; interpretation; and grounds for understanding and analyzing interviewees and their motivations, capacities, and expectations. As you plan interviews, you must learn to blend questions of all six types. This blend is called an *interview schedule.*

Interview Schedules

An interview schedule is your effort to organize specific questions in such a way as to systematically elicit the materials and opinions you are looking for. Like any other organizational pattern, an interview schedule should have a rationale, one that (1) permits you to acquire systematic information or opinion and (2) seems reasonable to the interviewee, avoiding confusing repetitions and detours. Interview schedules normally are built in one of two forms—the *traditional* and the *branching schedule:*

Traditional Schedule of Questions

I. "How many speech communication courses did you take at Jackson University?" (primary, direct, open question)

A. "Are those quarter-hour or semester-hour courses?" (secondary, direct, closed question)
B. "What kinds of practical experiences in communication with others did you get in the public speaking class?" (secondary, direct, open question)
  1. "What are your strengths as a speaker?" (secondary, indirect, open question)
  2. "What communication skills do you still feel a need to work on?" (secondary, direct, open question)
  3. "Would you say you're better at platform speaking or at informal-but-purposive chit-chat?" (secondary, direct, closed question)

Branching Schedule of Questions

1. "Did you take courses in speech communication while attending Jackson University?"

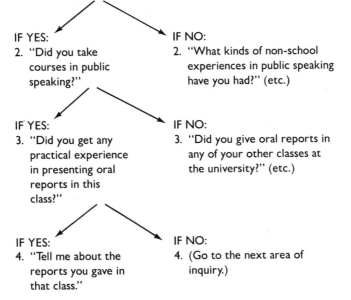

IF YES:
2. "Did you take courses in public speaking?"

IF NO:
2. "What kinds of non-school experiences in public speaking have you had?" (etc.)

IF YES:
3. "Did you get any practical experience in presenting oral reports in this class?"

IF NO:
3. "Did you give oral reports in any of your other classes at the university?" (etc.)

IF YES:
4. "Tell me about the reports you gave in that class."

IF NO:
4. (Go to the next area of inquiry.)

Notice that the traditional schedule of questions uses an organizational pattern that first extracts information and then follows with more probing questions. This pattern allows the interviewee to think through his or her experiences concretely before you ask for self-reflection or evaluation. Were that reversed, the interviewee might be asked to evaluate an experience before having recalled it clearly, most likely producing a less-than-complete evaluation. Notice, too, the mixing of types of questions in the traditional schedule to keep the interaction progressing.

A branching schedule is used in situations in which the interviewer knows rather specifically what he or she is looking for. Survey or polling interviewers often use this schedule. In our example, an employment interviewer is using a branching schedule to explore fully the relevant communication experience of a job applicant. In a complete branching schedule, the *"If no"* questions would likewise have "branches" beneath them; nonetheless, our illustration indicates the essential logic of the pattern.

No matter what type of questions you use and what specific organizational pattern for questions you devise, the important points to remember are these:

1. *Plan your questions* before going into an interview so that you know your goals and proceed toward them.

2. *Organize your questions* in a manner that seems rational and prepares interviewees adequately before asking them to make abstract, complex evaluations.

COMMUNICATION SKILLS FOR SUCCESSFUL INTERVIEWERS

From this discussion of interviewing and structures for getting the job done, it should be clear that adept interviewers must have some specific communication skills:

A good interviewer is a good listener. Unless you take care to understand what someone is saying and to interpret the significance of those comments, you may misunderstand the person. Because questioning and answering are alternated in an interview, there is plenty of opportunity to clarify remarks and opinions. You can achieve clarification only if you are a good listener (see Chapter 2).

A good interviewer is open. Many of us may have become extremely wary of interviewers. We are cynical enough to believe that they have *hidden agenda*—unstated motives or purposes—that they are trying to pursue. Too often interviewers have said they "only want a little information" when actually they were selling magazine subscriptions or a religious ideal. If, as an interviewer, you are "caught" being less than honest, your chances for success are vastly diminished. Frankness and openness should govern all aspects of your interview communication.

A good interviewer builds a sense of mutual respect and trust. Feelings of trust and respect are created by revealing your own motivation, by probing the other party and getting the person to talk, and by expressing sympathy and understanding. Sometimes, of course, your assumptions of integrity and goodwill can be proved wrong. To start with suspicion and distrust, however, is to condemn the relationship without giving it a fair chance.

CHAPTER SUMMARY

An interview is an interpersonal, usually one-on-one, communication transaction, characterized by mutually recognized goals, communicative turn taking, and often specific role playing. Three main kinds of interviews are *informative interviews* used in gathering ideas, materials, and opinions from others; *evaluative interviews* used to interpret and judge the performance of another person or of an object; and *persuasive interviews*, wherein one person tries to convince another to use a certain product, to accept a particular idea, to vote for a candidate, and the like. Regardless of type, all interviews are *purposive, interactive,* and *structured.* Interviewers learn to make use of six kinds of questions: (1) *primary questions,* which introduce a topic, as well as (2) *follow-up questions,* which probe more deeply; (3) *direct questions,* which ask what they appear to ask, and (4) *indirect questions,* which force people to think on their feet and let interviewers "see" thinking and communication skills; (5) *open questions,* wherein the interviewee gets to choose the possible answers, vs. (6) *closed questions,* wherein the interviewer specifies possible answers. These questions may be arranged in either a *traditional schedule* or a *branching schedule* of questions. Overall, a good interviewer is a good listener, is open, and builds a sense of mutual respect and trust.

Oral Activities

1. Along with several members of your class, consider the following situations and then formulate specific questions that an interviewer might use to get information, to evaluate job performance, or to persuade someone of something. What types of questions—direct, indirect, open, closed—did you choose and why?
   a. The interviewee worked only six months at the last job listed on his or her résumé.
   b. The interviewer wants to know how many employees are using electric typewriters, rather than computers, at work.
   c. An interviewer wants to ascertain whether Jane realizes that her work has become progressively poorer.

    d. The interviewer seeks to account for a switch in a major from predentistry to accounting.

    e. An interviewee wishes to find out what starting salary he or she might receive if a job is offered.

2. Your instructor will divide the class into pairs of partners. Meet briefly with your partner to decide on a type of interview and the specific situation that you will simulate, as well as who will be the interviewer and who will be the interviewee. Develop a series of questions for a ten-minute interview and execute the assignment on an appointed day.

Reference Notes

1. For additional information on types of questions as well as most other aspects of interviewing, see Charles J. Stewart and William B. Cash, Jr., *Interviewing: Principles and Practices,* 4th ed. (Dubuque, IA: William C. Brown Company Publishers, 1985). To concentrate particularly on all-important employment interviewing skills, see Lois J. Einhorn, Patricia Hayes Bradley, and John E. Baird, Jr., *Effective Employment Interviewing: Unlocking Human Potential* (Glenview, IL: Scott, Foresman and Company, 1982).

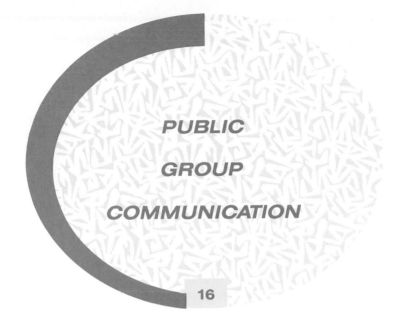

PUBLIC

GROUP

COMMUNICATION

16

In most of this book, we have talked about public speaking with a particular vision in mind—that of a single speaker standing on a podium or behind a lectern, addressing a sizeable collection of people seated some distance away. There are public speaking arrangements, however, in which you will be talking before a collection of people, but in a different role situation.

This chapter is devoted to some of those situations, especially those in which you are *part of* or *representative of* a *group*. An essential characteristic of the public speaking situations we will examine in this chapter is your relationship to others—as part of a group or team that is seeking knowledge or making decisions; as a member of a group or team that is making a collective presentation to an audience; or as a representative of a group or body that is making announcements, answering questions, and so on. You may be part of a *discussion* of an idea or problem; part of a team functioning as a *panel or symposium* before an audience; or a *group representative*—a spokesperson—addressing the public.

We call this chapter "public group communication" because in all cases, your messages go to a kind of "public," be it the rest of the group or society at large and because group membership—interdependence—is operative to a degree in every situation we will discuss.

DISCUSSIONS

Businesses and other professional organizations depend heavily on oral communication for their successful operation. It can even be said that what makes an organization an organization (rather than a collection of isolated individuals) is the opportunity for face-to-face oral interaction—the exchange of information, ideas, beliefs, perceptions, interpretations, and thoughts about what to do in any given situation. Businesspeople and professionals are constantly calling on committees, task forces, and more informal groups to formulate ideas, evaluate courses of action, and put proposals into effect. These exchanges generally are termed "group discussions." *A group discussion is a shared, purposive communication transaction in which a small group of people exchange and evaluate ideas and information in order to understand a subject or solve a problem.*

As this definition suggests, there are two major sorts of discussions: In a *learning, or study, discussion,* participants seek to educate each other, to come to a fuller understanding of a subject or problem. A number of people interested in art or literature or coin collecting, for example, may gather monthly to share thoughts and expertise; book clubs, genealogical societies, and Sunday School classes are learning groups. Businesses use such discussions to educate new employees and to explore problems creatively.

In an *action,* or *decision-making, group,* participants try to reach an agreement on what the group as a whole should believe or do or look for ways to implement a decision already made. In discussions of this kind, conflicting facts and values are examined, differences of opinion are evaluated, and proposed courses of action are explored for their practicality, in an effort to arrive at a consensus. So, a neighborhood homeowners' association may gather periodically to decide on projects to undertake. A city council must decide what to do with its federal revenue-sharing funds. A subcommittee in a business may be asked to find ways to expand markets. Once such decisions are made, these groups may meet later as action teams, discussing ways to implement their plans.

Essentials for the Participant

For the participant in group communication, the most important requirement is a *knowledge of the subject* being considered. If you know what you are talking about, you will be forgiven many faults. Of equal importance and usefulness is an *acquaintance with the other members of the group,* but it may not always be possible for you to know a great deal about them. To the extent that you can acquaint yourself with their values and interests, you will be able to judge more accurately the importance of their remarks and to determine more fairly the role you must play in order to make the group process profitable. Equally important is *close attention to the discussion* as it progresses. Unless you listen to what is going on, you will forget what already has been said or lose track of the direction in which the thinking of the group seems to be moving. As a result, you may make foolish or irrelevant comments, require the restatement of points already settled, or misunderstand the positions taken by other participants.

Essentials for the Leader

If a discussion is to prove fruitful, the leader of the group must be alert, quick witted, and clear thinking—able to perceive basic issues, to recognize significant ideas, to sense the direction of an interchange, to note common elements in diverse points of view, and to strip controversial matters of unnecessary complexity. Moreover, a good discussion leader must be capable of the *effective expression* needed to state the results of the group's analyses clearly and briefly or to make an essential point stand out from the others.

Another important quality of a discussion leader is *impartiality*. The leader must make sure that minority views are allowed expression and must phrase questions and comments fairly. In this way, a spirit of cooperation and conciliation will be promoted among participants who may differ from one another vigorously. Discussion groups are no different from other groups in preferring leaders who are fair. There is no place for a leader who takes sides in a personal argument or who openly favors some of the members at the expense of others. To help ensure that all may participate in a democratic, representative way—especially if the discussion is a formal, decision-making one—the leader should have a working knowledge of parliamentary procedure and the commonly used motions. For a brief discussion of parliamentary procedure and a table of such motions, see pages 345–48.

Finally, a discussion leader should have an *encouraging or permissive attitude* toward the participants. There are times, especially at the beginning of a discussion, when people are hesitant to speak out. Provocative questions may stimulate them to participate, but even more helpful is a leader whose manner conveys confidence that the group members have important things to say about an important subject.

DEVELOPING A DISCUSSION PLAN

When people communicate in groups, they can lose much time by needless repetition or by aimless wandering from point to point. A carefully developed discussion plan will guard against this danger.

Ideally, the entire group should cooperate in framing the discussion plan, but if this is impossible, the leader must take the responsibility for formulating it. In the following pages, we consider separate plans for learning discussions and decision-making discussions. Although these can be used in most situations, at times they may have to be modified because of peculiarities in the composition of the group or because in a decision-making discussion the problem has already received considerable attention, either by individuals or by the group, in earlier meetings.

A Plan for Learning Discussions

Sometimes a learning discussion concerns a book or parts of it or is based on a study outline or syllabus prepared by an authority in a given field. In such cases, the discussion generally should follow the organizational pattern used in the book or outline. The ideas in that resource, however, should be related to the experience of the individuals in the group, and an effort should be made to give proper emphasis to the more important facts and principles. When the group finds that previously prepared outlines are out of date or incomplete, the leader and/or the other participants should modify them to bring the missing information or points of view to the group's attention.

When learning discussions are not based on a book or outline, the leader and/or the group must formulate a plan. The first step in this process is to *phrase the subject for discussion as a question.* Usually the question is framed before the actual discussion begins. If not, the leader and the members of the group must work it out together. Ordinarily, it is phrased as a question of fact or of value. (See pages 292–93.) Questions of fact, such as "What is this community doing to increase the number of small businesses in town?" or "What range of courses and internship experiences are important to a public relations or advertising major?" seek an addition to or a clarification of knowledge within the group. Questions of value, such as "Is the United States' Middle Eastern policy effective?" or "Are there viable alternatives to this school's grading system?" seek judgments, appraisals, or preferences.

Leaders of groups are tempted to simply announce a topic, not frame their concerns in a question. That can get them into trouble.

A group in one speech class selected 'summer orientation,' a meaty topic, for their learning discussion. But, as group members went about their business of gathering information, some learned about competency testing; some, about the desirability of having new students stay in the dorms; others, about registration procedures; and another, about what parents want to learn about the university while they are in town. A focused question—'What do new students want from summer orientation?'—would have produced more focused information gathering and in-class discussion.

The following suggestions should help you develop a satisfactory discussion plan for either type of question we have just described.

Introduction

The introduction consists of a statement of the discussion question by the leader, together with one or two examples showing its importance or its relation to individuals in the group.

Analysis

In this step the group explores the nature and meaning of the question and narrows the scope of the discussion to those phases that seem most important. These considerations are pertinent:

1. Into what major topical divisions may this question conveniently be divided? (See pages 129–30 for some suggestions.)
2. To which of these phases should the discussion be confined?
   a. Which phases are of the greatest interest and importance to the group?
   b. On which phases are the members of the group already so well informed that detailed discussion would be pointless?

At this point the leader summarizes for the group, listing in a logical sequence the particular aspects of the questions that have been chosen for discussion.

Investigation

In the investigative phase of the discussion, the members focus on the topics they have chosen in the preceding step. *Under each topic,* they may consider the following questions:

1. What terms need definition? How should these terms be defined?

2. What factual material needs to be introduced as background for the discussion (historical, social, geographic, and so on)?

3. What personal experiences of group members might illuminate and clarify the discussion?

4. What basic principles or causal relationships can be inferred from this information and these experiences?

5. On which facts or principles is there general agreement and on which points is information still lacking or conflicting?

Final Summary

At the close of the discussion, the leader briefly restates (1) the reasons given for considering the question important and (2) the essential points brought out under each of the main topics. A summary need not be exhaustive; its purpose is merely to review the more important points and make clear their relationships to each other and to the general subject.

A Plan for Decision-Making Discussions

Decision-making discussions characteristically raise questions of policy. (See page 293.) Examples of such questions are "What can be done to give students a more effective voice in the affairs of our college?" and "How can our company meet competition from foreign imports?"[1] As you will see in the following suggested procedure, answering such questions also requires answering subsidiary questions of fact and of value.

The steps in this plan for decision-making discussions are adapted from John Dewey's analysis of how we think when we are confronted with a problem.[2] Although presented here in some detail, this plan is only one of several possible ways of deciding on a course of action and, therefore, is intended to be suggestive rather than prescriptive. Any plan that is developed, however, probably should follow—in general—a problem-solution order. Moreover, steps in the plan should always be stated as a series of questions.

Defining the Problem

After the leader's introductory remarks touching on the general purpose of the discussion and its importance, the group should consider:

1. How can the problem for discussion be phrased as a question? (*Note:* Usually the question has been phrased before the discussion begins. If not, it should be phrased at this time.)

2. What terms need defining?
   a. What do the terms in the question mean?
   b. What other terms or concepts should be defined?

Analyzing the Problem

This step involves evaluating the problem's scope and importance, discovering its causes, singling out the specific conditions that need correction, and setting up the basic requirements of an effective solution. The following sequence of questions is suggested for this step:

1. What evidence is there that an unsatisfactory situation exists?
   a. In what ways have members of the group been aware of the problem, how have they been affected by it, or how are they likely to be affected?
   b. What other people or groups does the situation affect, and in what ways are they affected?
   c. Is the situation likely to improve itself, or will it become worse if nothing is done about it?
   d. Is the problem sufficiently serious to warrant discussion and action at this time? (If not, further discussion is pointless.)
2. What are the causes of this unsatisfactory situation?
   a. Are they primarily financial, political, social, or what?
   b. To what extent is the situation the result of misunderstandings or emotional conflicts between individuals or groups?
3. What specific aspects of the present situation must be corrected? What demands must be met, what desires satisfied?
   a. What evils does everyone in the group wish corrected?
   b. What additional evils does a majority in the group wish corrected?
   c. What desirable elements in the present situation must be retained?
4. In light of the answers to Questions 1, 2, and 3 above, by what criteria should any proposed plan or remedy be judged?
   a. What must the plan do?
   b. What must the plan avoid?
   c. What restrictions of time, money, and so on must be considered?
5. In addition to the above criteria, what supplementary qualities of a plan are desirable, although not essential?

At this stage the leader summarizes the points agreed on thus far. Particularly important is a clear statement of the agreements reached on Questions 4 and 5, since the requirements set forth there provide the standards by which proposed remedies are judged. Moreover, agreement on such criteria tends to make further discussion more objective and to minimize disagreements based on personal prejudices.

Suggesting Solutions

In this step, every possible solution is presented. The group asks:

1. What are the various ways in which the difficulty could be solved? (If the group is meeting to discuss the merits of a previously proposed plan, it asks: What are the alternatives to the proposed plan?)
   a. What is the exact nature of each proposed solution? What cost, actions, or changes does it entail or imply?
   b. How may the various solutions best be grouped for initial consideration? It is helpful to list all solutions, preferably on a chalkboard.

Evaluating the Proposed Solutions

When the discussants have presented all possible solutions that have occurred to them, they examine and compare these solutions and try to agree on a mutually satisfactory plan. The following questions may be asked:

1. What elements are common to all the proposed solutions and are therefore probably desirable?
2. How do the solutions differ?
3. How do the various solutions meet the criteria set up in Questions 4 and 5 of the analysis step? (This question may be answered either by considering each plan or type of plan separately in the light of the criteria agreed on, or by considering each criterion separately to determine which solution best satisfies it.)
4. Which solutions should be eliminated and which ones retained for further consideration?
5. Which solution or combination of solutions should finally be approved?
   a. Which objectionable features of the approved solution or solutions should be eliminated or modified?
   b. If a number of solutions are approved, how may the best features of all the approved solutions be combined in a single superior plan?

As soon as agreement is reached on these matters, the leader sums up the principal features of the accepted plan. In groups that have no authority to act, this statement normally concludes the discussion.

Deciding How to Put the Approved Solution into Operation

When a group has the power to put its solution into operation, the following additional questions are pertinent:

1. What persons or committees should be responsible for taking action?
2. When and where should the solution go into effect?
3. What official action, what appropriation of money, and so on is necessary? (*Note:* If several divergent methods of putting the solution into effect are suggested, the group may need to evaluate these methods briefly to decide on the most satisfactory one.)

When these matters have been determined, the leader briefly restates the action agreed on to be sure it is clear and acceptable to the group.

Discussions Governed by Parliamentary Procedure

Sometimes, especially when groups are large or formal, your discussions are governed by parliamentary procedure. Parliamentary procedure is a set of *technical rules* that prescribes what may be said by whom, when, and to whom; they are designed to keep groups from being disorganized or dominated by a few overly powerful people. Among the most common of these technical rules are those recorded in *Robert's Rules of Order.* Because these technical rules are important and because you will probably encounter them, let us discuss them briefly.

As noted, parliamentary procedure limits *what* you can say (some motions are "out of order"), *whether* you can say it (you may not discuss an idea if your motion is not seconded), and even *when* you can say it (everything you say must be germane to the motion under consideration). The essential details of parliamentary procedure for handling motions are shown in the chart on pages 346–47.

If you are taking part in a meeting that is governed by parliamentary rules, there are several things you can do to increase your effectiveness:

1. *Know the appropriate rules yourself.* Do not depend on a good chair to keep you informed about the process. The more knowledgeable you are, the less confused you will become as the parliamentary process unfolds. Also, you will be able to counteract efforts to use the rules to create an unfair advantage for one or more persons.

2. *Listen carefully.* Be aware of what is going on. If the chair does not keep the group on track by constantly reminding members of what is pending, you may need to take that responsibility. A conscientious leader should keep you and others informed regarding what is on the floor.

3. *Ask questions.* If you are not sure about the procedures or become lost in the parliamentary thicket, do not hesitate to raise a question of personal privilege. Be specific in asking the chair or the parliamentarian (if one has been appointed) what is on the floor or what motions are appropriate under the circumstances.

4. *Speak to the motion.* Limit your remarks to the specific motion on the floor. Do not discuss the entire main motion if an amendment is pending; instead, comment directly on the merits of the amendment.

5. *Avoid unnecessary parliamentary gymnastics.* If the members of a group yield to the temptation to play with the rules, parliamentary procedure

Parliamentary Procedure for Handling Motions

Classification of motions	Types of motions and their purposes	Order of handling	Must be seconded	Can be discussed	Can be amended	Vote required [1]	Can be reconsidered
Main motion	(To present a proposal to the assembly)	Cannot be made while any other motion is pending	Yes	Yes	Yes	Majority	Yes
Subsidiary motions [2]	To postpone indefinitely (to kill a motion)	Has precedence over above motion	Yes	Yes	No	Majority	Affirmative vote only
	To amend (to modify a motion)	Has precedence over above motions	Yes	When motion is debatable	Yes	Majority	Yes
	To refer (a motion) to committee	Has precedence over above motions	Yes	Yes	Yes	Majority	Until committee takes up subject
	To postpone (discussion of a motion) to a certain time	Has precedence over above motions	Yes	Yes	Yes	Majority	Yes
	To limit discussion (of a motion)	Has precedence over above motions	Yes	No	Yes	Two thirds	Yes
	Previous question (to take a vote on the pending motion)	Has precedence over above motions	Yes	No	No	Two thirds	No
	To table (to lay a motion aside until later)	Has precedence over above motions	Yes	No	No	Majority	No
Incidental motions [3]	To suspend the rules (to change the order of business temporarily)	Has precedence over a pending motion when its purpose relates to the motion	Yes	No	No	Two thirds	No
	To close nominations [4]	[4]	Yes	No	Yes	Two thirds	No
	To request leave to withdraw or modify a motion [5]	Has precedence over motion to which it pertains and other motions applied to it	No	No	No	Majority [5]	Negative vote only
	To rise to a point of order (to enforce the rules) [6]	Has precedence over pending motion out of which it arises	No	No	No	Chair decides [7]	No
	To appeal from the decision of the chair (to reverse chair's ruling) [6]	Is in order only when made immediately after chair announces ruling	Yes	When ruling was on debatable motion	No	Majority [1]	Yes
	To divide the question (to consider a motion by parts)	Has precedence over motion to which it pertains and motion to postpone indefinitely	[8]	No	Yes	Majority [8]	No
	To object to consideration of a question	In order only when a main motion is first introduced	No	No	No	Two thirds	Negative vote only
	To divide the assembly (to take a standing vote)	Has precedence after question has been put	No	No	No	Chair decides	No

	Motion						
Privileged motions	To call for the orders of the day (to keep meeting to order of business) [6, 9]	Has precedence over above motions	No	No	No	No vote required	No
	To raise a question of privilege (to point out noise, etc.) [6]	Has precedence over above motions	No	No	No	Chair decides [7]	No
	To recess [10]	Has precedence over above motions	Yes	No [10]	Yes	Majority	No
	To adjourn [11]	Has precedence over above motions	Yes	No [11]	No [11]	Majority	No
	To fix the time to which to adjourn (to set next meeting time) [12]	Has precedence over above motions	Yes	No [12]	Yes	Majority	Yes
Unclassified motions	To take from the table (to bring up tabled motion for consideration)	Cannot be made while another motion is pending	Yes	No	No	Majority	No
	To reconsider (to reverse vote on previously decided motion) [13]	Can be made while another motion is pending [13]	Yes	When motion to be reconsidered is debatable	No	Majority	No
	To rescind (to repeal decision on a motion) [14]	Cannot be made while another motion is pending	Yes	Yes	Yes	Majority or two thirds [14]	Negative vote only

1. A tied vote is always lost except on an appeal from the decision of the chair. The vote is taken on the ruling, not the appeal, and a tie sustains the ruling.

2. Subsidiary motions are applied to a motion before the assembly for the purpose of disposing of it properly.

3. Incidental motions are incidental to the conduct of business. Most of them arise out of a pending motion and must be decided before the pending motion is decided.

4. The chair opens nominations with "Nominations are now in order." A member may move to close nominations, or the chair may declare nominations closed if there is no response to his or her inquiry "Are there any further nominations?"

5. When the motion is before the assembly, the mover requests permission to withdraw or modify it, and if there is no objection from anyone, the chair announces that the motion is withdrawn or modified. If anyone objects, the chair puts the request to a vote.

6. A member may interrupt a speaker to rise to a point of order or of appeal, to call for orders of the day, or to raise a question of privilege.

7. Chair's ruling stands unless appealed and reversed.

8. If propositions or resolutions relate to independent subjects, they must be divided on the request of a single member. The request to divide the question may be made when another member has the floor. If they relate to the same subject but each part can stand alone, they may be divided only on a regular motion and vote.

9. The regular order of business may be changed by a motion to suspend the rules.

10. The motion to recess is not privileged if made at a time when no other motion is pending. When not privileged, it can be discussed. When privileged, it cannot be discussed, but can be amended as to length of recess.

11. The motion to adjourn is not privileged if qualified or if adoption would dissolve the assembly. When not privileged, it can be discussed and amended.

12. The motion to fix the time to which to adjourn is not privileged if no other motion is pending or if the assembly has scheduled another meeting on the same or following day. When not privileged, it can be discussed.

13. A motion to reconsider may be made only by one who voted on the prevailing side. It must be made during the meeting at which the vote to be reconsidered was taken, or on the succeeding day of the same session. If reconsideration is moved while another motion is pending, discussion on it is delayed until discussion is completed on the pending motion; then it has precedence over all new motions of equal rank.

14. It is impossible to rescind any action that has been taken as a result of a motion, but the unexecuted part may be rescinded. Adoption of the motion to rescind requires only a majority vote when notice is given at a previous meeting; it requires a two-thirds vote when no notice is given and the motion to rescind is voted on immediately.

becomes counterproductive. The rational process of decision making is undermined by such game playing. Refrain from piling one motion on top of another, cluttering the floor (and the minds of members) with amendments to amendments. Also guard against raising petty points of order. Parliamentary procedure is intended to ensure equal, fair, controlled participation by all members. It provides a systematic way to introduce and dispose of complex ideas. Unnecessary "gymnastics" will impede rather than foster group decision making.

As we conclude our examination of group discussions, one final point we have already hinted at must be made: *The key to successful group communication experiences is interdependency.* Even though people take turns talking—often disagreeing with each other, worrying about whether the leader has been too heavy-handed or not forceful enough, and occasionally having to quit talking for the moment out of sheer frustration—and even though a discussion can exhibit as much competition as it does cooperation, ultimately it is an interdependent activity:

- You share a part of yourself with others.
- Others share parts of themselves with you.
- Your own ideas are deflected, reshaped, or accepted by others so that they end up belonging to everybody.
- All group members leave parts of themselves in a final document or other product assembled by the group.
- You are changed, even if just a little, by having worked as part of a mini-society—a team.
- You leave a group more experienced at cooperative and competitive communication behavior.

If both discussants and leaders promote a sense of interdependency, group communication experiences in school, business, and the professions will be positive and productive.

PRESENTATIONS IN TEAMS: PANELS AND SYMPOSIA

When a group is too large to engage in effective roundtable discussion or when its members are not well enough informed to make such discussion profitable, a *panel* of individuals—usually from three to five— may be selected to discuss the topic for the benefit of others, who then become an audience. Members of a panel are chosen either because they are particularly well informed on the subject or because they represent divergent views on the matter at issue.

Panel and symposium members discuss an issue for the benefit of a larger group of listeners.

Another type of audience-oriented discussion is the *symposium.* In this format, several people—again, usually from three to five—present short speeches, each focusing on a different facet of the subject or offering a different solution to the problem under consideration. Especially valuable when recognized experts with well-defined points of view or areas of competence are the speakers, the symposium is the discussion procedure commonly used at large-scale conferences and conventions.

Various modifications of the panel and the symposium are possible, and sometimes the two formats may be successfully combined. Frequently, the set speeches of the symposium are followed by an informal exchange among the speakers. Then the meeting might be opened for audience questions, comments, and reactions. The essential characteristic of both the panel and the symposium is that a few people discuss a subject or problem while many people listen.

When you are asked to participate in a panel or symposium, remember that the techniques you use do not vary substantially from those used for any other type of speech. Bear in mind, however, that you are participating as a member of a *group* that is centering its remarks, information, and opinions on a specific topic or problem. Therefore, you have an obligation to function as *part of a team,* to do what you can to coordinate your communicative behaviors with the efforts of others in order to give your audience a full range of viewpoints and options. Thus, in a sense, you must sacrifice part of your individual freedom and latitude for the greater good of all. With this important caution in mind, we can discuss techniques useful in preparing for and participating in panels and symposia.

Preparation for Panels and Symposia

As one of a team of communicators in a panel or symposium, it is important that you take others into account as you plan your remarks. This team approach involves problems you do not face in other speaking situations. First, *you have to fit your comments into a general theme.* If, say, the theme of your panel is "The Role of the University in the Economic Development of the State," not only will you be expected to mention university programs and the needs of the state, but you will also be expected to talk *only* about programs that can reasonably aid in the creation of jobs, the attraction of new capital, and the growth of tax revenues. The theme, in other words, goes a long way in setting both the substantial limits and stylistic qualities of your speeches.

Second, *remember that you may be responsible for covering only a portion of a topic or theme.* In most panels and symposia, speakers divide the topic into parts to avoid duplication and to provide an audience with a variety of viewpoints. So, for example, you could divide up the aforementioned panel on economic development as follows:

The Role of the University in the Economic Development of the State

- Constitutional requirements for university service to the state
- Potential university contributions to the growth of hi-tech and bio-tech business expansion
- Potential university contributions to an increase in foreign trade
- Potential university contributions to plans for attracting new manufacturers to the state
- The dangers of focusing too many university resources on economic growth

Third, *the more you know about the subject under discussion, the better.* To be ready for any eventuality, you must have a flexibility born of broad knowledge. For each aspect of the subject or implication of the problem you think may possibly be discussed, make the following analysis:

1. *Review the facts you already know.* Go over the information you have acquired through previous reading or personal experience and organize it in your mind. Prepare as if you were going to present a speech on every phase of the matter. You will then be better qualified to discuss any part of it almost spontaneously.

2. *Bring your knowledge up to date.* Find out if recent changes have affected the situation. Fit the newly acquired information into what you already know.

3. *Determine a tentative point of view on each of the important issues.* Decide what your attitude will be. Do you think that Hemingway was a greater writer than Faulkner? If so, exactly how and why? What three or four steps might be taken to attract new members into your club? On what medical or health-related grounds should cigarette smoking be declared illegal? Stake out a tentative position on each question or issue that is likely to come before the group, and have the facts and reasons that support your view clearly in mind. Be ready to state and substantiate your opinion at whatever point in the discussion seems most appropriate, but also be willing to change your mind if information or points of view provided by other participants show that you are wrong.

Fourth, *to the best of your ability, anticipate the effect of your ideas or proposals on the other members of the group or the organization of which the group is a part.* Might your proposal make someone lose money or force someone to retract a promise that has been made? Forethought concerning such possibilities will enable you to understand possible opposition to your view and to make a valid and intelligent adjustment. The more thoroughly you organize your facts and relate them to the subject and to the people involved, the more effective and influential your contributions to the discussion will be.

Participating in Panels and Symposia

Your style and vocal tone will, of course, vary according to the nature and purpose of the discussion, the degree of formality that is being observed, and your frame of mind as you approach the task. In general, however, *speak in a direct, friendly, conversational style.* As the interaction proceeds, differences of opinion are likely to arise, tensions may increase, and some conflict may surface. Thus, you will need to be sensitive to these changes and to make adjustments in the way you voice your ideas and reactions.

Present your point of view clearly, succinctly, and fairly. Participation in a panel or symposium should always be guided by one underlying aim: to help the group think objectively and creatively to analyze the subject or solve the problem at hand. To this end, you should organize your contributions not in the way best calculated to win other people to your point of view, but rather in the way that will *best stimulate them to think for themselves.* Therefore, instead of stating your conclusion first and then supplying the arguments in favor of it, let your contribution recount how and why you came to think as you do. Begin by stating the nature of the problem as you see it; outline the various hypotheses or solutions that occurred to you as you were thinking about it; tell why you rejected certain solutions; and only after all this, state your own opinion and explain the reasons for it. In this way, you give other group members a chance to check the accuracy and completeness of your thinking and to point out any deficiencies or fallacies that may not have occurred to you. At the same time, you will be making your contribution in the most objective and rational manner possible.

Maintain attitudes of sincerity, open-mindedness, and objectivity. Above all, remember that a serious discussion is not a showplace for prima donnas or an arena for verbal combatants. When you have something to say, say it modestly and sincerely, and always maintain an open, objective attitude. Accept criticism with dignity and treat disagreement with an open mind. Your primary purpose is not to get your own view accepted, but to work out with the other group members the best possible choice or decision that all of you together can devise and, as a team, to present a variety of viewpoints to the audience.

RESPONSES TO QUESTIONS AND OBJECTIONS

In most meetings (and at other times as well), listeners are given a chance to ask speakers questions. Panelists frequently direct questions to each other; professors ask students to clarify points made in classroom reports; club treasurers are often asked to justify particular expenditures; political candidates normally must field objections to positions they have taken.

Sometimes, questions require only a short response—a bit of factual material, a "yes" or "no," or a reference to an authoritative source. These sorts of questions need not concern us. But at other times, questions from listeners can require a good deal more, specifically:

1. Some questions call for *elaboration* and *explanation.* So, after an oral report, you might be asked to elaborate on some statistical information you presented, or called on to explain how some financial situation arose.

2. Other questions call for *justification* and *defense.* Politicians often must defend stands they have taken. In open hearings, school boards seeking to cut expenditures justify their selection of school buildings to be closed. At city council meetings, the city manager often has to defend ways council policies are being implemented.

In these two situations, a brief "speech" is called for in response to questions and objections.

Techniques for Responding to Questions

Questions calling for elaboration and explanation are, in many ways, equivalent to requests for an informative speech. That is, think about them as you would any situation in which you are offering listeners ideas and information in response to their needs and interests. This means:

Give a "whole" speech. Your response should include an introduction, a body, and a conclusion. Even though you may be offering an impromptu speech (see Chapter 10), nonetheless you are expected to structure ideas and information clearly and rationally. A typical pattern for an elaborative remark might look like this:

1. Introduction: a rephrasing of the question to clarify it for the other audience members; an indication of why the question is a good one; a forecast of the steps you will take in answering it.

2. Body: first point, often a brief historical review; second point, the information or explanation called for.

3. Conclusion: a very brief summary (unless the answer was extraordinarily long); a direct reference to the person asking the question to see if further elaboration or explanation is called for.

Directly address the question as it has been asked. Nothing is more frustrating to a questioner than an answer that misses the point or drifts into territory irrelevant to the query. Suppose, after you have advocated a "pass-fail" grading system for all colleges, you are questioned about how graduate schools can evaluate potential candidates for advanced degrees. The questioner is calling for information and an explanation. If, in response, you launch a tirade against the unfairness of letter grades or the cowardice of professors who refuse to give failing grades, you probably will not satisfy the questioner. Better would be an explanation of all the factors—letters of recommendation, standardized tests, number of advanced courses taken, and so on—other than grade point averages that graduate schools can use to evaluate candidates. If you are unsure what the point of the question is, do not hesitate to ask before you attempt an answer.

Be succinct. While you certainly do not want to give a terse "yes" or "no" in response to a question calling for detail, neither should you talk for eight minutes when two minutes will suffice. If you really think a long, complex answer is called for, you can say, "To understand why we should institute a summer orientation program at this school, you should know more about recruitment, student fears, problems with placement testing, and so on. I can go into these topics if you would like, but for now, in response to the particular question I was asked, I would say that . . . . " In this way, you are able to offer a short answer yet are leaving the door open for additional questions from auditors wishing more information.

Be courteous. During question periods, you may well be amazed that one person asks a question you know you answered during your talk, and another person asks for information so basic you realize your whole presentation probably went over his or her head. In such situations, it is easy to become flippant or overly patronizing. Avoid those temptations. Do not embarrass a questioner by pointing out you have already answered that query, and do not treat listeners like children. If you really think it would be a waste of the audience's time for you to review fundamental details, simply say that the group does not have time to discuss them, but that you are willing to talk with individuals after the meeting to go over that ground.

Techniques for Responding to Objections

A full, potentially satisfying response to an objection is composed of two sorts of verbal-intellectual activities. *Rebuttal* is an answer to an objection or counterargument, and *re-establishment* is a process of rebuilding the ideas originally attacked. (See Chapter 13.)

Suppose, for example, that at an office meeting you propose that your division institute a "management-by-objectives" system of employee evaluation. With this approach, the supervisor and employee together plan goals for a specified period of time; so, you argue, it tends to increase productivity, it makes employees feel they are in part determining their own future, and it makes company expectations more concrete. During a question period, another person might object to management-by-objectives, saying that such systems are mere busywork, that supervisors are not really interested in involving underlings in work decisions, and that job frustration rather than job satisfaction is the more likely result.

You then return to the podium, *rebutting* those objections with the results of studies at other companies much like your own (reasoning from parallel case); those studies indicate that paperwork is not drastically increased, that supervisors like having concrete commitments on paper from employees, and that employee satisfaction must increase because job turnover rates usually go down (reasoning from sign). Furthermore, you *re-establish* your original arguments by reporting on the results of interviews with selected employees in your own company, almost all of whom think the system would be a good one.

In this extended illustration, we see most of the principal communicative techniques used by successful respondents:

Be constructive as well as destructive when responding to objections. Do not simply tear down the other person's counterarguments. Constructively bolster your original statements as well. Re-establishment not only rationally shores up your position, but it psychologically demonstrates your control of the ideas and materials, thereby increasing your credibility.

Answer objections in an orderly fashion. If two or three objections are raised by a single questioner, sort them out carefully and answer them one at a time. Such a procedure helps guarantee that you respond to each objection, and it helps listeners sort out the issues being raised.

Attack each objection in a systematic fashion. A speech that rebuts the counterarguments of another ought to be shaped into a series of steps, to maximize its clarity and acceptability. A so-called "unit of rebuttal" proceeds in four steps:

1. State the opponent's claim that you seek to rebut. ("Joe has said that a management-by-objectives system won't work because supervisors don't want input from their underlings.")

2. State your objection to it. ("I'm not sure what evidence Joe has for that statement, but I do know of three studies done at businesses much like ours, and these studies indicate that . . . .")

3. Offer evidence for your objection. ("The first study was done at the XYZ Insurance Company in 1976; the researchers discovered that . . . . The second . . . . And, the third . . . .")

4. Indicate the significance of your rebuttal. ("If our company is pretty much like the three I've mentioned—and I think it is—then I believe our supervisors will likewise appreciate specific commitments from their subordinates, quarter by quarter. Until Joe can provide us with more hard data to support his objection, I think we will have to agree . . . .")

Keep the exchange on an impersonal (intellectual) level. All too often counterarguments and rebuttals degenerate into name-calling exchanges.

We all are tempted to strike out at objectors. When you become overly sensitive to attacks on your pet notions and other people feel similarly threatened, a communicative free-for-all can ensue. Little is settled in such verbal fights. Reasoned decision making can occur only when the integrity of ideas is paramount. And the calm voice of reason is more likely to be listened to than emotionally charged ranting.

In sum, answering questions and responding to objections can be a frightening experience. Many of us feel threatened when we are made accountable for what we say by questioners and counterarguers. Yet, we must overcome our natural reticence in such situations if we are to weed out illogic, insufficient evidence, prejudices, and infeasible plans of action from our group deliberations.

We have now come full circle. We have reviewed in *Principles of Speech Communication* most of the forms of everyday public oral communication. We have concentrated on the steps through which a public speaker proceeds when constructing and delivering informative, persuasive, and more specialized sorts of speeches. And we have examined in less detail the kinds of public discourses that comprise the world of work and social interaction, a discussion of which began this book.

While you cannot learn everything there is to know about public oral communication in a single course or in one brief book, you are now ready to take up the challenges of public oral expression. As you think through the rhetorical decisions you must make each time you rise to speak, we hope you will find a wealth of personal fulfillment and public service. You will then be putting the principles of speech communication to work in your life. If you do, we will have accomplished these purposes.

CHAPTER SUMMARY

A *group discussion* is a shared, purposive communication transaction in which a small group of people exchange and evaluate ideas and information in order to understand a subject *(learning or study discussion)* or to solve a problem *(action or decision-making discussion)*. To be a successful *participant* in a discussion, you must know the subject, acquaint yourself with the others, and pay close attention to the progress of the discussion. To be a successful *leader* of a discussion, you need effective expression, impartiality, and an encouraging or permissive attitude toward others. You may also be responsible for developing a discussion plan. In learning discussions, this calls for *introduction, analysis, investigation, and summary.* The plan for a decision-making discussion includes: *defining the problem, analyzing the problem, suggesting solutions, evaluating the proposed solutions, and deciding how to put the approved solution into operation.* When speaking as part of a *panel or symposium,* fit your comments to the general theme, remember that you may be responsible for only a portion of the topic or theme, and have a broad base of knowledge so that you can work well with the others. When speaking on a panel or at a symposium, present your point of view clearly, succinctly, and fairly and maintain attitudes of sincerity, open-mindedness, and objectivity. Responses to *questions and objections* likewise demand special techniques. When responding to questions, give a brief but complete speech and answer the questions as they were asked. When responding to objections, (1) be both constructive and destructive, (2) answer them in an orderly manner, (3) attack each objection in a systematic fashion, and (4) keep the exchange on an impersonal level.

Oral Activities

1. Divide into groups of four or five and select a topic for a learning or decision-making discussion. Prepare a panel forum that you will present to your class in twenty-five minutes (or more, if your instructor gives you the time). Decide on the degree of audience involvement you will allow for, the kind of interaction among panelists you will encourage, and the desirability of having audience members critique you after the discussion. The following are possible topics:
   a. How effective is our freshman orientation program?
   b. How are American cities solving their traffic problems?
   c. What features make a novel/play/film/speech great?
   d. What are the social and ethical implications of organ transplant surgery?
   e. How can we reconcile the demands of both the ecological and the energy crises in this country?
   f. What can be done about America's child abuse problems?
   g. How can the basic public speaking course be taught?
   h. What reasonable legal controls can be placed over pornography?
   i. What has the United Nations accomplished?
2. Conduct press conferences. Speakers will select or be given a situation in which the conference is to be held. They will prepare an opening statement, and the rest of the class will serve as members of the press,

asking clarifying or probing questions. You may wish to be the president, disagreeing with legislation Congress has passed; a board chair indicating that your company has signed a trade agreement with China; or the like.

Reference Notes

1. Not all discussions of this kind deal with problems or policies over which the group has immediate control. For example, a decision-making group may discuss "Should we de-emphasize intercollegiate athletes?" or "What can the government do to ensure a stable food supply at reasonable prices?" The systematic investigation of these subjects, however, requires the same steps as would the exploration of matters over which the group does have control. The only difference is that instead of asking "What shall we *do?*" the group, in effect, asks "What shall we *recommend* to those in authority?" or "What *would* we do if we ourselves were in positions of authority?"

2. See John Dewey, *How We Think* (Boston: D. C. Heath, 1933), Chapter 7, "Analysis of Reflective Thinking." Cf. pages 271–74 of this textbook, where these steps are discussed in connection with the motivated sequence.

SAMPLE

SPEECH

MATERIALS

. . . A **S**peech to **I**nform . . . .

Some speeches to inform give listeners detailed information, instructions, background data, and the like. For example, "The Geisha" (page 255) provides historical background and descriptions of geishas' duties for an audience essentially ignorant of both. Some speeches to inform, however, try to orient audiences. Rather than concentrating on detail, they offer "ways of thinking about and looking at" an idea, event, or object.

Architect Myron Goldsmith's speech, "We Shape Our Buildings, and Thereafter They Shape Us," is an example of an informative speech that concentrates on orientation. It was delivered as an introduction to a symposium presented to the citizens of Columbus, Indiana. The purpose of the symposium was to present the revised Master Plan for that city. Goldsmith's speech introducing the symposium had as its primary purpose orientation—showing the participants the value of the dual concerns for utility and esthetic appeal in the architectural environment. Notice that Mr. Goldsmith (1) uses his introduction to stress the importance of his subject and to forecast the development of the speech; (2) carefully divides the body of his talk into "utilitarian" and "aesthetic" considerations; and (3) presents a short conclusion (because the other members of the symposium presumably will develop more particular conclusions). The resulting speech is short, clear, and efficient.

WE SHAPE OUR BUILDINGS, AND THEREAFTER THEY SHAPE US
Myron Goldsmith

The theme of our symposium is "We Shape Our Buildings, and Thereafter They Shape Us." I would like to explore the truth of that statement in terms of architectural merit and the architecture of your community.   /1

Scholars all over the world study the impact of environment on human behavior. It is a new and burgeoning field of research activity for anthropologists, sociologists, psychologists, and communication specialists. For these scholars, it is a fresh area of inquiry that is enjoying a surge of attention and scrutiny. It is widely covered and discussed in journal literature, in publications, and in symposiums such as the one we enjoy today.   /2

But the impact of environment on human behavior is *not* a new idea to architects: It's something we've known for hundreds of years. I will address its significance in reference to the two broad aspects or dimensions of architecture—the utilitarian and the aesthetic—and I will explain why I think great architecture combines both of these.   /3

First, the utilitarian. In the field of domestic architecture, we know that some houses are easier and more pleasant to live in than others and promote positive interaction among family members. The large kitchen of our past and its legacy in the post-World-War II family room encourage family interaction. On the other hand, a too-formal and forbidding room can discourage use. A similar effect occurs in a neighborhood. Arrangement of houses in a common cul de sac promotes interaction among families and children in the cul de sac. Or, dwellings can be set back—behind fences, through gates. Such devices provide greater privacy and security; they convey messages that say: Stay Out.   /4

In places of work, we know that a pleasant, well-organized factory or office fosters better efficiency, happier employees, and less absenteeism. The layout of a building can promote or restrict accessibility to people. In some banks, for example, the president is in the open, accessible to any person who wants to discuss something. The opposite can also be true, where top executives are on the upper floor of a building, reached only through a battery of receptionists and secretaries, or even in a separate building with separate dining and parking facilities. This too affects interaction, the style of management, and the priorities of the corporation.   /5

I know of a conglomerate that was nearly ruined because all the top managers of the constituent companies were moved to a single, isolated building on the theory that the interaction of the top management was the most important priority. For them, horizontal communication at the upper echelons was more important than vertical communication. And meanwhile, no one was minding the company store.   /6

In other words, we have learned and are learning by trial and error about architectural spaces—public and private, accessible and formal. We understand more about what makes a building function well and efficiently.   /7

What about the aesthetic? In the best architecture, the utilitarian is combined with the aesthetic. And when that occurs, architecture represents more than the sum of its parts. While it is easy to define and evaluate the functional aspect, it is much more difficult to define and evaluate the aesthetic aspect. To do this, we must be able to recognize and make informed judgments about aesthetics and decide how much we are willing to invest in it. The return may be many times the investment in the improved quality of life. /8

How does the aesthetic aspect serve us and our community? Does it only give people pleasure? Or does it meet other basic human needs as well? The most dramatic example of this concept is the church or cathedral. How can one explain Chartres Cathedral, built 700 years ago in a town the size of Columbus, Indiana? What prompted the prodigious effort in engineering and craftsmanship, in art and architecture? What made those people build a nave over 120 feet high, the height of a 12-story building, and towers almost 300 feet high? If the utilitarian dimension was the sole criterion, they could have built a nave 15 to 20 feet high. But there were other things at stake in the 13th century—the glory of God and civic pride, to name but two. The worship of God was heightened and exalted by the beauty of man's unparalleled artistic achievement. And the pride of the community was enhanced by the size, the proportions, and the majesty of the cathedral—bigger and more beautiful than its counterpart in Paris, only 40 miles away. /9

But we need not go to thirteenth century France to see a proper example of the combination of the utilitarian and the aesthetic in historic architecture. Your own county courthouse, built in 1874, is a good example. Not to put it in the same class as Chartres, but it is a fine building. It provides centralized, efficient working space for the county functions, but it also aesthetically represents a good example of late nineteenth century civic architecture. Buildings constitute a large part of the tangible reality we experience. Size and scale are not necessarily the measure of their significance. /10

Your own town is a notable example of the impact of a distinguished architectural environment on the quality of community life: where informed clients and distinguished architects have confronted with honesty and solved with integrity the problems of space and use, where the functional and aesthetic aspects of architecture have forged a standard of excellence that any community in the world might envy. Through a combination of clear vision, good fortune, and unusual circumstances, you have provided for your citizens the finest our profession has to offer in churches, schools, and buildings—public, commercial, and industrial. You have given your young people something beautiful to grow up with, and you have given your own population something beautiful to live with. /11

So, then, what value do we place on the environment where we live and work and learn? How important is it that the community as well as the leadership—clients, architects, teachers, and business people—are knowledgeable about architecture and have some aesthetic judgments? It is of immense value and in Columbus you are better informed about architecture than any city I know of. Columbus is the proper training ground for the architects and clients of the future. You shape your buildings, and thereafter they shape you. /12

• • • • • • • • • • • • • • • • • • • •

• • •*A* **S***peech to* **A***ctuate* • • • • • • • • • • •

Most beginning speakers do not realize the potential power of the Visualization Step. Most of us offer our solutions in the Satisfaction Step and then move as quickly as possible into the Action Step. Opportunities to hit an audience hard may thus be lost.

Consider the following speech by Melissa Phillips of Ohio State University. She devotes eight of twenty-one paragraphs (12–19)—almost 40 percent of the speech— to the Visualization Step. Why? She obviously has reasoned that while most people agree something should be done about child abuse, they do not know what. By visualizing ways the Child Assault Prevention Project (CAP) of Columbus, Ohio, can be operationalized on a larger scale, Ms. Phillips is attempting to show that the solution will work. The Visualization Step, therefore, can be a key in demonstrating the practicality of your proposed solution.

PREVENTION—THE FIRST STEP
Melissa Phillips

We usually get our best education through trial and error. As children we learn that a hot stove burns, a big brother always wins, a sharp knife cuts. A kiss is the reward for our education and a Band-aid helps to heal the wound. But a Band-aid doesn't help prevent the wound from occurring. Such band-aid solutions are often applied to the topic of child abuse, typically, pleas for harsher prosecution, counseling for victims and abusers and so forth. But these ideas, all well and good, are after the fact and do nothing to prevent child abuse. However, there is hope. The Child Assault Prevention Project, referred to as CAP, of Columbus, Ohio, seeks to end the victimization of children through the education of elementary school children and the adults in their communities.   /1

Sandra Butler, author of *The Conspiracy of Silence; The Trauma of Incest* says, "The Child Assault Prevention Project provides parents and all concerned people in the community with a welcome sense of hope. It helps us feel, not more vulnerable, but more confident." The CAP Project is relatively new, approximately five years old, and finds its strongest support in Ohio, California and New York. However, child abuse is nationwide. To understand the role we can play in the prevention of child abuse, let's first look at how CAP dispels myths to arrive at reasons for the vulnerability of children to assault. Second, how the CAP program actually works in reducing this vulnerability and finally, the role we can play in the growth of this prevention movement. /2

Before we can actually talk about prevention and CAP's resulting theories, we need first to consider the problem. Child assault, particularly sexual assault, has only recently become a subject that is discussable in public. Therefore, little information is available, as reported in the *Christian Science Monitor* of February 18, 1986. Hence most previous attempts to deal with the problem of child abuse were ineffective because they were based on myths and stereotypes. CAP works to dispel myths with facts. For instance, many people regard child sexual assault as a rare occurrence. FBI statistics show otherwise. It is conservatively estimated that one out of every four girls and one out of every seven boys will be sexually assaulted before the age of eighteen. The myth of "the stranger" also prevails. Unfortunately, over 80% of all children who are assaulted are assaulted by someone they know and usually trust—yet, these possibilities are rarely discussed with adults, let alone children. /3

Cathy Phelps, co-author of *Strategies for Free Children,* confirms our fears that "sexual assault has many long-range implications to a child. There is a strong correlation between alcoholism and drug abuse in adults who were assaulted as children, and the majority of men convicted of sex offenses were themselves sexually assaulted as children." /4

CAP tackles this problem by reasoning that assault by a stranger is actually rare, yet we prepare our children only for this one instance with our advice, "Don't take candy from a stranger." This simply is not adequate. /5

Therefore, we need to provide children with the information and specific strategies to assist them in preventing their own assault. A child is never sent out to play without first teaching them about cars and crossing the street safely. Similarly, we can prepare children for the dangers of assault. /6

CAP's approach to prevention focuses on reducing children's vulnerability to assault. Yvonne Lutter of "Women Against Rape" explains the three major reasons that make children vulnerable to assault are a lack of information, dependence and isolation. /7

First, children lack information about sexual assault. Afraid that children will not understand or will become fearful with the information, advice is often limited to "stranger-danger" warnings. Giving practical information can only give confidence to a child knowing that they have specific strategies to avoid this problem. /8

The second way that children are vulnerable to assault is through their dependence on adults. Prevention must seek strategies that empower children. If children understand that they have the right to say "No," to determine how their body can be touched and to get assistance in keeping these rights, we are empowering them to stop their own assault.   /9

The last way that children are vulnerable is their isolation from each other and from support in the community. CAP helps children to identify adults within the community that they could go to if they needed help.   /10

Overall, the prevention methods taught to the children are designed to reduce their vulnerability to sexual assault using three main strategies: self-assertion—standing up for yourself; peer support—standing up for the rights of others; and finally, telling a trusted adult.   /11

Now we can look at how CAP implements these strategies in an effort to reduce the vulnerabilities of children. CAP's program is targeted at three main audiences: educators, parents, and of course, children. "The teacher in-service training is crucial," according to Sally Cooper of the CAP Project, "because they spend so many hours with the children." The workshop provides teachers and staff with identifiable physical and emotional characteristics they should consider if they suspect a child is being abused. Learning how to talk to a child in crisis is another responsibility of school staff.   /12

The parent workshop of the project developed as an extension of the teacher/staff in-service, except the emphasis is prevention and communication with children rather than legalities and intervention.   /13

The children's workshops are facilitated by three CAP leaders. Using role plays and guided group discussions, CAP trains children to recognize potentially dangerous situations. The workhsop [sic] begins with a discussion of rights. For instance, a facilitator will ask the children if they have the right to eat. "Of course," they respond. "How about the right to go to the bathroom?," [sic] the facilitator continues, "Of course we do." The kids are asked, "What would happen if someone took away your right to eat or go to the bathroom?" As the children imagine this terrible prospect, the guide then talks about three other rights—to be "safe," "strong," and "free"—rights that children must be willing to fight for. Then the three facilitators act out a series of role plays representing the most common assault experiences a child might encounter: child against child (or the playground bully), adult stranger against child, and assault involving an adult the child knows. Each role play is enacted twice. The first time, the CAP leader, playing the role of the child, acts confused, frightened and passive. Group discussion focuses on the options available to the potential victim. Role plays are then redone as "success stories" incorporating positive prevention techniques.   /14

Now, obviously, child assault is pervasive; but it's a problem that CAP is attacking head-on. Linda Sanford, author of *The Silent Children* comments, "This is the most innovative, effective and practical program in the country." And this is where you and I come in, particularly as future parents and educators ourselves. CAP's goal is to thwart child assault in every community by reaching and educating as many children as possible. They only need to be invited.   /15

CAP offers a three-day consultation to train persons in project implementation. This seminar covers the issues discussed earlier—getting started, funding, administration, and training people to become CAP facilitators.   /16

CAP also tries to make itself accessible to the individual community by looking at its specific needs. In moving to more multi-cultural areas, particularly the Hispanic and Oriental regions of our country, CAP realizes that they needed to be sensitive to their language and culture and willingly makes the necessary adaptations.   /17

Because it is an innovative project, the possibility of securing foundation monies to pilot the CAP Project in a particular community is very good. Many counties in California which are replicating the project have been able to obtain grants for prevention work. However, if such grants are unavailable, then financing becomes part of the school negotiation process.   /18

"To judge the effectiveness of this program with facts and numbers is difficult," according to Laura Kagy, Director of the CAP Project. "Longitudinally, you're measuring something that hopefully doesn't happen. It's better judged anectodally, [sic] or through 'success stories,' and we have thousands of them. And most importantly, studies show that the children are retaining and employing the information."   /19

If any of you would like more information about getting involved yourself, setting up a CAP program in your community, or just want to learn more about how the program works, I have some flyers with the address and phone number of the CAP headquarters in Columbus, Ohio, that I can give you after the round.   /20

Now, we know that there is a problem, child abuse. I could have given you example after example of children coming to school black and blue, the neighbor's kids disappearing ... but that's not why I'm here. We all know in our hearts the seriousness of the situation. What we need now is a viable solution. CAP is that viable solution. They only need to be invited. Child abuse doesn't go away just because we watch a documentary on television and feel sad. It goes away because we choose to take a positive step and do something about it.   /21

● ●

. . . *A* **S***peech to* **P***ersuade* . . . .

Often it is difficult to take immediate actions to make widespread problems go away. In such situations, about all a speaker can do is persuade an audience to think about such problems and not participate in their future increase. Such a problem is the near-mania Americans have developed in suing their medical personnel for malprac- tice. Calling for action—dropping suits—makes little sense, because, of course, most of us are not suing anybody at the moment. Rather, the rhetorically sensible course is to aim at persuasion rather than actuation, setting a mental frame that, the speaker hopes, will stay with audience members when they interact with medical personnel.

That is the course taken by Matthew Solomon of Northern Illinois University when talking about malpractice suits. Paragraphs 1–5 set up the speech, getting attention and focusing his talk on a claim. The Need Step is seen in paragraphs 6– 18, with paragraph 19 a transitional paragraph leading to the Satisfaction and Visualization Steps in paragraphs 20–27. Mr. Solomon combines those steps to let his audience see how the solutions work even as he proposes them. The concluding Action Step occupies the last three paragraphs.

A CASE OF LIABLE
Matthew J. Solomon

Debbie Cutler, mother of one, was preparing to become mother of two. The delighted Mrs. Cutler called her obstetrician in order to set up an appointment. Unfortunately for Debbie Cutler and many other Boston mothers-to-be, the obstetrician was [in] effect, on strike.   /1

Many Boston obstetricians are now refusing to deliver babies. Why this sudden aversion to birth? It's simple, the doctors cannot afford the insurance.   /2

An isolated case of New England eccentricity? Unfortunately not. Everyone from cities and school districts to bowling alleys and exterminators are facing liability insurance premiums that are up to 50, 100, and even 1,000%, according to the September 16, 1986, issue of *Time*.   /3

The insurance industry, which started out to protect the businessman, is now forcing him to pay premiums which are driving him out of business. While they once promised us "we're in good hands," insurance premiums are getting out of hand, injuring those they purport to protect.   /4

To insure ourselves against this out of control industry, I am filing a claim that first, these rising premiums are a problem for all of us; and second, I will investigate who is liable for this dilemma; and finally, offer a protection plan to safeguard us from further and future damage.   /5

All the doctors, architects and truck drivers who thought they had nothing in common, now know better. They all have difficulties with liability insurance. The problem: pay exorbitant premiums or don't be insured.   /6

Even our cities and schools are feeling the crunch. Says Don Benninghoven, Executive Director of the League of California Cities, "This is the most serious issue I can ever remember cities having to deal with." /7

When the city of Syilesville, Maryland, finally found coverage, they paid for it, with a 700% increase with reduced coverage, while Utica Mutual was in the process of cancelling the policies of 585 Ohio schools. /8

The Chicago Transit Authority was staggered when they were quoted a 600% increase with a 10 million dollar deductible. "No thanks" said the CTA, and they decided to insure themselves. /9

Unfortunately, most businesses cannot afford to do this and it is the individual who is paying for it, or not paying for it. As it is, 3,400 truck drivers who [sic] have lost operating authority for failing to afford increased premiums. /10

Architects and engineers who work with chemicals or waste find it impossible to get coverage at all. Even the people who sell hot dogs at Tiger Stadium saw their insurance rise from $50,000 to $1 million a year. /11

Some of the obstetricians I mentioned earlier would rather switch than fight these premiums. *Time* estimates that 18% of our nation's obstetricians will switch to other specialities [sic] this year, largely due to $72,000 insurance premiums. Many areas of the medical profession are being affected with disturbing results. Dr. Harry Cole, President of the St. Louis Metropolitan Society, states, "Unless we can get some relief, we're going to see high-risk patients having difficulty finding doctors to treat them." /12

From doctors to hot dog vendors our claim has been substantiated, rising insurance rates are a problem for everyone. But who is liable for the damages? Not surprisingly, one culprit is the insurnace [sic] industry itself. *U.S. News and World Report* of October 7, 1985, blames part of the problem on a six year premium price war among major insurers. The effects of the premium slashing finally caught up with insurers last year. However, according to *Time* this was only a small part of the problem. /13

The greater problem is the growing number and size of personal injury lawsuits. According to *Forbes* July 15, 1985, there was one private lawsuit last year for every 15 Americans. As Rudolph F. Landolt, President of Kemper Group Insurance, puts it, "You have an accident and everyone is sued. We live in litigious times." Litigious times, indeed. And who can blame the suer for trying? Last year the average liability award was $1.07 million dollars! /14

Unfortunately, it seems that some of the big winners aren't necessarily deserving. For example, two men in Maryland decided to dry their hot air balloon in their laundry dryer. The explosion wasn't as big as their award, $885,000. An overweight man with history of coronary disease suffered a heart attack trying to start his Sears' lawnmower. He charged that the mower required too much yank power. Then it was Sears' turn for a heart attack, paying the man $1.7 million in damages! /15

Suddenly it seems everyone is doing [it]. Liability lawsuits doubled from 1978 to 1984. /16

The picture should be becoming clear. When 360 injury cases were awarded at least $1 million dollars last year alone, someone has to pay. That someone is you and I. Because insurers aren't in the business of losing money, when their costs go up due to liability claims that cost is passed on to us. /17

If you are still unconvinced that these lawsuits are affecting us personally, consider the fact that last year the paperwork alone cost us, the taxpayers, over 360 million dollars. /18

The evidence is submitted. These excessive liability suits are causing sky high premiums. Some sort of protection plan is needed to affect some changes. /19

According to Illinois Governor James Thompson, one of the first changes to be made is a change in our attitude. Says Thompson, "We have to understand that if we hope to produce goods that are going to compete on a world market, we can't have a society in which everybody spends all their time suing everybody else." /20

He also calls for the overthrow of the so-called "deep pocket theory," of making awards for negligence. According to the *Chicago Tribune*, February 9, 1986, "deep pocket theory" is the tendency of some juries and judges to make unusually high awards to injured parties on the theory that insurance companies can afford to pay. /21

Obviously, the insurance companies can no longer afford to pay such awards and just as obvious, such an attitude change is not going to happen over night. [sic] In the meantime, experts propose that the only solution to excessive litigation is legislation. Such as the idea suggested by Dr. Robert Wheelock on a February 4, 1986, edition of *Nightline*. He suggests a panel of doctors and lawyers who would screen cases before they even get to court, similar to the grand juries in our criminal courts. This system would more than pay for itself by saving valuable court time and lawyers' fees. However, according to *Forbes*, the insurance industry cannot recover until Congress or state legislatures step in and impose order on our legal system. Pennsylvania has already made a start, passing legislation that curbs pain and suffering awards. Senator Robert Kasten of Wisconsin proposes among other things, limiting lawyer's [sic] fees and jury awards to a reasonable amount. Enactment of such a bill says Kasten, would "put money back in the hand of the victims and out of the pockets of the lawyers." /22

Not surprisingly, the National Bar Association has been successful in preventing such legislation. The reason for this success is that they have remained unchallenged. By joining local groups affected by the rising insurance rates, like the PTA and school boards, we can help counter the lobbying power of the Bar Association.   /23

Finally, experts propose changes that would limit liability to cases of actual negligence. For example, a drunk driver jumps a curb and smashes into a phone booth, injuring the man inside. Who gets sued? You guessed it, the manufacturer of the phone booth, and the man collects. Obviously, some of our courts are stretching liability too far and the result is outrageous premiums.   /24

While this proposed legislation will solve insurance problems in the long term, many of us need affordable insurance today. Unfortunately, short-term solutions also exist.   /25

Some large companies, like the Chicago Transit Authority are able to self-insure. For smaller institutions, like a Peoria, Illinois, group of day care centers, you can ban [sic] together and purchase insurance as a group, which effectively solved their insurance woes, for the time being.   /26

But short-term solutions don't last forever, to solve this problem we need the legislative action I have discussed before.   /27

As potential jurors, as parents whose children's athletic programs are being cancelled, as employees of businesses who can no longer afford insurance, we must realize we are the ones paying the price.   /28

The insurance industry, which once promised us a piece of the rock, has now become a millstone around our necks. It seems for everyone involved, the prevention has become worse than the disease. The protection plan I propose must be put into action, for when it comes to insuring our own security, we are all liable.   /29

● ● ● ● ● ● ● ● ● ● ● ● ● ● ● ● ● ●

● ● ● ● *An* **Argumentative** **Speech** *(Claim of Policy)* ● ● ● ●

In a technology-intensive society, especially one caught up in innovation, it is difficult to stop a stampede toward new labor-saving devices and money-saving processes. Those were the problems faced by Samantha Hubbard of Anchorage Community College when she fought the Food and Drug Administration's recent approval of irradiation of food as a preservation process.

Notice how she set up her argumentative speech: Paragraphs 1–3 provided basic orientation to the problem area; paragraphs 4–5 offered her claim and forecast; and paragraphs 6–7 offered historical background on present policy. She now was ready for the argumentative core of the speech: paragraph 8 outlined the affirmative case for irradiation, while paragraphs 9–11 bolstered the negative case in support of her claims. Paragraph 12 then added some additional support, and her concluding paragraph requested that her position be recognized by Congress.

IRRADIATION OF FOOD
Samantha L. Hubbard

On December 12, 1985, the United States Food and Drug Administration approved the irradiation of food—a method of preservation so controversial it has been debated for thirty years.   /1

Irradiation is a process by which the food is taken to a nuclear plant and bombarded with gamma rays or machine generated electrons. This activates the electrons within the food—which begin moving around, thereby changing the chemical makeup of the food itself. The Food and Drug Administration, the FDA, is now allowing the food industry to irradiate fruits and vegetables. Margaret Heckler, former Secretary of the U.S. Department of Health and Human Services, is one of the strong proponents, calling the use of irradiation a promising new technique.   /2

However, the opponents argue that the FDA has failed to prove this technique to be safe for the consumer. The Health Research Group for the Public Citizen contends that the FDA loses whatever scientific credibility it may have by declaring irradiation to be safe. In response, Sanford Miller, Director of the FDA's Center for Food Safety and Applied Nutrition, claims that people might be less worried if they knew that irradiation has been used for years to sterilize hospital equipment. Of course, we don't *eat* hospital equipment.   /3

Today I would like to urge you to recognize the startling lack of safety of this proposal and to help you see how unnecessary the "Federal Food Irradiation Development and Control Act of 1985" is.   /4

I will focus on the following areas: The history of its use, the pros and cons of this technique, and the importance of this issue to each and every one of us.   /5

The idea of using irradiation as a preservation technique was conceived more than thirty years ago. In 1953, during the Eisenhower Administration, the FDA okayed the U.S. Army to test the feasibility of irradiation as a means to prevent food spoilage. The Army spent 51 million dollars on testing between 1953 and 1978. It is estimated that 80 million dollars has now been spent by the U.S. Government on irradiation research. In 1958, the FDA classified irradiation as a food additive, thereby requiring users to test its safety as they would have to for any chemical additive. Then, in 1960, it was approved for use to disinfest wheat and limit sprouting potatoes; and then approved for use on bacon on the basis of U.S. Army test results in 1963. But this approval was reversed in 1968 when it was discovered that the test used in collecting the data had not been carried out scientifically, and in some cases was blatantly fraudulent. The further implication of this discovery is that it puts all the test data collected by the Army between 1953 to 1963 in question. In 1971, when the Army was ready to abandon the project, Congress unexpectedly granted a contract for long term animal feeding studies to be carried out by Industrial Biotest Laboratories, I.B.T., who had—by the way—conducted several of the Army studies. Tests were carried out by I.B.T. until 1977, and in 1983 three of their top executives were convicted of falsifying data.   /6

Irradiation has now been approved for use on fruits and vegetables . . . but in the near future possibility [sic] grains, meat, fish, and poultry. Included in these proposals are plans to reclassify irradiation so that it will no longer be considered a food additive. This means that irradiated foods may not have to [be] labeled.   /7

Let us look at the affirmative argument for the use of irradiation. When food is irradiated, the movement of the electrons damages the DNA, which is why radiation is so harmful to humans. This retards cell division, slows ripening, allows fruits and vegetables to be shipped farther, and allow[s] longer shelf lives. The irradiation process also kills any insects which may have infected crops. In fact, the recent outlawing of ethyline dibromide as a pesticide, because of its carcinogenic properties, has made irradiation seem to look more attractive at this time.   /8

But the argument against this technique is much stronger. First, not enough is known about the chemical changes that take place within the food when it is exposed to radiation. The movement of the electrons breaks chemical bonds— new chemical substances are created called radiolytic products; some of these are entirely unique to the food and there is no test data available at this time to show the implications of such new chemical creations. *Science Digest* of October, 1984 reported that the irradiation process may kill insects but promotes the growth of mold which produces aflatoxins . . . Aflatoxins are currently considered by the Environmental Protection Agency as being 1,000 times more carcinogenic than EDB. Furthermore, there are no guarantees that these crops will not become reinfested. Also, the irradiation process may kill organisms which cause smell and other signs of spoilage without killing the harmful organism itself. This means that irradiated food might look and smell perfectly fine, but may be rotten. In addition, animal feeding studies showed severe kidney disease, cancerous body lesions, chronic reproductive problems, and mutagenic assault. In fact, as of August, 1985, the FDA itself had to stop animal feeding studies because the laboratory animals were either dying or becoming violently ill after ingesting irradiated food. The United Nations Committee on Food Irradiation admits the possibility of these effects in humans, which might be latent and not become evident for 20, 30, or even 40 years. At present, tests involving food irradiation and humans have not been sufficiently long term.   /9

Environmental factors also must be considered. First, food has to be irradiated in nuclear plants, governed by the Nuclear Regulatory Commission whose record is poor insofar as protecting the workers are concerned. Also,

Cobalt 60, a highly radioactive substance, has to be transported to and from these plants, presumably by the nation's highways. And there is no technique available at this time to deal with the waste generated. This is no *small* problem. One irradiation plant has the potential to generate as much radioactive waste as all government and commercial nuclear facilities in 1981.   /10

This issue effects [sic] us all. We are already receiving foods treated by all the known methods of preservation. For example, fruits and vegetables that are picked while still green, and bananas that are gassed to make them yellow before they are ripe. Irradiated foods are now going to be put on our shelves . . . food that has been changed enough to inhibit nutritive value. This means that we could conceivably eat a diet of what we think is only fresh fruit, vegetables and grains and still suffer the consequences of a poor diet.   /11

After reviewing both sides of this issue, I am outraged at the prospect of irradiated foods. While the food will not be radioactive, it will not be what it appears to be. The fact that the FDA is willing to allow this process despite the fact that 80 million dollars of research has not provided any proof that this technique is safe or necessary seem[s] to me to be in complete disregard of its role as a protective agency. What of the laboratory animals that died during testing and the mortality rate of their offspring? If the FDA will not protect us, we must protect outselves. [sic] Oppose the "Federal Food Irradiation Development and Control Act of 1985." Ban the sale of irradiated food and the construction of irradiation facilities.   /12

It should now be apparent to all that, even though this bill has just been passed in the U.S. Senate, we must seek to repeal it. The FDA has not proven this technique to be safe or necessary. Without an outcry from the public, irradiated foods are going to be imposed on us . . . and if not banned now, we will have to suffer the consequences in the next generation.   /13

● ● ● ● ● ● ● ● ● ● ● ● ● ● ● ● ● ● ● ●

● ● ● *An* **A***cceptance* **S***peech* ● ● ● ● ● ● ● ● ●

"*Brutus is an honourable man*"—*Mark Antony used that phrase four times in his speech at the reading of Caesar's will in Shakespeare's play* Julius Caesar *(III.ii). The more he used it, the more ironic became the assertion and the more the crowd called for revenge. In 1964, too, after a heart-rending film tribute to John F. Kennedy was played to the Democratic National Convention, then vice-presidential nominee Hubert H. Humphrey presented a rousing speech to bring the delegates back to practical politics. He used a refrain—"But not Mr. Goldwater!"—to attack the GOP candidate, and the auditorium was rocking to that refrain inside five minutes. In the speech that*

*follows, songwriter Marilyn Bergman uses a refrain—"Interesting things, words"—
with humor and irony when talking to an audience of Women in Film. It involves the
audience with her thoughts; it shows off her own verbal skills; and it provides a
structure for a short speech that otherwise might have been perceived as formless.*

INTERESTING THINGS, WORDS
Marilyn Bergman

Thank you. This award is particularly meaningful to me as it comes from women in film—both very important in my life—women and film. Not *girls* in film. Not *ladies* in film. But *women* in film. /1

Interesting things, words. /2

Girl: non-threatening, unimpowered, non-authoritative. According to Webster: "A female servant." /3

Lady: identifying class or social position. Not free—belonging to, a mistress of a lord. Webster again: "well-bred, of refined and gentle manner." /4

Woman: clearly and cleanly identifying gender. Independent, responsible, empowered. According to Webster: "an adult female person." /5

Interesting things, words. /6

I've had a love affair with them for as long as I can remember. As a writer, I spend my days in pursuit of the right word. Words can be used to express or repress, to release or restrain, to enlighten or obscure. Through words we can adore each other and abhor each other. Nations can offend or befriend one another. Words can enslave and keep people in their place. They're easy prey for those who would tamper with the integrity of their meaning. Like those who use the words "peacekeeper" for an instrument of death and destruction—who refer to the contras of Nicaragua as "freedom fighters." And "moral majority." To my mind, neither moral nor the majority. Or those who call themselves "pro-life," a word which makes it appear that those who oppose them are anti-life. /7

Interesting things, words. /8

How stealthily they can enter the vocabulary and lose their real identity in the crowd. "Fall-out" for example: a word that was born with the bomb. Meaning radioactive particles in the atmosphere as a result of nuclear explosion. How benign the word has become through usage. We use it now to mean, "the result of something"—a meeting, a conversation—with no positive or negative implication, and certainly no danger. "Melt-down"—I dare say before too long it will wend its way into the vernacular, stripped of its malignant meaning. /9

Are we not creating a language with which to describe the indescribable? To make thinkable the unthinkable. And the sinister innocent, so that people are not outraged. So that these horrors are taken as a part of life, a fact of life. When in reality they are the facts of death and we should not accept them. /10

Interesting things, words.   /11

Message movies: That invariably means that a movie is not commercial and is left of center. And yet, aren't "Rambo" and "Cobra" perfect message movies? Their message is loud and clear : "Violent solutions are the only solutions." According to the *New York Times* review of "Cobra," its message is: "the good guys can't win if they have to play by the rules." In this case, the rules are the Constitution of the United States, the courts, and the laws of due process. All drowned in blood—in orgies of murder and weapon worship, and all for the almighty buck. Aren't we selling our souls?   /12

I remember the "Grapes of Wrath," about the hungry and homeless in America in the 1930s. "To Kill a Mockingbird," about racism. "Doctor Strangelove," which addressed the insanity of war, and "Tootsie," perhaps one of the most insightful movies about sexism ever made. Highly successful, all of them.   /13

Sure we want to entertain and be entertained, and made to forget the fear, the violence, the wars, slums, the greed. The sounds of people devouring each other and the earth. But don't we have to make sure that there's always a place for films that reaffirm the best in us? That elevate, that illuminate. That call upon us to hold out a vision of ourselves in relationship to others—to *all* others. To not deny the problems of our times, but to raise questions in our work and perhaps even help find some answers.   /14

We are the communicators. We deal with words and images. We must remember that words need the resonance of ideas—of thought. Otherwise they wear out—become deprived of their levels, their richness. We live in an atmosphere of slogans—where content is not questioned, and unless something can be reduced to a bumber sticker [sic] or a ten second news bite it is discarded.   /15

We help provide the mirror into which America—if not the world—looks to see itself. That's power—and with it comes responsibility.   /16

I remember when I first read Rachel Carson's *The Silent Spring* in which she warned us of the consequences of destroying the balance of nature. I remember thinking: "but *they* won't allow that to happen. *They* know better. *They* won't allow the seas to die, the air to become polluted. *They* won't allow the food chain to become poisoned." I was wrong. Not only has all that happened, but who are *"they?"*   /17

I've come to think that there is no "they." Trusting that there is, is a way of abdicating responsibility, of copping out, of leaving it to others. But we mustn't. For it's becoming more and more clear, that "we" are "they."   /18

Thank you again for this wonderful award and for letting me get all these words off my chest.   /19

• •

...An After-Dinner Speech ....

After-dinner speeches usually are one of two kinds: Some speakers try for humor organized loosely around a theme; others go for an inspirational theme appropriate to the audience being addressed. Richard L. Weaver II, Professor of Interpersonal and Public Communication at Bowling Green State University, used that second tactic when talking to the school's Golden Key National Honors Society. He talked about creativity to creative people—a topic designed to please the audience. He organized the speech around two sets of characteristics—the characteristics of creative people and the means one can use to achieve full potential. The characteristics and means were easy to understand, well illustrated, and organized so they could be remembered. The result is a pleasant, satisfying, and even elevating speech; it is light enough to go after dinner, yet strong enough to fit a bright audience.

SECOND WIND: CAPITALIZING ON YOUR FULL CREATIVE POTENTIAL
Richard L. Weaver II

First, I want to thank all of those people who were involved in the decision to have me come and speak. I want to thank you because this opportunity gives me a chance to say something important to people who should *really* care. I like talking to the créme de la créme of our students. Congratulations to all of you.   /1

Let me begin with a story: "A Zen master invited one of his students over to his house for afternoon tea. They talked for a while, and then the time came for tea. The teacher poured the tea into the student's cup. Even after the cup was full, he continued to pour. The cup overflowed and tea spilled out onto the floor.   /2

"Finally, the student said, 'Master you must stop pouring; the tea is overflowing—it's not going into the cup.'   /3

"The teacher replied, 'That's very observant of you. And the same is true with you. If you are to receive any of my teachings, you must first empty out what you have in your mental cup.' "   /4

The moral to this story is that we need the ability to unlearn what we know—*and* the important ability to go well beyond (flow over) what we already know. We need second wind.   /5

Our minds are cluttered with ready-made answers; we do not have the freedom to strike off the beaten path in new directions. Our attitudes, approaches, and responses have created mental locks. We need to be able to unlearn some of what we know, and we need to learn to go well beyond (flow over) what we already know. This flowing-over process will help us unlearn and learn again. We need second wind.   /6

"Creativity," by definition, means artistic or intellectual inventiveness. Inventiveness . . . bringing things together in new ways, for example. We need to find ways to stimulate insight. Insight is the wisdom of the soul. And insight comes to the *prepared* mind. See, that's why I enjoy talking to you—people with prepared minds. You have laid the foundation—at least some of the essential footings—for developing creativity—or, for capitalizing on your full creative potential. Who better than *you*, as a prospect for creative endeavor? Who better than you to capitalize on second wind?   /7

All right, let me give you a little quiz. When was the last time you came up with a creative idea? This morning? Yesterday? Last week? Last month? Last year? What was it? What is it that motivates you to be creative?   /8

Some of the answers might be: "I found a new way to debug a computer program." "I decorated my room with a new poster." "I got a unique idea for a paper I had to write, or a speech that I had to give." "I found a new way to make lasagna taste even better." "I found a quicker way to get from my dorm room to McDonald's or Wendy's." Being creative is fun, and being creative results in change.   /9

Do you know what a "creative self" looks like? There are four character-istics. Ask yourself if any of these (or all of these!) fit you: (1) Creative people are *more adventurous*. They dare and are willing to fail. They are more experimental; they're curious to see what happens. Sometimes they're even considered to be rebellious. Let me share with you a great quotation about failing. This is one you can hang onto and state, forthrightly, to your parents as you traverse the creative path: "If you're not failing occasionally, then you're not reaching out as far as you can."   /10

In addition to being adventurous, (2) creative people are also *more spontaneous*. They don't fear expressing their thoughts and feelings. That's how we generate reactions and discussions. Most people stop and ask, "How good is this thought?" Or "How will it make me look?"—then they suppress the thought. You need to take to heart the folk wisdom of Will Rogers, who said, "Everybody is ignorant, only on different subjects." Most people will be open and receptive to your ideas if you will just share them. Spontaneous people are people who stick their neck out; if they never stick their neck out, they'll never get their head above the crowd. James B. Conant, a famous educator and former president of Harvard University, had a poster on his office wall of a turtle. It read, "Behold the turtle, he makes progress only when he sticks his neck out."   /11

In addition to being adventurous and spontaneous, (3) creative people have *more of a sense of humor*. Humorous situations often result from seeing the old in a new way. I think we take life too seriously. When our primary goal is to get good grades, our vision is blurred and our goal blocks out the beauty, variety, and richness of our lives. One of the best things people can have up their sleeves is a funny bone. One thing I've noticed is that people are about as happy as they make up their minds to be. If you change your self and the way you come at the world, your work will seem different.   / 12

In addition to being adventurous, spontaneous, and having a sense of humor, (4) creative people *have and use intuition,* and have the courage to express it. Intuition equals instantaneous apprehension. Intuition comes from experience. The broader the experience, the more the materials we have to draw upon. Experience provides the materials of creativity. And the courage and confidence to express our ideas comes, too, from knowing more. Listen to this advice of an anonymous sage:

> You can't control the length of your life—but you can control its width and depth. You can't control the contour of your face—but you can control its expression. You can't control the weather—but you can control the atmosphere of your mind. Why worry about things you can't control when you can keep yourself busy controlling the things that depend on *you.* / 13

Adventurous . . . spontaneous . . . having a sense of humor. . . and having and using intuition . . . how many of you see yourselves as having at least three out of the four characteristics of the creative person? (Ask for a show of hands.) I thought so; perfect candidates for second wind.   / 14

We know that [sic] creativity means, and we know what the creative self looks like. Now, how can you capitalize on your full creative potential? There are numerous suggestions and many possibilities; let me share just three that, if followed, will change you from a caterpillar into a butterfly: the launching pad to freedom of flight.   / 15

To begin with, we need *courage.* Creative people are *not* necessarily talented people. Talent suggests that you have an area in which you are accomplished—like music, writing, athletics, art, etc. A talented person can write prose, for example, that is fine, clear, and proper—but creative people can make it soar! It's more a matter of degree.   / 16

Courage means willingness to frolic in new territory. Opening your mind to the unaccustomed. Trying things you've never tried before. Courage means taking risks. Courage means feeling something strongly enough and having the courage to try it. Putting yourself on the line. Passionate involvement. Living life with both arms—not with one attached to something secure *before* reaching out with the other. Let me share a personal story. Since ninth grade I had wanted to go into medicine—from the time we had to write our career projects in ninth-grade social studies. It was both a personal *and* a public commitment for me. In my sophomore year of college, I had to take a required speech course as part of my pre-medical program at the University of Michigan.

It was *courage*, as I look back on it now, that caused me to break a six-year commitment to medicine and to become a speech major. It was a break that, once made, became a passionate commitment.   /17

I ask you, how do *you* know what you'd really like until you've experienced more, seen more, done more, tried more? I am a teacher of speech not a doctor of medicine because I had the courage to open myself to a new possibility. It is the courage of second wind.   /18

Are you in a rut? Someone described a rut as a grave with both ends pushed out. Want to try something new? Did you know that there are more than 130 student organizations on this campus? How many have you tried? Explore more; be active. Read more, travel more, make more friends, do more things because the more you experience the more you will have to bring to each new encounter.   /19

In addition to courage, we need *curiosity*. Curiosity is a state of mind. Curiosity will stimulate your imagination. We need new visions—new ways of looking at things. Acts of creation are often unstructured and loose. And we've been taught to be so organized, routinized, formal—follow the rules. Let me read you what one frustrated 16-year old boy wrote:

He always wanted to explain things
But no one cared.
The teacher came and spoke to him.
She told him to wear a tie like all the other boys.
He said it didn't matter.
After that they drew.
And he drew all yellow and it was the way he felt about the morning
And it was beautiful.
The teacher came and smiled at him.
"What's this?" she said. "Why don't you draw something like Ken's
    drawing
Isn't that beautiful?"
After that his mother bought him a tie.
And he always drew airplanes and rocketships like everyone else.
And he threw the old picture away.
And when he lay out alone looking at the sky
It was big and blue and all of everything.
But he wasn't anymore.
He was square inside and brown
And his hands were still
And he was like everyone else.
And the things inside that needed saying didn't need it anymore.
It had stopped pushing.

It was crushed.
Stiff
Like everything else.

Just after writing this, this 16-year old boy committed suicide. Curiosity stifled. No chance for second wind.   /20

What makes creativity difficult is fear. Fear of retribution; fear of authority; fear of breaking the rules; fear of failure. We need to allow our minds to wander into fantasy, daydreams, and reverie—fanciful imagination. We need to let our minds roam. A preoccupation with grades keeps us safe and secure—structured and rigid. We're doing what society expects, what our parents want; what our teachers think is right. But do you know what? We can have it both ways! Listen to your inner voices. We are our own biggest hurdle, our biggest handicap, our biggest restriction, our biggest burden. We need to loosen the bridle that society has placed on us, and we need to remove the chains that shackle us. We need the freedom to experience second wind.   /21

We need courage; we need curiosity; and, third, we need to *think beyond*— to flow over. So often, insights have occurred because we have been willing to ask, "What else?" We are restricted in our creativity by people who say, "It can't be done," "That's absolutely impossible," "It goes against the facts," or "This is the only way to do it." Most new ideas *are* at variance with what is known as the "facts." The airplane is, perhaps, the best example. "If God had intended that man should fly," they said, "He would have given him wings." The development of the rifle was another; bows and arrows were thought to be far superior when the rifle was first introduced. But the more experiences we have, the more our ideas can flow over. Just look sometime at the resources that creative people depend upon—they are pulling ideas from everywhere. They depend upon *all* their resources and they are limited only by the extent of their ability to imagine. What is it that is stopping us? Fear that we may be wrong? The person who is never wrong is one who never does anything— wrong *or* right! Enthusiasm is the lubricant that oils the machinery of action. Ask the questions "What if?" and "What about?" but don't stop there. Ask, "But what else?" and then keep on asking, "But what else?"   /22

The reason I jumped at the opportunity to talk with you is because you are students who have already established a base of operations. Everybody in this room knows what you can do with your first breath—your first wind. That's why you're here! Let me end with a brief story: "A certain youth was fond of swimming but he had never swum farther than one-half mile in his life. One day he was challenged to attempt a five-mile swim. When he passed the first half-mile, he naturally began to lose his wind. Very soon his heart began to pound, he gasped for breath, and his face assumed an agonized look. Just as he was about to give up, he suddenly drew a deep breath then another and another, and his troubles were gone. Since he had never before experienced "second wind," it seemed a miracle to him. His new-found strength propelled him on and on and he finished the five miles tired of muscle, but breathing easily and confidently.   /23

"To him this was a new discovery, for he had never known that power was within him. It's true that every distance runner knows the power of second wind. In every long race the runners are tempted to give up, just before second wind comes. Always they go through the breathless stage, and always follows the miracle to carry them onward. Yes, here is a power, unknown to many, that can take men *ten times as far* as most people can go.   /24

"In every man not only is there a vast lung power in reserve, but there is also an amazing reserve supply of mind power and general physical power." /25

Ahhhh, yes, we all know what you can do with first wind. Your presence here is evidence of that. To capitalize on *your* full creative potential . . . to put yourself together in a new way—inventiveness—you need to discover second wind. It's that amazing reserve supply of power—creative power—at *your* command. Just remember, it's what you can do with second wind that counts! /26

• •

BIBLIOGRAPHY

OTHER PUBLIC SPEAKING TEXTBOOKS

Ayres, Joe, and Janice M. Miller. *Effective Public Speaking.* 2nd ed. Dubuque, IA: Wm. C. Brown Publishers, 1987.

Bryant, Donald C., Karl Wallace, and Michael C. McGee. *Oral Communication: A Short Course in Speaking.* 5th ed. Englewood Cliffs, NJ: Prentice-Hall, Inc., 1982.

DeVito, Joseph A. *The Elements of Public Speaking.* 3rd ed. New York: Harper & Row, 1987.

Dance, Frank E. X., and Carl C. Zak-Dance. *Public Speaking.* New York: Harper & Row, 1986.

Gronbeck, Bruce E. *The Articulate Person: A Guide to Everyday Public Speaking.* 2nd ed. Glenview, IL: Scott, Foresman and Company, 1983.

Hanna, Michael S., and James W. Gibson. *Public Speaking for Personal Success.* Dubuque, IA: Wm. C. Brown Publishers, 1987.

Hart, Roderick, Gustav Friedrich, and Barry Brummett. *Public Communication.* 2nd ed. New York: Harper & Row, 1984.

Haskins, William A., and Joseph M. Staudacher. *Successful Public Speaking: A Practical Guide.* Glenview, IL: Scott, Foresman and Company, 1987.

Jeffrey, Robert, and Owen Peterson. *Speech.* 2nd ed. New York: Harper & Row, 1984.

Katula, Richard A. *Principles and Patterns of Public Speaking.* Belmont, CA: Wadsworth Publishing Co., 1987.

Logue, Cal M., et al. *Speaking: Back to Fundamentals.* 3rd ed. Boston: Allyn and Bacon, 1982.

Lucas, Stephen. *The Art of Public Speaking.* 2nd ed. Westminster, MD: Random House, 1986.

Minnick, Wayne C. *Public Speaking.* 2nd ed. Palo Alto, CA: Houghton Mifflin, 1983.

Nelson, Paul Edward, and Judy Cornelia Pearson. *Confidence in Public Speaking.* 3rd ed. Dubuque, IA: Wm. C. Brown Publishers, 1987.

Osborn, Michael. *Speaking in Public.* Palo Alto, CA: Houghton Mifflin, 1982.

Patton, Bobby R., Kim Giffin, and Wil A. Linkugel. *Responsible Public Speaking.* Glenview, IL: Scott, Foresman and Company, 1983.

Powers, John H. *Public Speaking: The Lively Art.* Belmont, CA: Wadsworth Publishing Co., 1987.

Samovar, Larry A., and Jack Mills. *Oral Communication: Message and Response.* 6th ed. Dubuque, IA: Wm. C. Brown Publishers, 1986.

Thrash, Artie, and John I. Sisco. *The Basic Skills of Public Speaking.* Minneapolis, MN: Burgess Publishing Co., 1984.

Verderber, Rudolph F. *The Challenge of Effective Speaking.* 6th ed. Belmont, CA: Wadsworth Publishing Co., 1985.

Walter, Otis M., and Robert L. Scott. *Thinking and Speaking.* 5th ed. New York: Macmillan, 1984.

White, Eugene E. *Basic Public Speaking.* New York: Macmillan, 1984.

Zeuschner, Raymond Bud. *Building Clear Communication.* Glenview, IL: Scott, Foresman and Company, 1985.

SUPPLEMENTARY READING FOR THE CHAPTERS

Addington, David W. "The Relationship of Selected Vocal Characteristics to Personality Perception." *Speech Monographs,* 35 (November 1968): 492–503.

Andrews, James R. *The Practice of Rhetorical Criticism.* New York: Macmillan, 1983.

Arnold, Carroll C., and John Waite Bowers, eds. *Handbook of Rhetorical and Communication Theory.* Boston: Allyn and Bacon, 1984.

Becker, Samuel L., and Leah V. Ekdom. "That Forgotten Basic Skill: Oral Communication." *Association for Communication Administration Bulletin,* #33 (August 1980).

Bem, Daryl. *Beliefs, Attitudes, and Human Affairs.* Belmont, CA: Brooks/Cole Publishing Co., 1980.

Bettinghaus, Erwin P. *Persuasive Communication.* 3rd ed. New York: Holt, Rinehart & Winston, 1980.

Bitzer, Lloyd. "The Rhetorical Situation." *Philosophy & Rhetoric,* 1 (January 1968): 1–14.

Bormann, Ernest G. *Communication Theory.* New York: Holt, Rinehart & Winston, 1980.

Burgoon, Judee K., and Thomas Saine. *The Unspoken Dialogue: An Introduction to Nonverbal Communication.* Dallas: Houghton Mifflin, 1978.

DeVito, Joseph A., Jill Giattino, and T. D. Schon. *Articulation and Voice: Effective Communication.* Indianapolis: The Bobbs-Merrill Co., Inc., 1975.

Einhorn, Lois J., Patricia Hayes Bradley, and John E. Baird, Jr. *Effective Employment Interviewing: Unlocking Human Potential.* Glenview, IL: Scott, Foresman and Company, 1982.

Floyd, James J. *Listening: A Practical Approach.* Glenview, IL: Scott, Foresman and Company, 1985.

Harper, Nancy L., and John Waite Bowers. "Communication and Your Career." In Douglas Ehninger, Bruce E. Gronbeck, and Alan Monroe, *Principles of Speech Communication.* 9th brief ed. Glenview, IL: Scott, Foresman and Company, 1984.

Harte, Thomas. "The Effects of Evidence in Persuasive Communication." *Central States Speech Journal,* 27 (Spring 1976): 42–46.

Knapp, Mark L. *Essentials of Nonverbal Communication.* New York: Holt, Rinehart & Winston, 1980.

Littlejohn, Stephen W. "A Bibliography of Studies Related to Variables of Source Credibility." *Bibliographical Annual in Speech Communication: 1971.* Ned A. Shearer, ed. New York: Speech Communication Association, 1972, pp. 1–40.

Littlejohn, Stephen W., and David M. Jabusch, *Persuasive Transactions.* Glenview, IL: Scott, Foresman and Company, 1987.

Malandro, Loretta A., and Larry Barker. *Nonverbal Communication.* Reading, MA: Addison-Wesley, 1983.

Ong, Walter J., S. J. *Orality and Literacy: The Technologizing of the Word.* New Accents Series. New York: Methuen, 1982.

Osborn, Michael. *Orientations to Rhetorical Style.* Procomm Series. Chicago: Science Research Associates, 1976.

Rieke, Richard D., and Malcolm O. Sillars. *Argumentation and Decision Making Processes.* 2nd ed. Glenview, IL: Scott, Foresman and Company, 1984.

Salomon, Gavriel. *Interaction of Media, Cognition, and Learning.* San Francisco: Jossey-Bass, Inc., 1979.

Satterthwaite, Les. *Graphics: Skills, Media and Materials.* 4th ed. Dubuque: Kendall/ Hunt, 1980.

Severin, Werner J., and James W. Tankard, Jr. *Communication Theories: Origins Methods Uses.* Humanistic Studies in the Arts. New York: Hastings House, 1979.

Shimanoff, Susan B. *Communication Rules: Theory and Research.* Sage Library of Social Research, No. 97. Beverly Hills: Sage Pub. Inc., 1980.

Simons, Herbert W. *Persuasion: Understanding, Practice, and Analysis.* 2nd ed. Reading, MA: Random House, 1986.

Smith, Mary John. *Persuasion and Human Action: A Review and Critique of Social Influence Theories.* Belmont, CA: Wadsworth Publishing Co., 1982.

Steil, Lyman K., Larry L. Barker, and Kittie W. Watson. *Effective Listening.* Reading, MA: Addison-Wesley, 1983.

Stewart, Charles S., and William B. Cash, Jr. *Interviewing: Principles and Practices.* 4th ed. Dubuque, IA: Wm. C. Brown Publishers, 1985.

Toulmin, Stephen, Richard Rieke, and Allan Janik. *An Introduction to Reasoning.* 2nd ed. New York: Macmillan, 1984.

Vernon, Magdalen D. "Perception, Attention, and Consciousness." *Foundations of Communication Theory.* Kenneth K. Sereno and C. David Mortensen, eds. New York: Harper & Row, 1970, pp. 137–51.

Wilcox, Roger P. "Characteristics and Organization of the Technical Report." *Communicating Through Behavior.* William E. Arnold and Robert O. Hirsch, eds. St. Paul: West Publishing Co., 1977, pp. 201–6

Wolfgang, Aaron, ed. *Nonverbal Behavior: Perspectives, Applications, Intercultural Insights.* New York: C. J. Hogrefe, Inc., 1984.

Wolvin, Andrew D., and Carolyn G. Coakley. *Listening.* Dubuque, IA: Wm. C. Brown Publishers, 1982.

Zimbardo, Philip G., Ebbe B. Ebbesen, and Christina Maslach. *Influencing Attitudes and Changing Behavior.* 2nd ed. Reading, MA: Addison-Wesley, 1977.

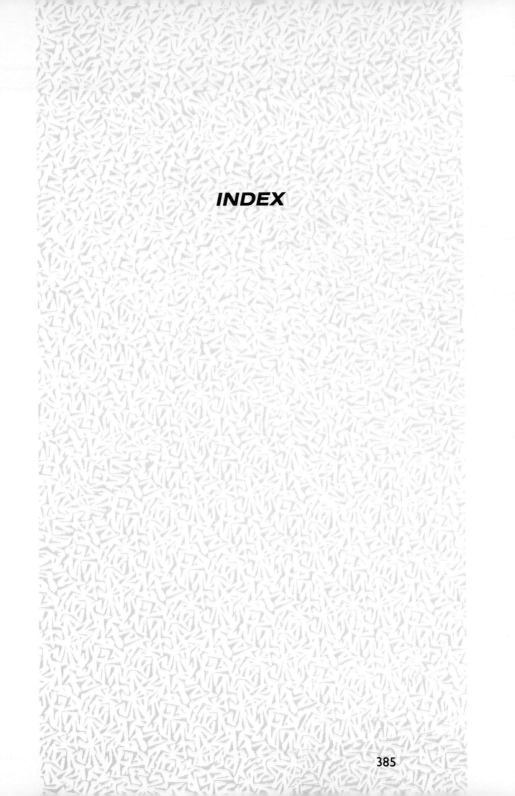

INDEX

CREDITS

LITERARY CREDITS

p. 8   "Inventory of Shyness Reactions" from "The Silent Prison of Shyness" by P. G. Zimbardo, P. A. Pilkonis, and R. M. Norwood. The Office of Naval Research Technical Report Z-17, November 1974. Reprinted by permission of Philip G. Zimbardo.

p. 24   Chart based on Chapter Two, "Theoretic Bases of Persuasion" in *The Art of Persuasion*, second edition, by Wayne C. Minnick. Copyright © 1968 by Houghton Mifflin Company. Reprinted by permission.

p. 359 "We Shape Our Buildings, and Thereafter They Shape Us" by Myron Goldsmith. Reprinted by permission of the author.

p. 362 "Prevention—the First Step" by Melissa Phillips. Reprinted from *Winning Orations* by special arrangement with the Interstate Oratorical Association, Larry Schnoor, Executive Secretary, Mankato State College, Mankato, Minnesota.

p. 366 "A Case of Liable" by Matthew J. Solomon. Reprinted from *Winning Orations* by special arrangement with the Interstate Oratorical Association, Larry Schnoor, Executive Secretary, Mankato State College, Mankato, Minnesota.

p. 370 "Irradiation of Food" by Samantha L. Hubbard. Reprinted from *Winning Orations* by special arrangement with the Interstate Oratorical Association, Larry Schnoor, Executive Secretary, Mankato State College, Mankato, Minnesota.

p. 373 "Interesting Things, Words" by Marilyn Bergman. Delivered to Women in Film, Los Angeles, California, May 30, 1986. Reprinted by permission of Freedman, Kinzelberg & Broder.

p. 375 "Second Wind: Capitalizing on Your Full Creative Potential" given by Richard L. Weaver II at the Golden Key National Honors Society Fall Reception and Initiation at Bowling Green State University, December 7, 1986. Reprinted by permission of Richard L. Weaver II.

PHOTO CREDITS

All photographs not credited are the property of
Scott, Foresman and Company.

p. 3	James H. Pickerell
p. 31	Michael Evans/The White House
p. 46	Julie Houck/Stock Boston
p. 85	Ellis Herwig/Marilyn Gartman Agency
p. 89	Thomas M. Pantages
p. 155	Russell Abraham/Stock Boston
p. 181	Bettmann Newsphoto
p. 205	James H. Pickerell
p. 227	Tom Grill/Comstock
p. 228	Brent Jones
p. 230	Cary Wolinsky/Stock Boston
p. 232	Brent Jones
p. 240	Dick Wade/Berg & Associates
p. 246	Bobbe Wolf
p. 262	Brent Jones
p. 266	Reprinted by permission. Courtesy AT&T Communications
p. 294	James H. Pickerell
p. 312	Kirk Schlea/Berg & Associates
p. 349	James H. Pickerell

AIDS TO CHOOSING SPEECH TOPICS

The beginning speaker often has difficulty in selecting a suitable speech subject. If you find yourself in this situation, we suggest that you study the following list of subject categories. These categories are not speech subjects; rather, they are types or classes of material in which speech subjects may be found. To decide on a suitable subject for a public speech, consider them in terms of your own interests and knowledge, the interests of your audience, and the nature of the occasion on which you are to speak.

● *Personal Experience*

1. Jobs you have held
2. Places you have been
3. Military service
4. The region you come from
5. Schools you have attended
6. Friends and enemies
7. Relatives you like—and dislike
8. Hobbies and pastimes

● *Foreign Affairs*

1. Foreign-policy aims:
   – What they are
   – What they should be
2. The implementation of policy aims
3. Ethics of foreign-policy decisions
4. History of the foreign policy of the United States (or of some other nation)
5. Responsibility for our foreign policy
6. How foreign policy affects domestic policy
7. War as an instrument of national policy
8. International peacekeeping machinery

● *Domestic Affairs*

1. Social problems:
   – Crime
   – The family (marriage, divorce, adjustments)
   – Problems of cities
   – Problems of rural areas
   – Problems of races and ethnic groups
   – Problems of juveniles or the aged
   – Child abuse
   – Abortion, adoption
   – The drug culture
   – Sexual mores
   – Pollution
2. Economic problems:
   – Federal fiscal policy
   – Economically deprived persons and areas
   – Fiscal problems of state and local governments
   – Taxes and tax policies
   – Inflation and price controls
   – Unemployment
   – International monetary affairs
   – Energy
3. Political problems:
   – Powers and obligations of the federal government
   – Relations between the federal government and the states
   – Problems of state and local governments
   – Parties, campaigns, and nominating procedures
   – The courts:
     –Delays in justice
     –The jury system
   – Congress versus the president
   – Careers in government